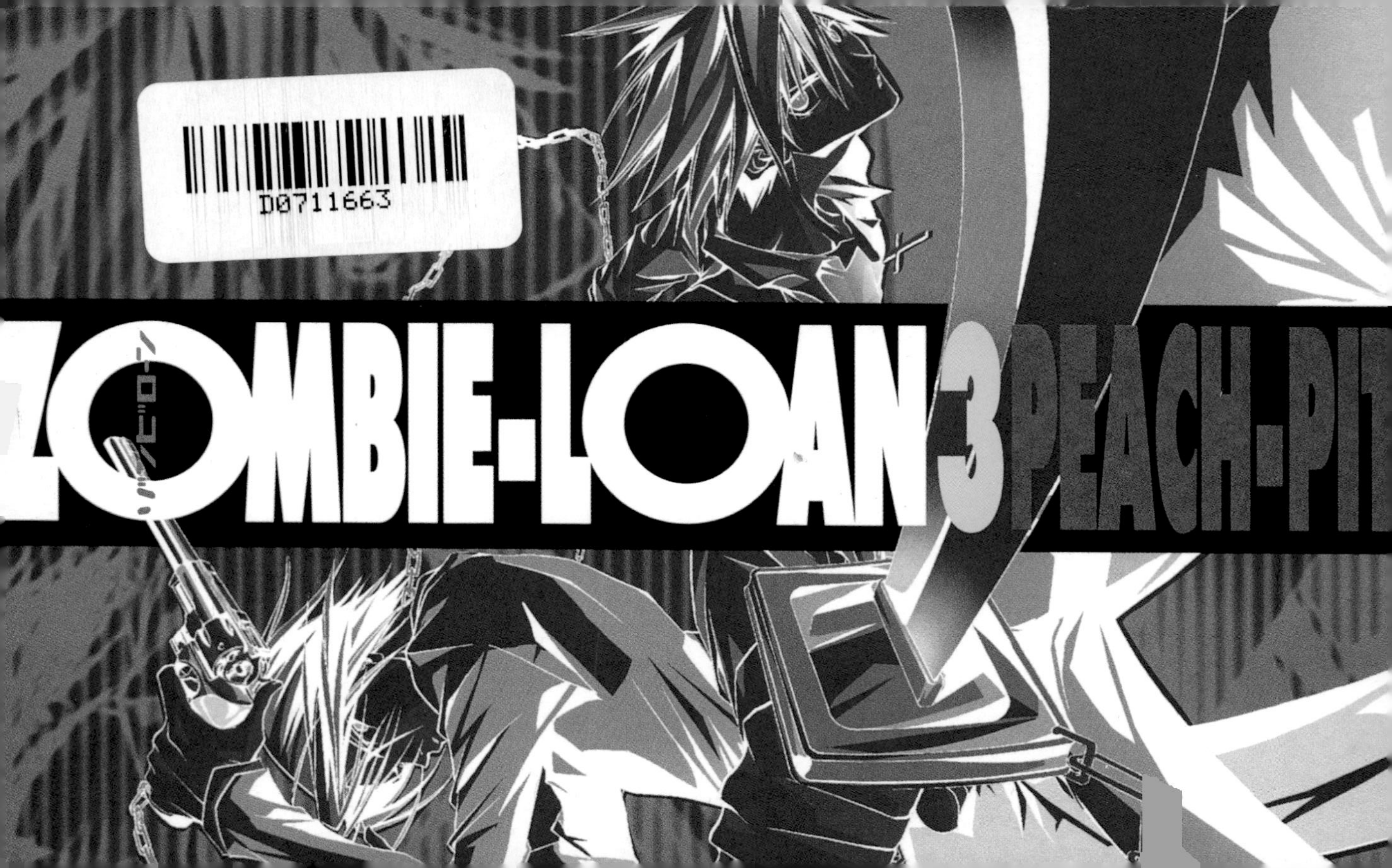
ZOMBIE-LOAN
ゾンビローン
3
PEACH-PIT

C O N T E N T S

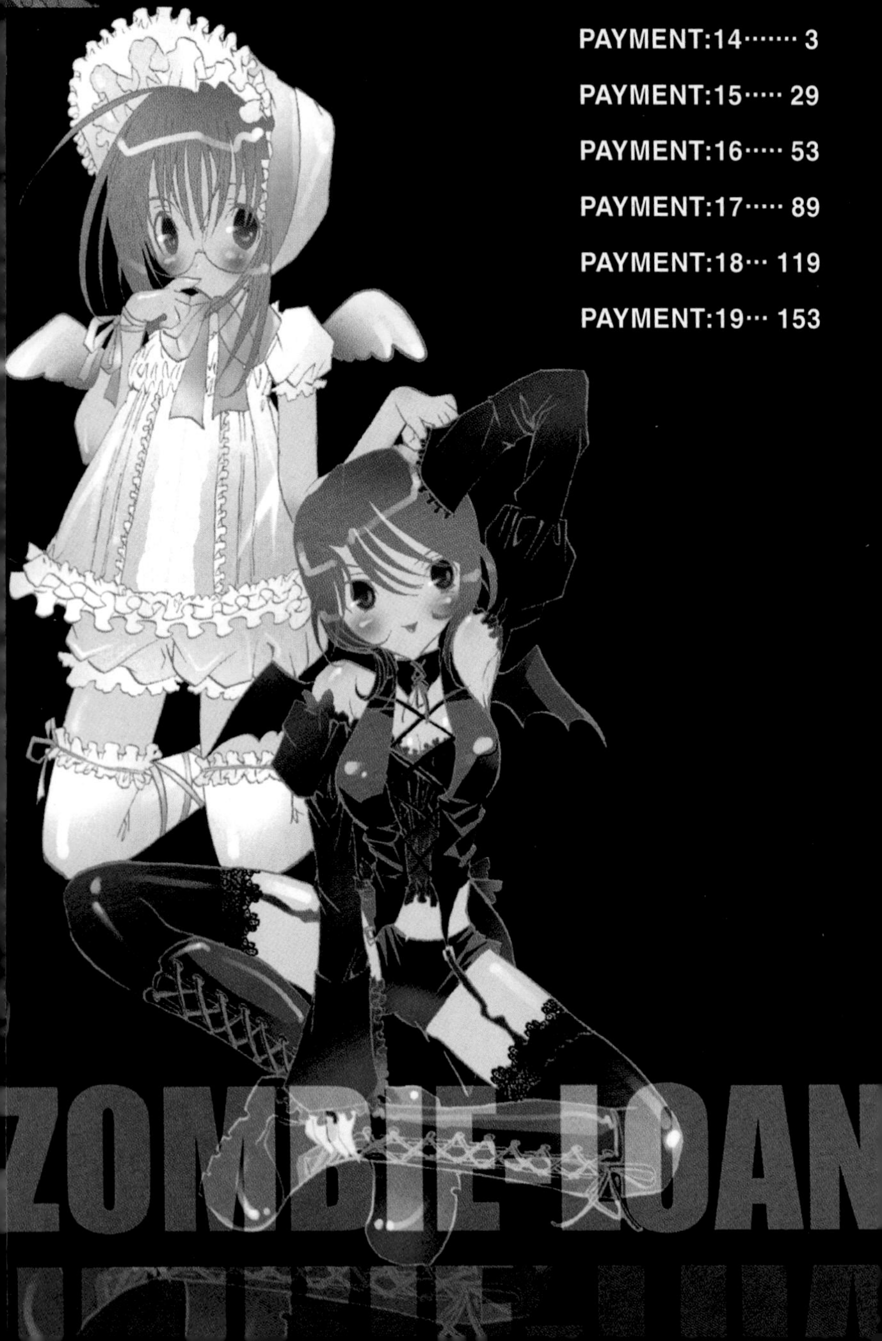
ZOMBIE LOAN

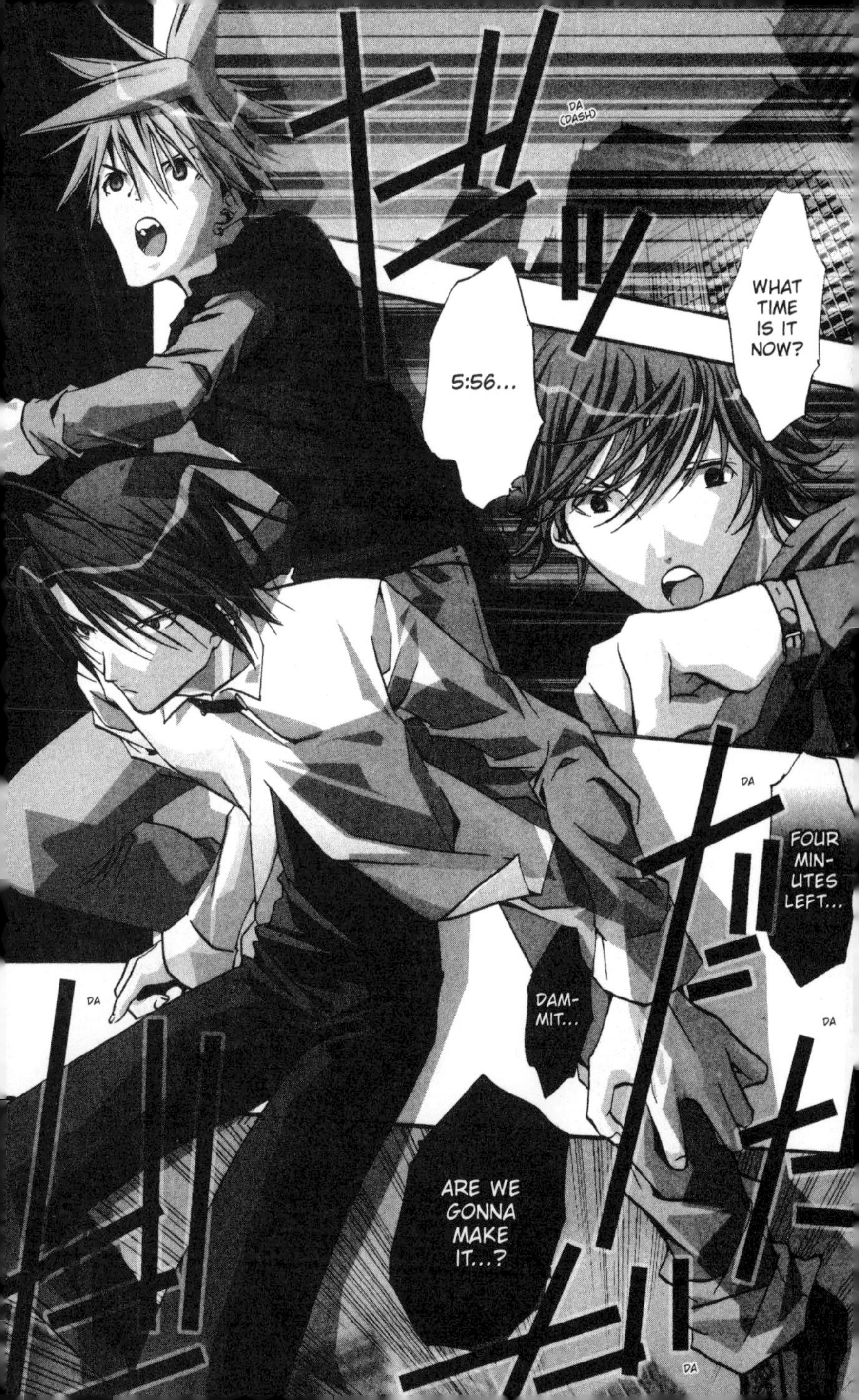
DA (DASH)
WHAT TIME IS IT NOW?
5:56...
DA
FOUR MIN-UTES LEFT...
DA
DAM-MIT...
ARE WE GONNA MAKE IT...?
DA
DA

PAYMENT:14

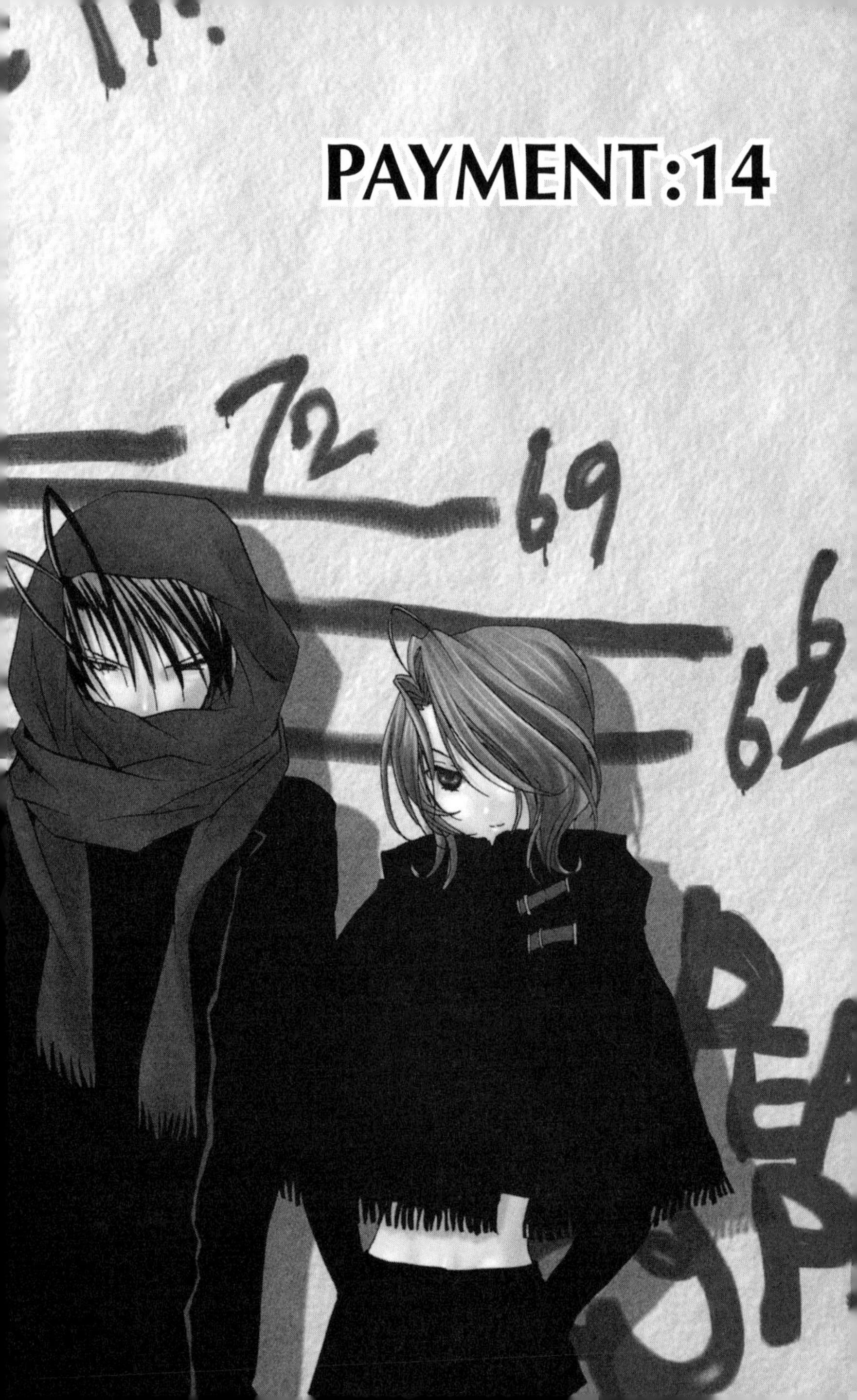
72
69
62

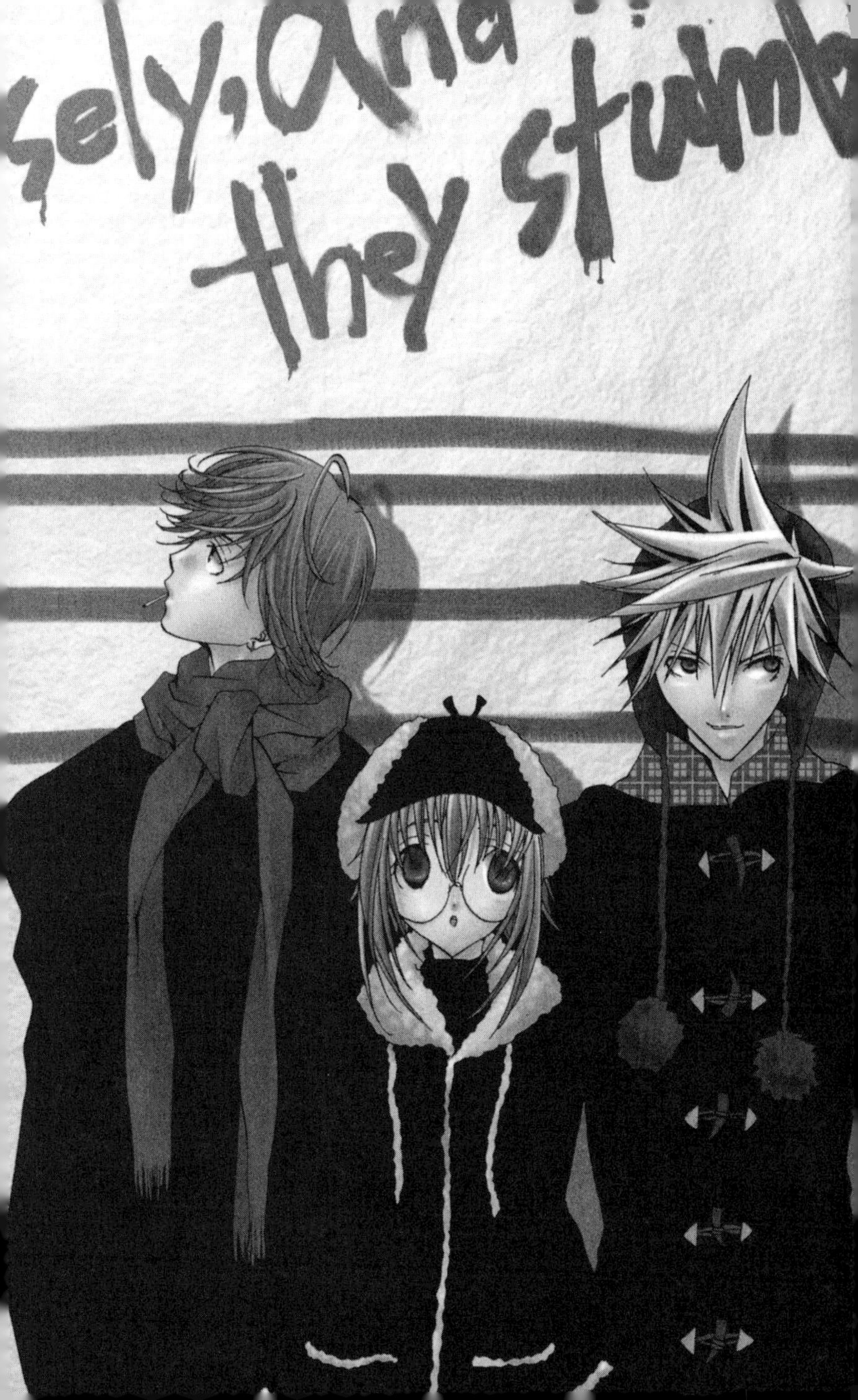
sely, and
they stumb

ZOMBIE-LOAN MANIAX-DX

SHITO TACHIBANA

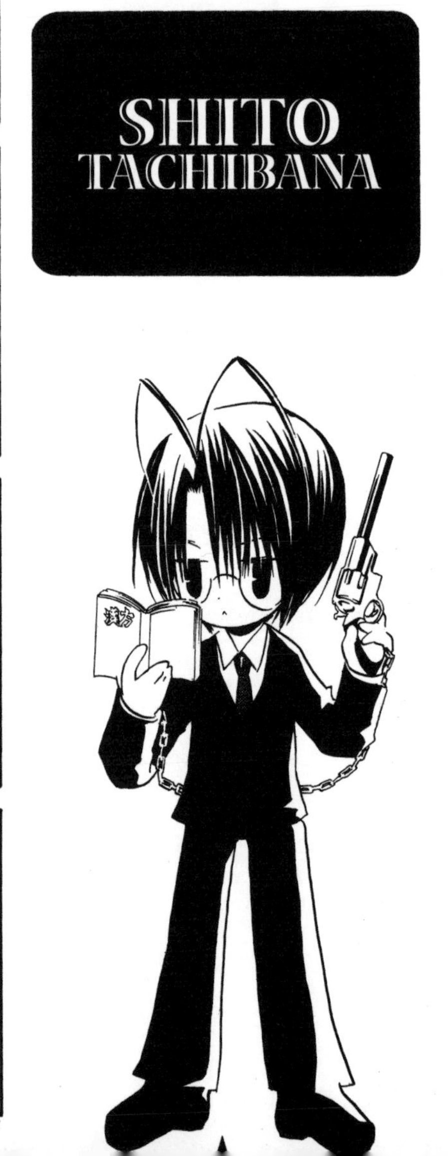

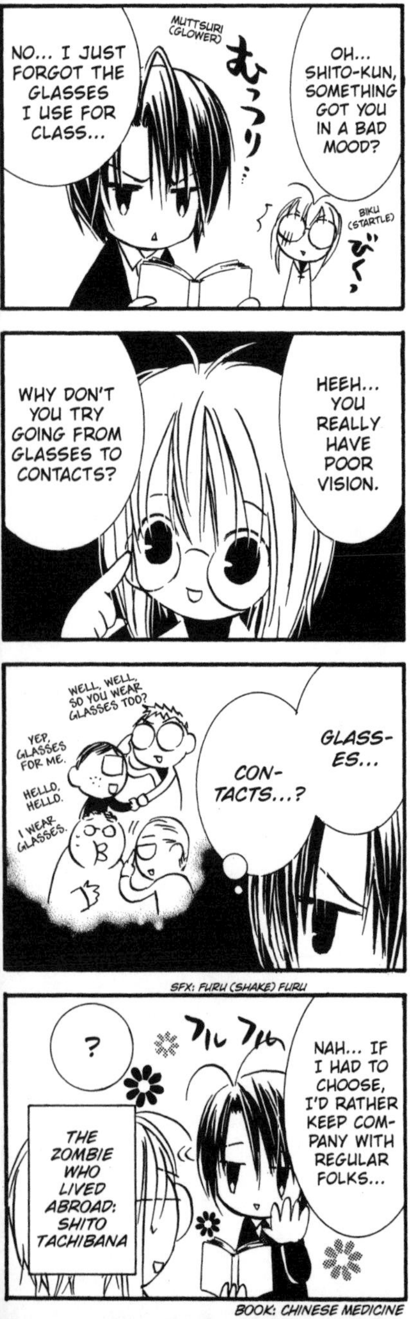

OH... SHITO-KUN, SOMETHING GOT YOU IN A BAD MOOD?
BIKU (STARTLE)
MUTTSURI (GLOWER)
NO... I JUST FORGOT THE GLASSES I USE FOR CLASS...
HEEH... YOU REALLY HAVE POOR VISION.
WHY DON'T YOU TRY GOING FROM GLASSES TO CONTACTS?
GLASS- ES...
CON- TACTS...?
WELL, WELL, SO YOU WEAR GLASSES TOO?
YEP, GLASSES FOR ME.
HELLO, HELLO.
I WEAR GLASSES.
SFX: FURU (SHAKE) FURU
NAH... IF I HAD TO CHOOSE, I'D RATHER KEEP COM- PANY WITH REGULAR FOLKS...
?
THE ZOMBIE WHO LIVED ABROAD: SHITO TACHIBANA
BOOK: CHINESE MEDICINE

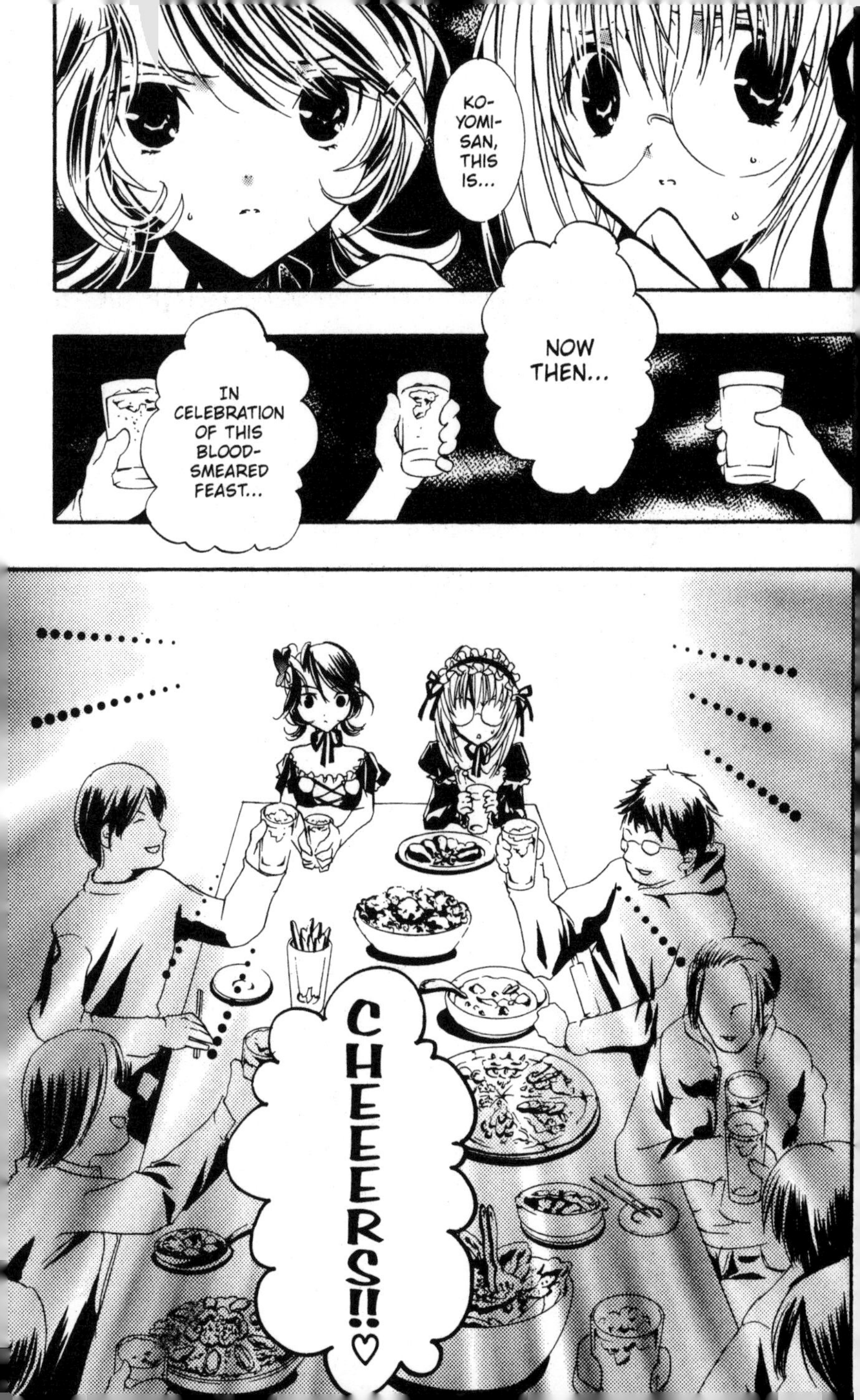
KO-YOMI-SAN, THIS IS...
NOW THEN...
IN CELEBRATION OF THIS BLOOD-SMEARED FEAST...
CHEERS!!♡

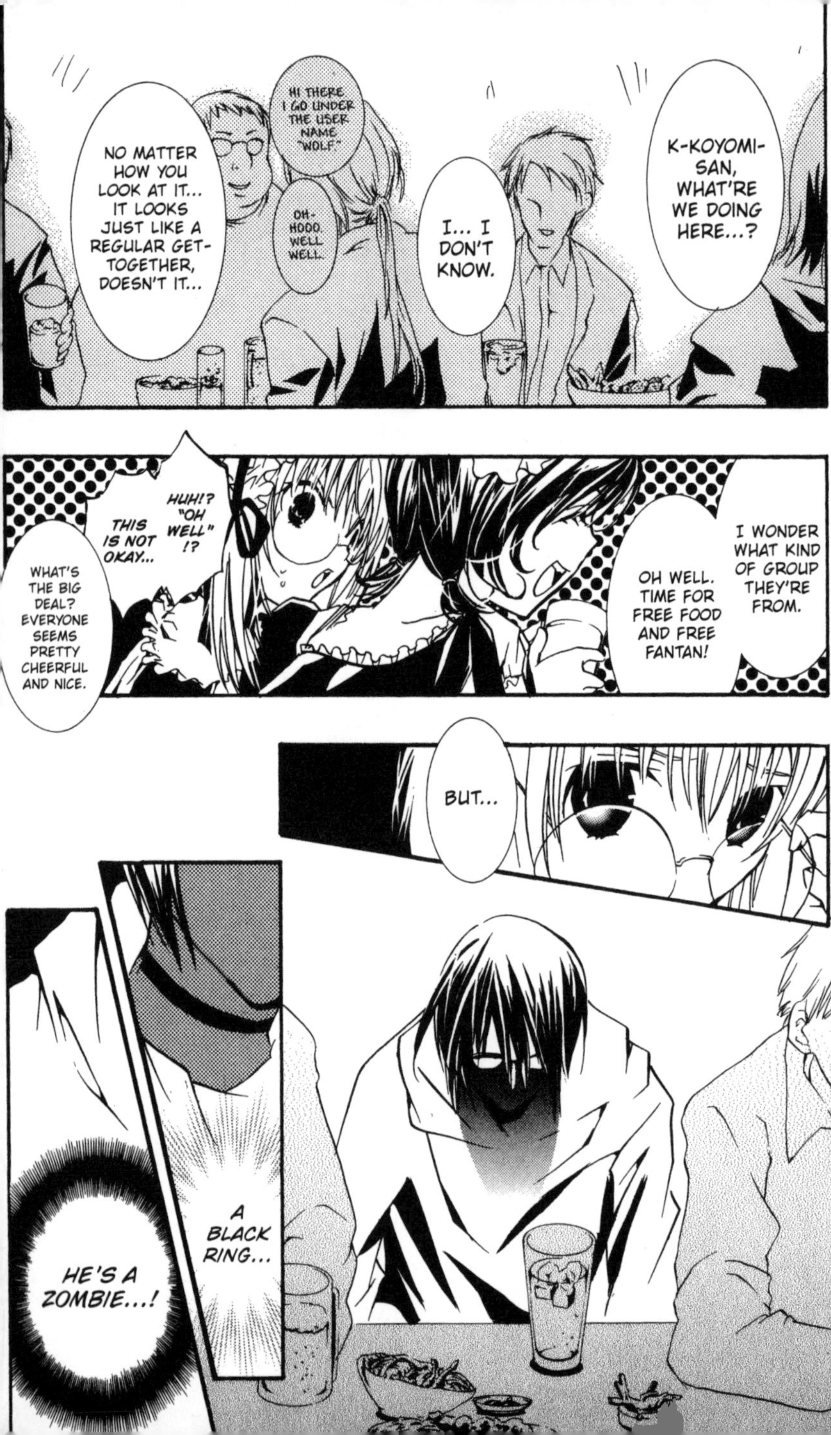
K-KOYOMI-SAN, WHAT'RE WE DOING HERE...?
I... I DON'T KNOW.
HI THERE I GO UNDER THE USER NAME "WOLF."
OH-HOOO. WELL WELL.
NO MATTER HOW YOU LOOK AT IT... IT LOOKS JUST LIKE A REGULAR GET-TOGETHER, DOESN'T IT...
I WONDER WHAT KIND OF GROUP THEY'RE FROM.
OH WELL. TIME FOR FREE FOOD AND FREE FANTAN!
HUH!? "OH WELL" !?
THIS IS NOT OKAY...
WHAT'S THE BIG DEAL? EVERYONE SEEMS PRETTY CHEERFUL AND NICE.
BUT...
A BLACK RING...
HE'S A ZOMBIE...!

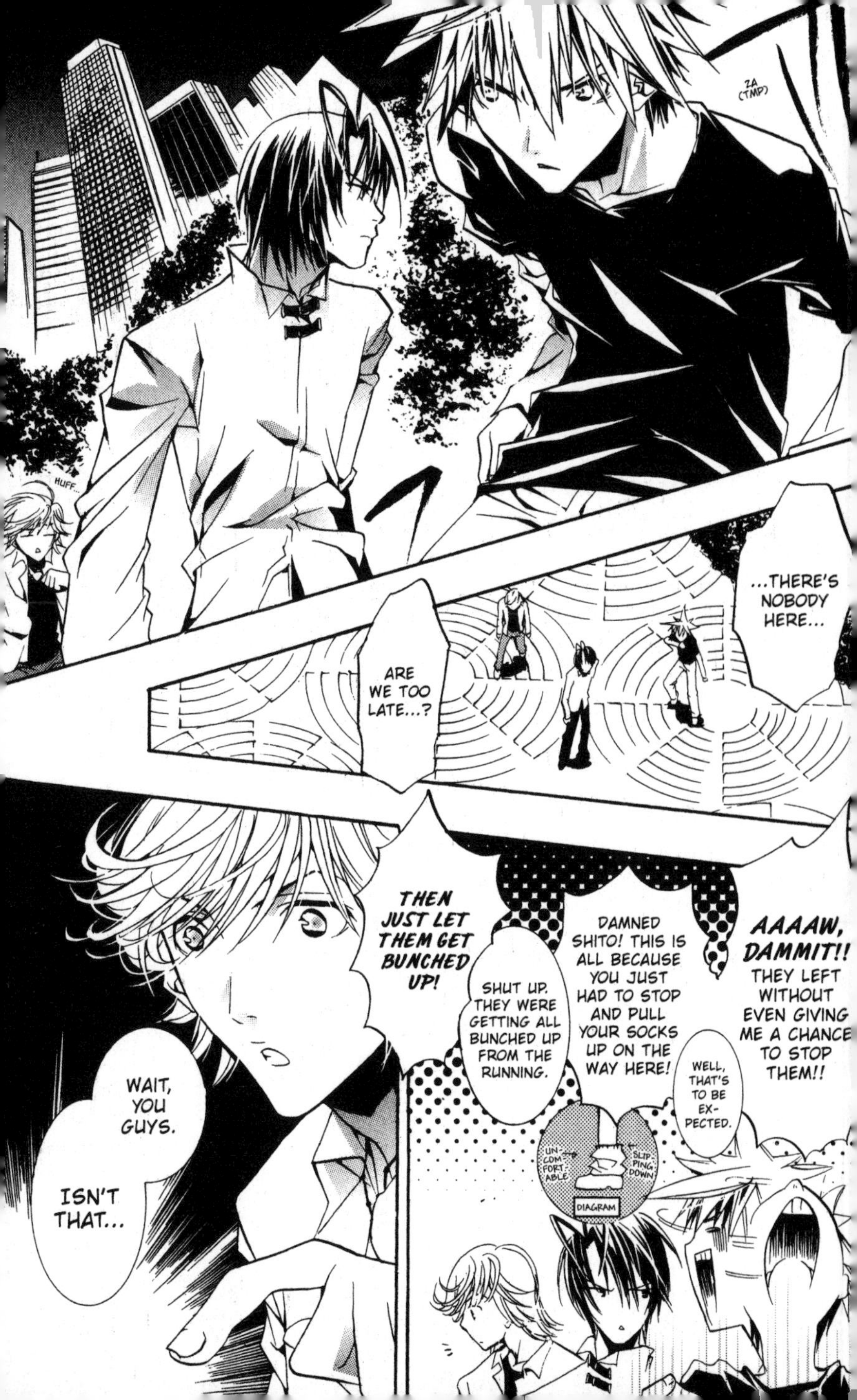
ZA (TMP)
HUFF...
...THERE'S NOBODY HERE...
ARE WE TOO LATE...?
AAAAW, DAMMIT!! THEY LEFT WITHOUT EVEN GIVING ME A CHANCE TO STOP THEM!!
WELL, THAT'S TO BE EX-PECTED.
DAMNED SHITO! THIS IS ALL BECAUSE YOU JUST HAD TO STOP AND PULL YOUR SOCKS UP ON THE WAY HERE!
SHUT UP. THEY WERE GETTING ALL BUNCHED UP FROM THE RUNNING.
THEN JUST LET THEM GET BUNCHED UP!
UN-COM-FORT-ABLE
SLIP-PING DOWN
DIAGRAM
WAIT, YOU GUYS.
ISN'T THAT...

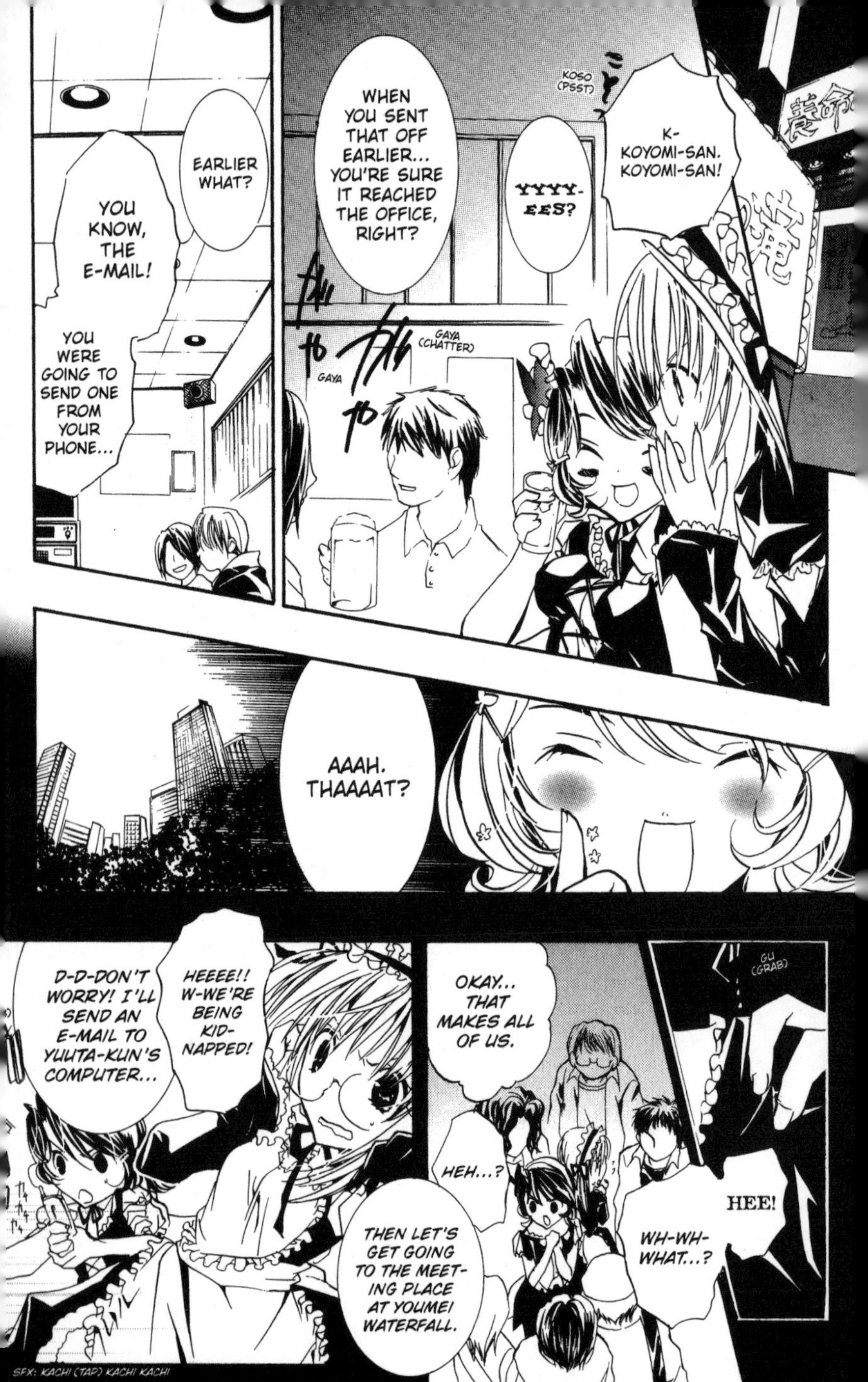
KOSO (PSST)
K-KOYOMI-SAN. KOYOMI-SAN!
YYYY-EES?
WHEN YOU SENT THAT OFF EARLIER... YOU'RE SURE IT REACHED THE OFFICE, RIGHT?
GAYA (CHATTER)
GAYA
EARLIER WHAT?
YOU KNOW, THE E-MAIL!
YOU WERE GOING TO SEND ONE FROM YOUR PHONE...
AAAH. THAAAAT?
OKAY... THAT MAKES ALL OF US.
THEN LET'S GET GOING TO THE MEET-ING PLACE AT YOUMEI WATERFALL.
GU (GRAB)
HEE!
HEH...?
WH-WH-WHAT...?
HEEEE!! W-WE'RE BEING KID-NAPPED!
D-D-DON'T WORRY! I'LL SEND AN E-MAIL TO YUUTA-KUN'S COMPUTER...
SFX: KACHI (TAP) KACHI KACHI

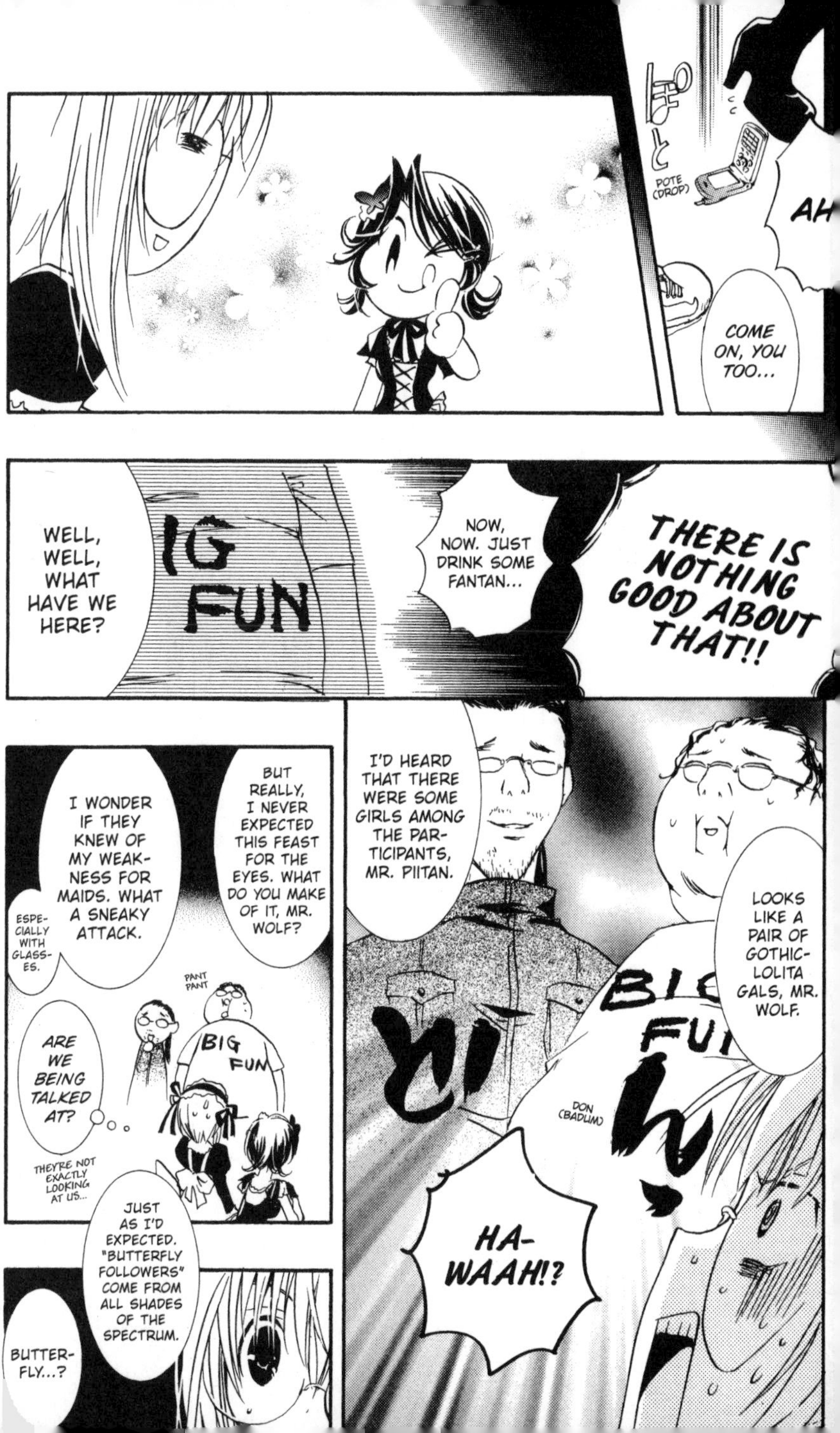

AH
POTE (DROP)
COME ON, YOU TOO...
THERE IS NOTHING GOOD ABOUT THAT!!
NOW, NOW. JUST DRINK SOME FANTAN...
IG FUN
WELL, WELL, WHAT HAVE WE HERE?
I'D HEARD THAT THERE WERE SOME GIRLS AMONG THE PARTICIPANTS, MR. PIITAN.
LOOKS LIKE A PAIR OF GOTHIC-LOLITA GALS, MR. WOLF.
DON (BADUM)
HA-WAAH!?
BUT REALLY, I NEVER EXPECTED THIS FEAST FOR THE EYES. WHAT DO YOU MAKE OF IT, MR. WOLF?
I WONDER IF THEY KNEW OF MY WEAKNESS FOR MAIDS. WHAT A SNEAKY ATTACK.
ESPECIALLY WITH GLASSES.
PANT PANT
BIG FUN
ARE WE BEING TALKED AT?
THEY'RE NOT EXACTLY LOOKING AT US...
JUST AS I'D EXPECTED. "BUTTERFLY FOLLOWERS" COME FROM ALL SHADES OF THE SPECTRUM.
BUTTERFLY...?

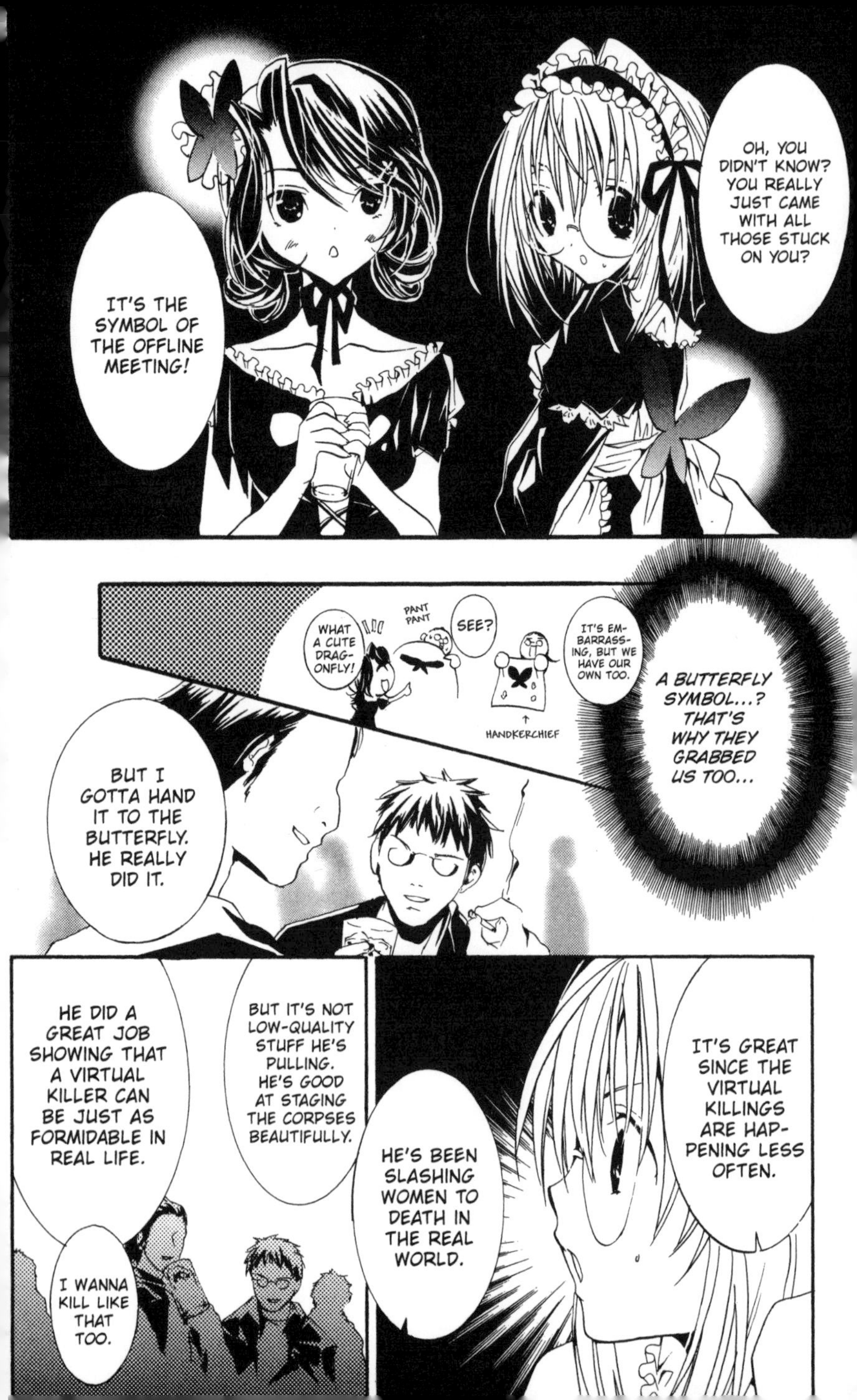
OH, YOU DIDN'T KNOW? YOU REALLY JUST CAME WITH ALL THOSE STUCK ON YOU?
IT'S THE SYMBOL OF THE OFFLINE MEETING!
A BUTTERFLY SYMBOL...? THAT'S WHY THEY GRABBED US TOO...
IT'S EM-BARRASS-ING, BUT WE HAVE OUR OWN TOO.
HANDKERCHIEF
SEE?
PANT PANT
WHAT A CUTE DRAG-ONFLY!
BUT I GOTTA HAND IT TO THE BUTTERFLY. HE REALLY DID IT.
IT'S GREAT SINCE THE VIRTUAL KILLINGS ARE HAP-PENING LESS OFTEN.
HE'S BEEN SLASHING WOMEN TO DEATH IN THE REAL WORLD.
BUT IT'S NOT LOW-QUALITY STUFF HE'S PULLING. HE'S GOOD AT STAGING THE CORPSES BEAUTIFULLY.
HE DID A GREAT JOB SHOWING THAT A VIRTUAL KILLER CAN BE JUST AS FORMIDABLE IN REAL LIFE.
I WANNA KILL LIKE THAT TOO.

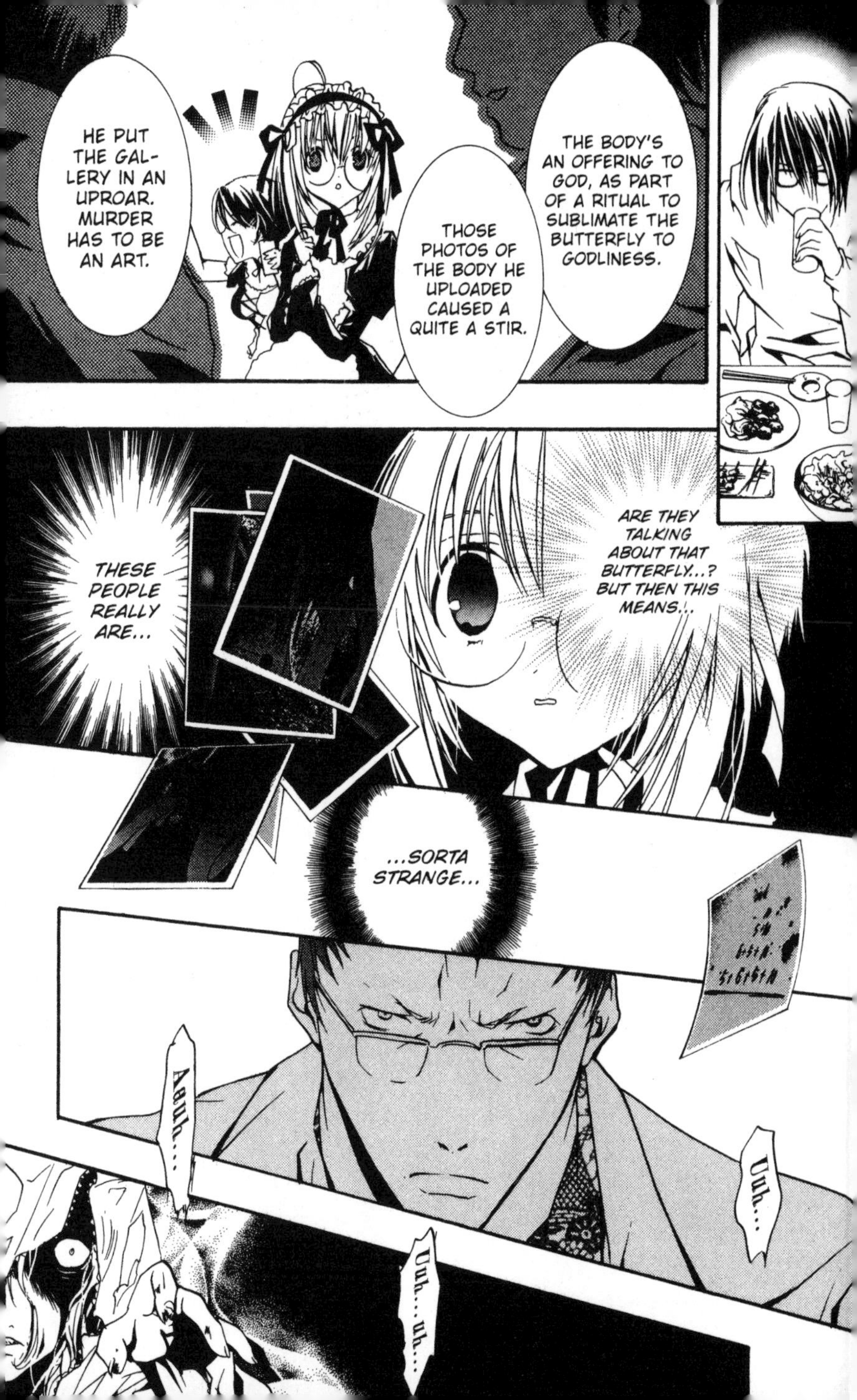
THE BODY'S AN OFFERING TO GOD, AS PART OF A RITUAL TO SUBLIMATE THE BUTTERFLY TO GODLINESS.
THOSE PHOTOS OF THE BODY HE UPLOADED CAUSED A QUITE A STIR.
HE PUT THE GALLERY IN AN UPROAR. MURDER HAS TO BE AN ART.
ARE THEY TALKING ABOUT THAT BUTTERFLY...? BUT THEN THIS MEANS...
THESE PEOPLE REALLY ARE...
...SORTA STRANGE...
Uuh...
Uuh...uh...
Aauh...

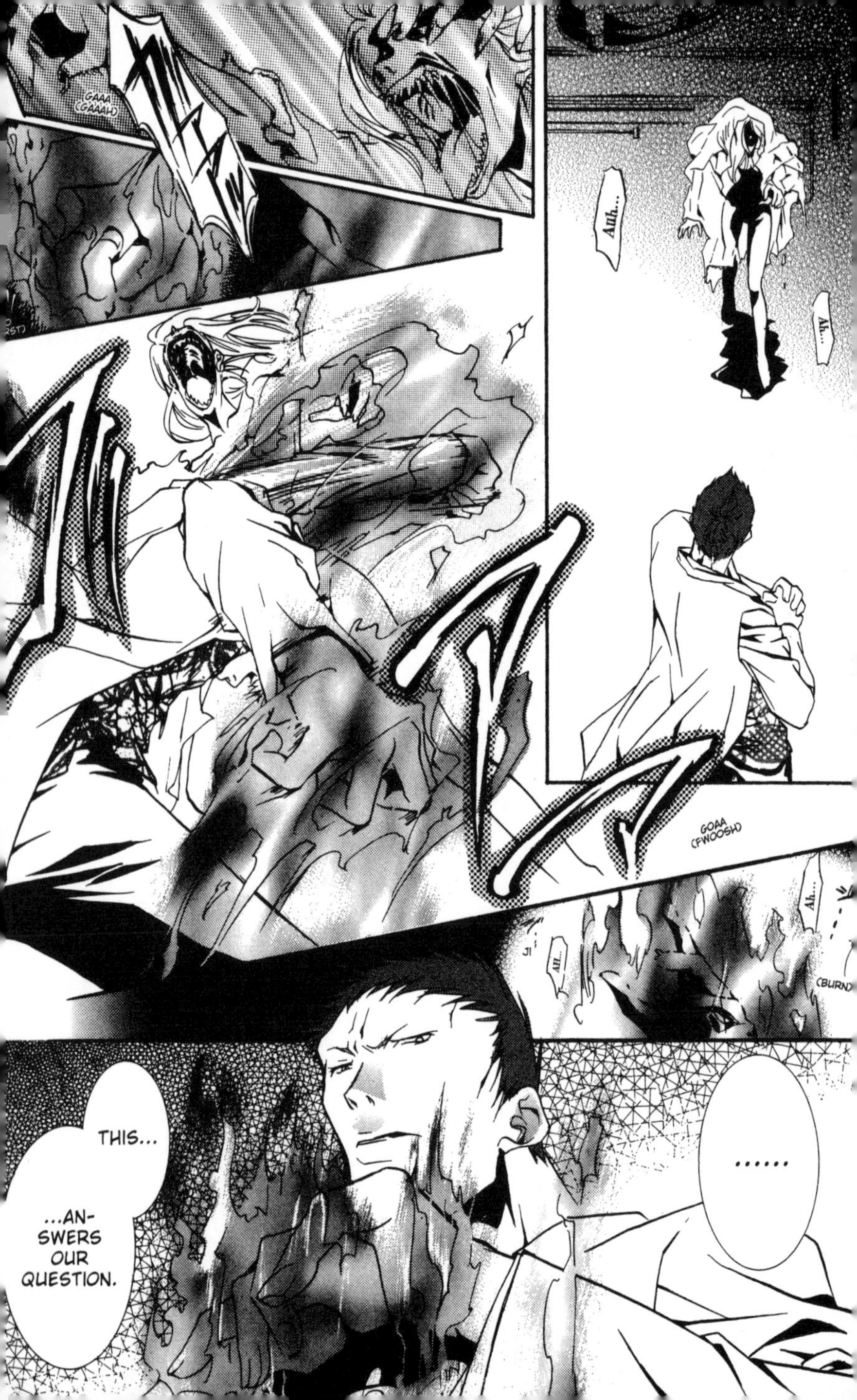
Auh...
Ah...
GAAA (GAAAH)
GOAA (FWOOSH)
Ah...
(BURN)
JI
AH...
....
THIS...
...AN-SWERS OUR QUESTION.

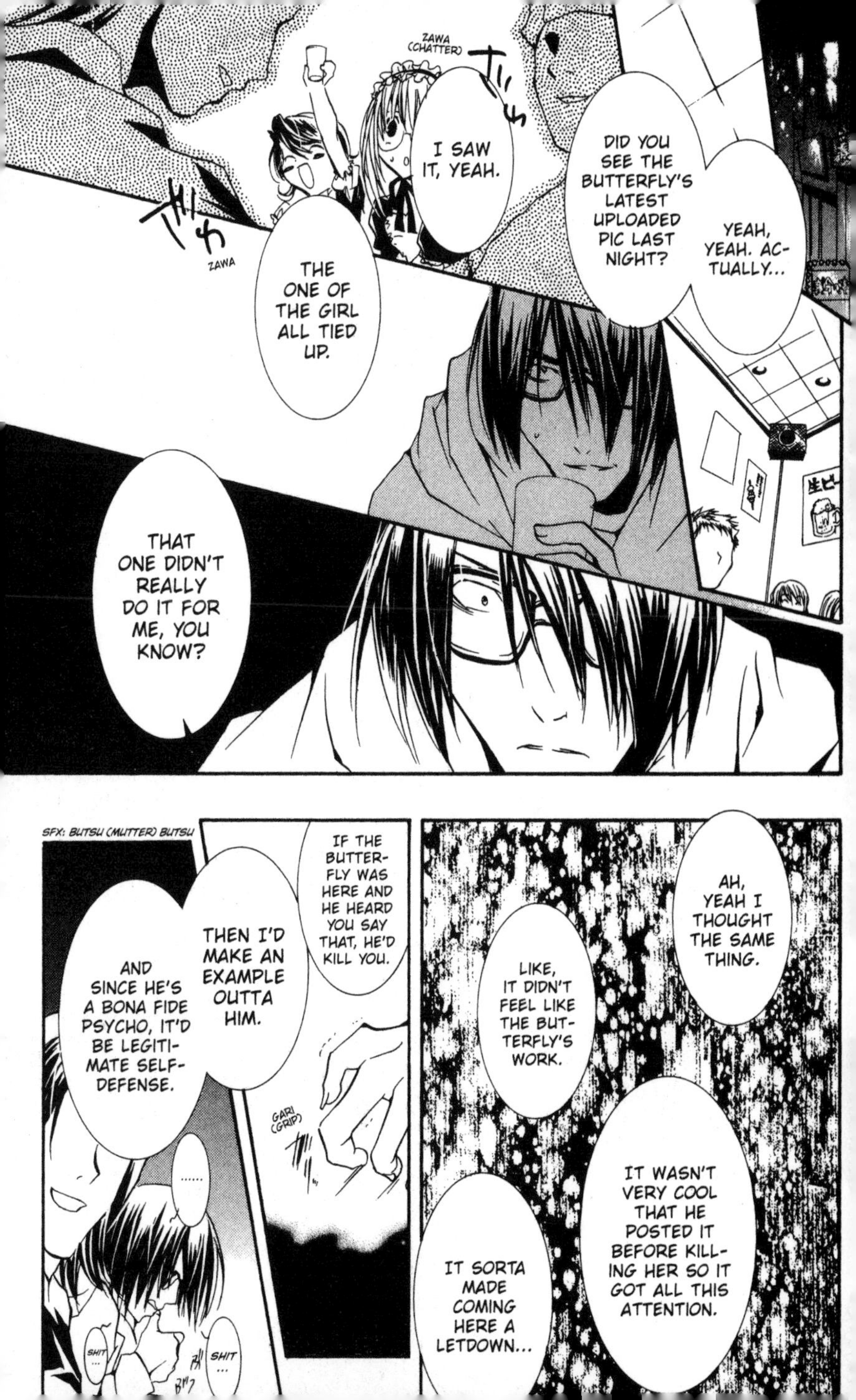

DID YOU SEE THE BUTTERFLY'S LATEST UPLOADED PIC LAST NIGHT?
YEAH, YEAH. AC-TUALLY...
ZAWA (CHATTER)
I SAW IT, YEAH.
THE ONE OF THE GIRL ALL TIED UP.
ZAWA
THAT ONE DIDN'T REALLY DO IT FOR ME, YOU KNOW?
AH, YEAH I THOUGHT THE SAME THING.
LIKE, IT DIDN'T FEEL LIKE THE BUT-TERFLY'S WORK.
IT WASN'T VERY COOL THAT HE POSTED IT BEFORE KILL-ING HER SO IT GOT ALL THIS ATTENTION.
IT SORTA MADE COMING HERE A LETDOWN...
SFX: BUTSU (MUTTER) BUTSU
IF THE BUTTER-FLY WAS HERE AND HE HEARD YOU SAY THAT, HE'D KILL YOU.
THEN I'D MAKE AN EXAMPLE OUTTA HIM.
AND SINCE HE'S A BONA FIDE PSYCHO, IT'D BE LEGITI-MATE SELF-DEFENSE.
GARI (GRIP)
......
SHIT...
SHIT...

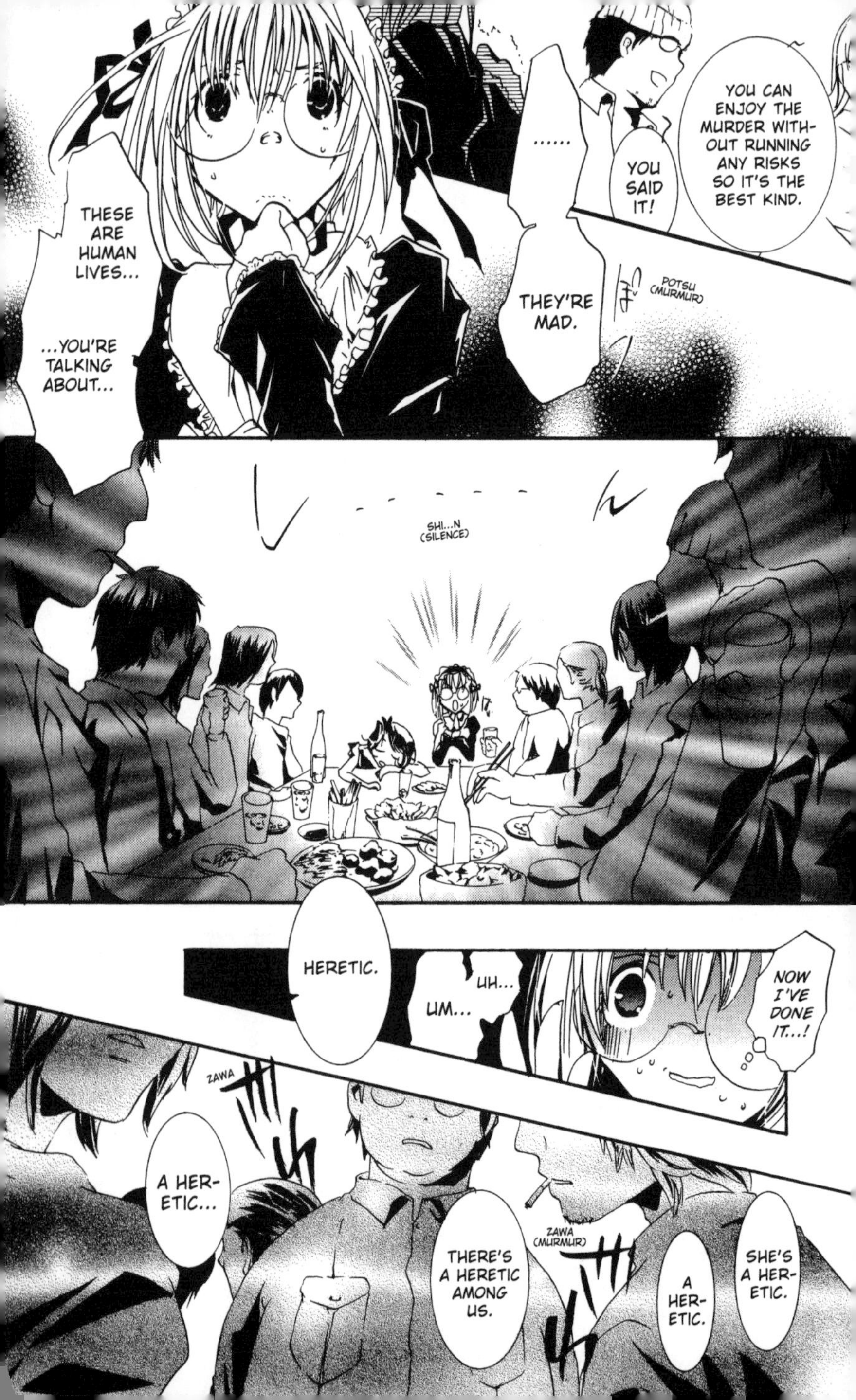
YOU CAN ENJOY THE MURDER WITHOUT RUNNING ANY RISKS SO IT'S THE BEST KIND.
YOU SAID IT!
......
POTSU (MURMUR)
THEY'RE MAD.
THESE ARE HUMAN LIVES...
...YOU'RE TALKING ABOUT...
SHI...N (SILENCE)
NOW I'VE DONE IT...!
UH...
UM...
HERETIC.
SHE'S A HERETIC.
A HERETIC.
ZAWA (MURMUR)
THERE'S A HERETIC AMONG US.
A HERETIC...
ZAWA

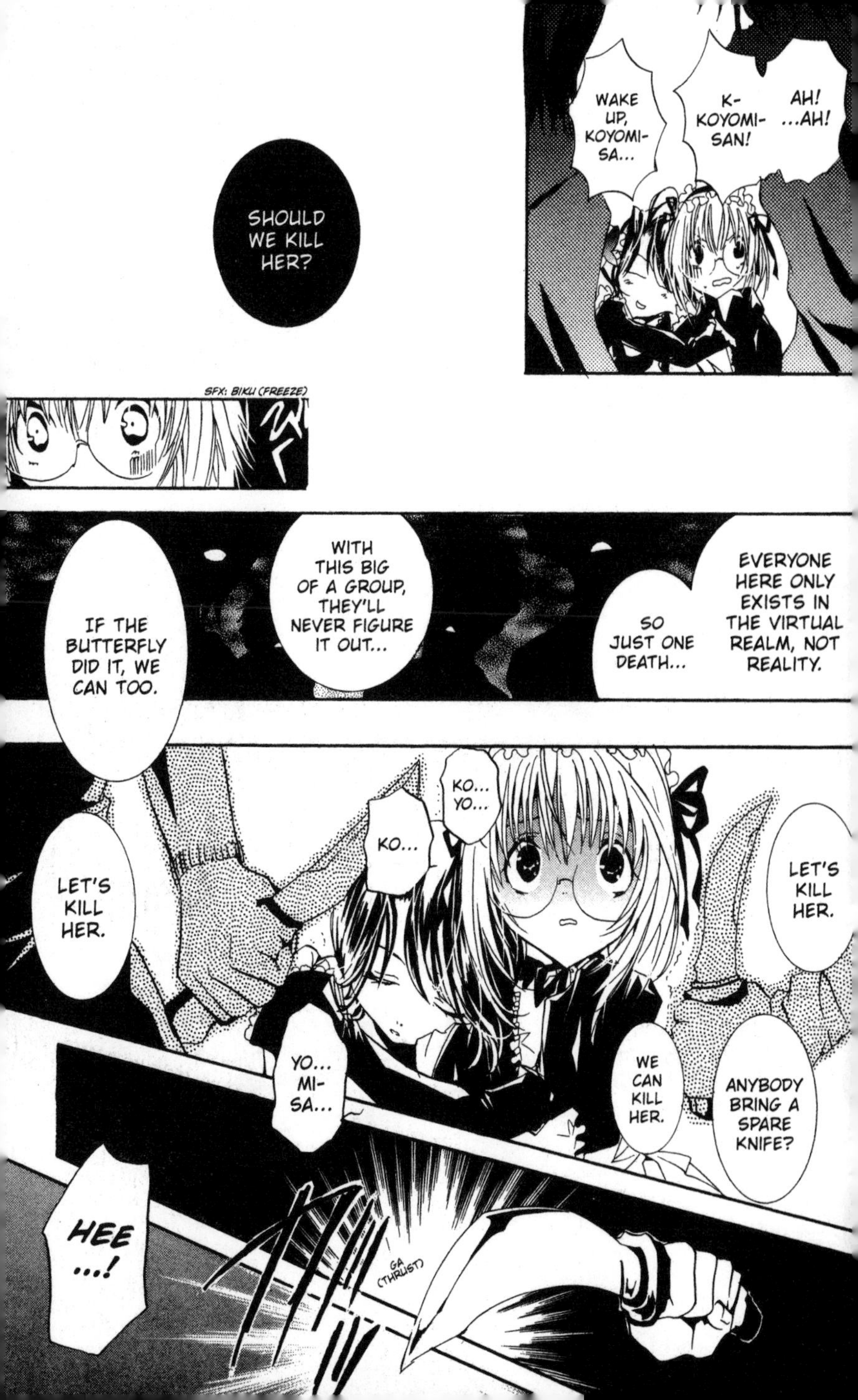
AH! ...AH!
K-KOYOMI-SAN!
WAKE UP, KOYOMI-SA...
SHOULD WE KILL HER?
SFX: BIKU (FREEZE)
EVERYONE HERE ONLY EXISTS IN THE VIRTUAL REALM, NOT REALITY.
SO JUST ONE DEATH...
WITH THIS BIG OF A GROUP, THEY'LL NEVER FIGURE IT OUT...
IF THE BUTTERFLY DID IT, WE CAN TOO.
LET'S KILL HER.
KO... YO...
KO...
LET'S KILL HER.
ANYBODY BRING A SPARE KNIFE?
WE CAN KILL HER.
YO... MI-SA...
GA (THRUST)
HEE ...!

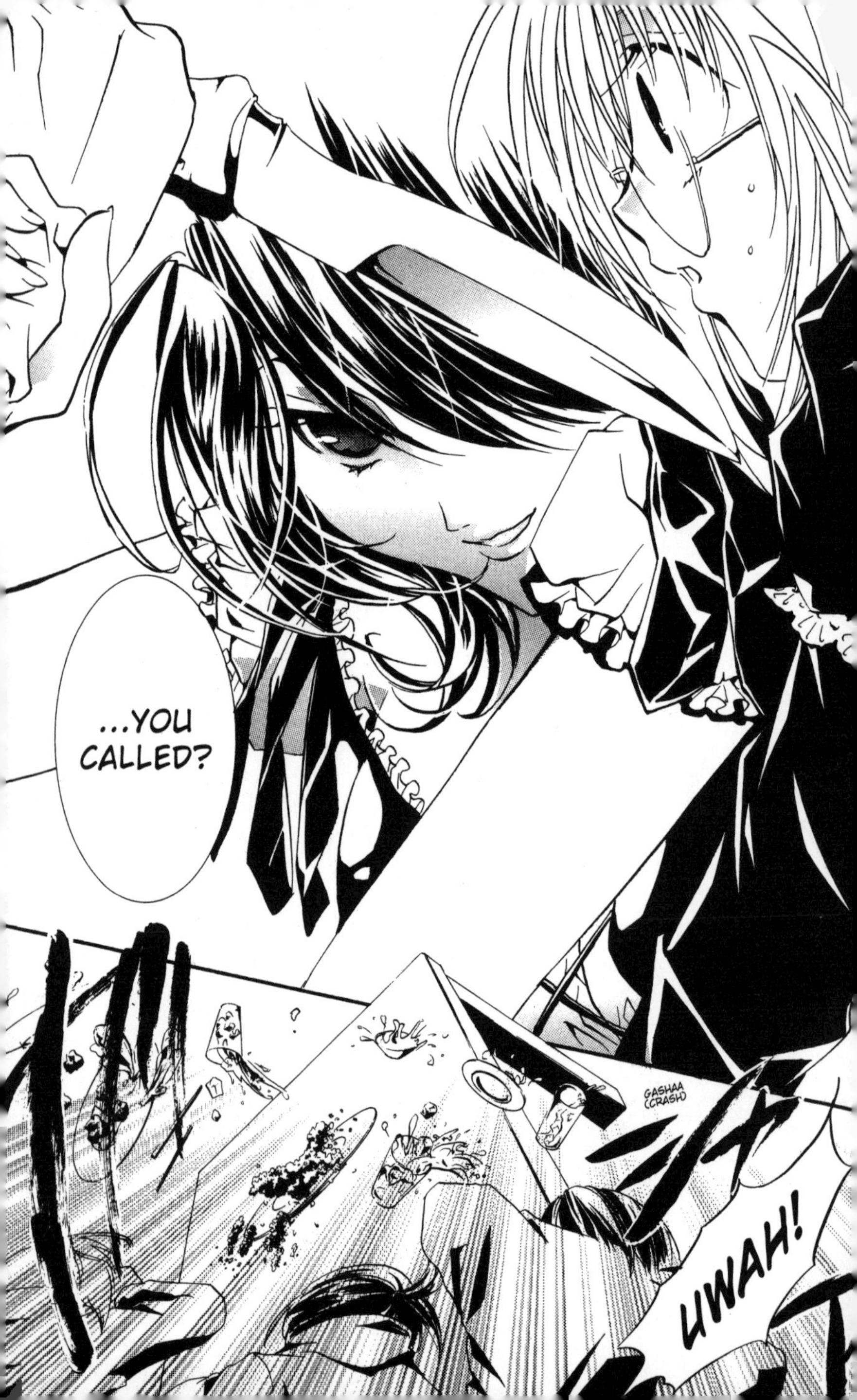
...YOU CALLED?
GASHAA (CRASH)
UWAH!

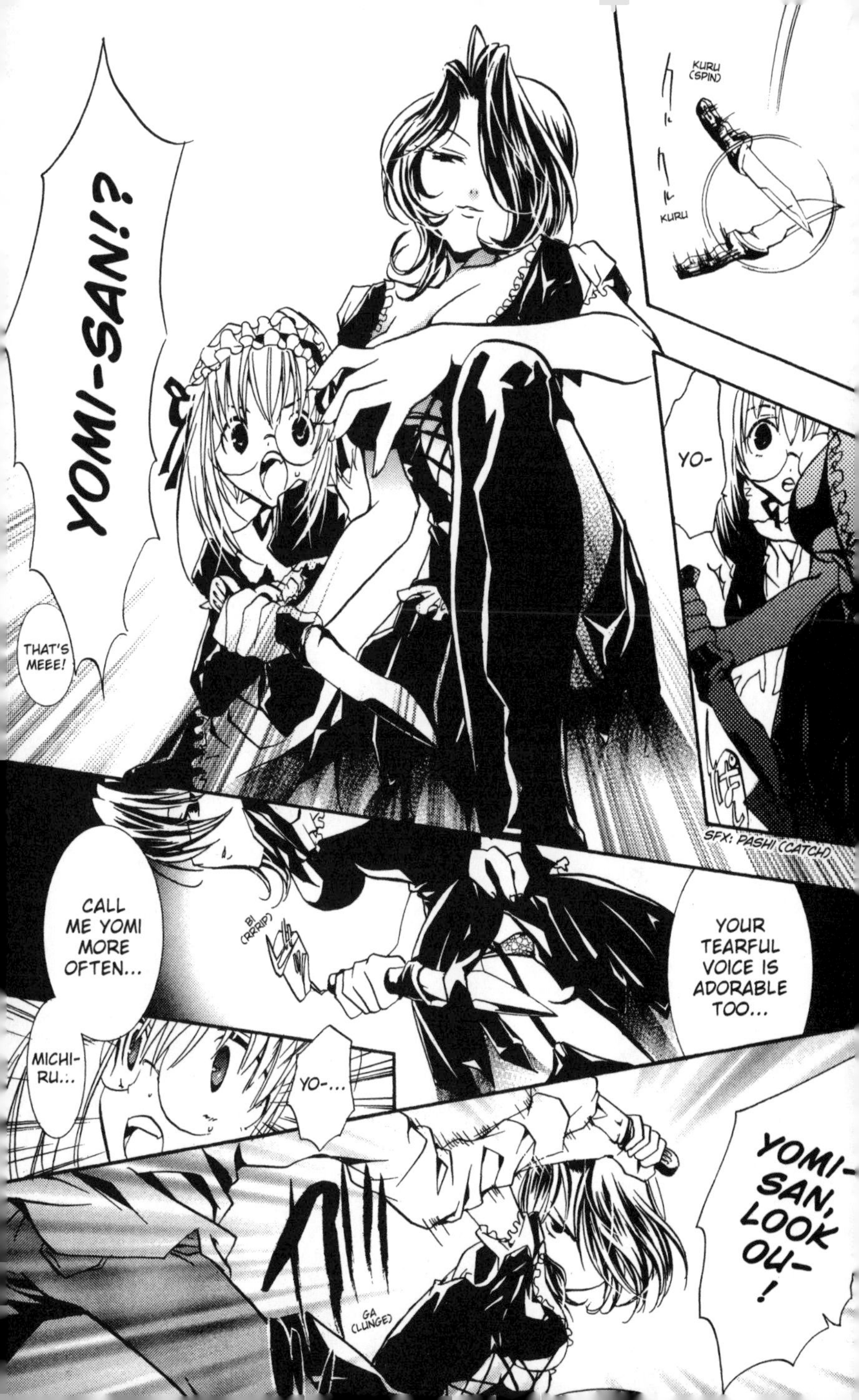

KURU (SPIN)
KURU
YOMI-SAN!?
THAT'S MEEE!
YO-
SFX: PASHI (CATCH)
BI (RRRIP)
YOUR TEARFUL VOICE IS ADORABLE TOO...
CALL ME YOMI MORE OFTEN...
MICHI-RU...
YO-...
YOMI-SAN, LOOK OU-!
GA (LUNGE)

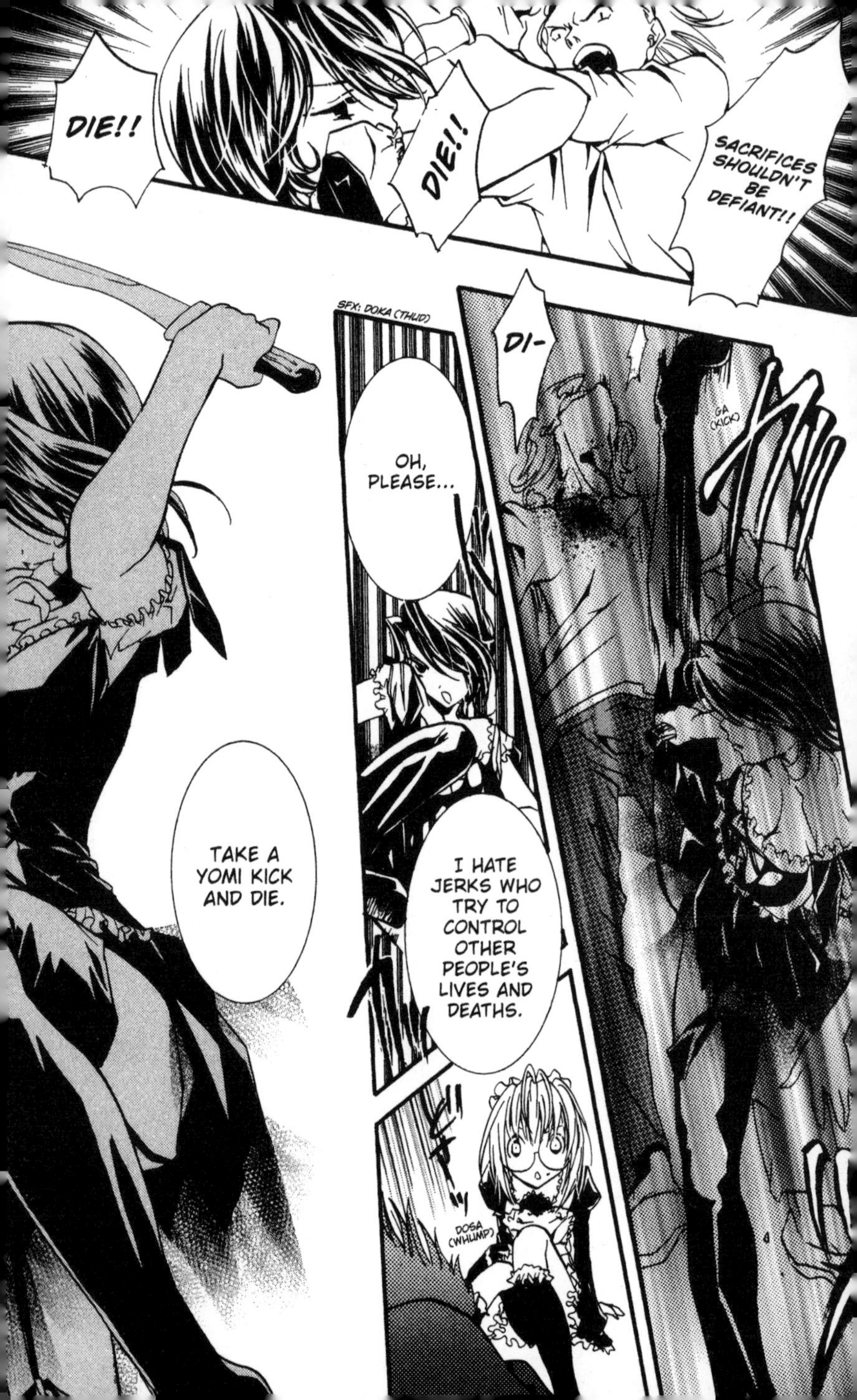
SACRIFICES SHOULDN'T BE DEFIANT!!
DIE!!
DIE!!
DI-
GA (KICK)
SFX: DOKA (THUD)
OH, PLEASE...
I HATE JERKS WHO TRY TO CONTROL OTHER PEOPLE'S LIVES AND DEATHS.
DOSA (WHUMP)
TAKE A YOMI KICK AND DIE.

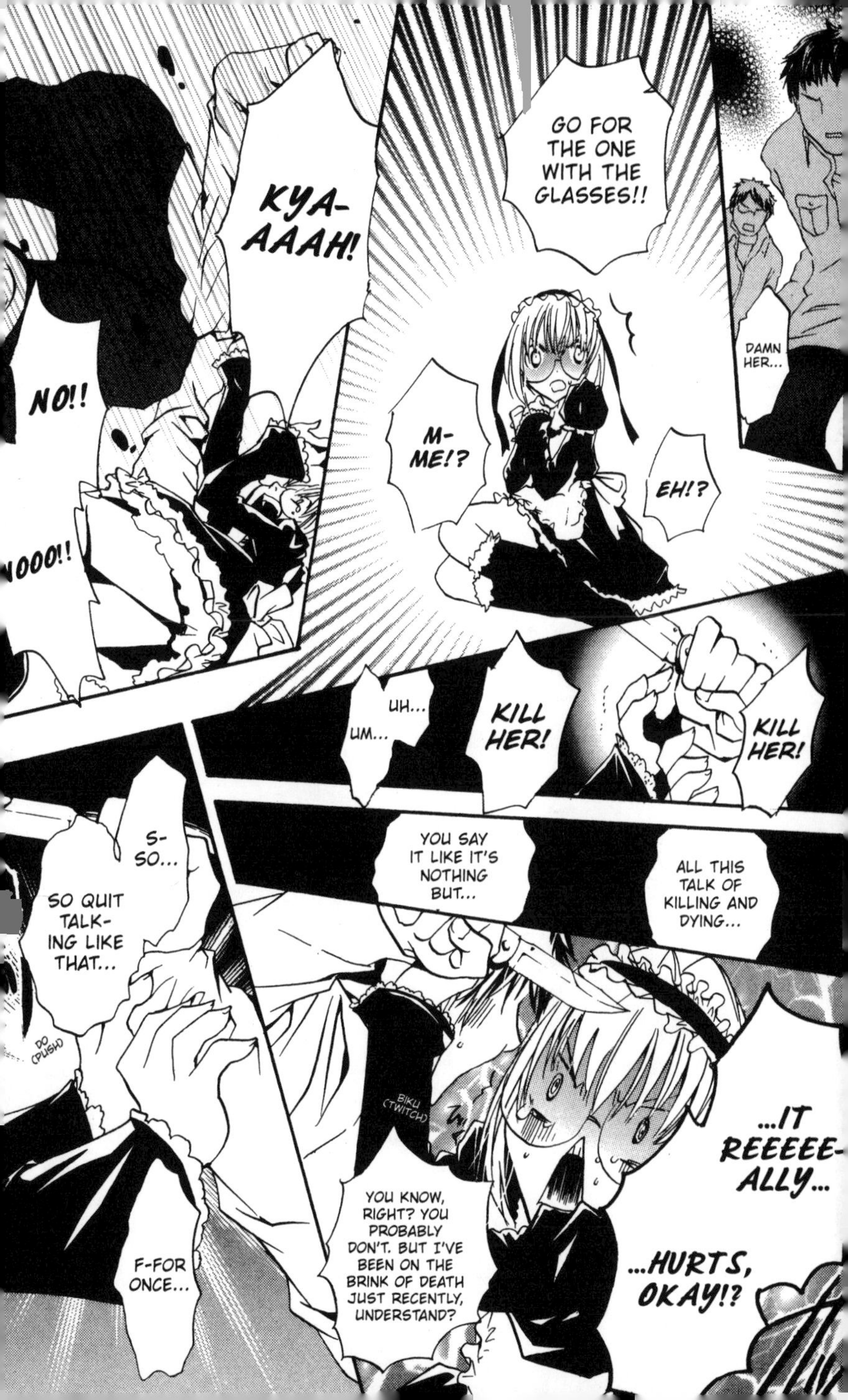

GO FOR THE ONE WITH THE GLASSES!!
DAMN HER...
EH!?
M-ME!?
KYA-AAAH!
NO!!
NOOO!!
KILL HER!
KILL HER!
UH...
UM...
ALL THIS TALK OF KILLING AND DYING...
YOU SAY IT LIKE IT'S NOTHING BUT...
BIKU (TWITCH)
...IT REEEEEE-ALLY...
...HURTS, OKAY!?
YOU KNOW, RIGHT? YOU PROBABLY DON'T. BUT I'VE BEEN ON THE BRINK OF DEATH JUST RECENTLY, UNDERSTAND?
S-SO...
SO QUIT TALK-ING LIKE THAT...
DO (PUSH)
F-FOR ONCE...

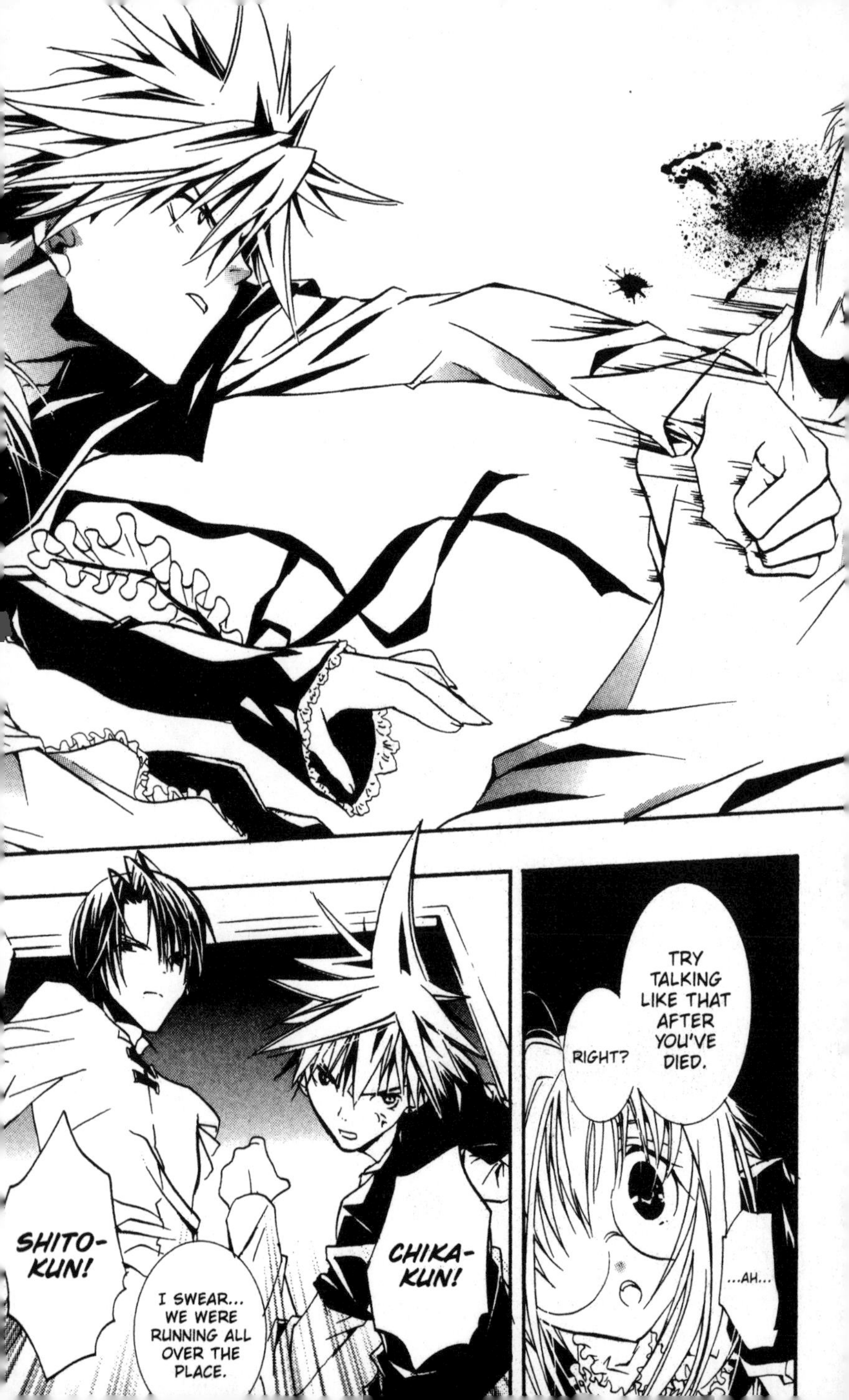
TRY TALKING LIKE THAT AFTER YOU'VE DIED.
RIGHT?
...AH...
CHIKA-KUN!
SHITO-KUN!
I SWEAR... WE WERE RUNNING ALL OVER THE PLACE.

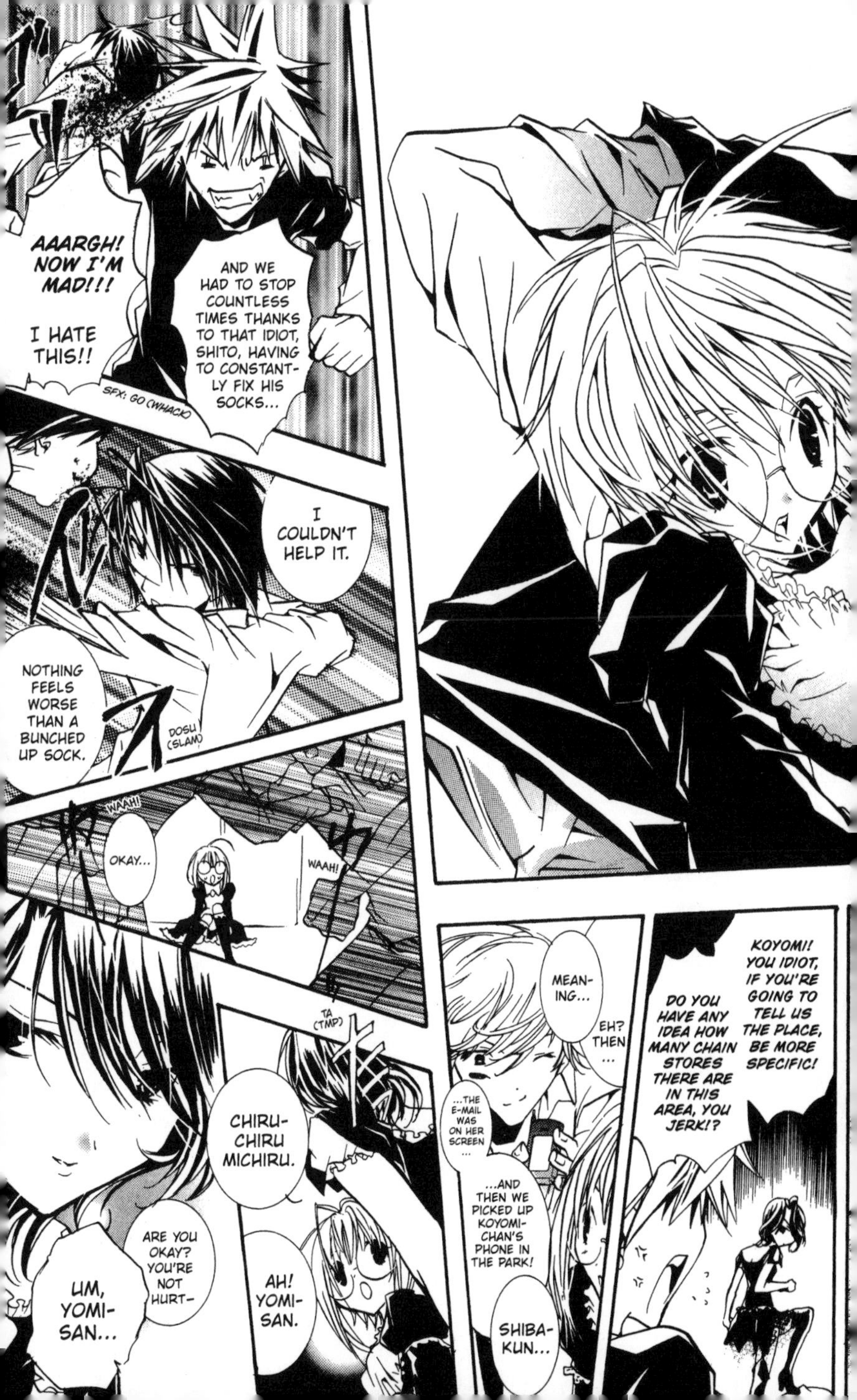
AND WE HAD TO STOP COUNTLESS TIMES THANKS TO THAT IDIOT, SHITO, HAVING TO CONSTANTLY FIX HIS SOCKS...
SFX: GO (WHACK)
AAARGH! NOW I'M MAD!!!
I HATE THIS!!
I COULDN'T HELP IT.
DOSU (SLAM)
NOTHING FEELS WORSE THAN A BUNCHED UP SOCK.
WAAH!
OKAY...
WAAH!
KOYOMI! YOU IDIOT, IF YOU'RE GOING TO TELL US THE PLACE, BE MORE SPECIFIC!
DO YOU HAVE ANY IDEA HOW MANY CHAIN STORES THERE ARE IN THIS AREA, YOU JERK!?
MEANING...
EH? THEN...
...THE E-MAIL WAS ON HER SCREEN...
...AND THEN WE PICKED UP KOYOMI-CHAN'S PHONE IN THE PARK!
SHIBA-KUN...
TA (TMP)
CHIRU-CHIRU MICHIRU.
ARE YOU OKAY? YOU'RE NOT HURT-
AH! YOMI-SAN.
UM, YOMI-SAN...

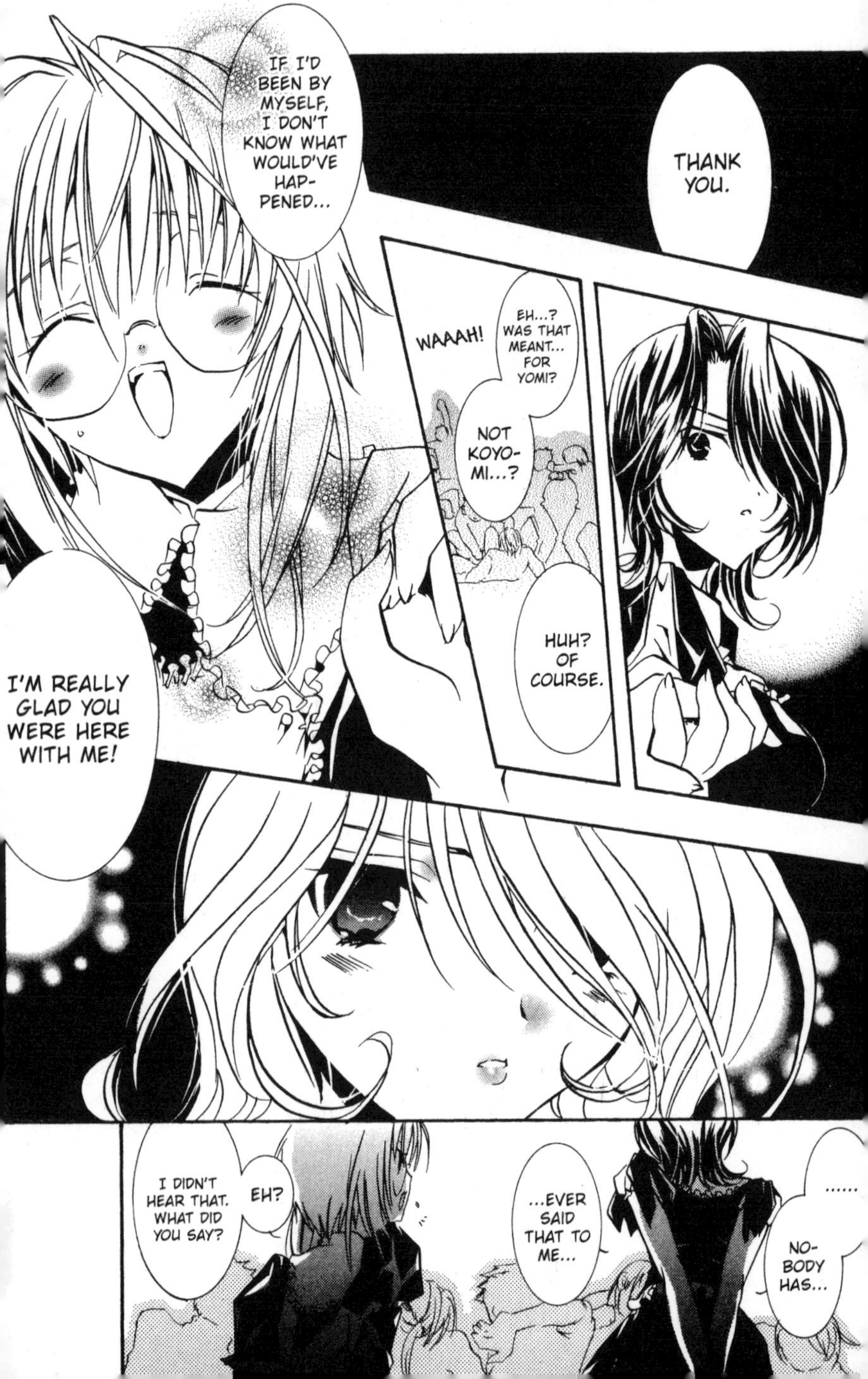
THANK YOU.
IF I'D BEEN BY MYSELF, I DON'T KNOW WHAT WOULD'VE HAP-PENED...
I'M REALLY GLAD YOU WERE HERE WITH ME!
HUH? OF COURSE.
EH...? WAS THAT MEANT... FOR YOMI?
NOT KOYO-MI...?
WAAAH!
......
NO-BODY HAS...
...EVER SAID THAT TO ME...
EH?
I DIDN'T HEAR THAT. WHAT DID YOU SAY?

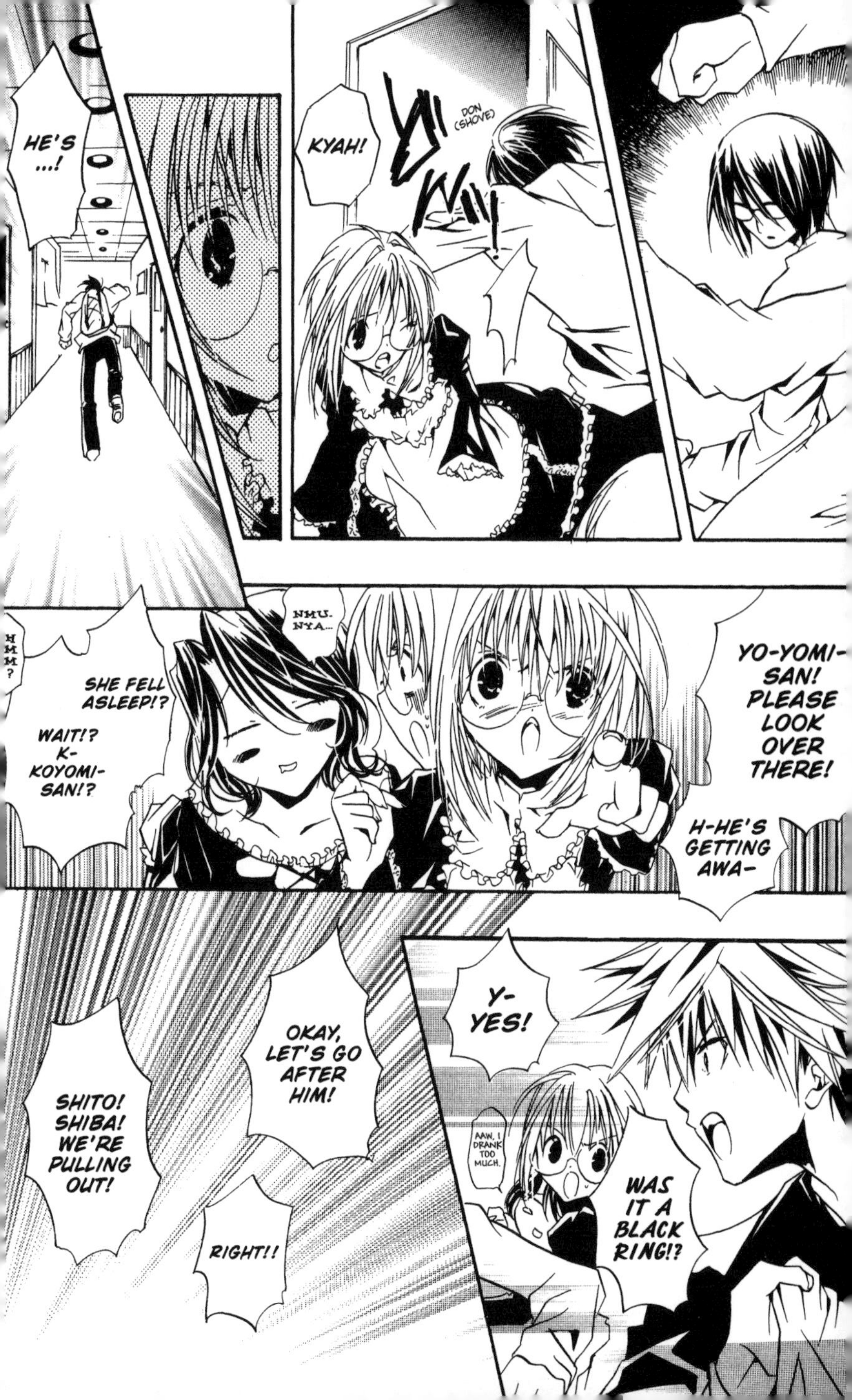
DON (SHOVE)
KYAH!
HE'S ...!
YO-YOMI-SAN! PLEASE LOOK OVER THERE!
H-HE'S GETTING AWA-
NMU. NYA...
SHE FELL ASLEEP!?
WAIT!? K-KOYOMI-SAN!?
HMM?
Y-YES!
WAS IT A BLACK RING!?
AAW, I DRANK TOO MUCH.
OKAY, LET'S GO AFTER HIM!
SHITO! SHIBA! WE'RE PULLING OUT!
RIGHT!!

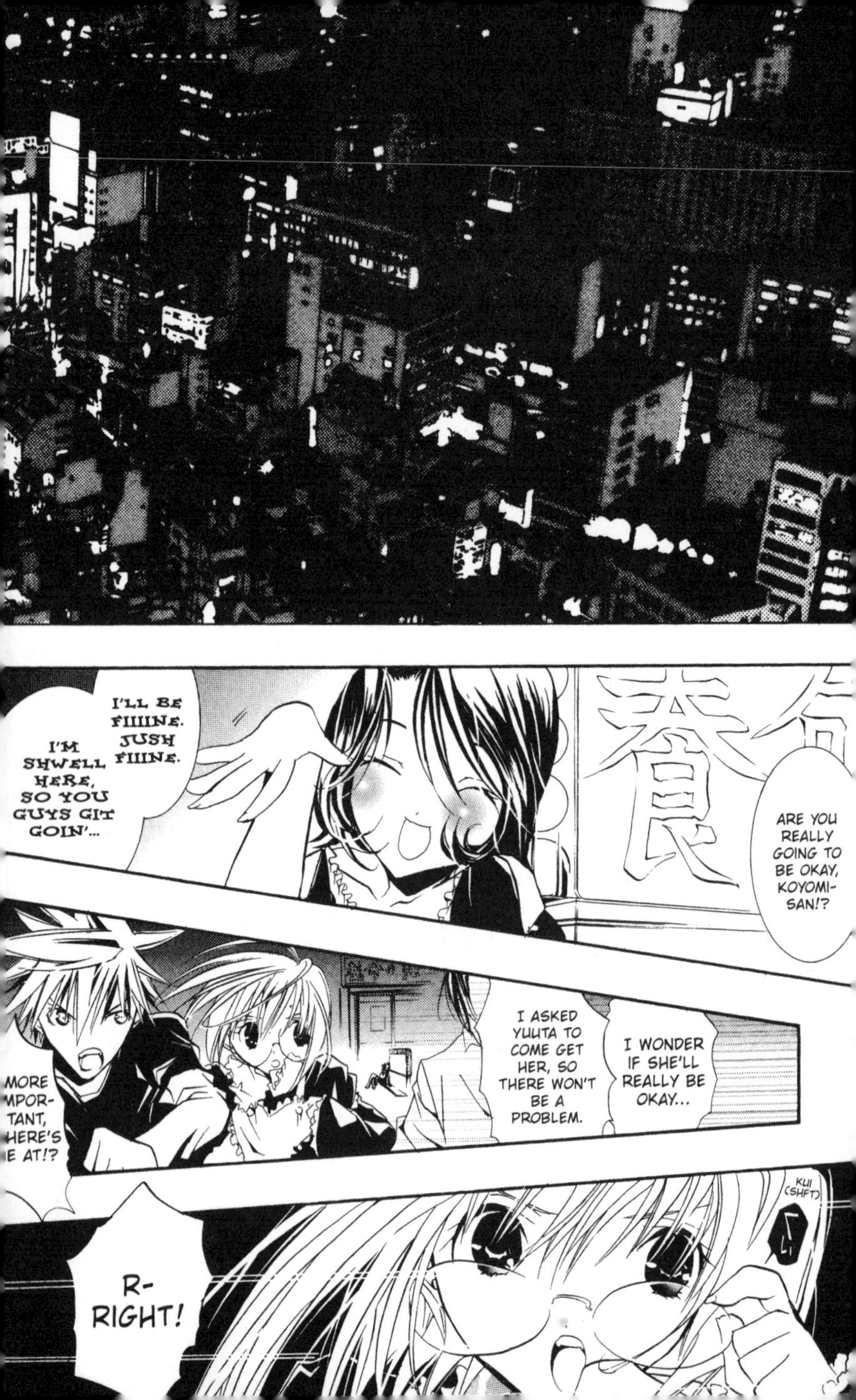
ARE YOU REALLY GOING TO BE OKAY, KOYOMI-SAN!?
I'LL BE FIIIINE. JUSH FIIIINE.
I'M SHWELL HERE, SO YOU GUYS GIT GOIN'...
I WONDER IF SHE'LL REALLY BE OKAY...
I ASKED YUUTA TO COME GET HER, SO THERE WON'T BE A PROBLEM.
MORE MPOR-TANT, HERE'S E AT!?
KUI (SHFT)
R- RIGHT!

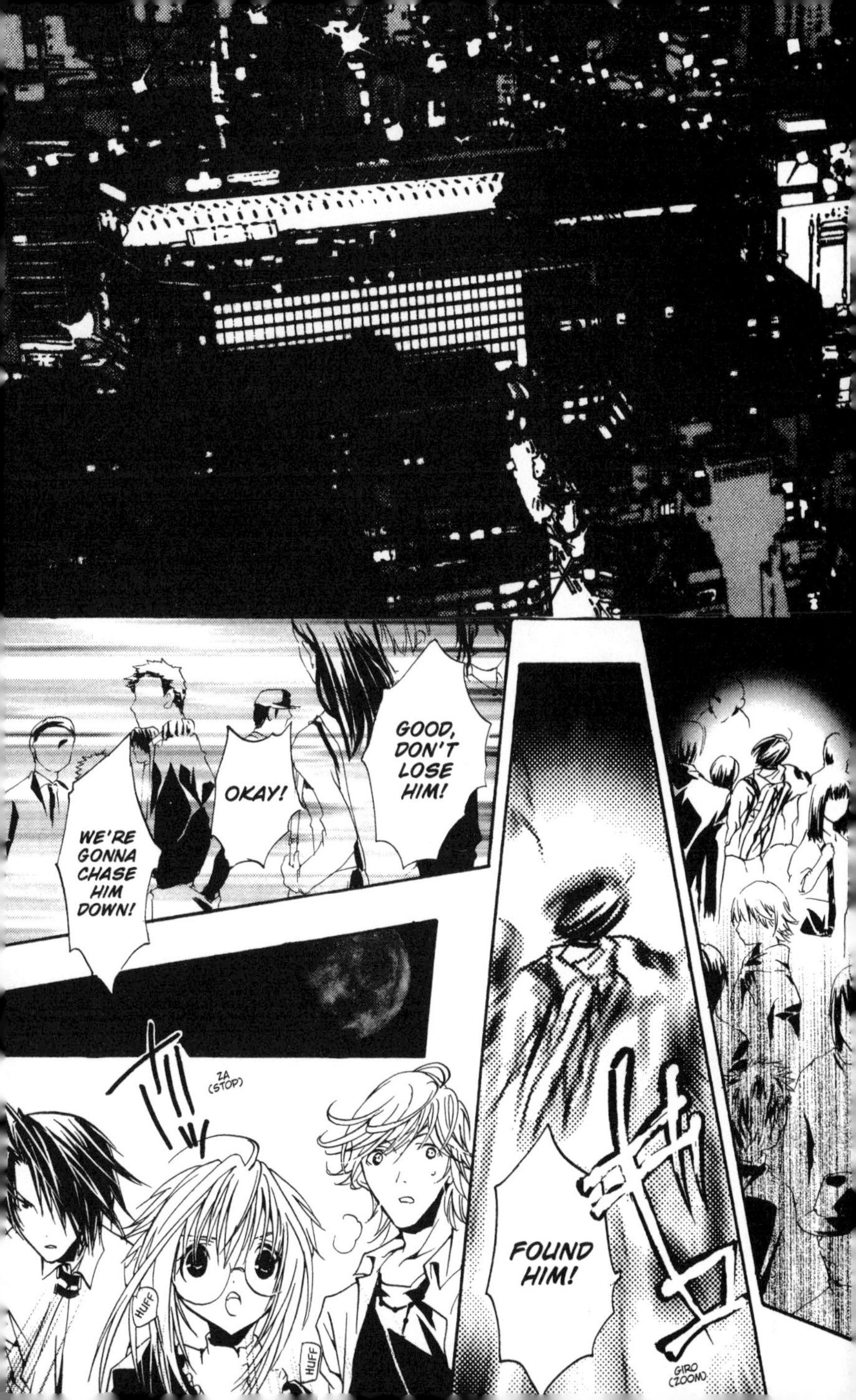
FOUND HIM!
GIRO (ZOOM)
GOOD, DON'T LOSE HIM!
OKAY!
WE'RE GONNA CHASE HIM DOWN!
ZA (STOP)
HUFF
HUFF

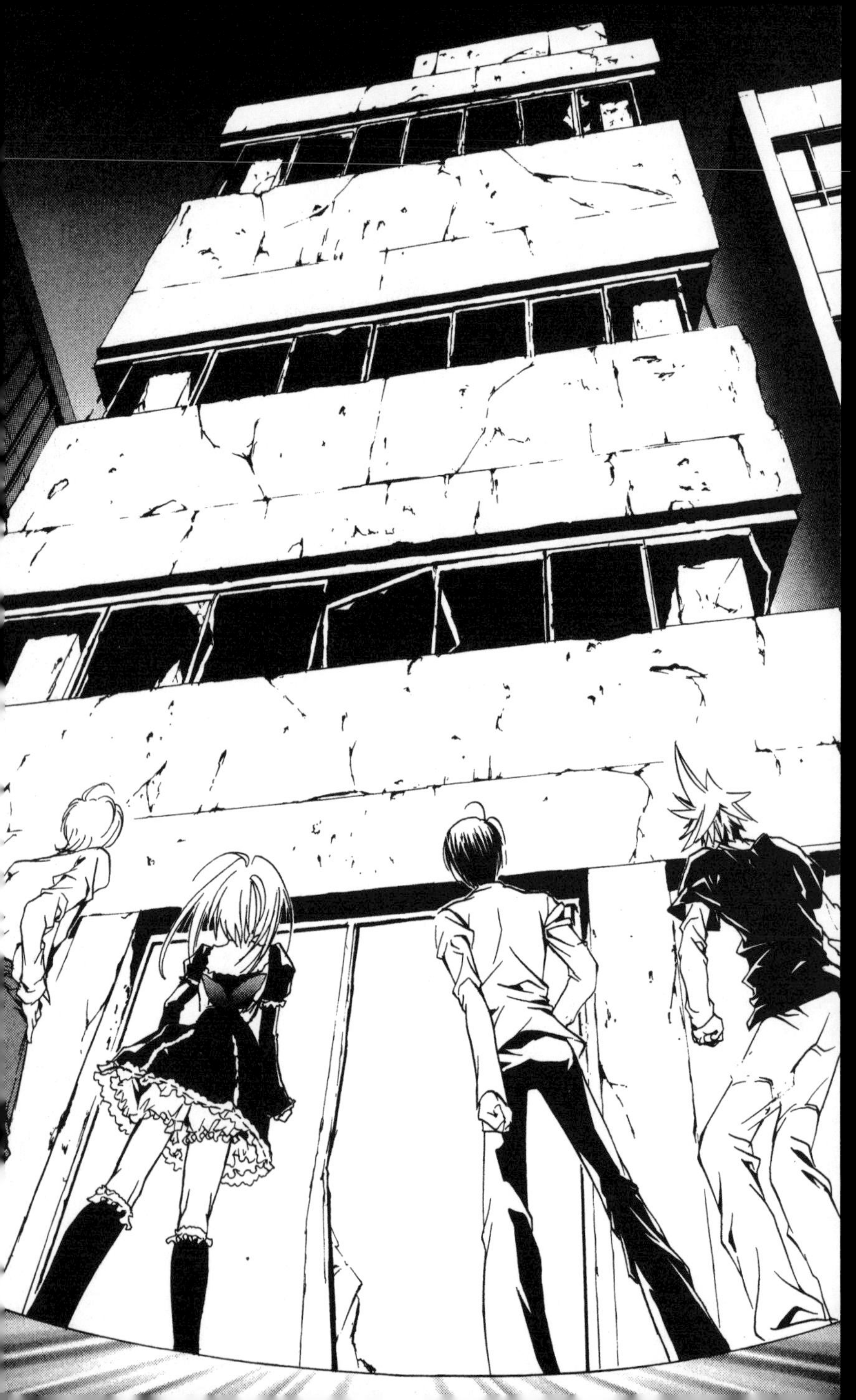

ZOMBIE-LOAN

PAYMENT:15

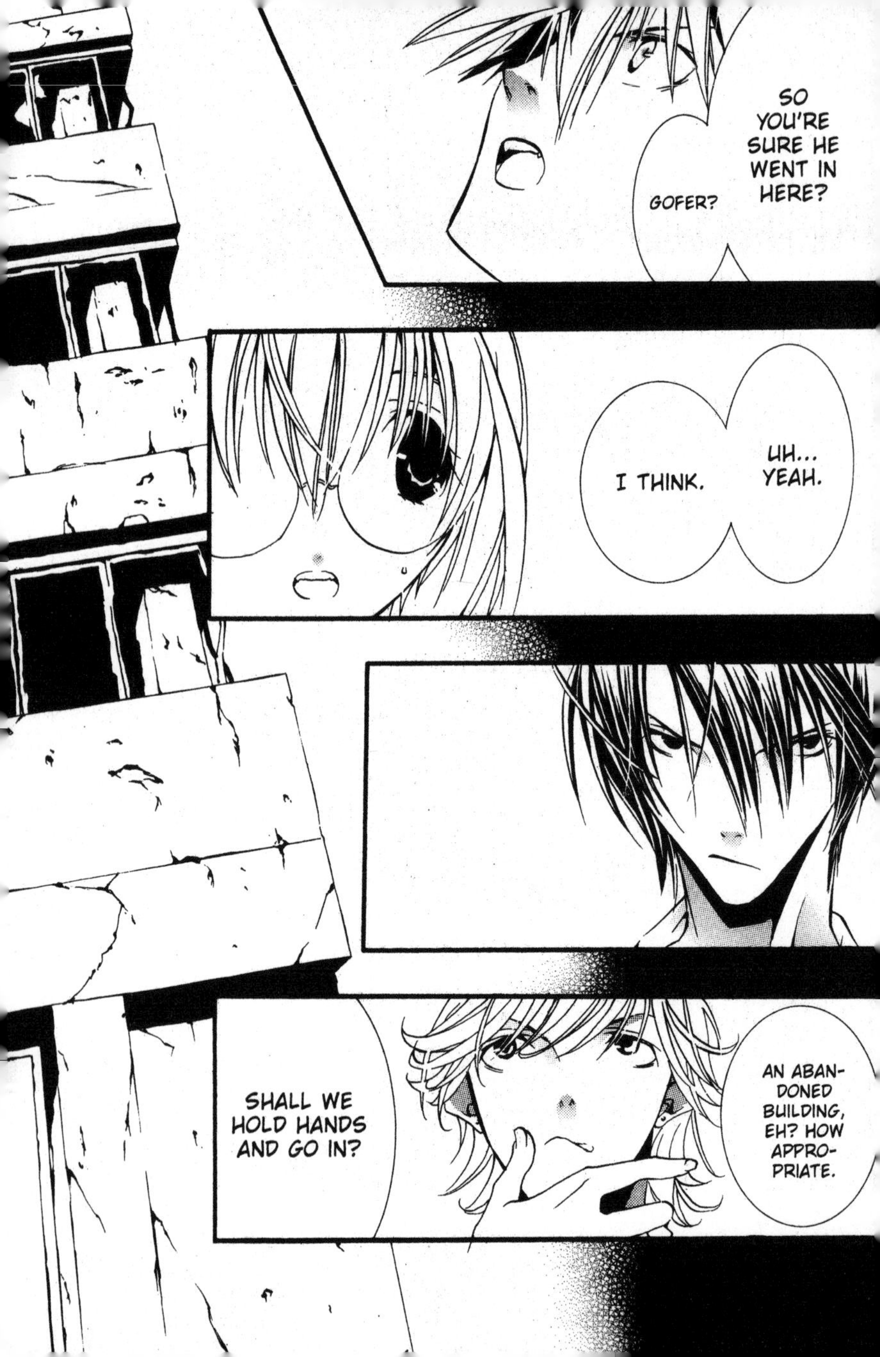
SO YOU'RE SURE HE WENT IN HERE?
GOFER?
UH... YEAH.
I THINK.
AN ABAN-DONED BUILDING, EH? HOW APPRO-PRIATE.
SHALL WE HOLD HANDS AND GO IN?

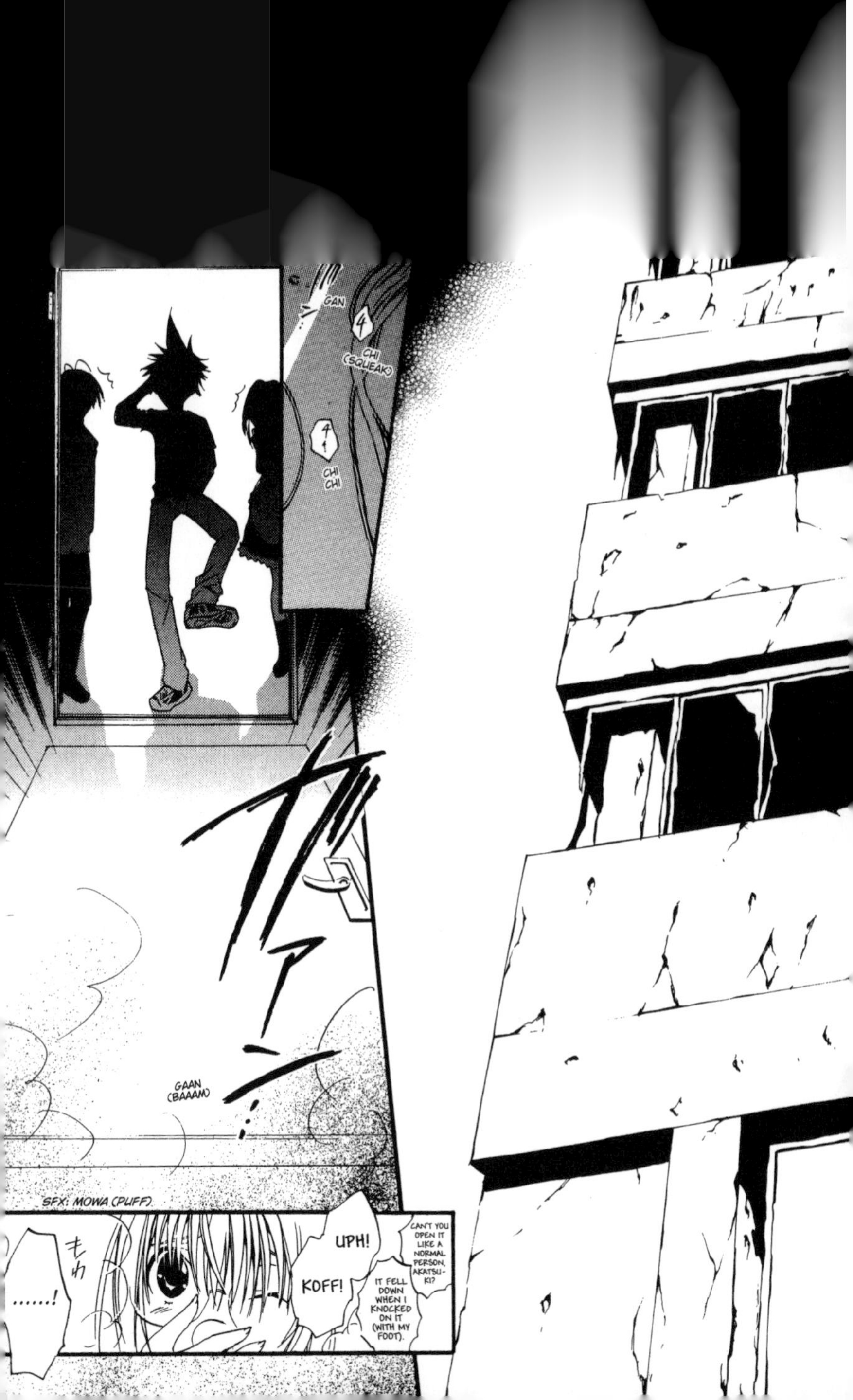
GAN
CHI (SQUEAK)
CHI CHI
GAAN (BAAAM)
SFX: MOWA (PUFF)
CAN'T YOU OPEN IT LIKE A NORMAL PERSON, AKATSUKI?
IT FELL DOWN WHEN I KNOCKED ON IT (WITH MY FOOT).
UPH!
KOFF!
......!

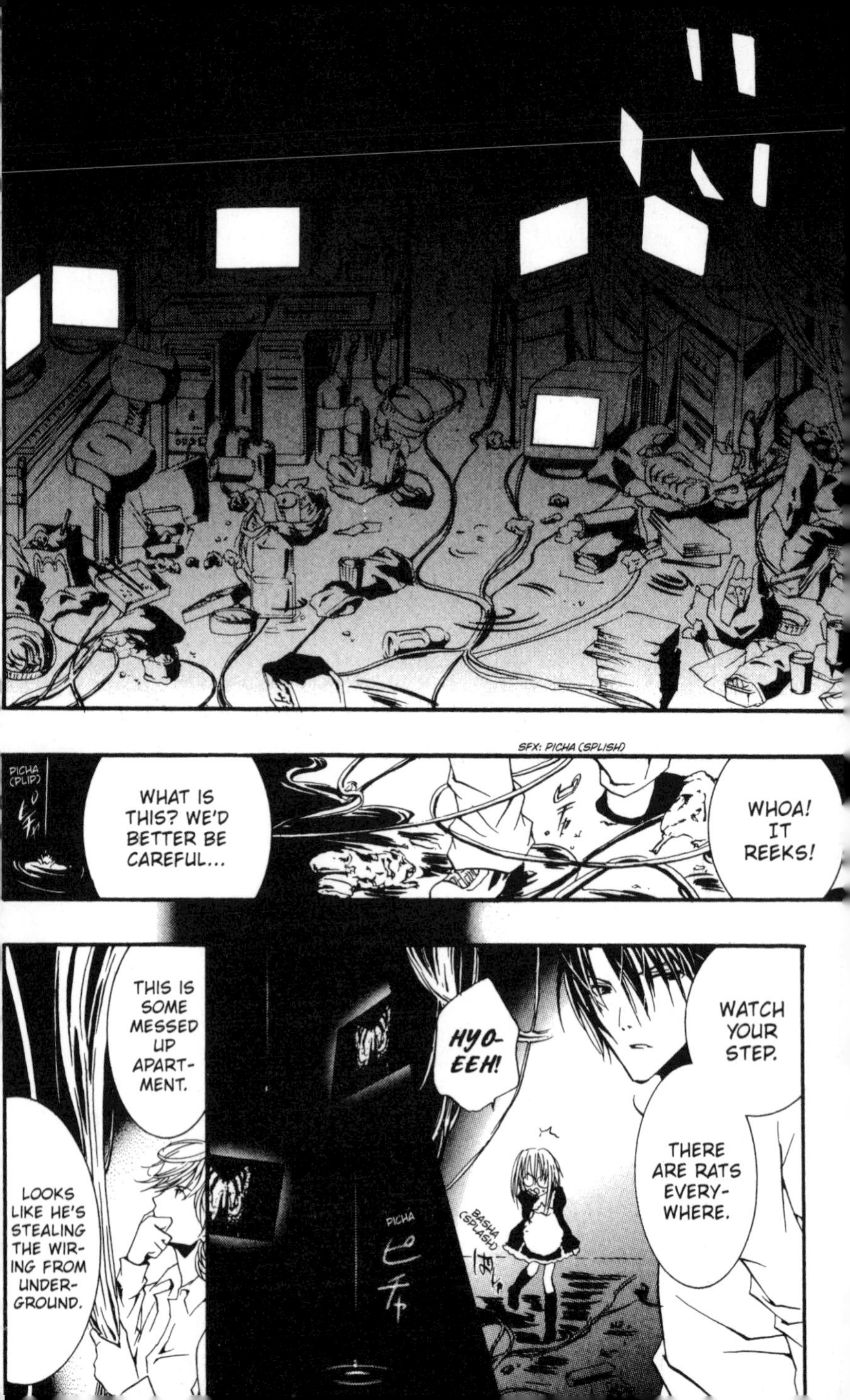
SFX: PICHA (SPLISH)
WHOA! IT REEKS!
WHAT IS THIS? WE'D BETTER BE CAREFUL...
PICHA (PLIP)
WATCH YOUR STEP.
THERE ARE RATS EVERY-WHERE.
HYO-EEH!
BASHA (SPLASH)
PICHA
THIS IS SOME MESSED UP APART-MENT.
LOOKS LIKE HE'S STEALING THE WIR-ING FROM UNDER-GROUND.

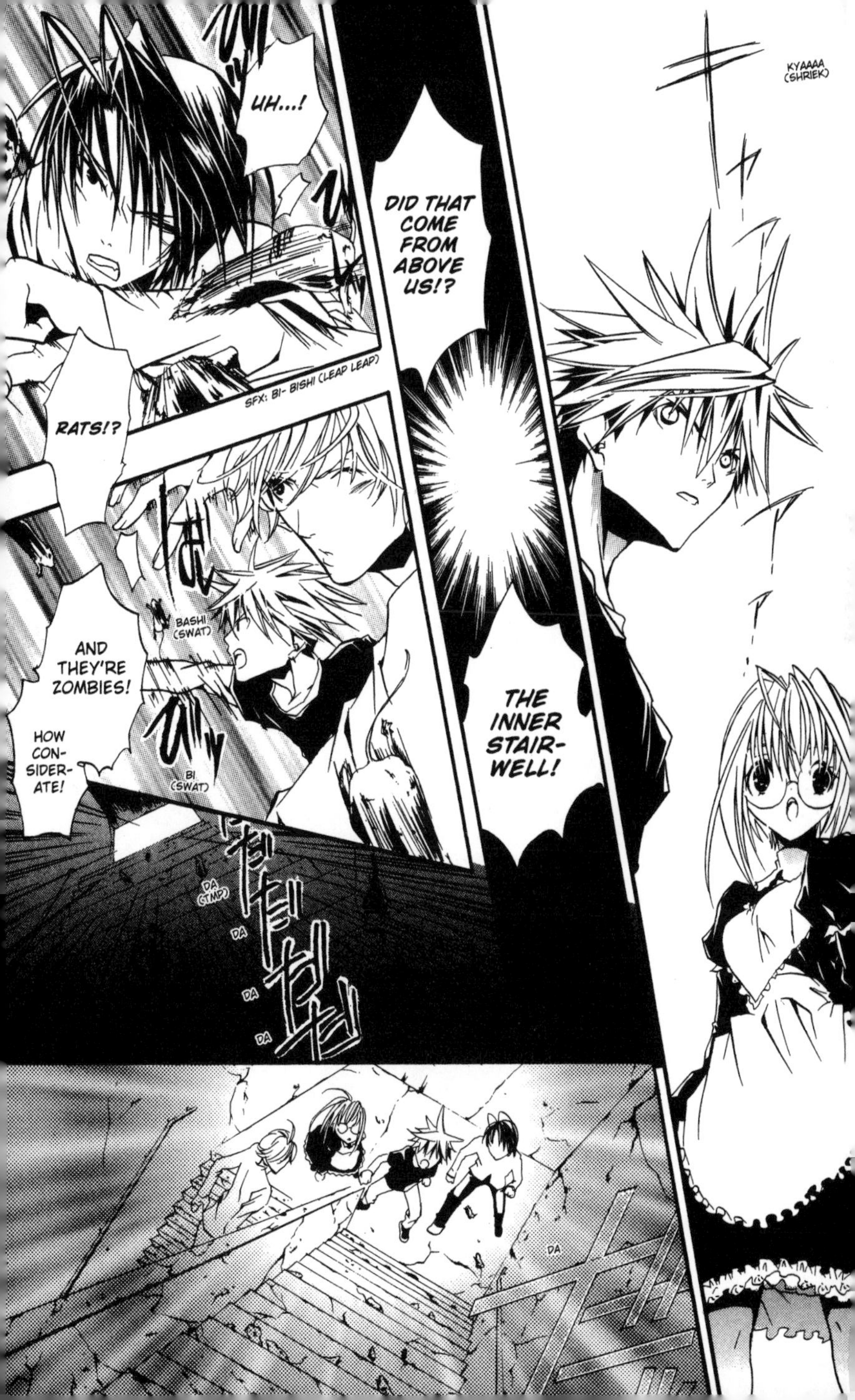
KYAAAA (SHRIEK)
DID THAT COME FROM ABOVE US!?
THE INNER STAIR-WELL!
UH...!
SFX: BI- BISHI (LEAP LEAP)
RATS!?
BASHI (SWAT)
AND THEY'RE ZOMBIES!
HOW CON-SIDER-ATE!
BI (SWAT)
DA (TMP)
DA
DA
DA
DA

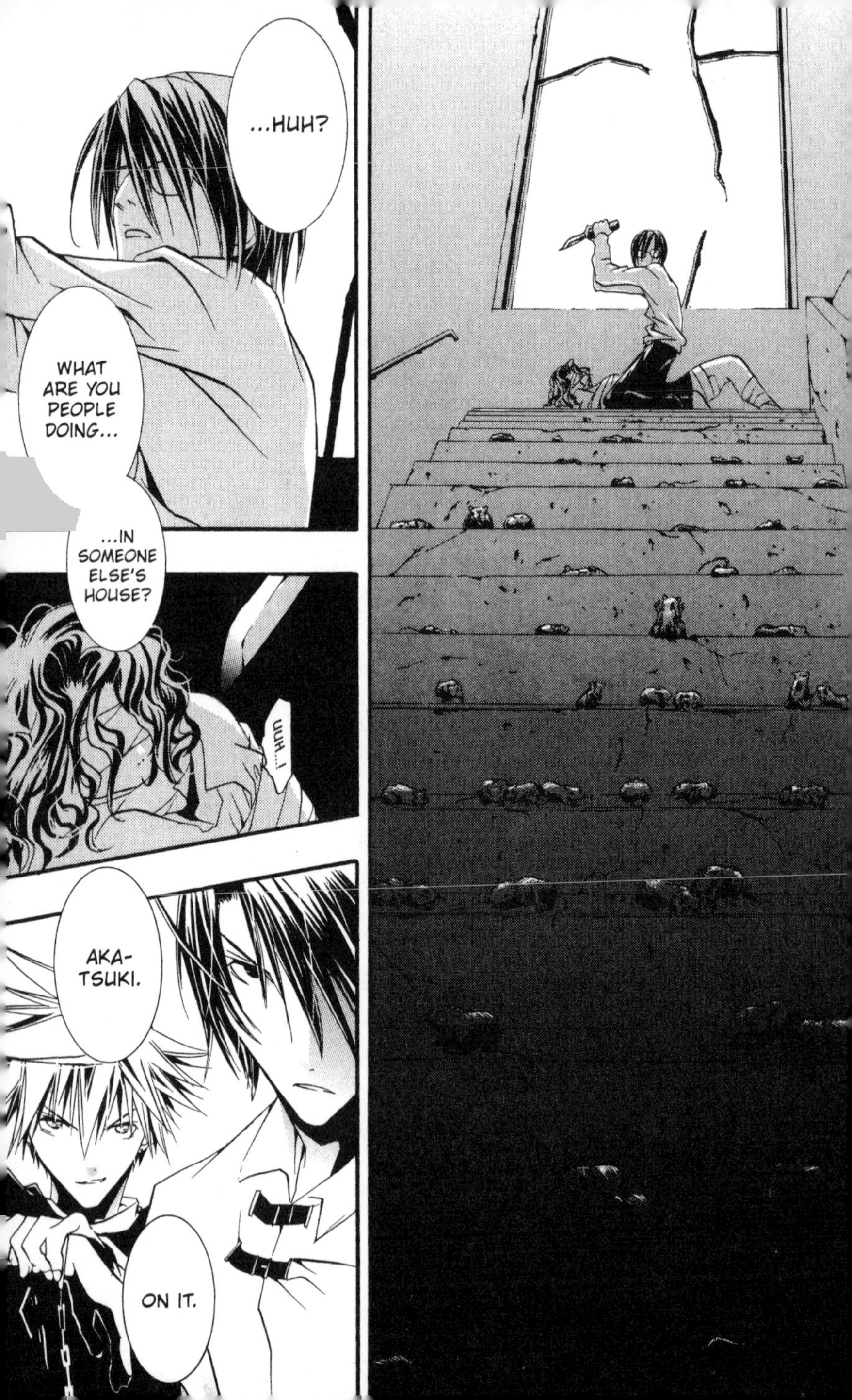
...HUH?
WHAT ARE YOU PEOPLE DOING...
...IN SOMEONE ELSE'S HOUSE?
UUH...!
AKA-TSUKI.
ON IT.

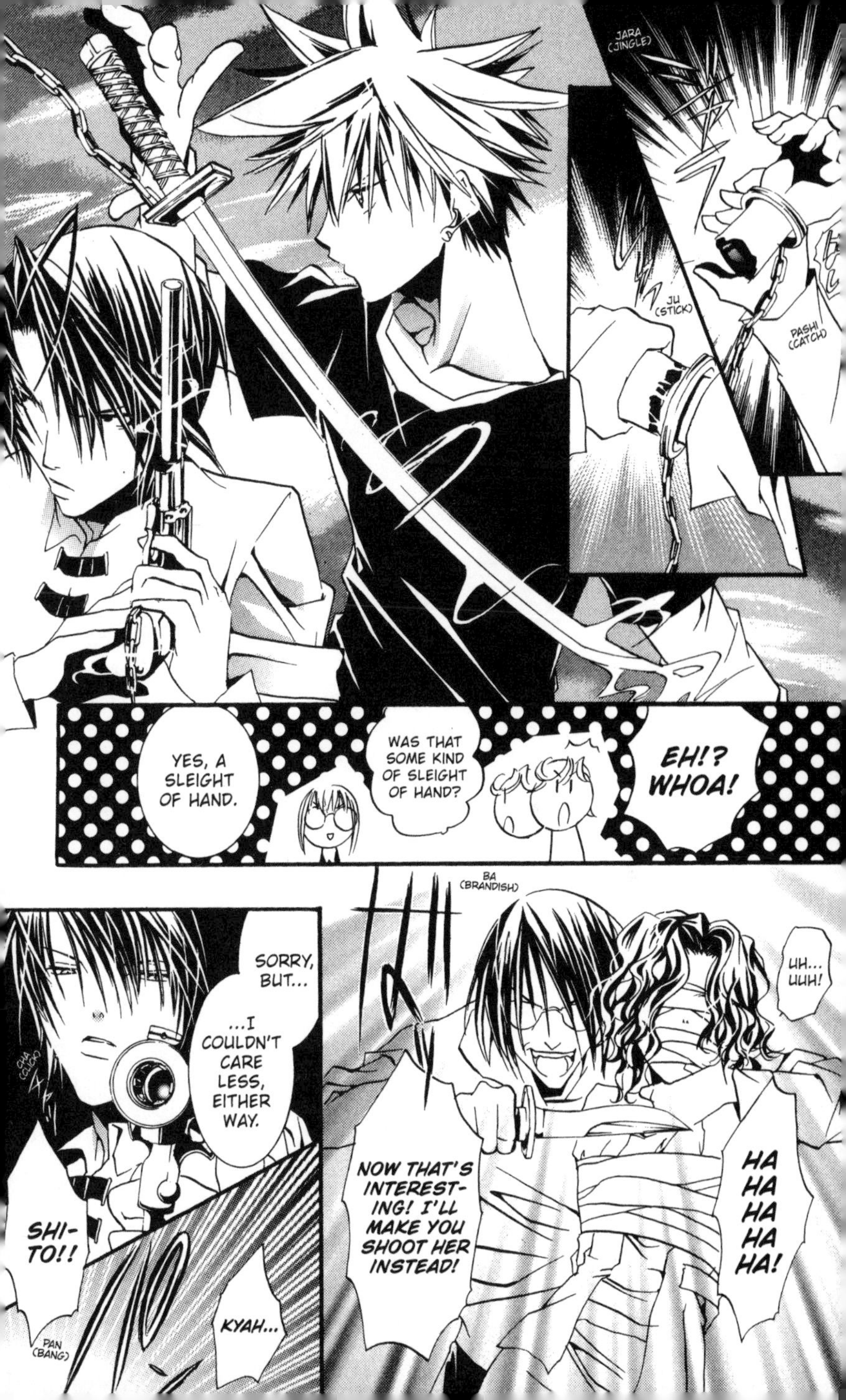
JARA (JINGLE)
PASHI (CATCH)
JU (STICK)
EH!? WHOA!
WAS THAT SOME KIND OF SLEIGHT OF HAND?
YES, A SLEIGHT OF HAND.
UH... UUH!
BA (BRANDISH)
HA HA HA HA HA!
NOW THAT'S INTEREST-ING! I'LL MAKE YOU SHOOT HER INSTEAD!
SORRY, BUT...
...I COULDN'T CARE LESS, EITHER WAY.
CHA (CLICK)
SHI-TO!!
KYAH...
PAN (BANG)

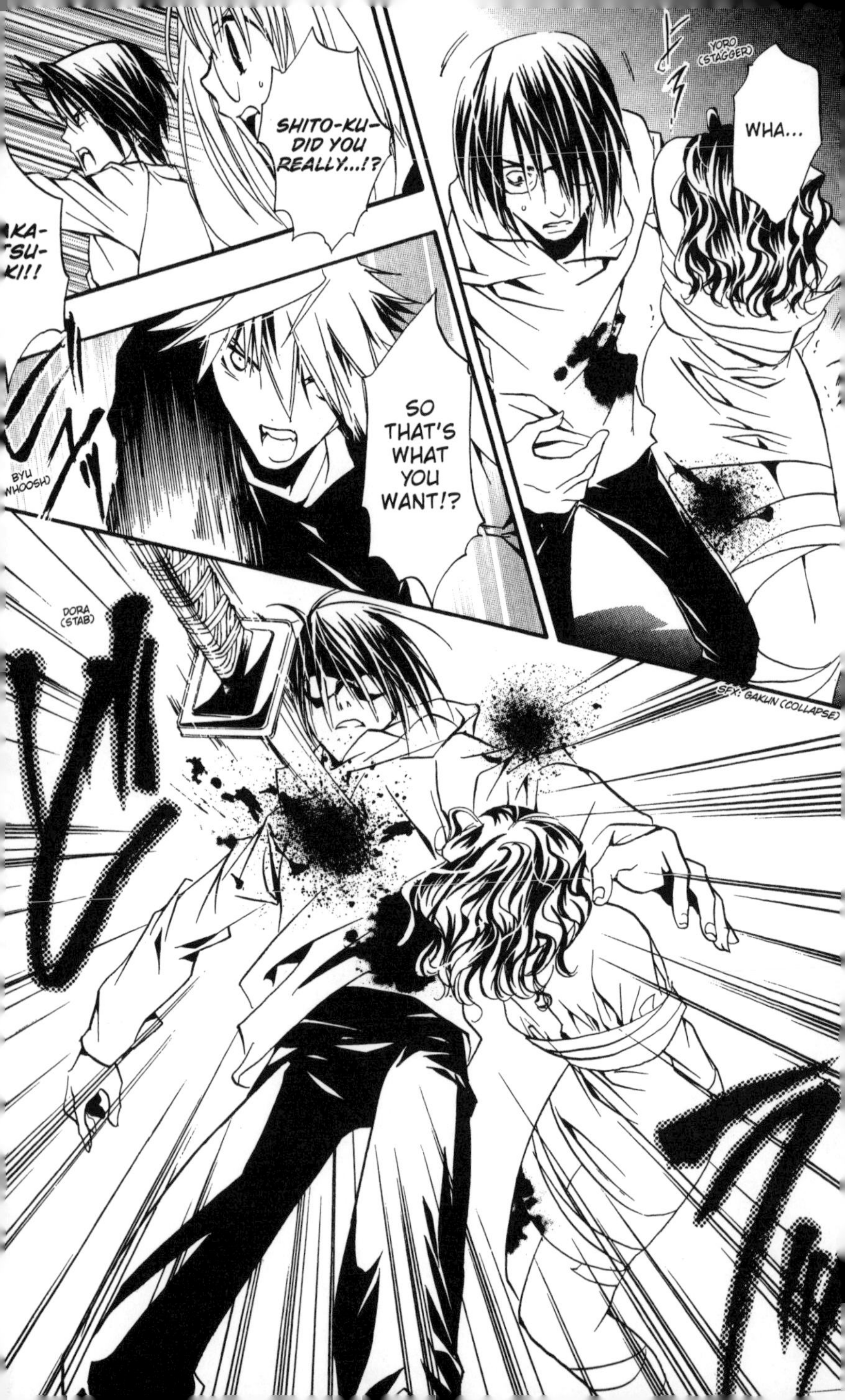
YORO (STAGGER)
WHA...
SHITO-KU- DID YOU REALLY...!?
AKA-TSU-KI!!
SO THAT'S WHAT YOU WANT!?
BYU (WHOOSH)
SFX: GAKUN (COLLAPSE)
DORA (STAB)

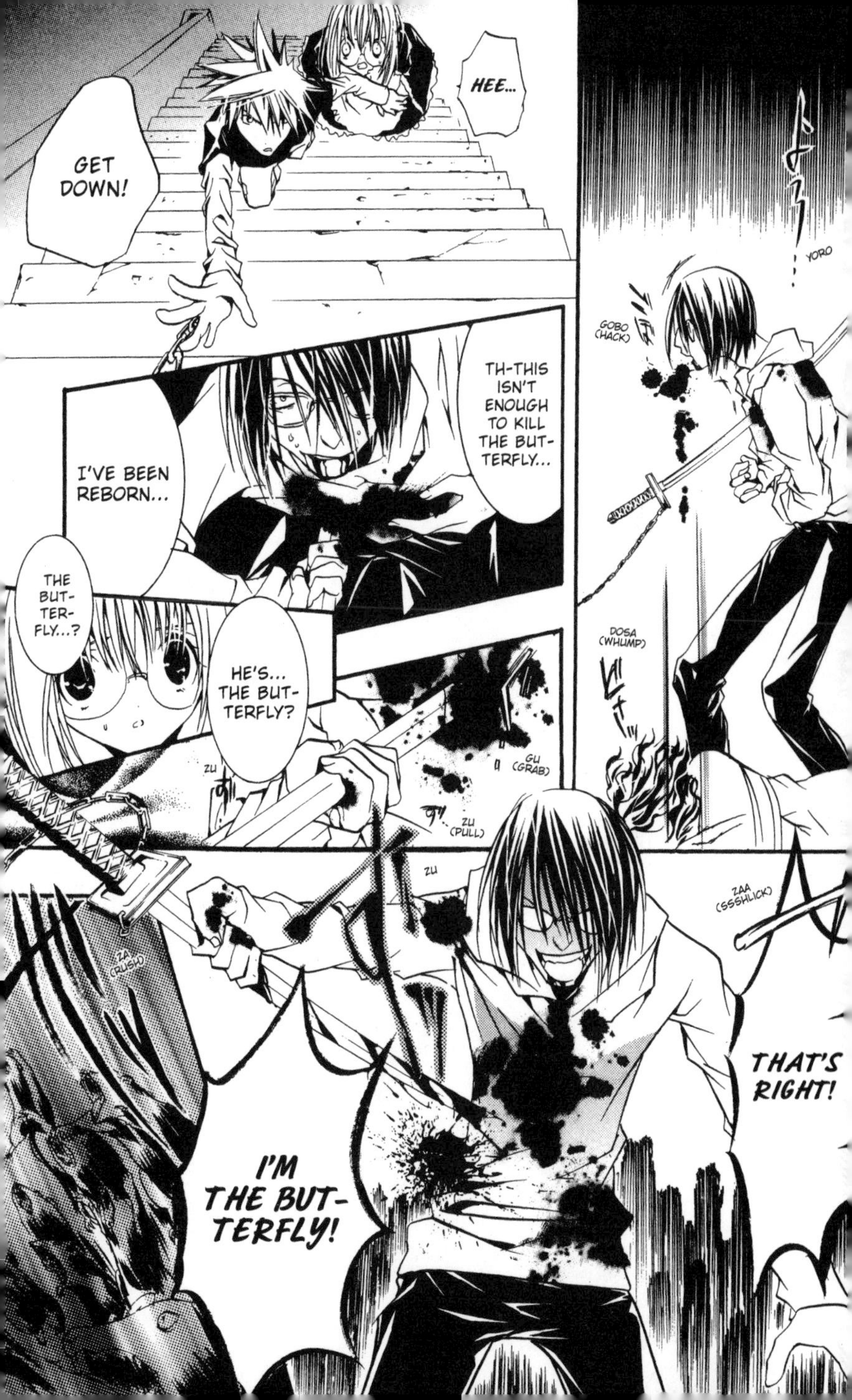
YORO
GOBO (HACK)
DOSA (WHUMP)
HEE...
GET DOWN!
TH-THIS ISN'T ENOUGH TO KILL THE BUT-TERFLY...
I'VE BEEN REBORN...
GU (GRAB)
ZU (PULL)
HE'S... THE BUT-TERFLY?
THE BUT-TER-FLY...?
ZU
ZAA (SSSHLICK)
ZU
THAT'S RIGHT!
I'M THE BUT-TERFLY!
ZA (RUSH)

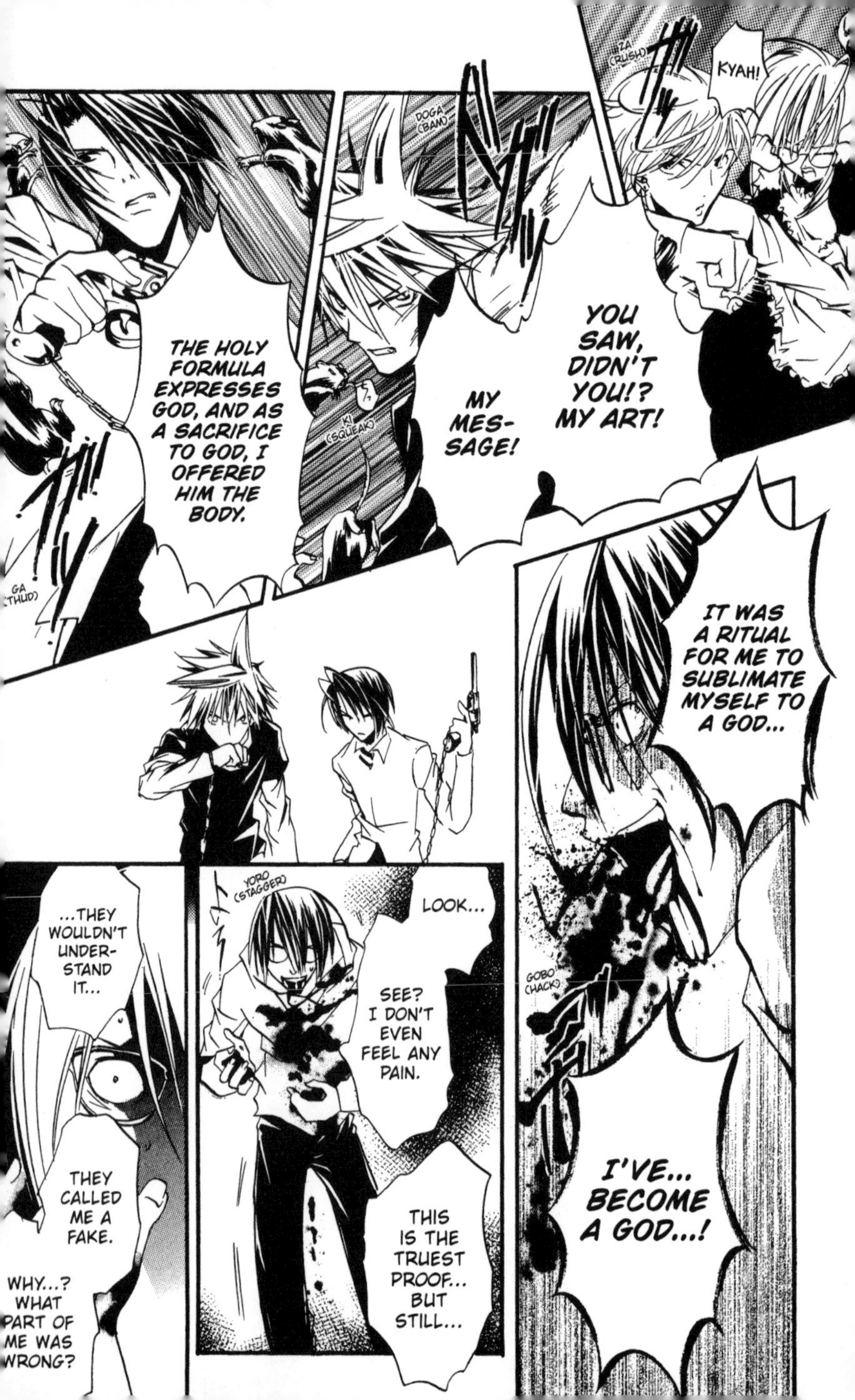
ZA (RUSH)
KYAH!
YOU SAW, DIDN'T YOU!? MY ART!
DOGA (BAM)
KI (SQUEAK)
MY MES-SAGE!
THE HOLY FORMULA EXPRESSES GOD, AND AS A SACRIFICE TO GOD, I OFFERED HIM THE BODY.
GA (THUD)
IT WAS A RITUAL FOR ME TO SUBLIMATE MYSELF TO A GOD...
GOBO (HACK)
I'VE... BECOME A GOD...!
YORO (STAGGER)
LOOK...
SEE? I DON'T EVEN FEEL ANY PAIN.
THIS IS THE TRUEST PROOF... BUT STILL...
...THEY WOULDN'T UNDER-STAND IT...
THEY CALLED ME A FAKE.
WHY...? WHAT PART OF ME WAS WRONG?

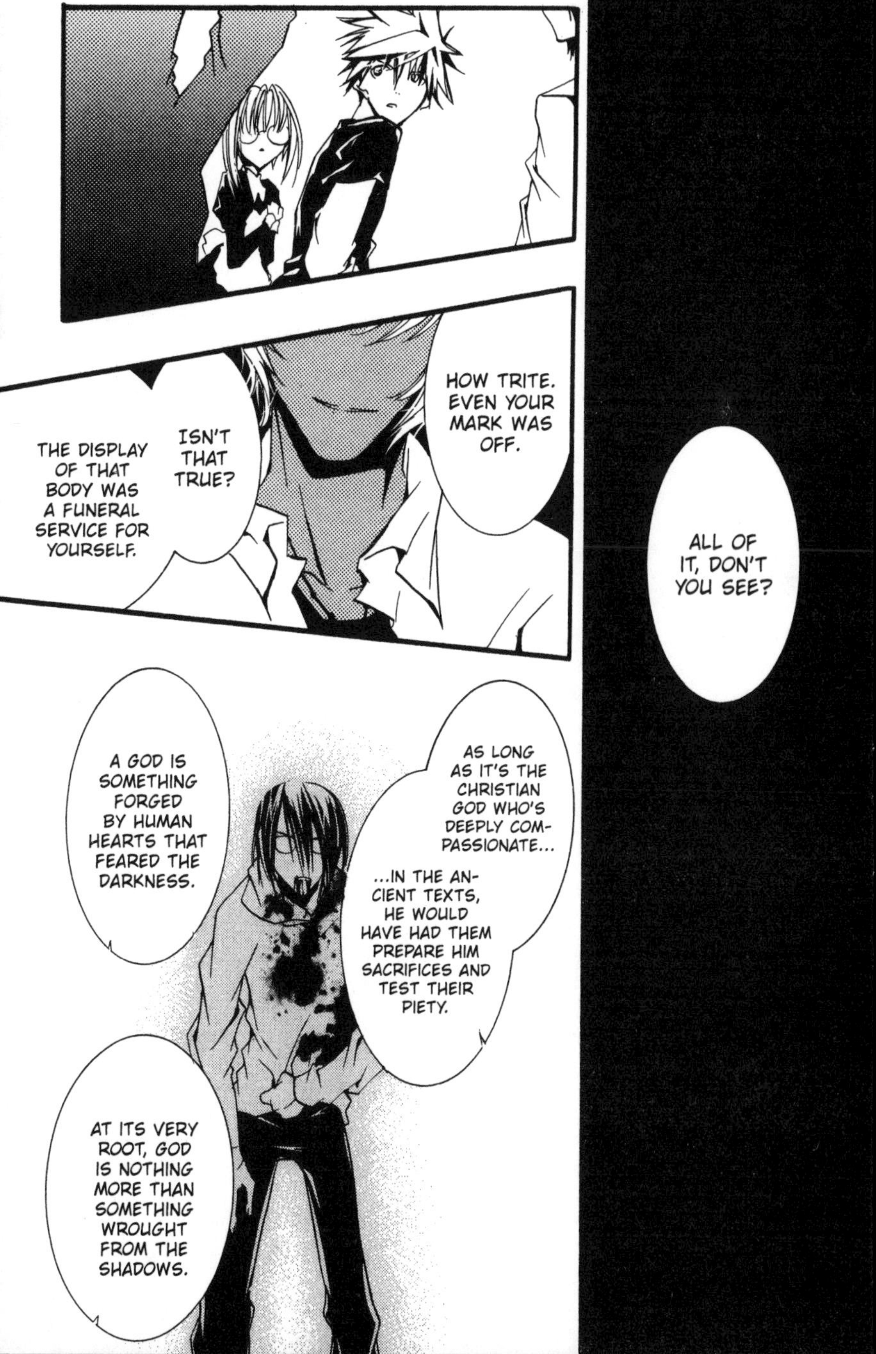
HOW TRITE. EVEN YOUR MARK WAS OFF.
ISN'T THAT TRUE?
THE DISPLAY OF THAT BODY WAS A FUNERAL SERVICE FOR YOURSELF.
ALL OF IT, DON'T YOU SEE?
AS LONG AS IT'S THE CHRISTIAN GOD WHO'S DEEPLY COM-PASSIONATE...
...IN THE AN-CIENT TEXTS, HE WOULD HAVE HAD THEM PREPARE HIM SACRIFICES AND TEST THEIR PIETY.
A GOD IS SOMETHING FORGED BY HUMAN HEARTS THAT FEARED THE DARKNESS.
AT ITS VERY ROOT, GOD IS NOTHING MORE THAN SOMETHING WROUGHT FROM THE SHADOWS.

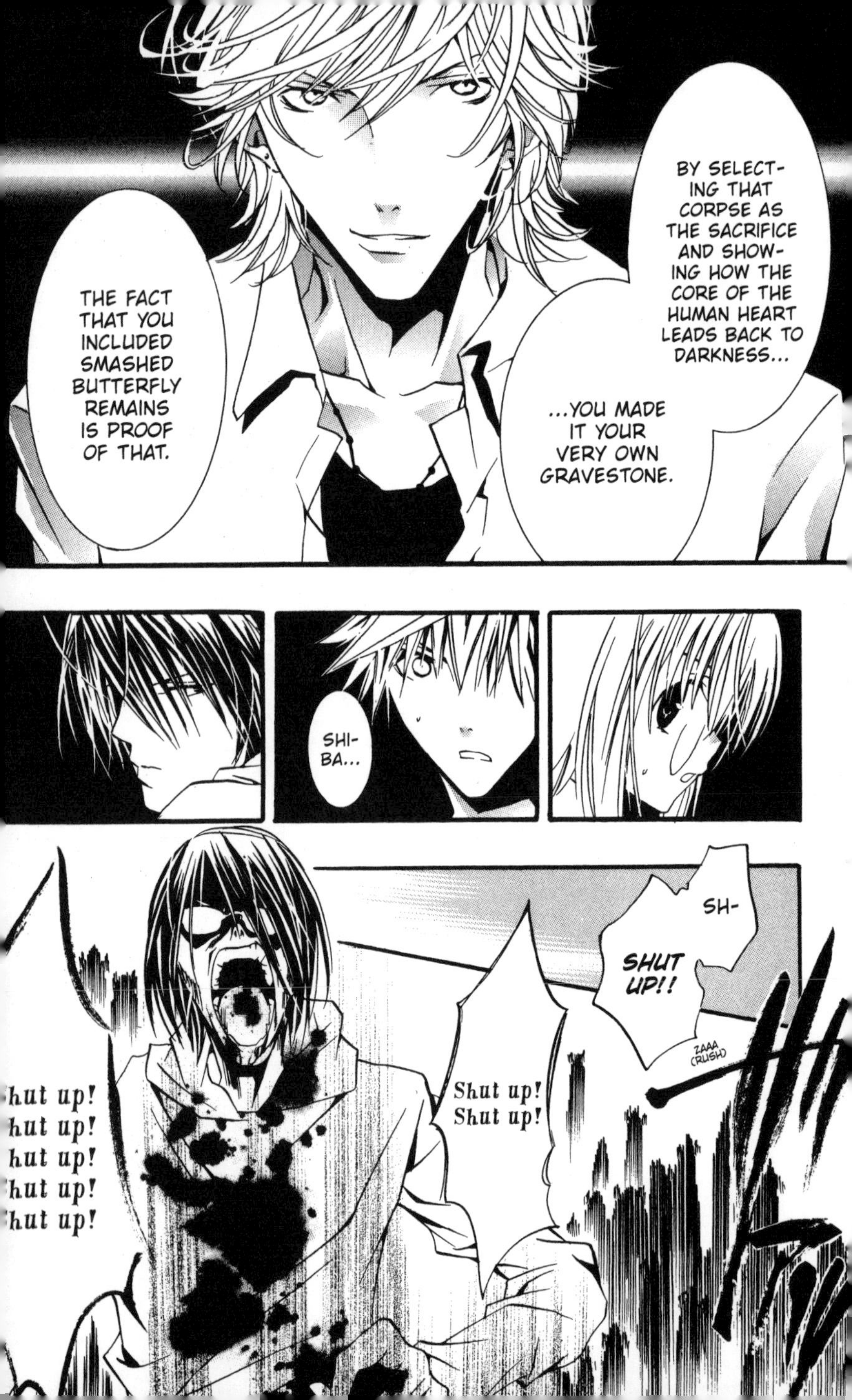
BY SELECTING THAT CORPSE AS THE SACRIFICE AND SHOWING HOW THE CORE OF THE HUMAN HEART LEADS BACK TO DARKNESS...
...YOU MADE IT YOUR VERY OWN GRAVESTONE.
THE FACT THAT YOU INCLUDED SMASHED BUTTERFLY REMAINS IS PROOF OF THAT.
SHI-BA...
SH- SHUT UP!!
ZAAA (RUSH)
Shut up! Shut up!
hut up! hut up! hut up! hut up! hut up!

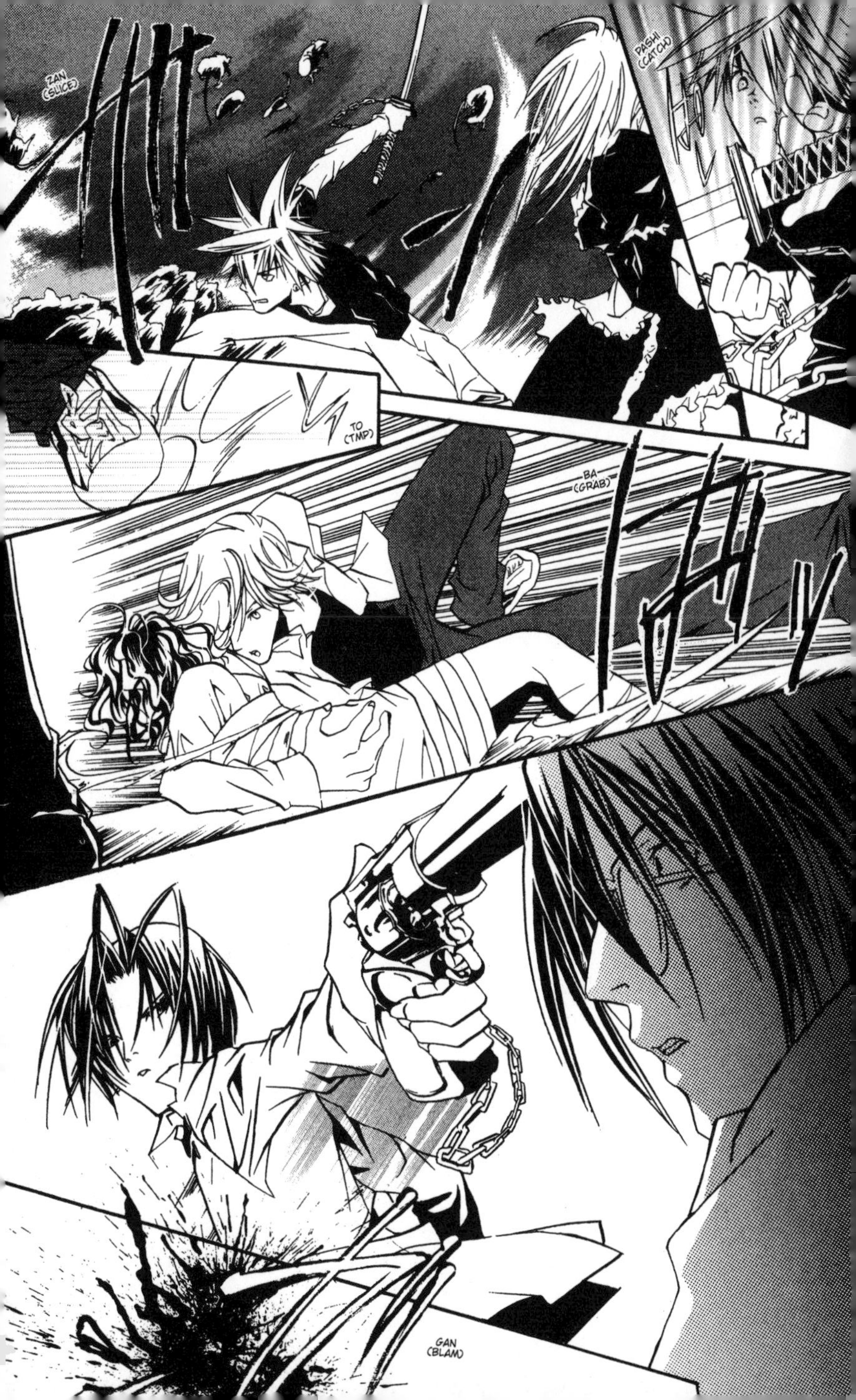
PASHI (CATCH)
ZAN (SLICE)
TO (TMP)
BA (GRAB)
GAN (BLAM)

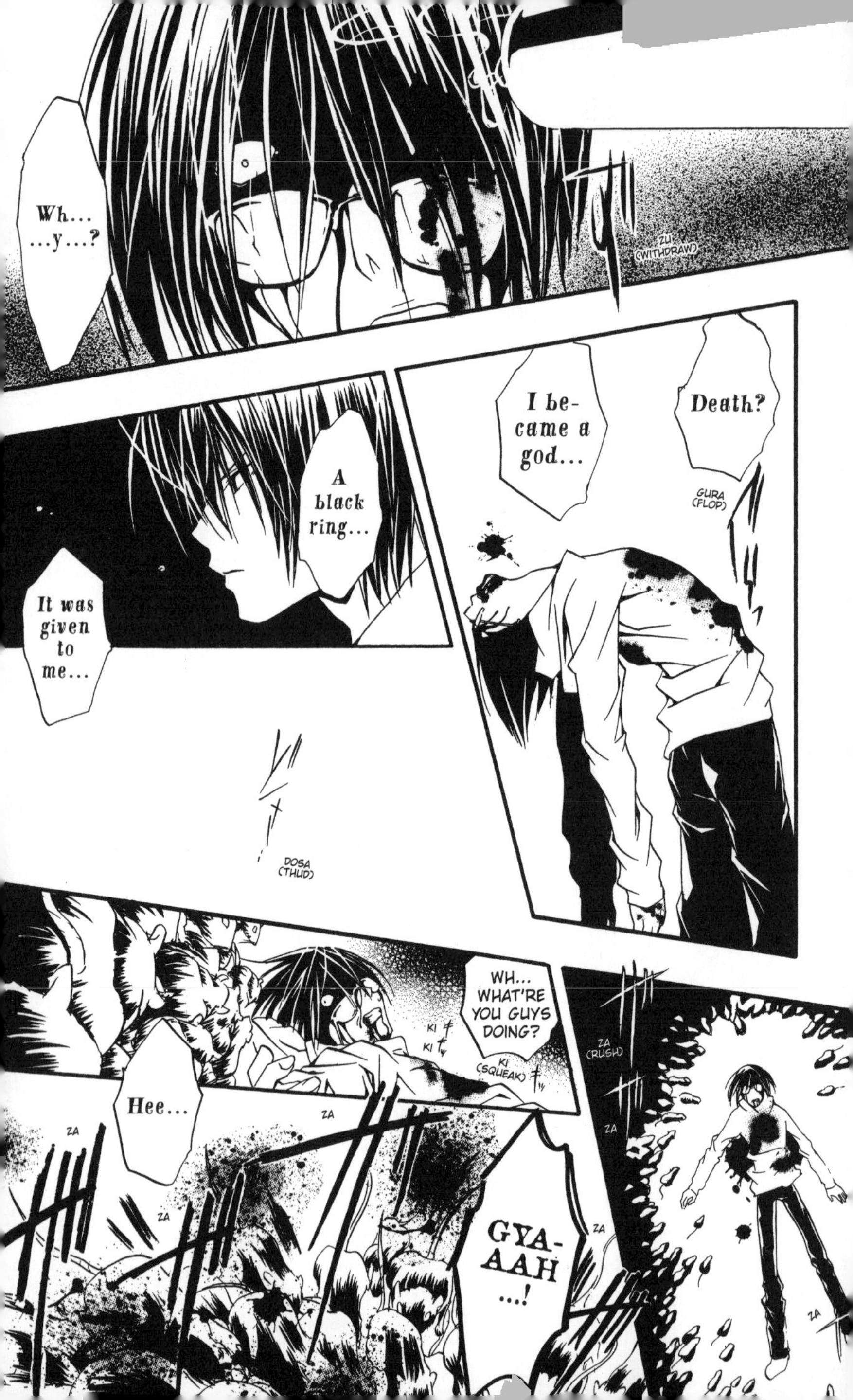
ZU (WITHDRAW)
Wh... ...y...?
Death?
I be- came a god...
GURA (FLOP)
A black ring...
It was given to me...
DOSA (THUD)
ZA (RUSH)
ZA
ZA
WH... WHAT'RE YOU GUYS DOING?
KI
KI
KI (SQUEAK)
Hee...
ZA
ZA
ZA
GYA-AAH ...!
ZA

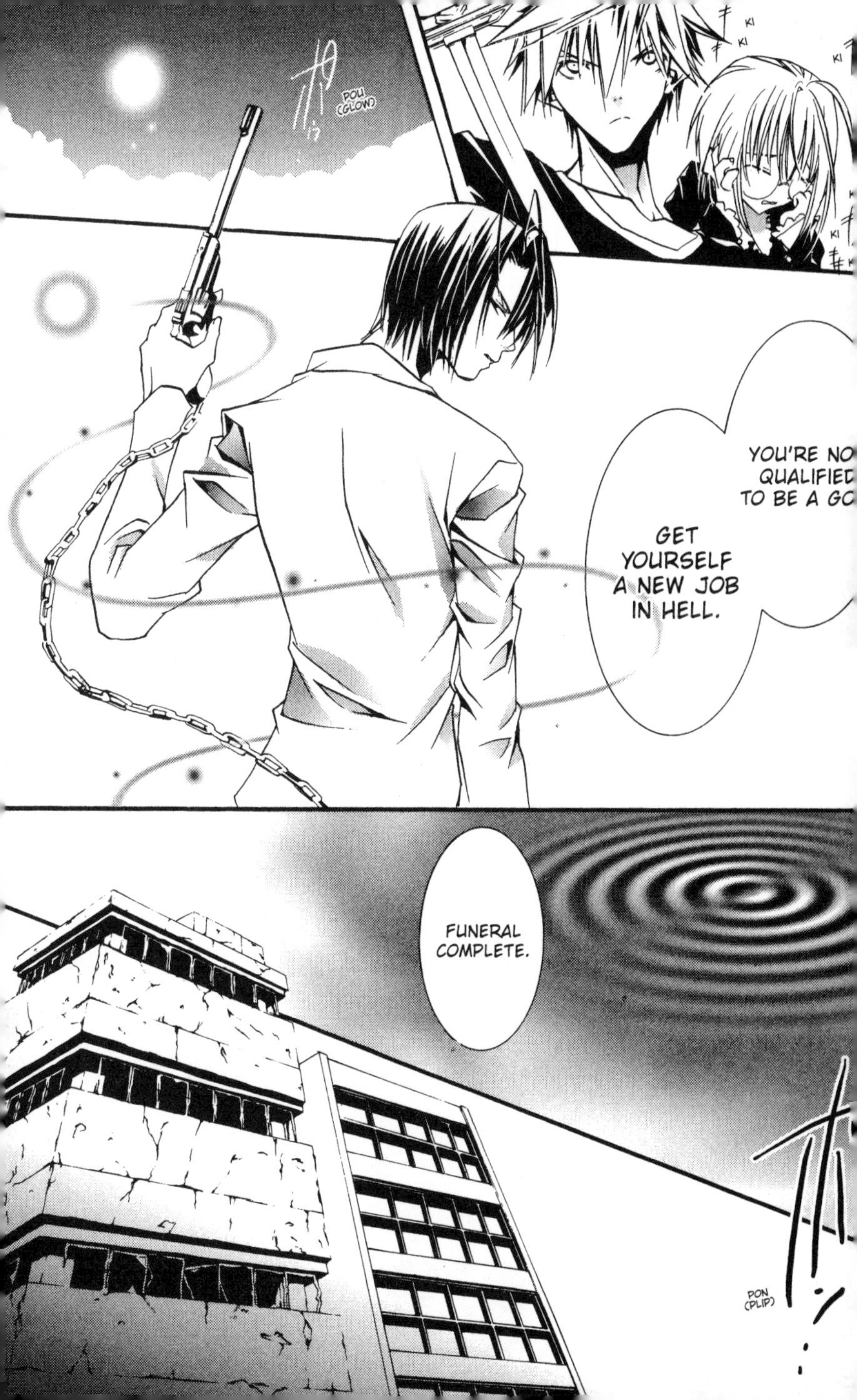
KI
KI
KI
KI
POU (GLOW)
YOU'RE NO
QUALIFIED
TO BE A GO
GET YOURSELF A NEW JOB IN HELL.
FUNERAL COMPLETE.
PON (PLIP)

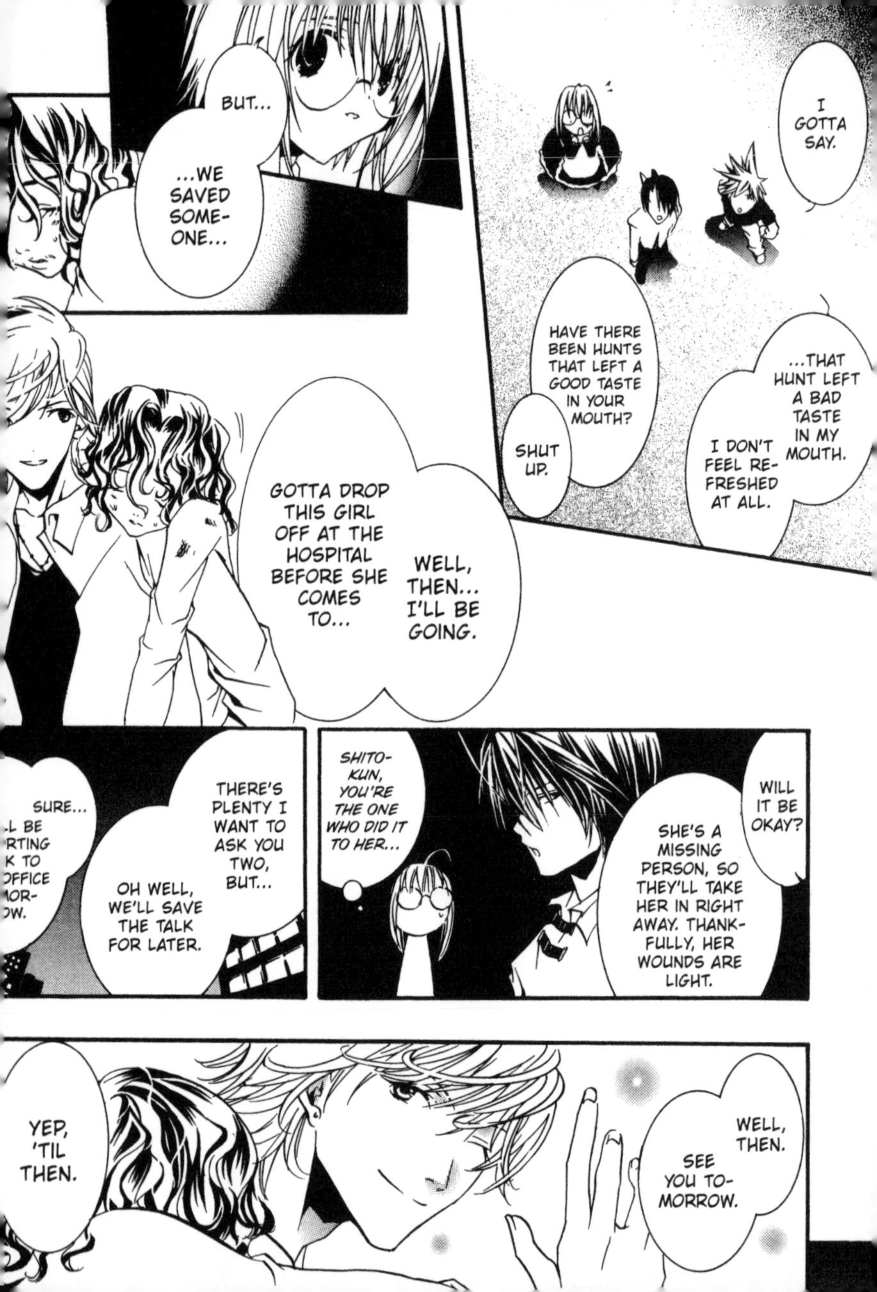

I GOTTA SAY.
...THAT HUNT LEFT A BAD TASTE IN MY MOUTH.
I DON'T FEEL RE-FRESHED AT ALL.
HAVE THERE BEEN HUNTS THAT LEFT A GOOD TASTE IN YOUR MOUTH?
SHUT UP.
BUT...
...WE SAVED SOME-ONE...
WELL, THEN... I'LL BE GOING.
GOTTA DROP THIS GIRL OFF AT THE HOSPITAL BEFORE SHE COMES TO...
WILL IT BE OKAY?
SHE'S A MISSING PERSON, SO THEY'LL TAKE HER IN RIGHT AWAY. THANK-FULLY, HER WOUNDS ARE LIGHT.
SHITO-KUN, YOU'RE THE ONE WHO DID IT TO HER...
THERE'S PLENTY I WANT TO ASK YOU TWO, BUT...
OH WELL, WE'LL SAVE THE TALK FOR LATER.
SURE...
WELL, THEN. SEE YOU TO-MORROW.
YEP, 'TIL THEN.

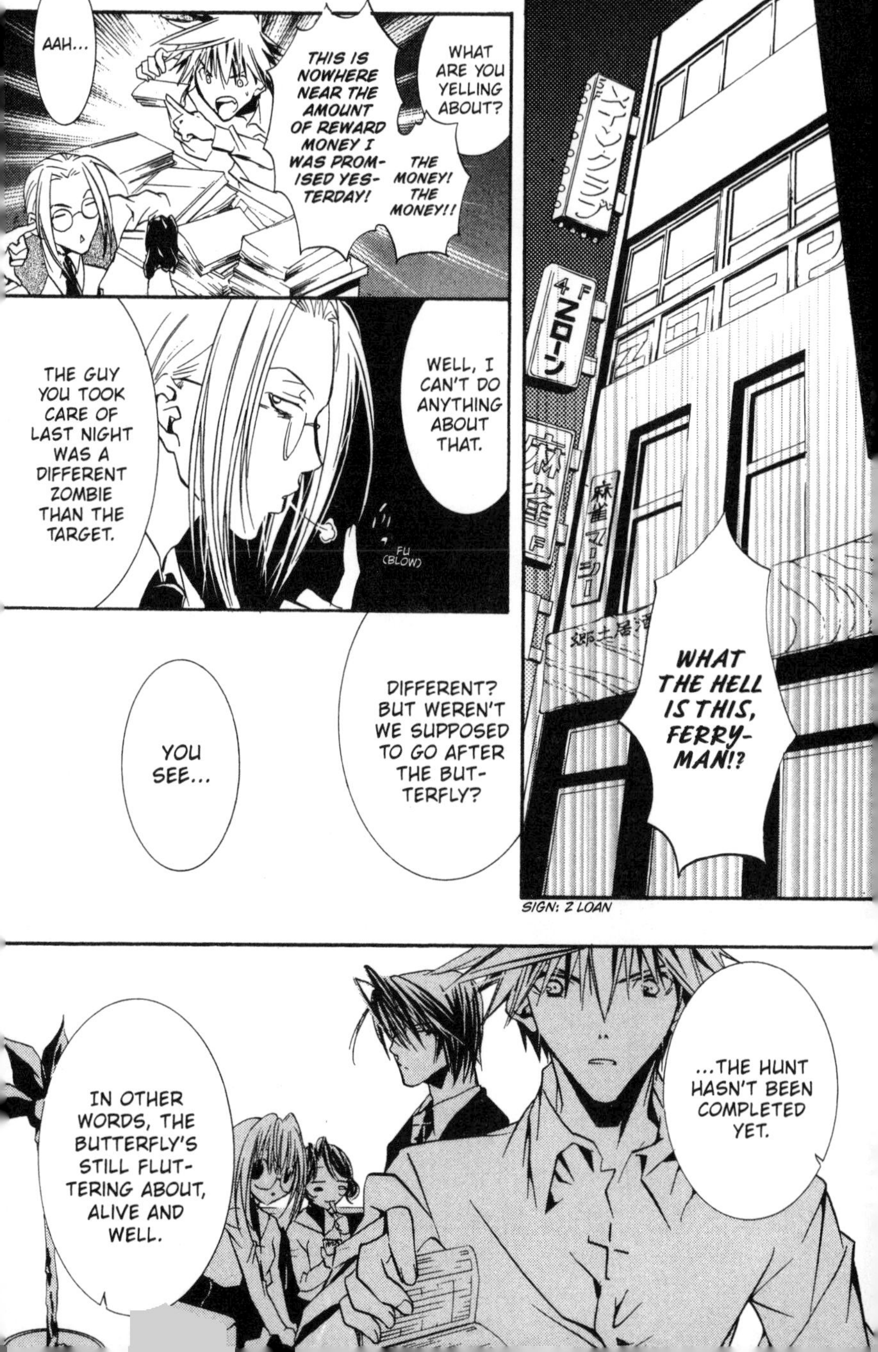
WHAT THE HELL IS THIS, FERRY-MAN!?
SIGN: Z LOAN
WHAT ARE YOU YELLING ABOUT? THE MONEY! THE MONEY!!
THIS IS NOWHERE NEAR THE AMOUNT OF REWARD MONEY I WAS PROM-ISED YES-TERDAY!
AAH...
WELL, I CAN'T DO ANYTHING ABOUT THAT.
FU (BLOW)
THE GUY YOU TOOK CARE OF LAST NIGHT WAS A DIFFERENT ZOMBIE THAN THE TARGET.
DIFFERENT? BUT WEREN'T WE SUPPOSED TO GO AFTER THE BUT-TERFLY?
YOU SEE...
...THE HUNT HASN'T BEEN COMPLETED YET.
IN OTHER WORDS, THE BUTTERFLY'S STILL FLUT-TERING ABOUT, ALIVE AND WELL.

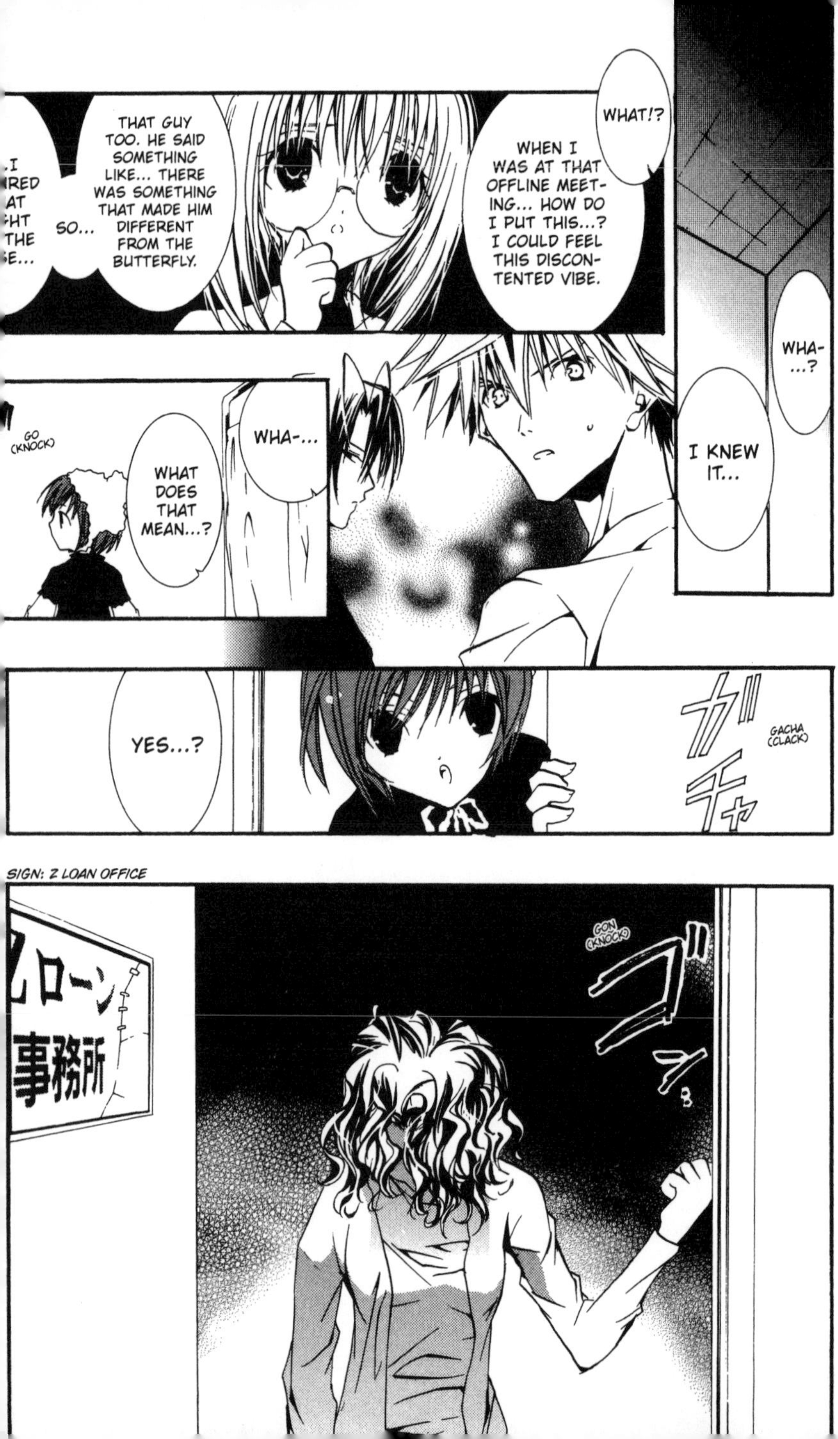
WHAT!?
WHEN I WAS AT THAT OFFLINE MEETING... HOW DO I PUT THIS...? I COULD FEEL THIS DISCONTENTED VIBE.
THAT GUY TOO. HE SAID SOMETHING LIKE... THERE WAS SOMETHING THAT MADE HIM DIFFERENT FROM THE BUTTERFLY.
SO...
.I IRED AT HT THE E...
WHA-...?
I KNEW IT...
WHA-...
WHAT DOES THAT MEAN...?
GO (KNOCK)
GACHA (CLACK)
YES...?
SIGN: Z LOAN OFFICE
ローン
事務所
GON (KNOCK)

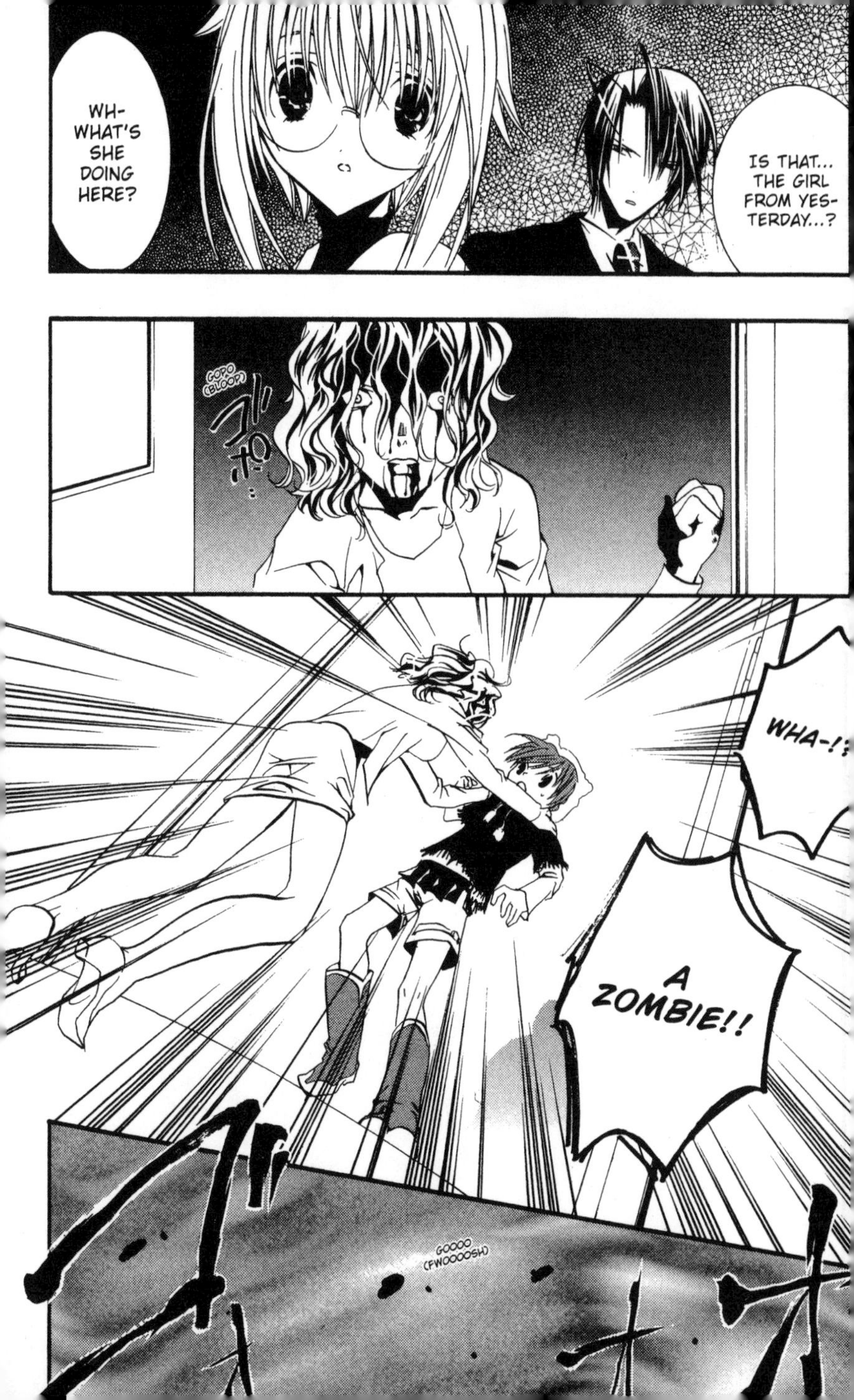
IS THAT... THE GIRL FROM YES-TERDAY...?
WH- WHAT'S SHE DOING HERE?
GOPO (BLOOP)
WHA-!?
A ZOMBIE!!
GOOOO (FWOOOOSH)

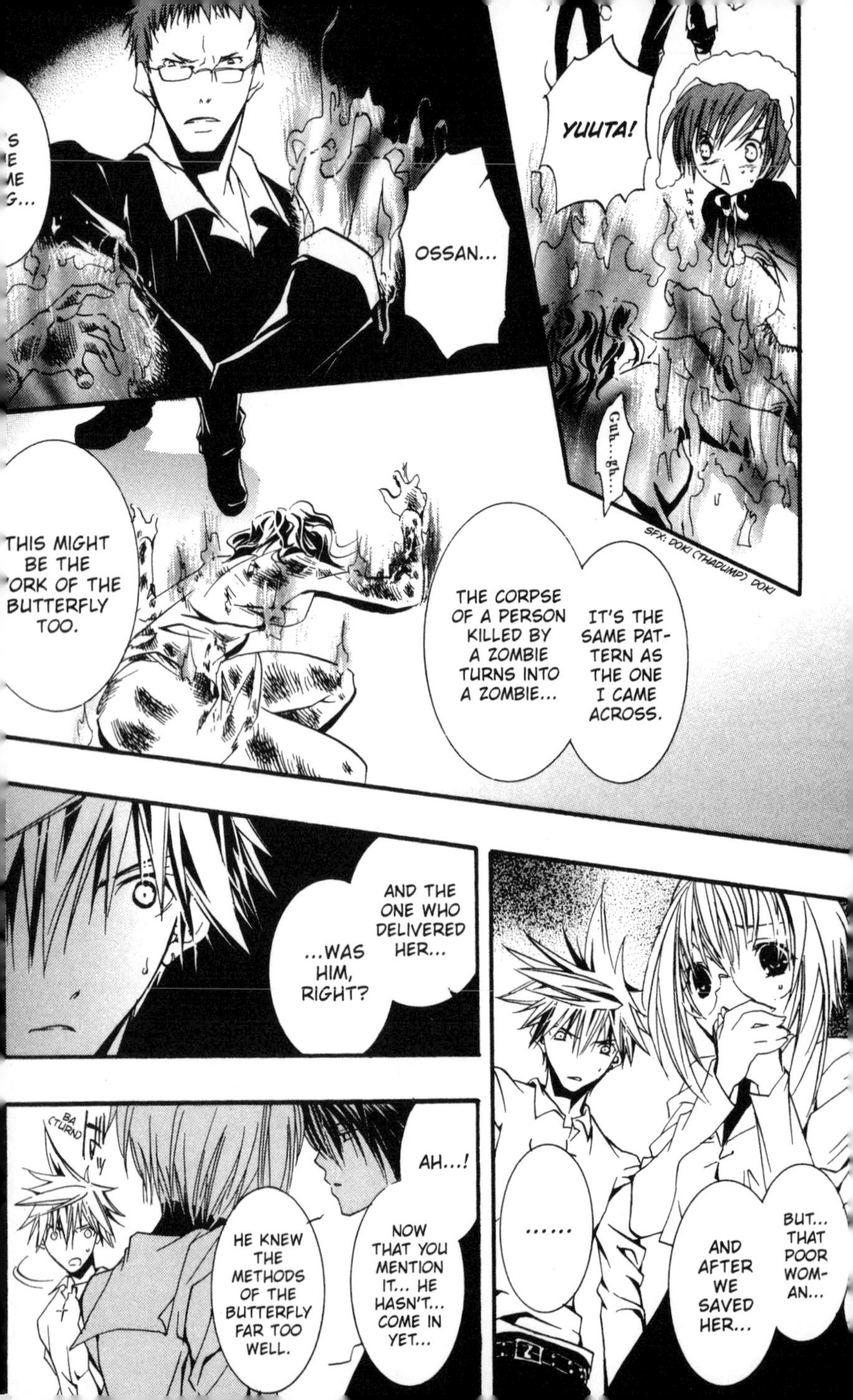
YUUTA!
Guh...gh...
SFX: DOKI (THADUMP) DOKI
'S
E
ME
G...
OSSAN...
IT'S THE SAME PAT-TERN AS THE ONE I CAME ACROSS.
THE CORPSE OF A PERSON KILLED BY A ZOMBIE TURNS INTO A ZOMBIE...
THIS MIGHT BE THE 'ORK OF THE BUTTERFLY TOO.
BUT... THAT POOR WOM-AN...
AND AFTER WE SAVED HER...
......
AND THE ONE WHO DELIVERED HER...
...WAS HIM, RIGHT?
AH...!
NOW THAT YOU MENTION IT... HE HASN'T... COME IN YET...
HE KNEW THE METHODS OF THE BUTTERFLY FAR TOO WELL.
BA (TURN)

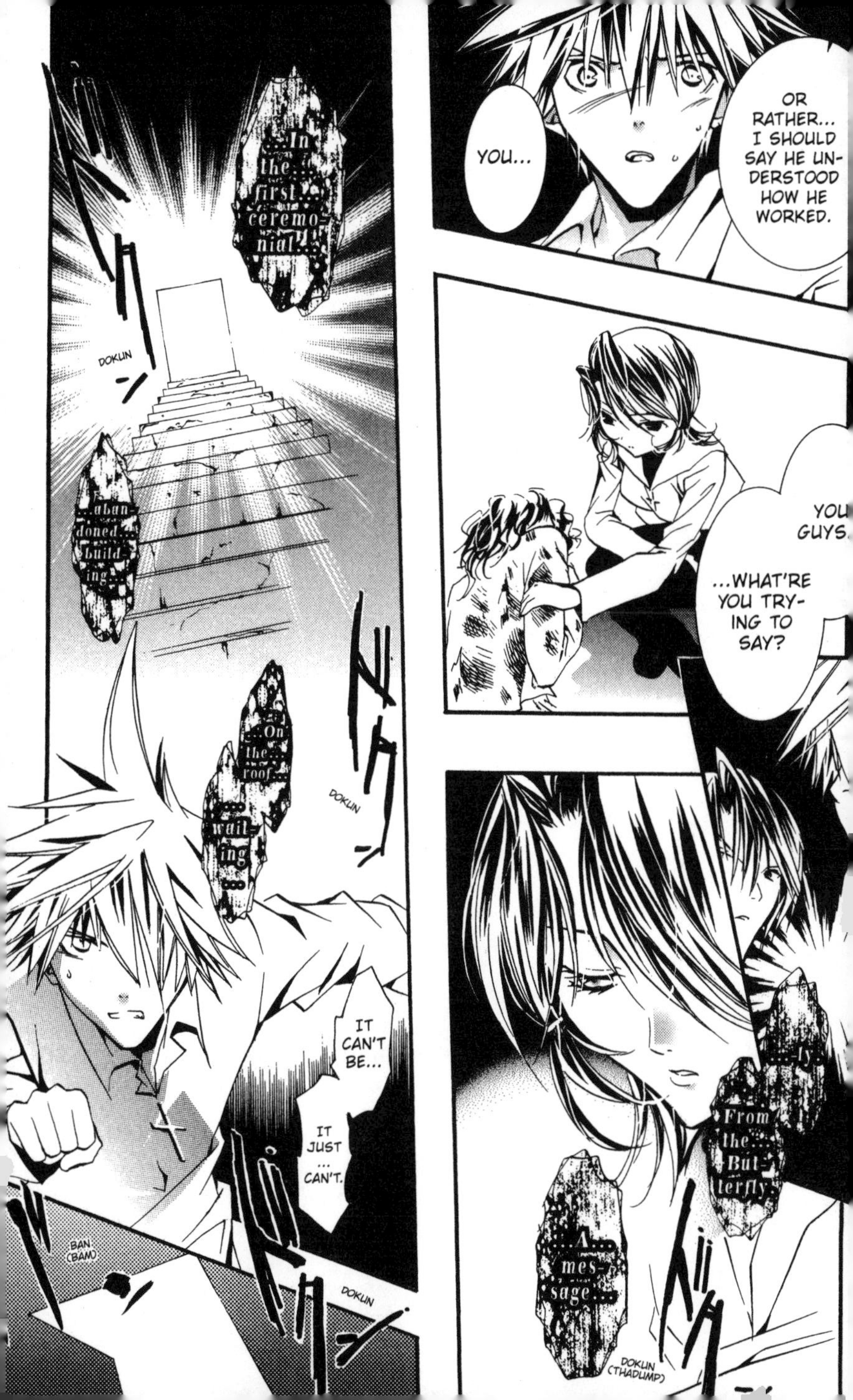
OR RATHER... I SHOULD SAY HE UNDERSTOOD HOW HE WORKED.
YOU...
YOU GUYS.
...WHAT'RE YOU TRYING TO SAY?
...ly. From the... Butterfly.
...A... message...
DOKUN (THADUMP)
...In the... first... ceremonial...
DOKUN
...abandoned... building...
...On the... roof... ...waiting...
DOKUN
IT CAN'T BE...
IT JUST ... CAN'T.
BAN (BAM)
DOKUN

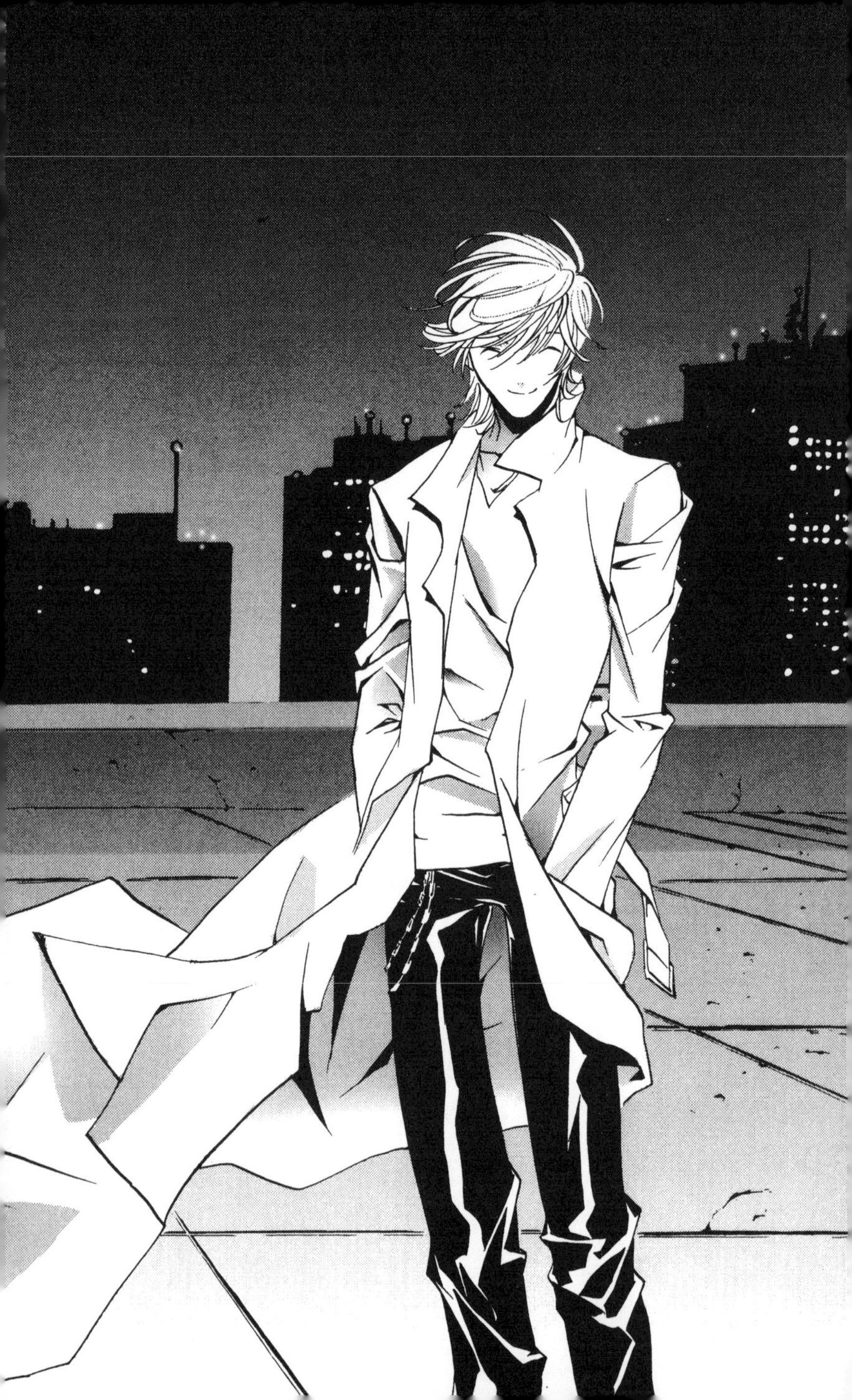

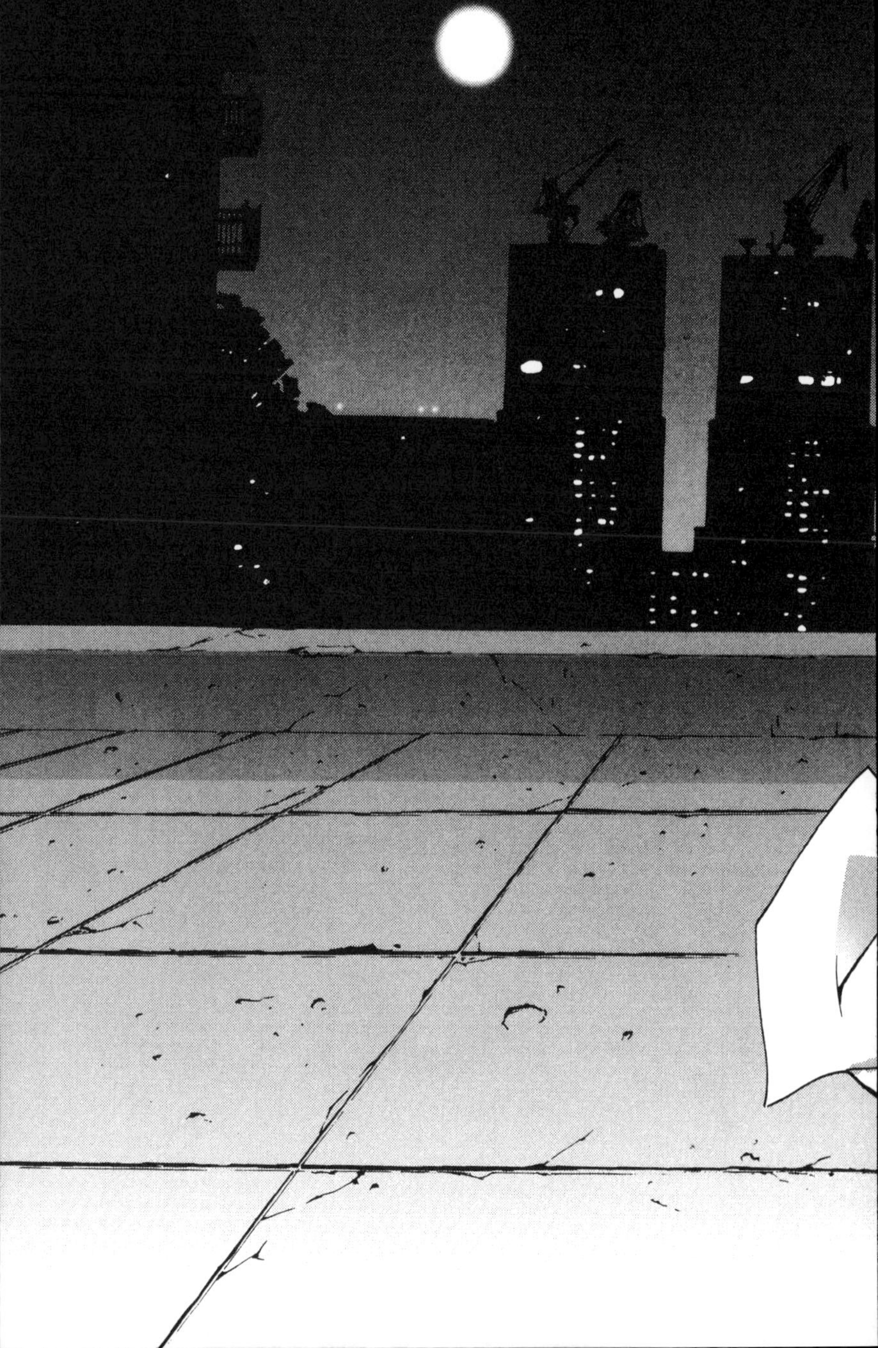

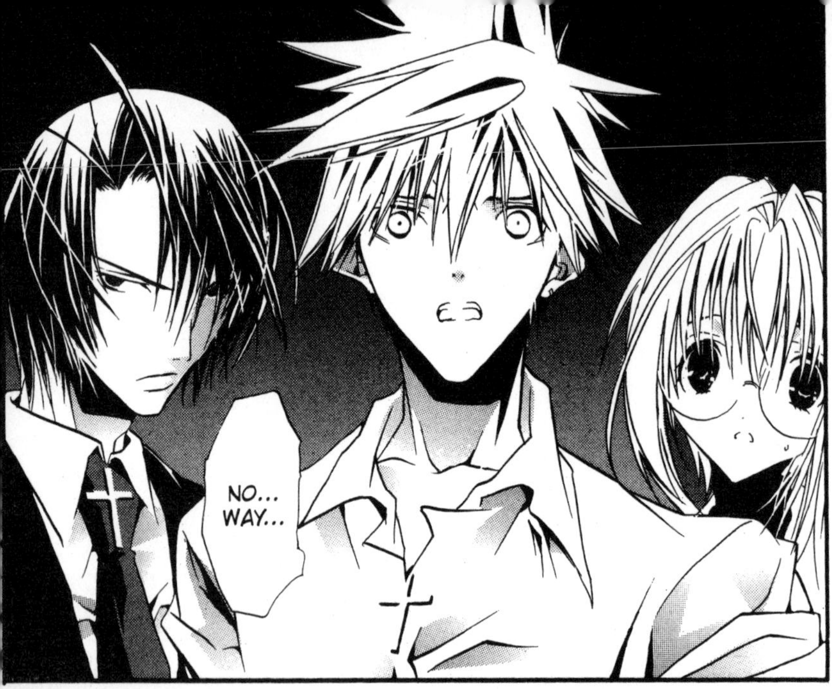
NO... WAY...
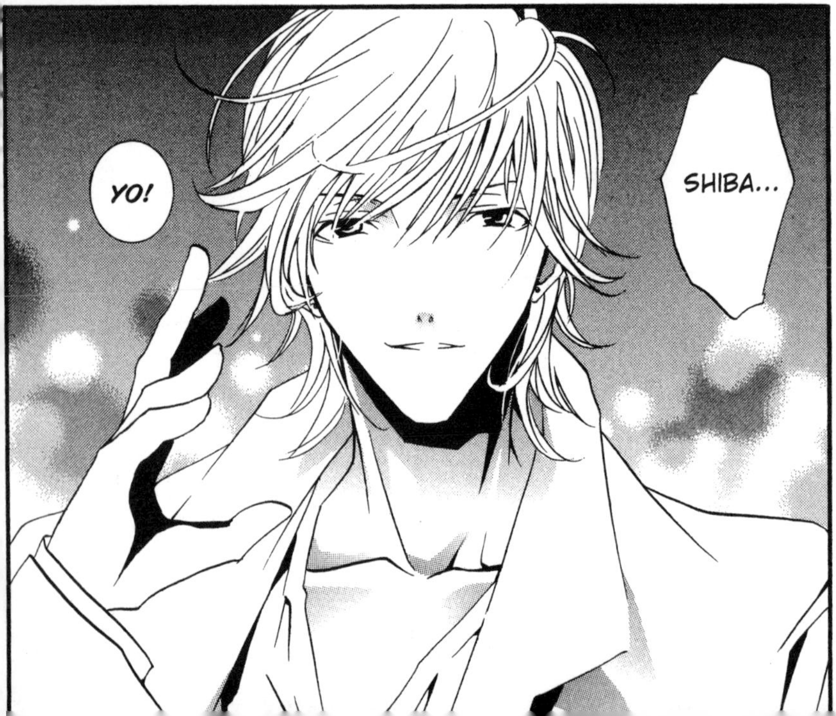
SHIBA...
YO!

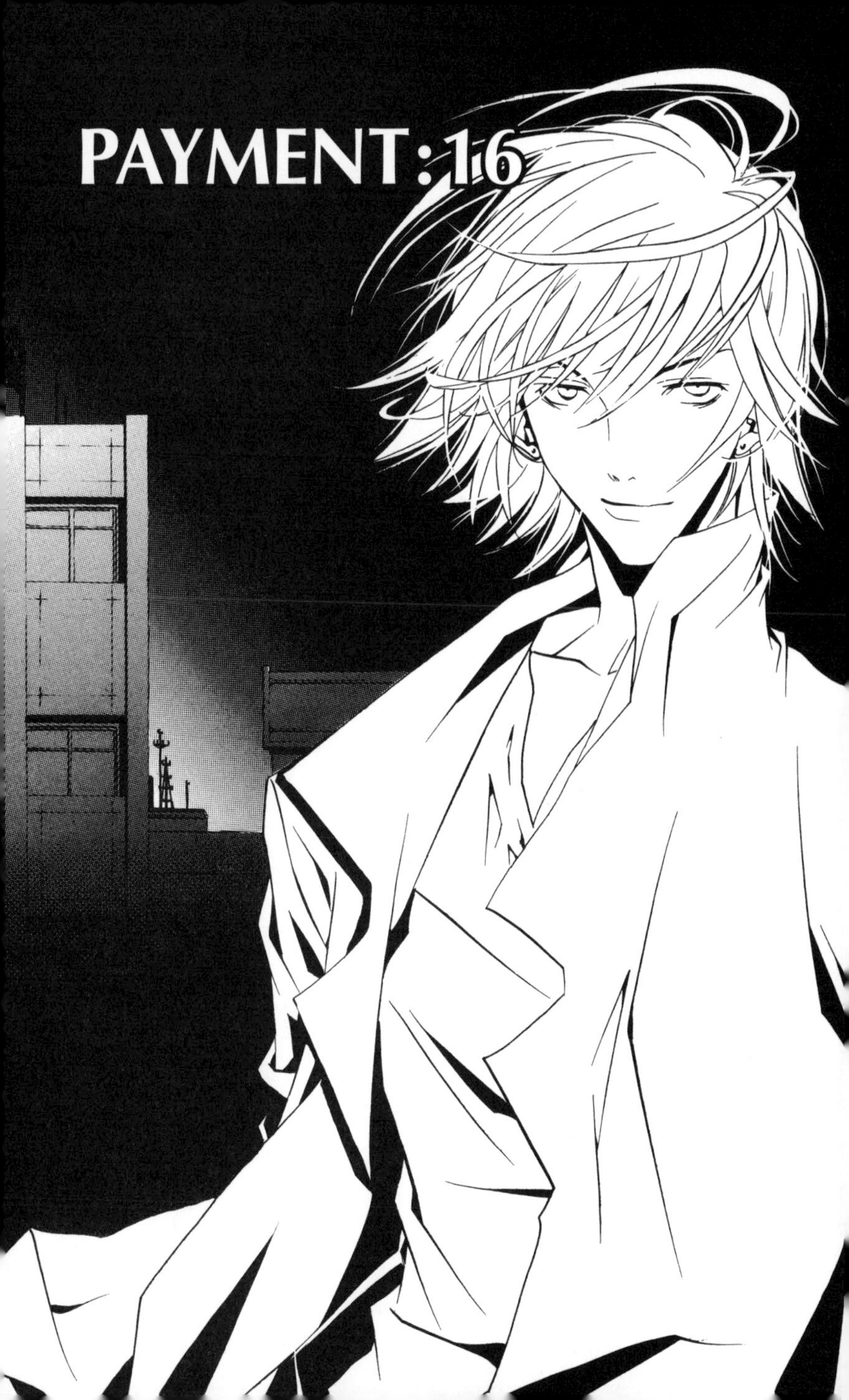
PAYMENT:16

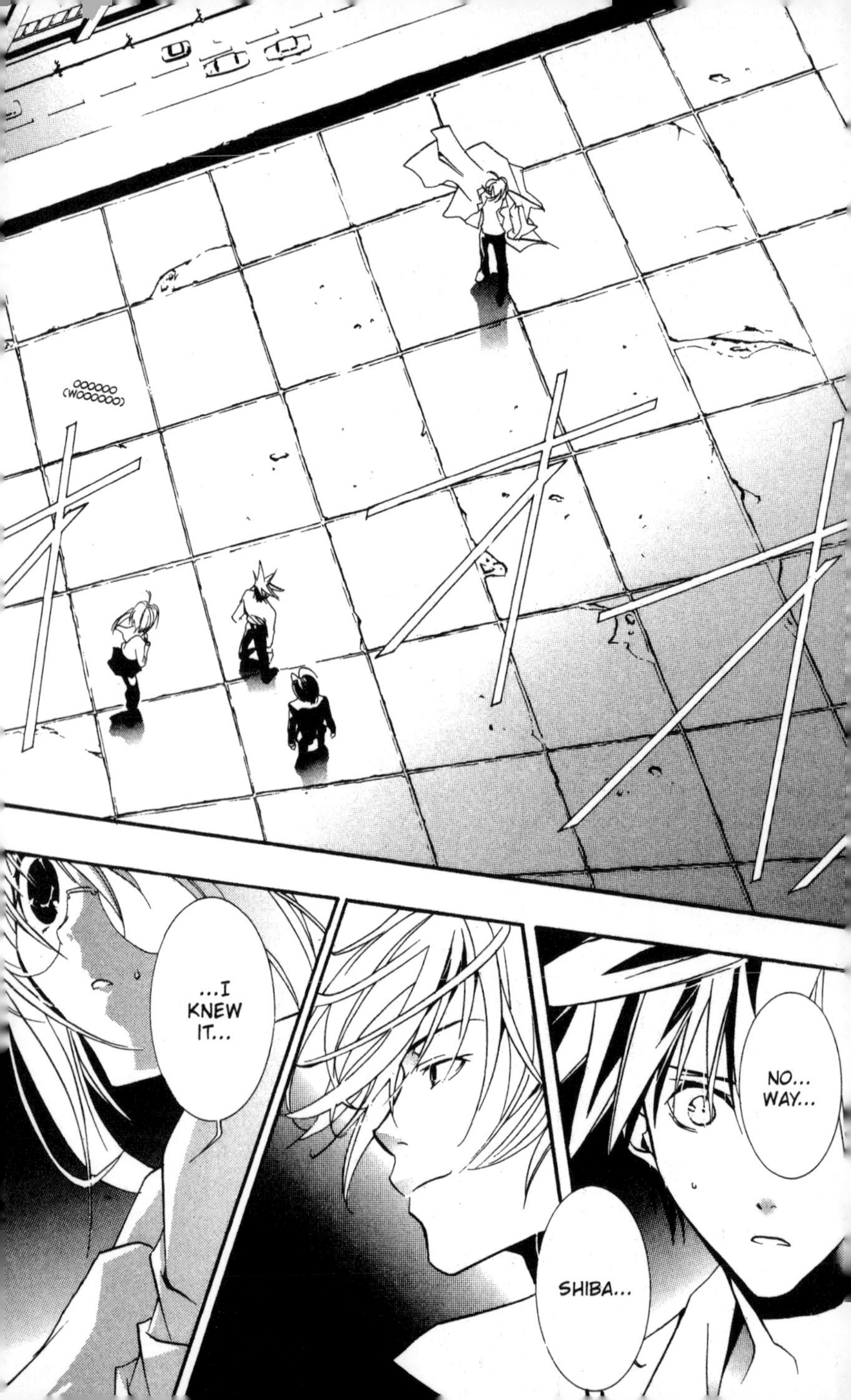
OOOOOO
(WOOOOOO)
NO... WAY...
SHIBA...
...I KNEW IT...

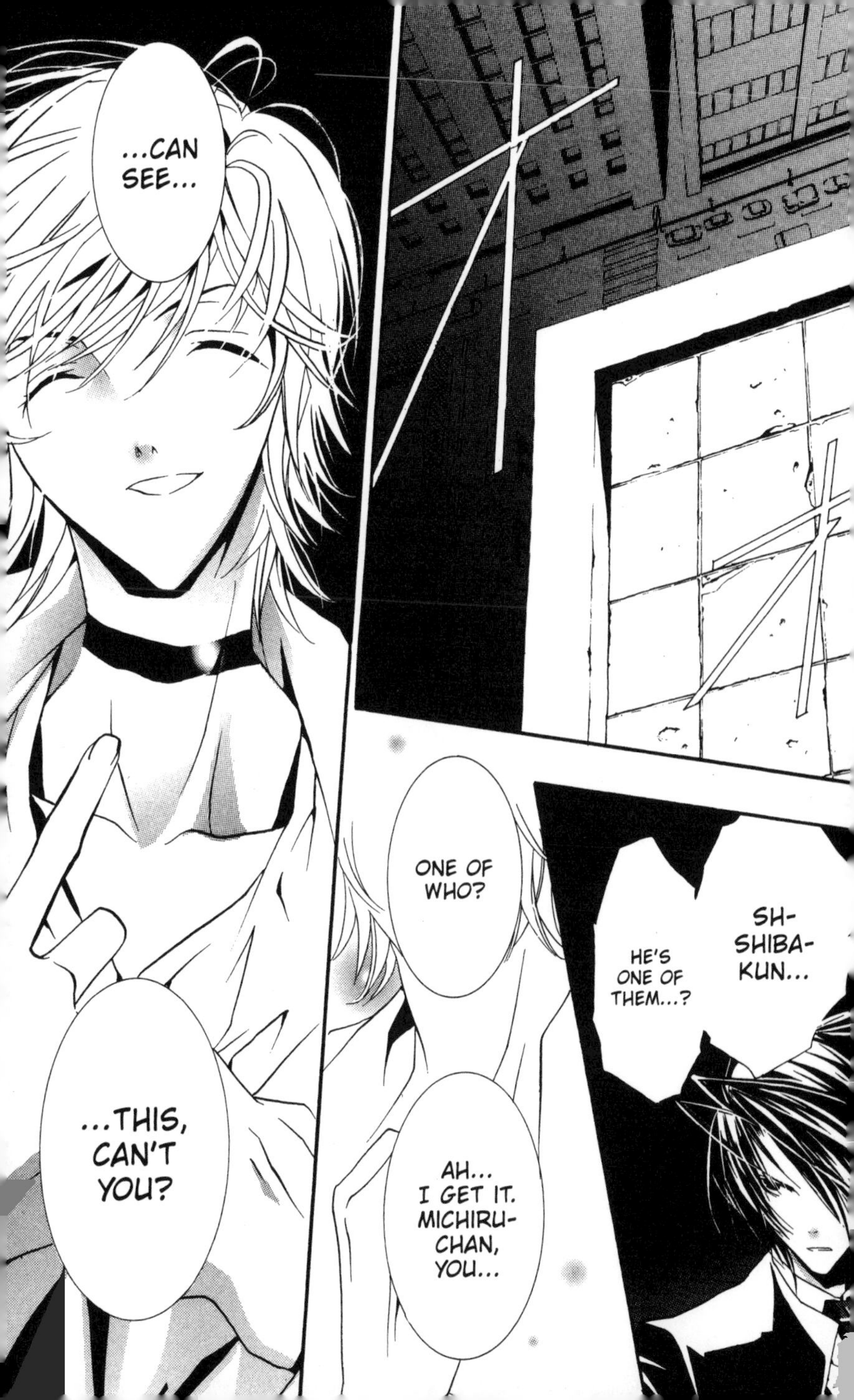
SH-SHIBA-KUN...
HE'S ONE OF THEM...?
ONE OF WHO?
AH... I GET IT. MICHIRU-CHAN, YOU...
...CAN SEE...
...THIS, CAN'T YOU?

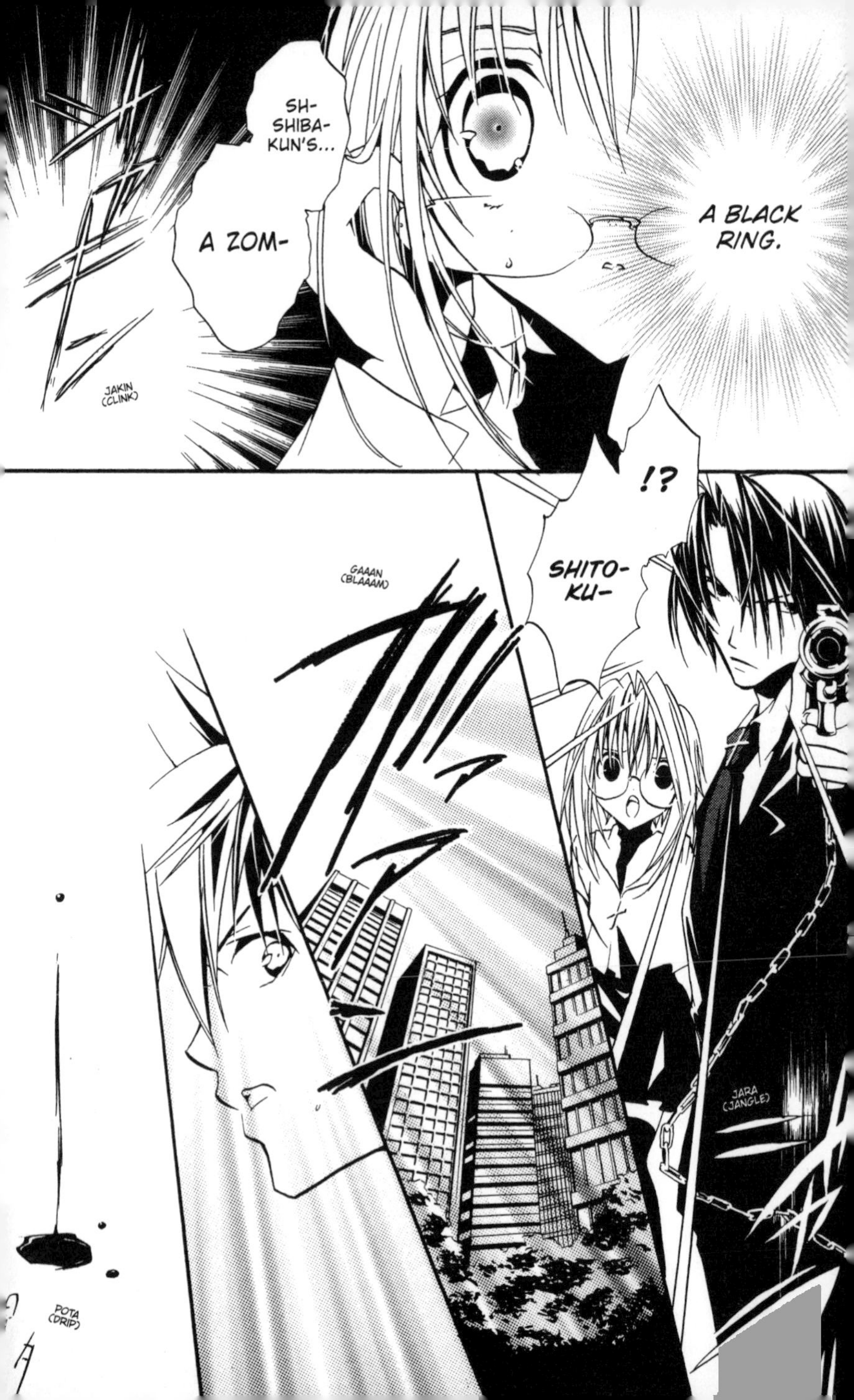
A BLACK RING.
SH-SHIBA-KUN'S...
A ZOM-
JAKIN (CLINK)
!?
SHITOKU-
GAAAN (BLAAAM)
JARA (JANGLE)
POTA (DRIP)

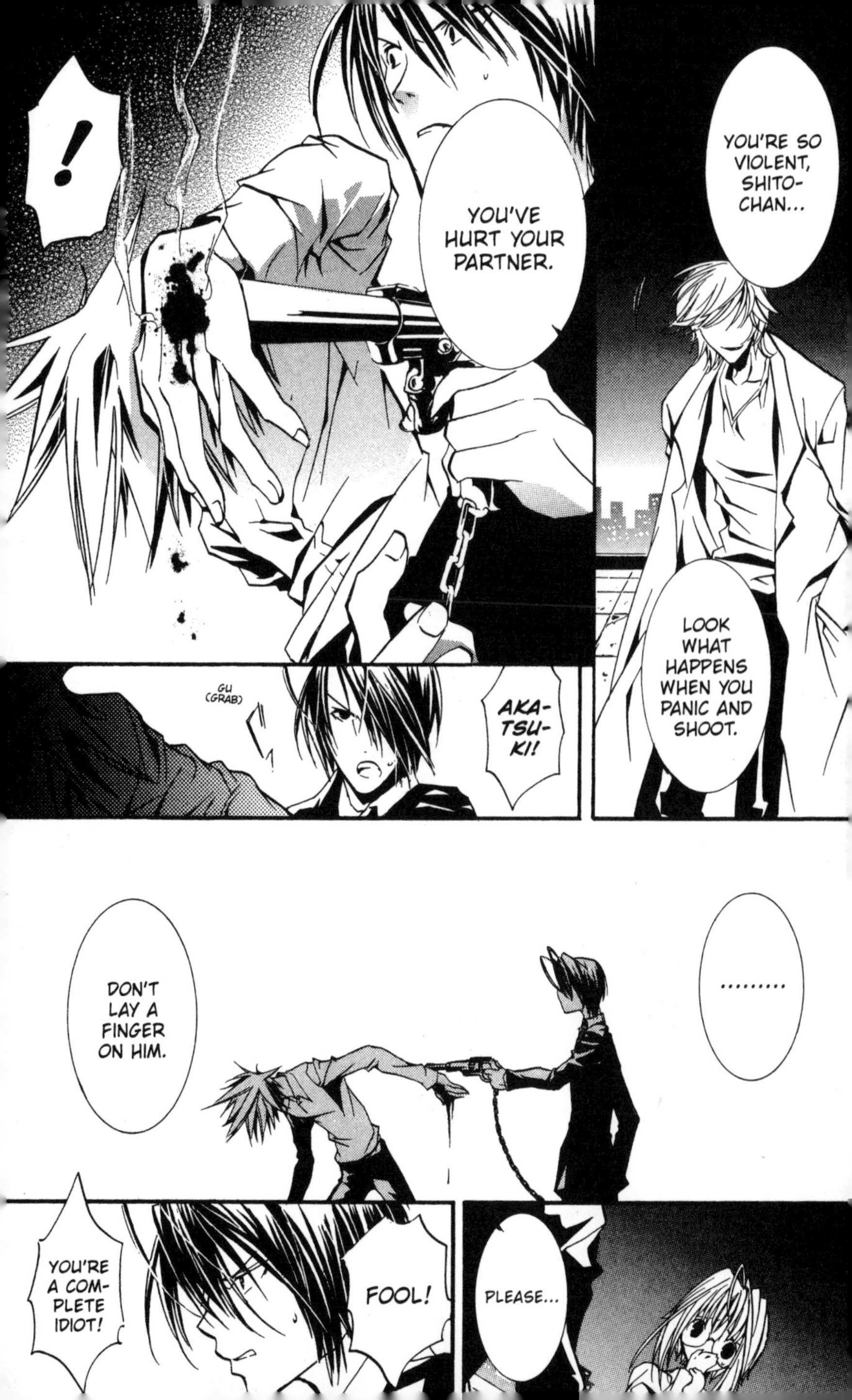
YOU'RE SO VIOLENT, SHITO-CHAN...
YOU'VE HURT YOUR PARTNER.
!
LOOK WHAT HAPPENS WHEN YOU PANIC AND SHOOT.
AKA-TSU-KI!
GU (GRAB)
....
DON'T LAY A FINGER ON HIM.
PLEASE...
FOOL!
YOU'RE A COM-PLETE IDIOT!

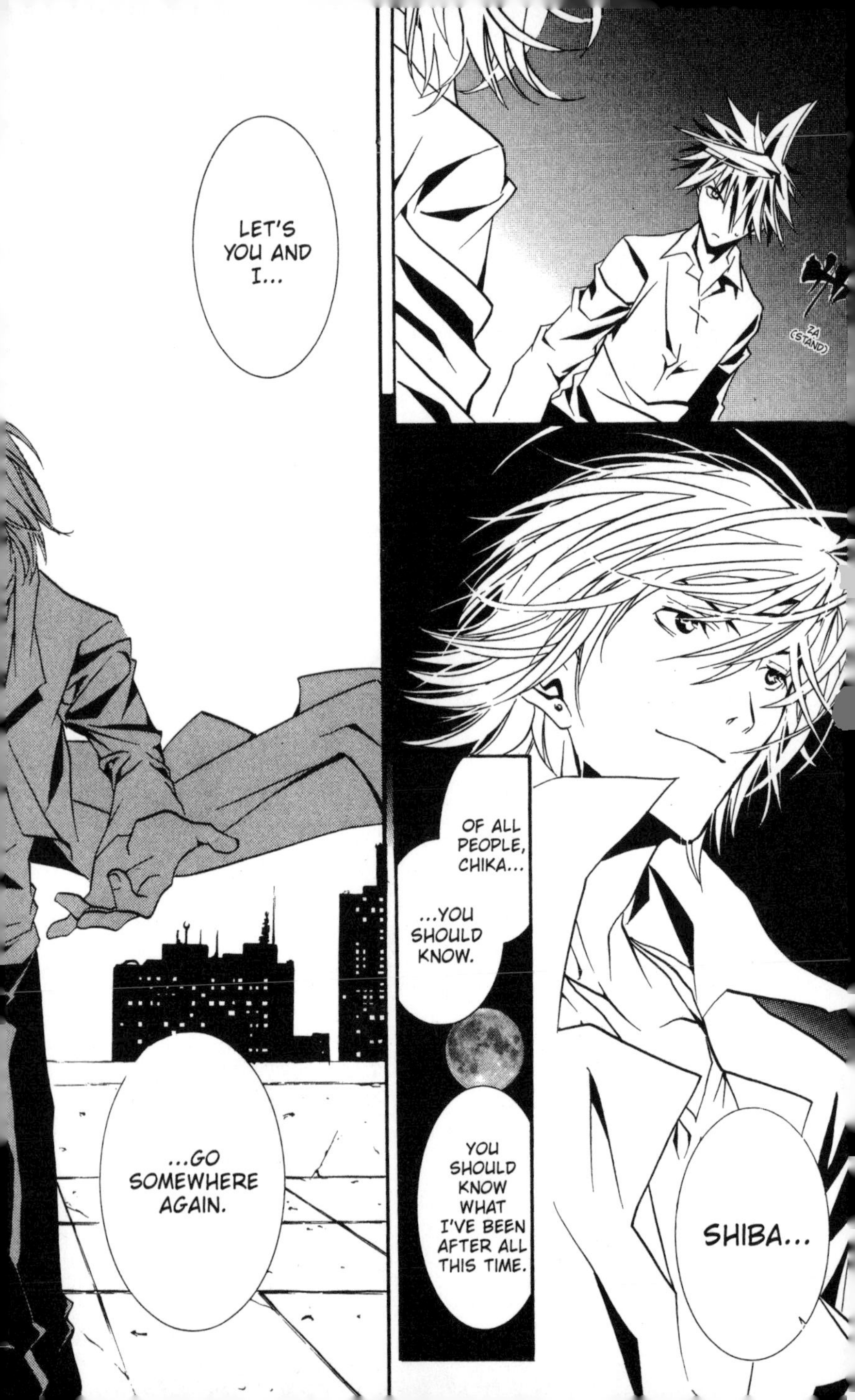

ZA (STAND)
SHIBA...
OF ALL PEOPLE, CHIKA...
...YOU SHOULD KNOW.
YOU SHOULD KNOW WHAT I'VE BEEN AFTER ALL THIS TIME.
LET'S YOU AND I...
...GO SOMEWHERE AGAIN.

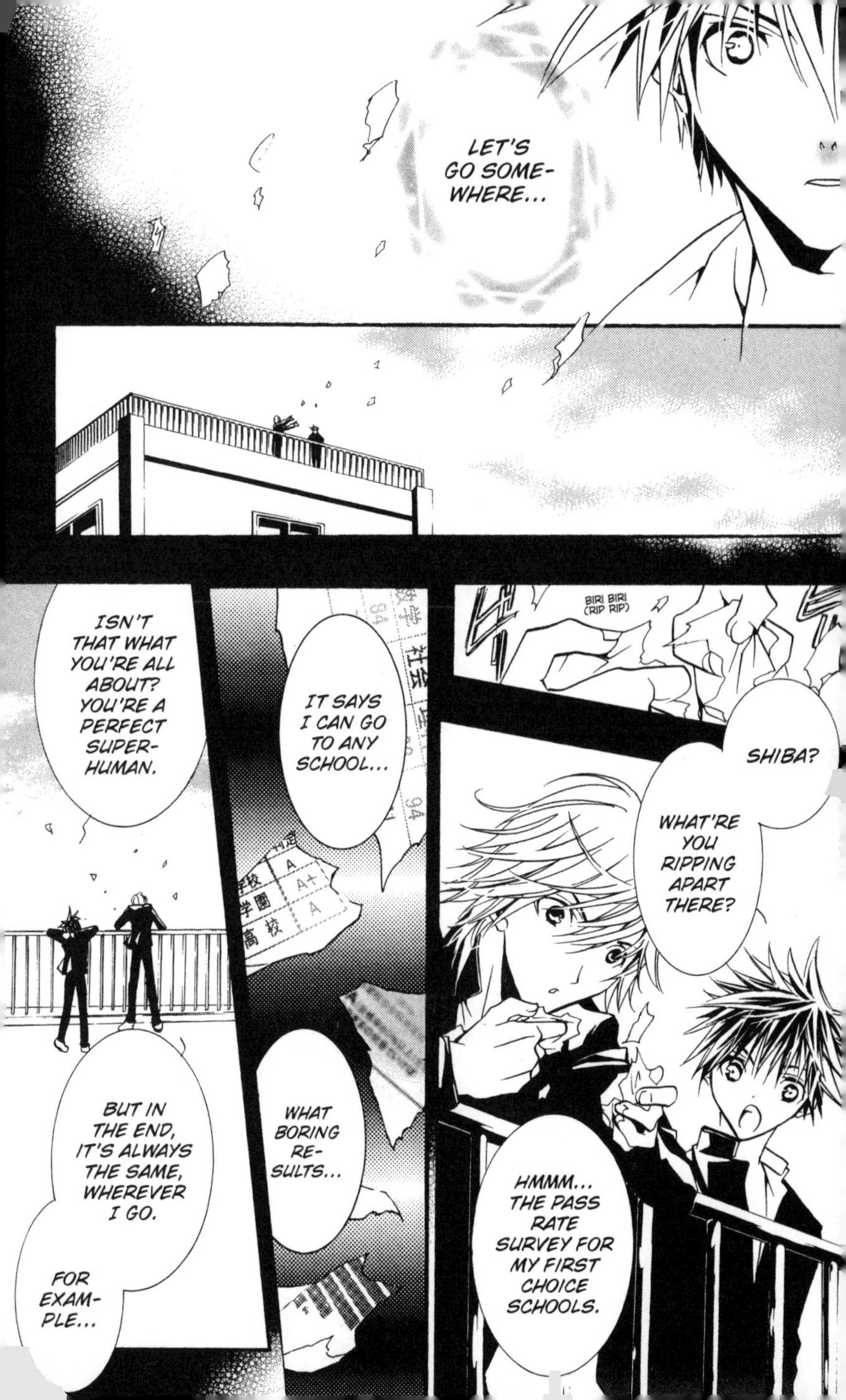
LET'S GO SOME-WHERE...
BIRI BIRI (RIP RIP)
SHIBA?
WHAT'RE YOU RIPPING APART THERE?
HMMM... THE PASS RATE SURVEY FOR MY FIRST CHOICE SCHOOLS.
IT SAYS I CAN GO TO ANY SCHOOL...
WHAT BORING RE-SULTS...
ISN'T THAT WHAT YOU'RE ALL ABOUT? YOU'RE A PERFECT SUPER-HUMAN.
BUT IN THE END, IT'S ALWAYS THE SAME, WHEREVER I GO.
FOR EXAM-PLE...

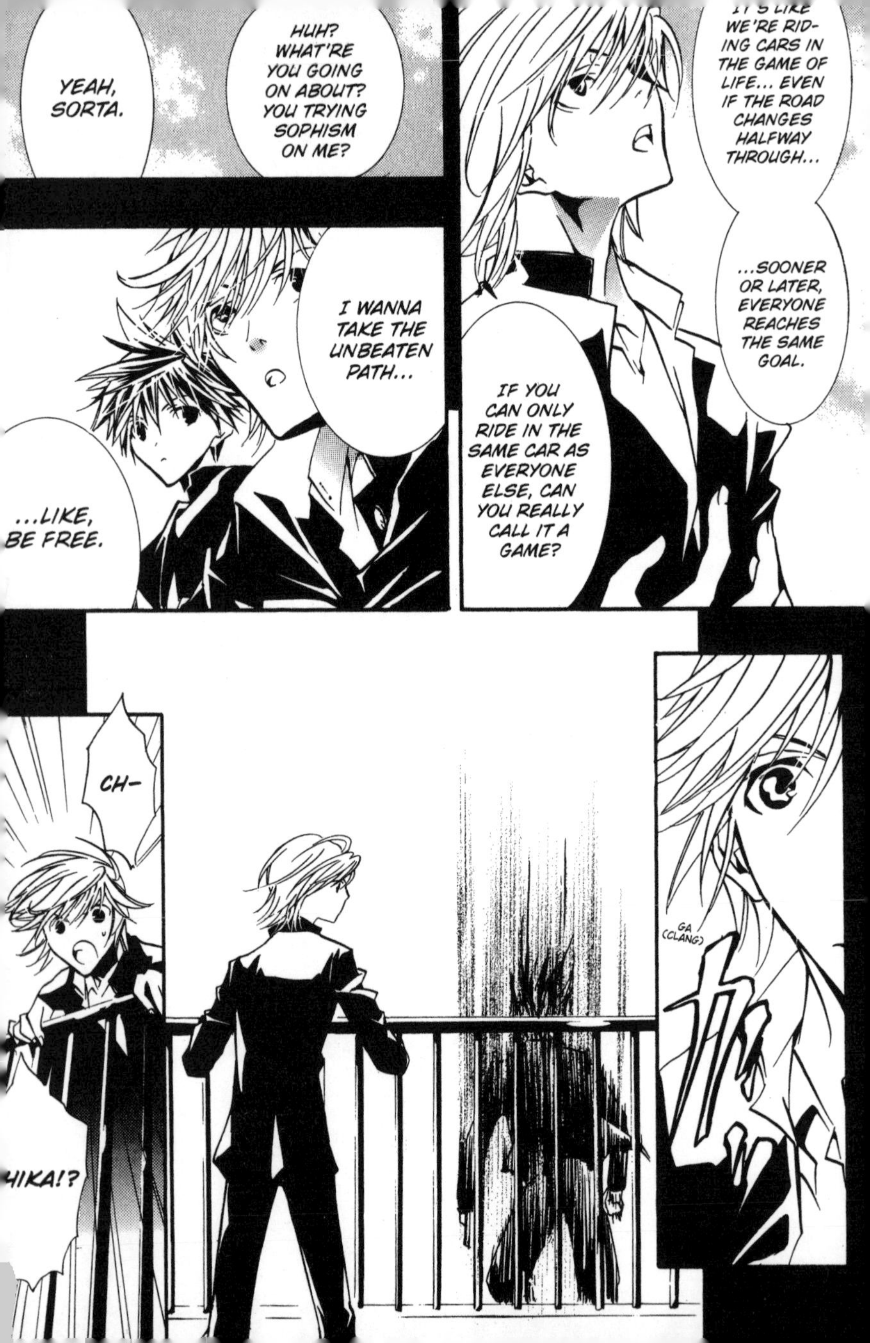
IT'S LIKE WE'RE RID-ING CARS IN THE GAME OF LIFE... EVEN IF THE ROAD CHANGES HALFWAY THROUGH...
...SOONER OR LATER, EVERYONE REACHES THE SAME GOAL.
IF YOU CAN ONLY RIDE IN THE SAME CAR AS EVERYONE ELSE, CAN YOU REALLY CALL IT A GAME?
HUH? WHAT'RE YOU GOING ON ABOUT? YOU TRYING SOPHISM ON ME?
YEAH, SORTA.
I WANNA TAKE THE UNBEATEN PATH...
...LIKE, BE FREE.
GA (CLANG)
CH-
HIKA!?

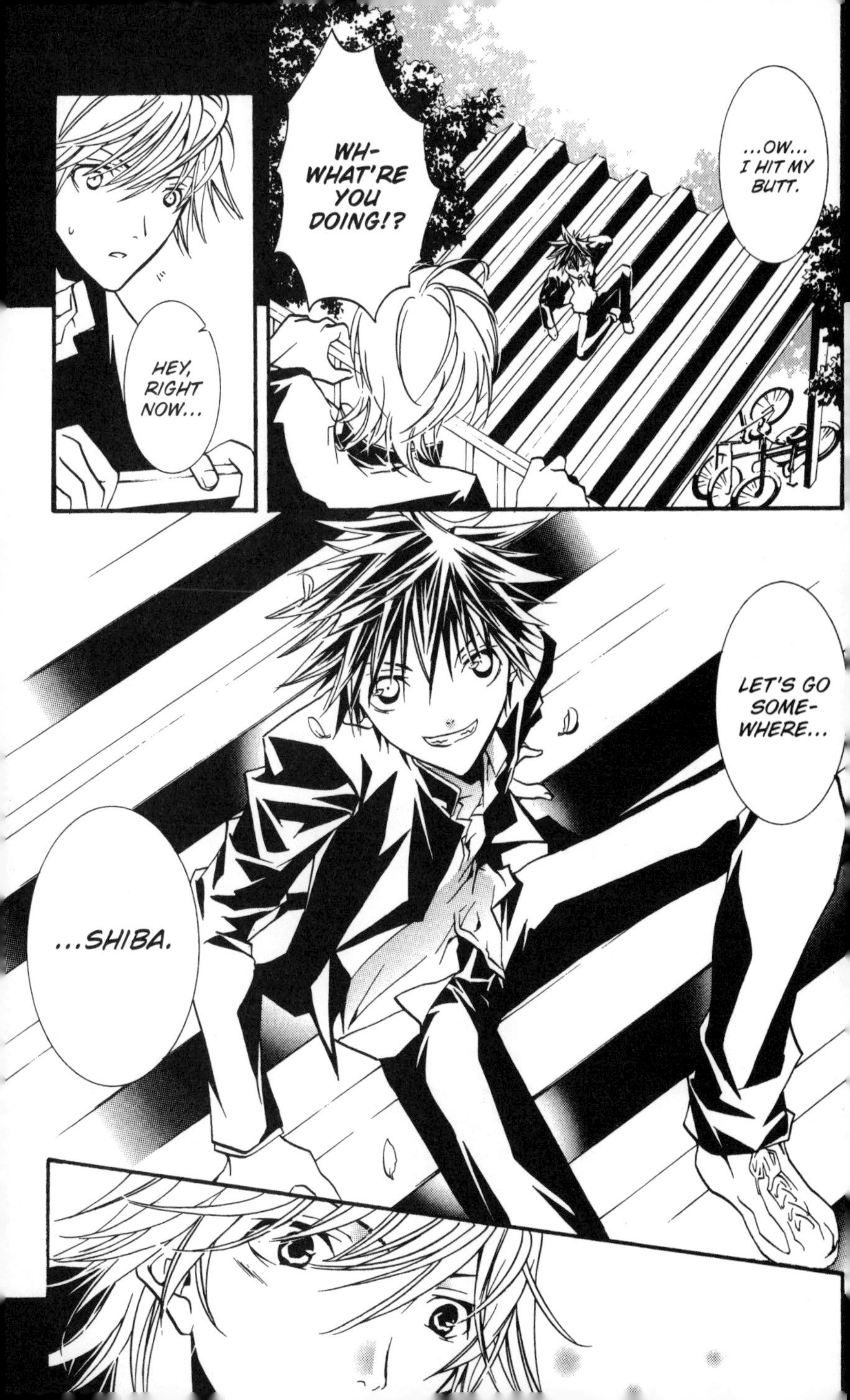
...OW... I HIT MY BUTT.
WH- WHAT'RE YOU DOING!?
HEY, RIGHT NOW...
LET'S GO SOME- WHERE...
...SHIBA.

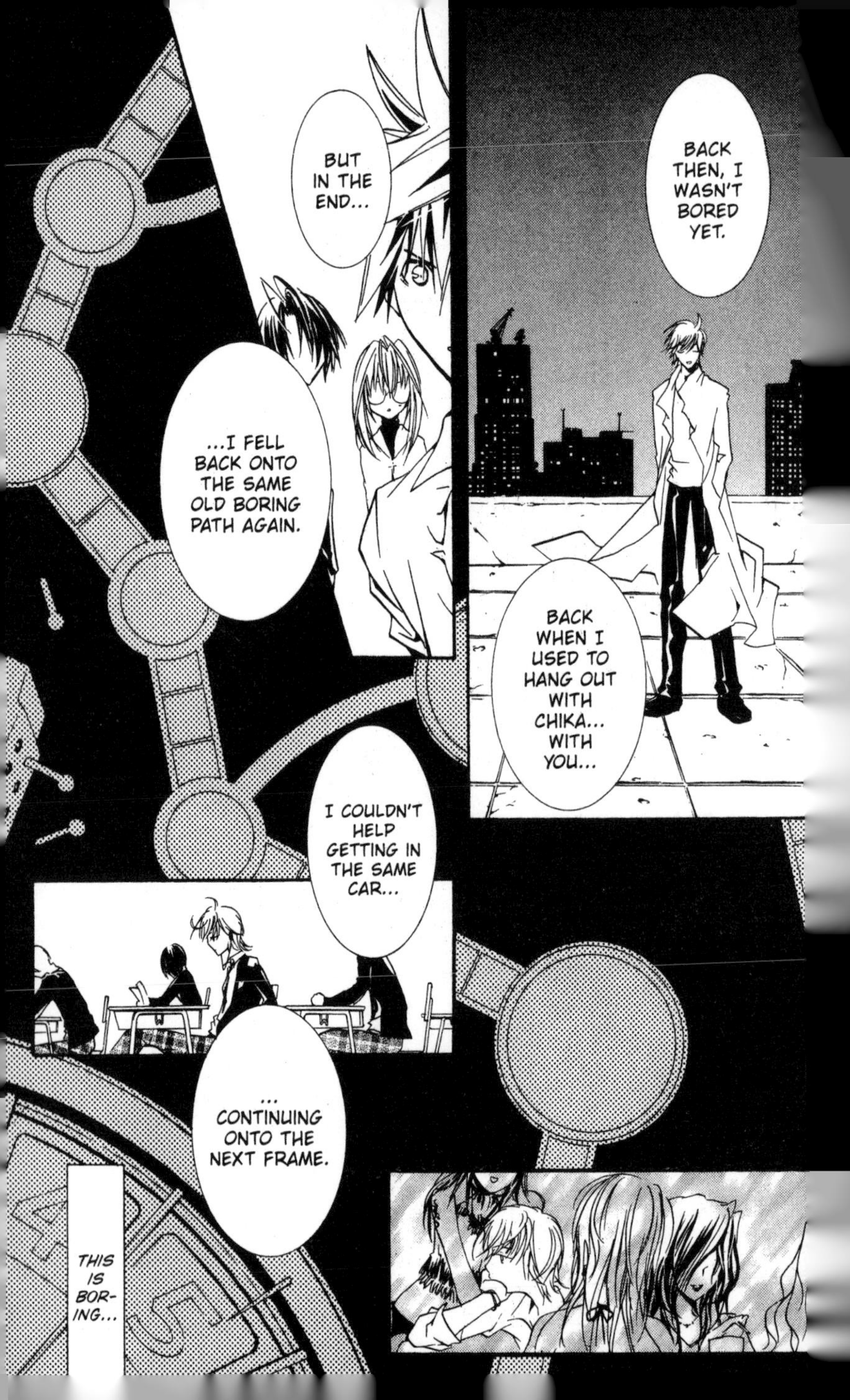
BACK THEN, I WASN'T BORED YET.
BACK WHEN I USED TO HANG OUT WITH CHIKA... WITH YOU...
BUT IN THE END...
...I FELL BACK ONTO THE SAME OLD BORING PATH AGAIN.
I COULDN'T HELP GETTING IN THE SAME CAR...
... CONTINUING ONTO THE NEXT FRAME.
THIS IS BOR-ING...

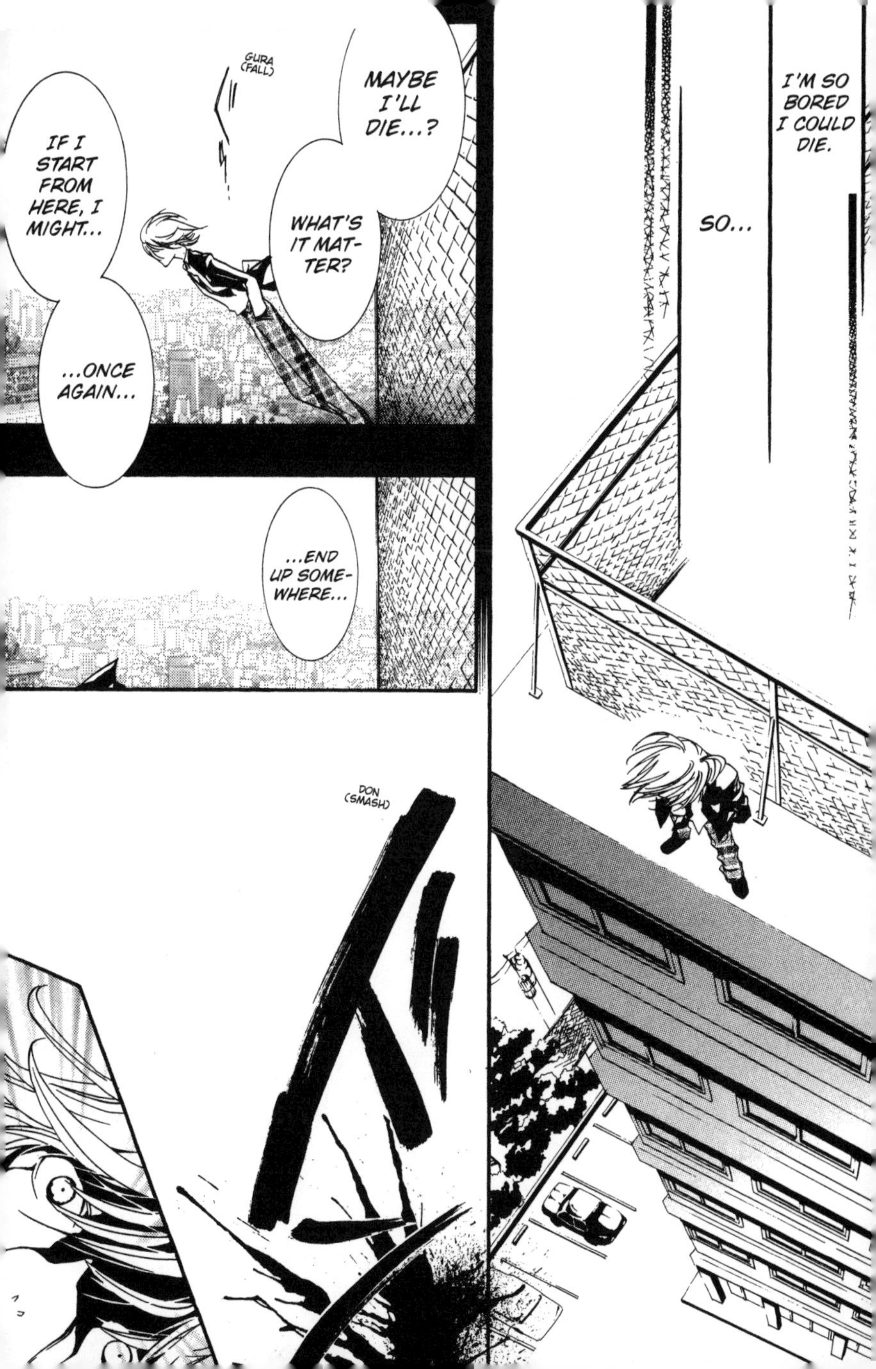
I'M SO BORED I COULD DIE.
SO...
MAYBE I'LL DIE...?
WHAT'S IT MAT-TER?
GURA (FALL)
IF I START FROM HERE, I MIGHT...
...ONCE AGAIN...
...END UP SOME-WHERE...
DON (SMASH)

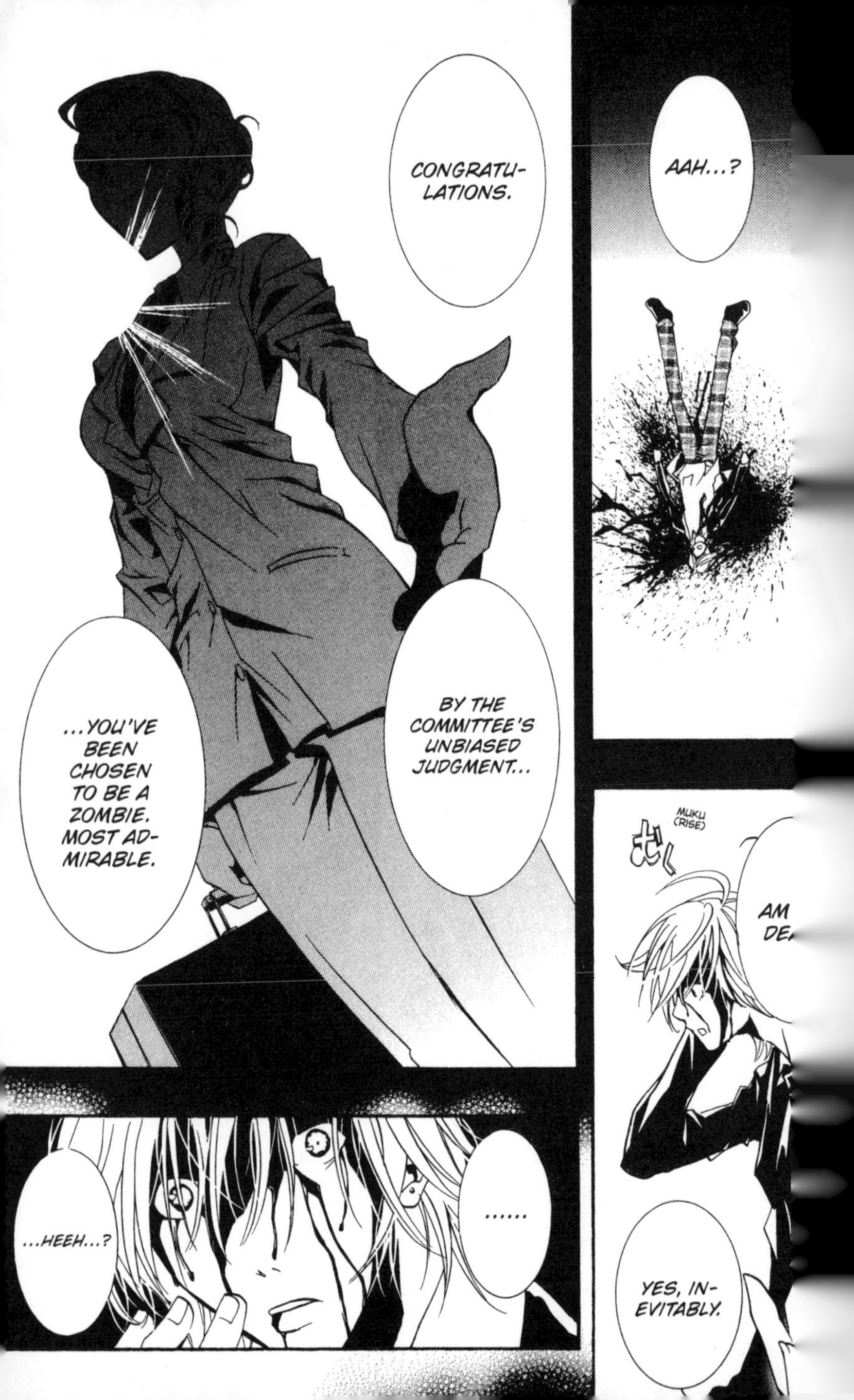
AAH...?
むく
MUKU (RISE)
AM
DE
YES, IN-EVITABLY.
CONGRATU-LATIONS.
BY THE COMMITTEE'S UNBIASED JUDGMENT...
...YOU'VE BEEN CHOSEN TO BE A ZOMBIE. MOST AD-MIRABLE.
......
...HEEH...?

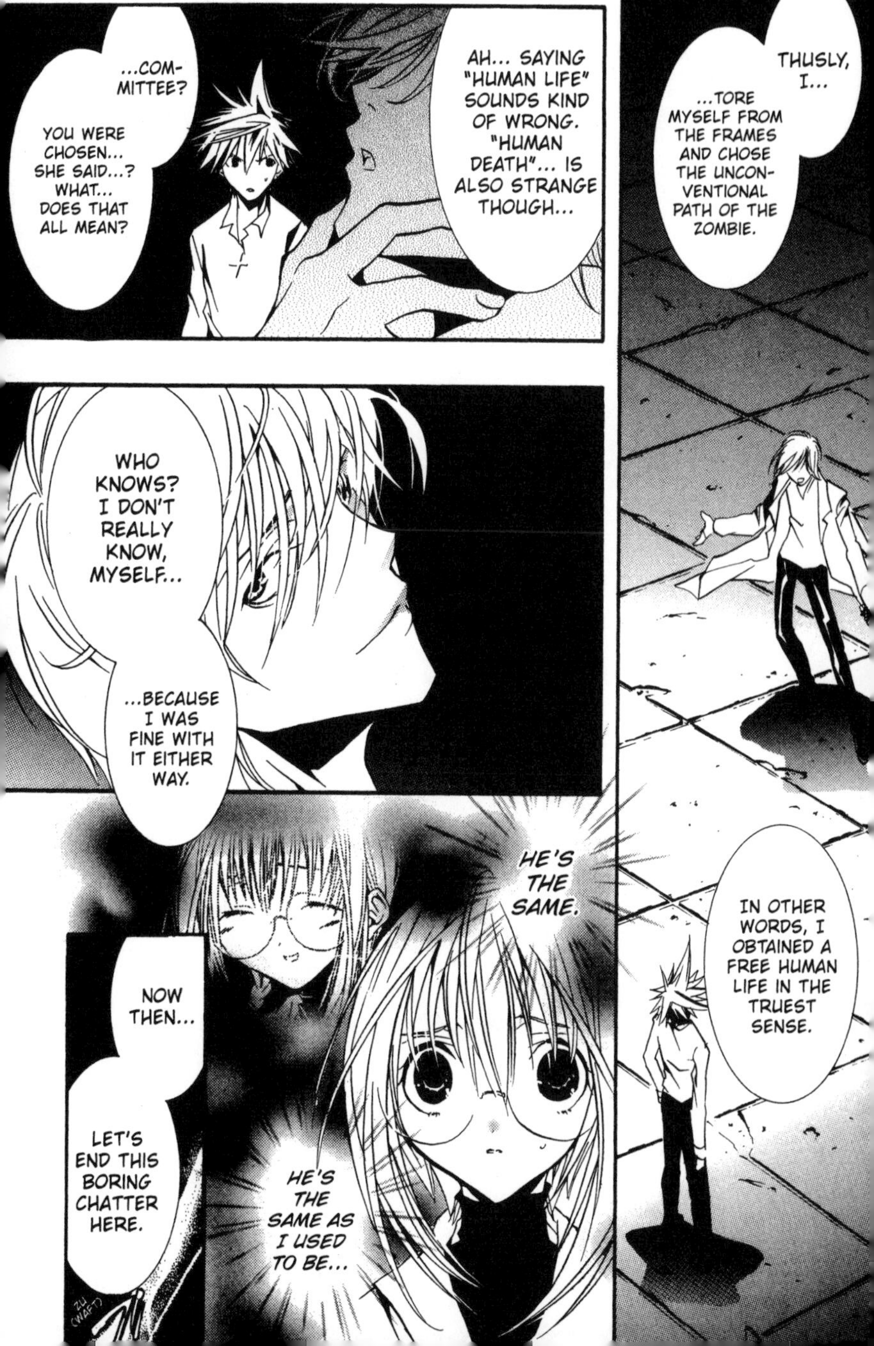
THUSLY, I...
...TORE MYSELF FROM THE FRAMES AND CHOSE THE UNCONVENTIONAL PATH OF THE ZOMBIE.
IN OTHER WORDS, I OBTAINED A FREE HUMAN LIFE IN THE TRUEST SENSE.
AH... SAYING "HUMAN LIFE" SOUNDS KIND OF WRONG. "HUMAN DEATH"... IS ALSO STRANGE THOUGH...
...COM-MITTEE?
YOU WERE CHOSEN... SHE SAID...? WHAT... DOES THAT ALL MEAN?
WHO KNOWS? I DON'T REALLY KNOW, MYSELF...
...BECAUSE I WAS FINE WITH IT EITHER WAY.
HE'S THE SAME.
NOW THEN...
LET'S END THIS BORING CHATTER HERE.
HE'S THE SAME AS I USED TO BE...
ZU (WAFT)

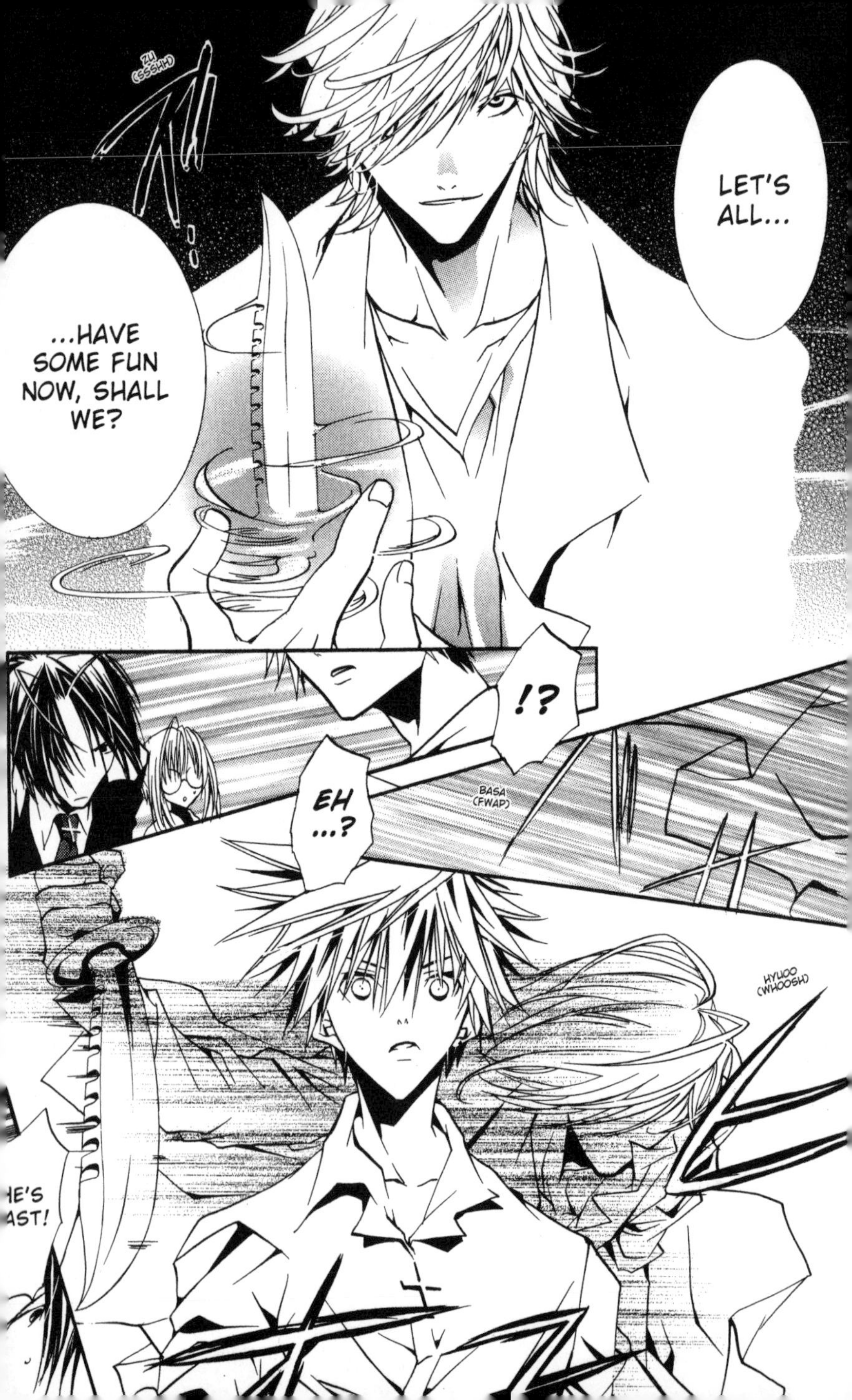
LET'S ALL...
ZU (SSSHH)
...HAVE SOME FUN NOW, SHALL WE?
!?
BASA (FWAP)
EH ...?
HYUOO (WHOOSH)

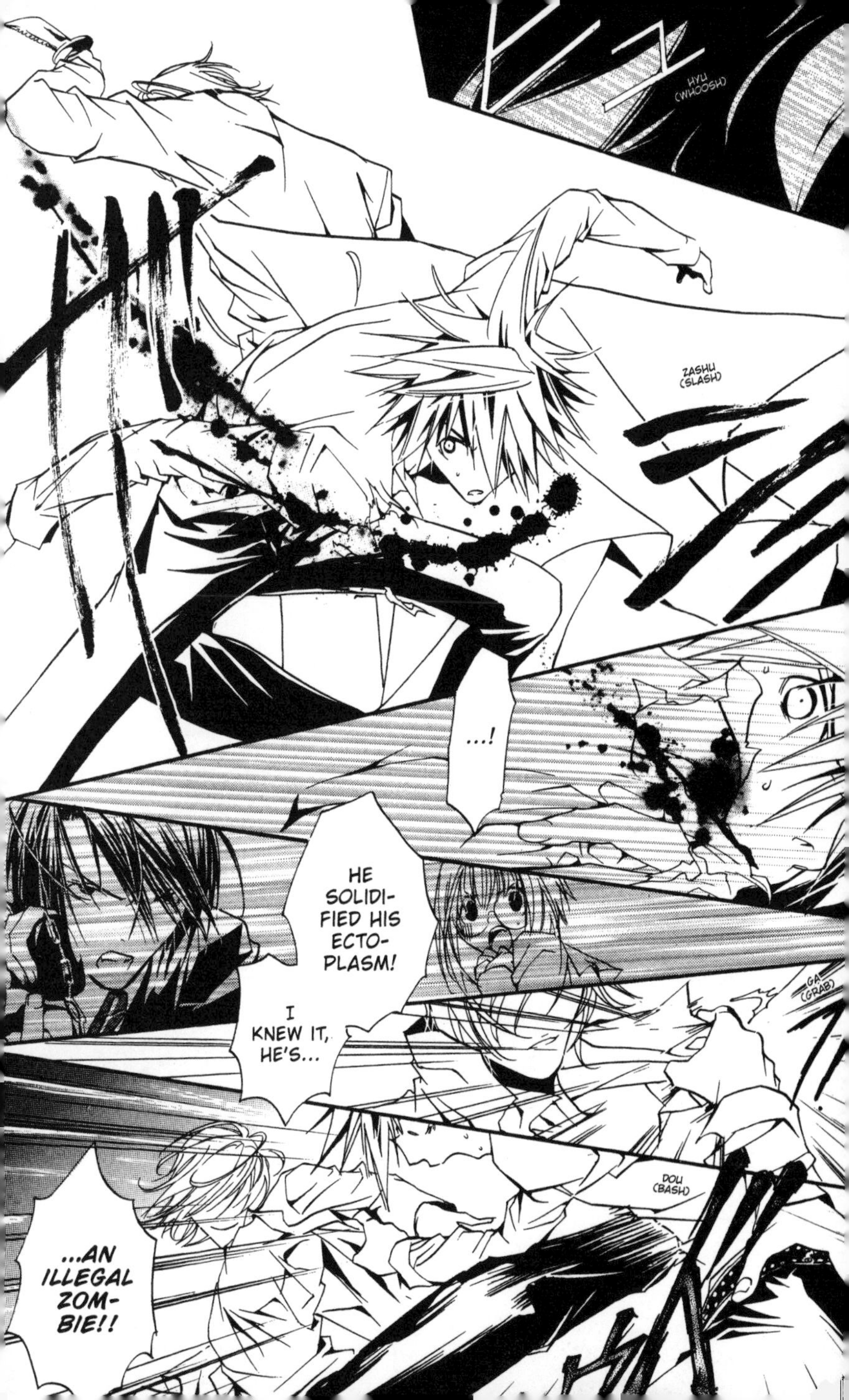
HYU (WHOOSH)
ZASHU (SLASH)
...!
HE SOLIDIFIED HIS ECTOPLASM!
I KNEW IT, HE'S...
GA (GRAB)
DOU (BASH)
...AN ILLEGAL ZOMBIE!!

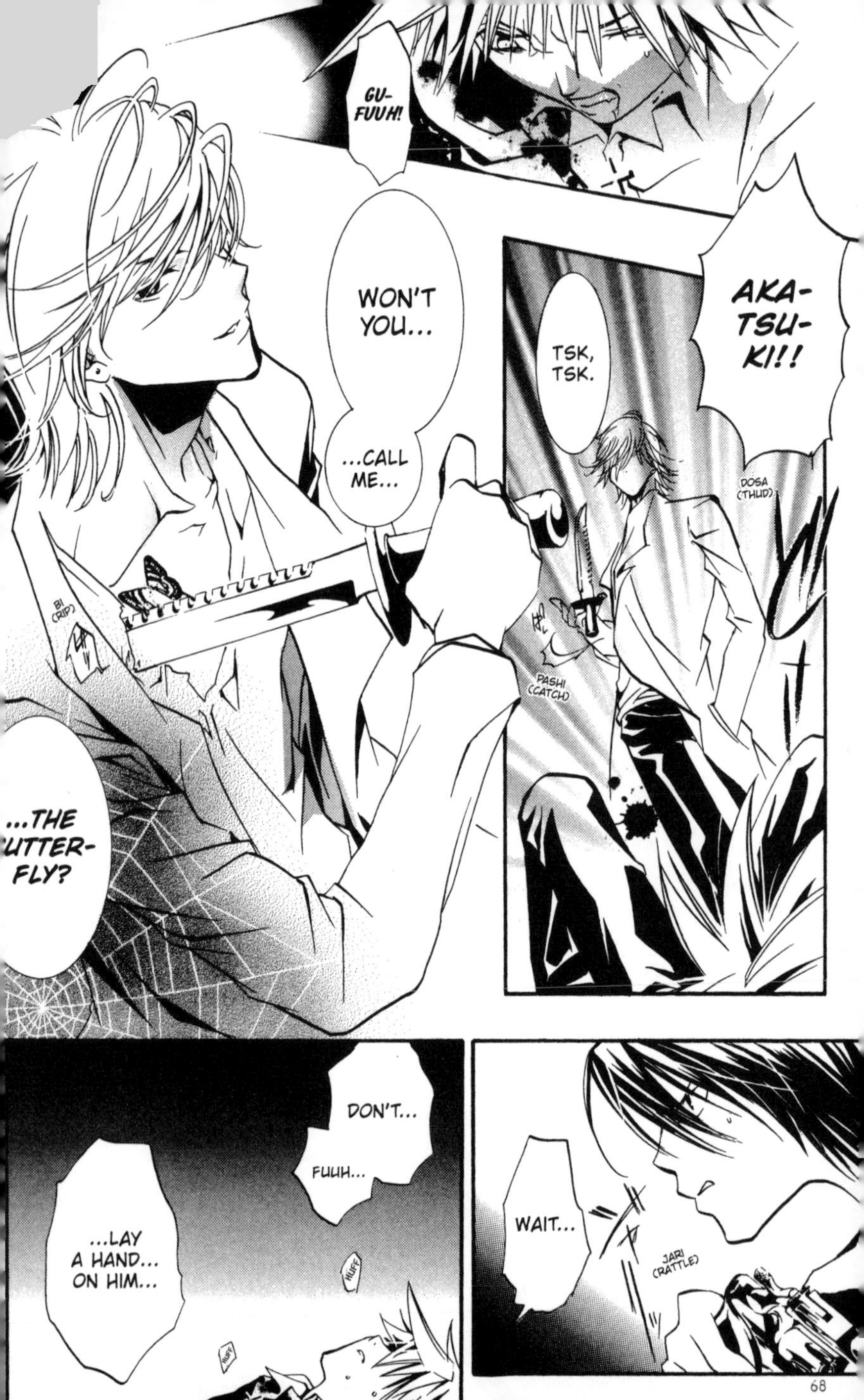
GU-FUUH!
AKA-TSU-KI!!
TSK, TSK.
DOSA (THUD)
PASHI (CATCH)
WON'T YOU...
...CALL ME...
BI (RIP)
...THE UTTER-FLY?
WAIT...
JARI (RATTLE)
DON'T...
FUUH...
...LAY A HAND... ON HIM...
HUFF
HUFF

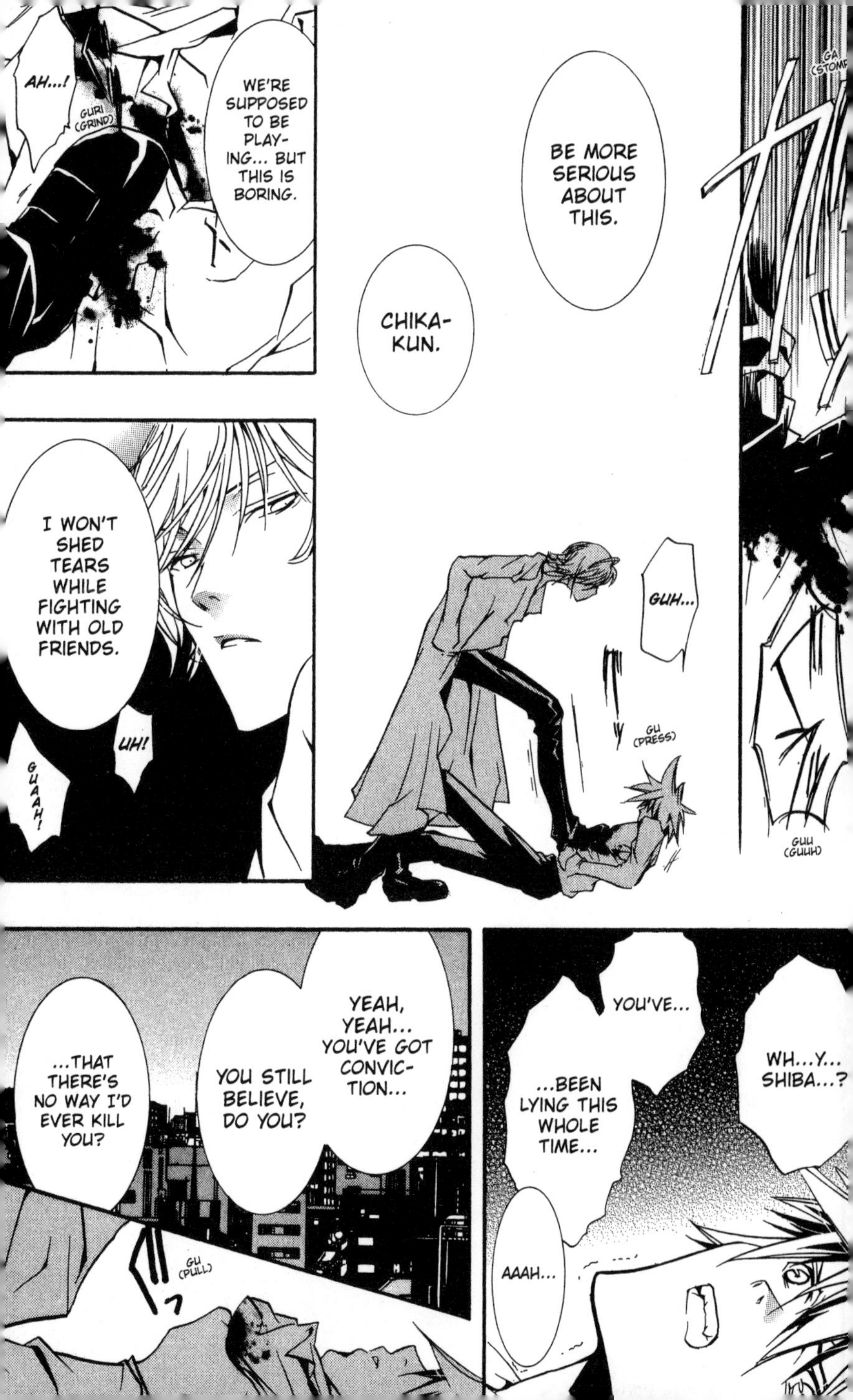
GA (STOMP)
GUU (GUUH)
BE MORE SERIOUS ABOUT THIS.
CHIKA-KUN.
WE'RE SUPPOSED TO BE PLAY-ING... BUT THIS IS BORING.
GURI (GRIND)
AH...!
GUH...
GU (PRESS)
I WON'T SHED TEARS WHILE FIGHTING WITH OLD FRIENDS.
UH!
GUAAAH!
WH...Y... SHIBA...?
YOU'VE...
...BEEN LYING THIS WHOLE TIME...
AAAH...
YEAH, YEAH... YOU'VE GOT CONVIC-TION...
YOU STILL BELIEVE, DO YOU?
...THAT THERE'S NO WAY I'D EVER KILL YOU?
GU (PULL)

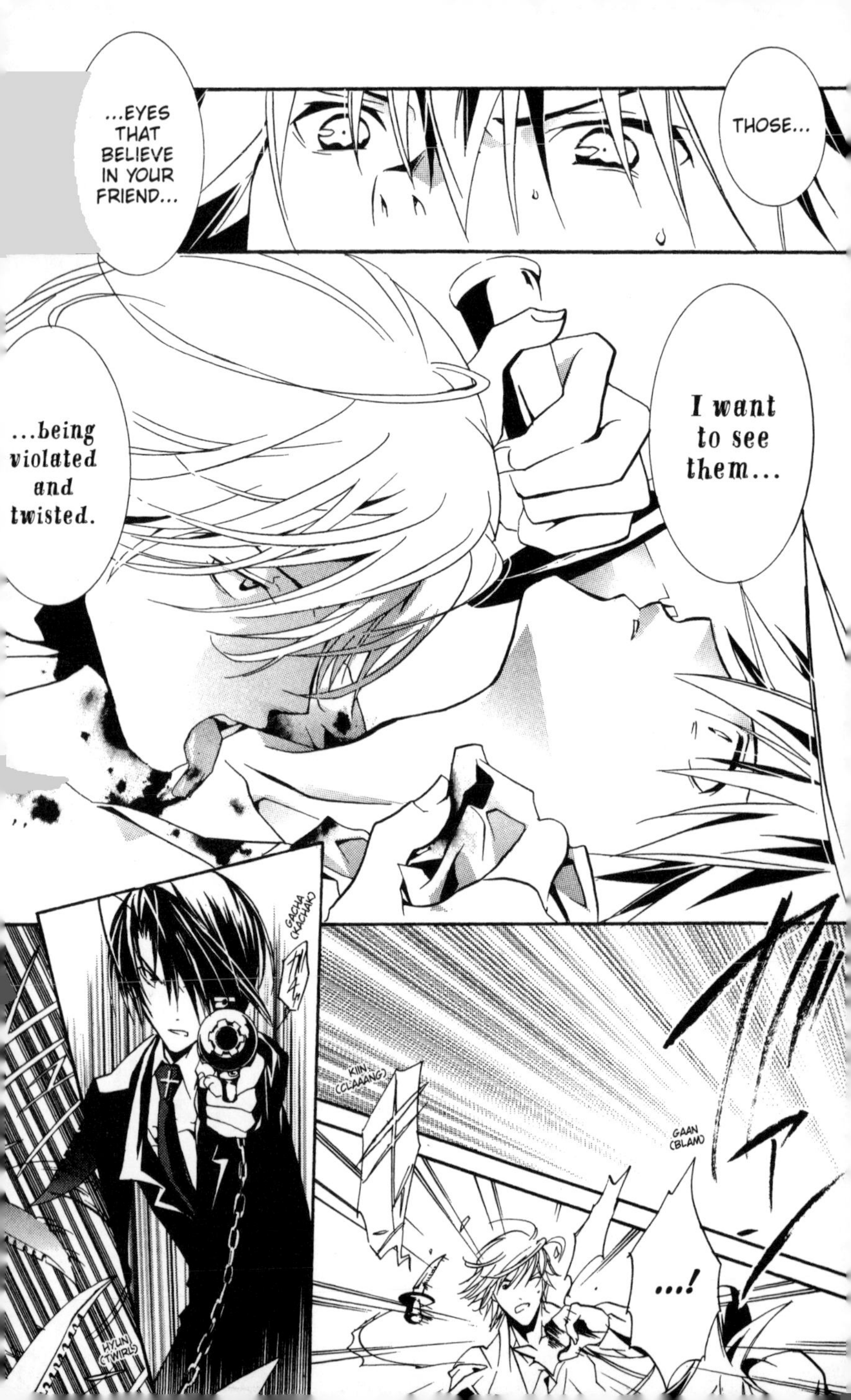
THOSE...
...EYES THAT BELIEVE IN YOUR FRIEND...
I want to see them...
...being violated and twisted.
GAAN (BLAM)
...!
KIIN... (CLAAANG)
GACHA (KACHAK)
HYUN (TWIRLS)

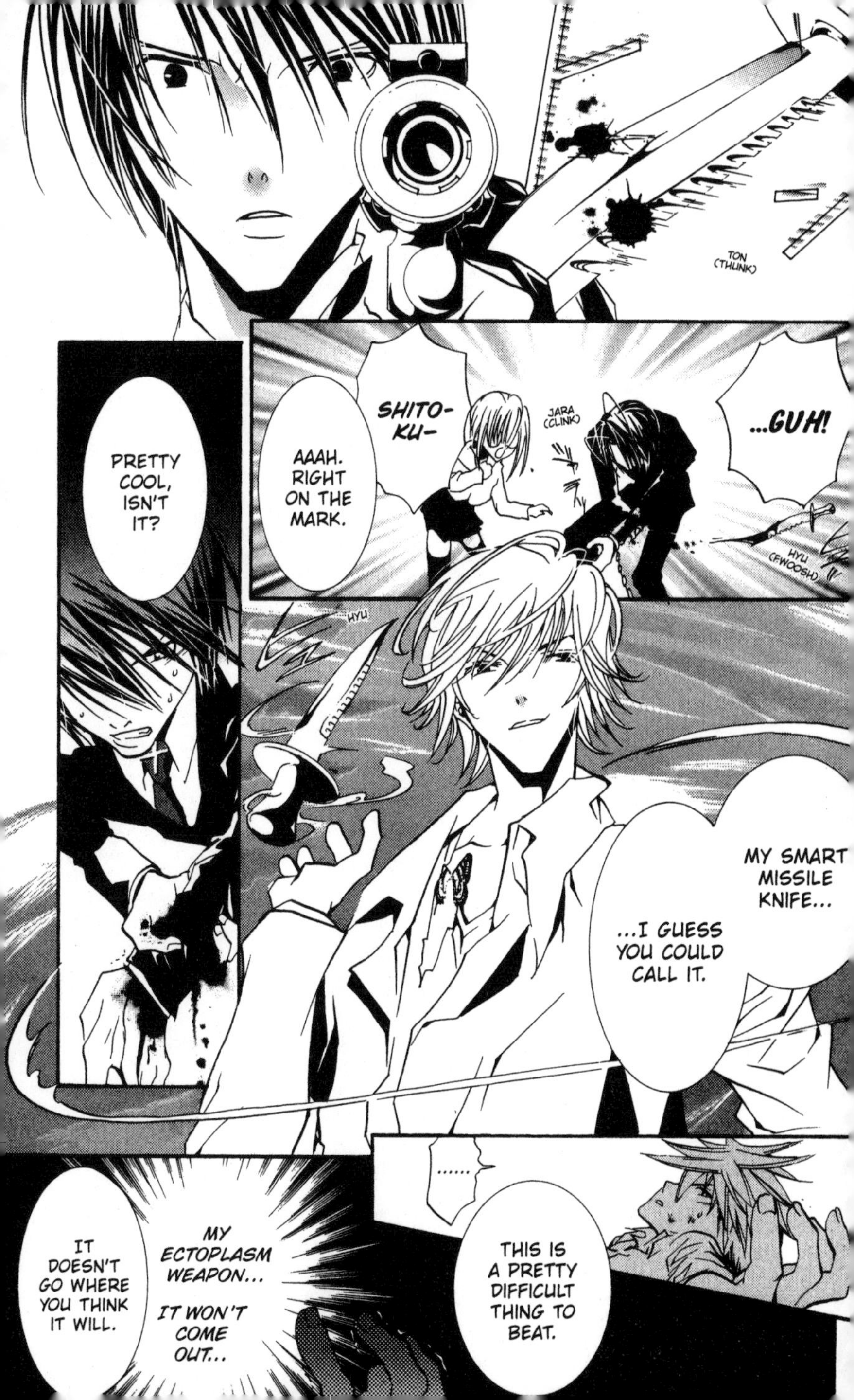
TON (THUNK)
...GUH!
JARA (CLINK)
SHITO-KU-
AAAH. RIGHT ON THE MARK.
HYU (FWOOSH)
HYU
MY SMART MISSILE KNIFE...
...I GUESS YOU COULD CALL IT.
PRETTY COOL, ISN'T IT?
......
THIS IS A PRETTY DIFFICULT THING TO BEAT.
MY ECTOPLASM WEAPON...
IT WON'T COME OUT...
IT DOESN'T GO WHERE YOU THINK IT WILL.

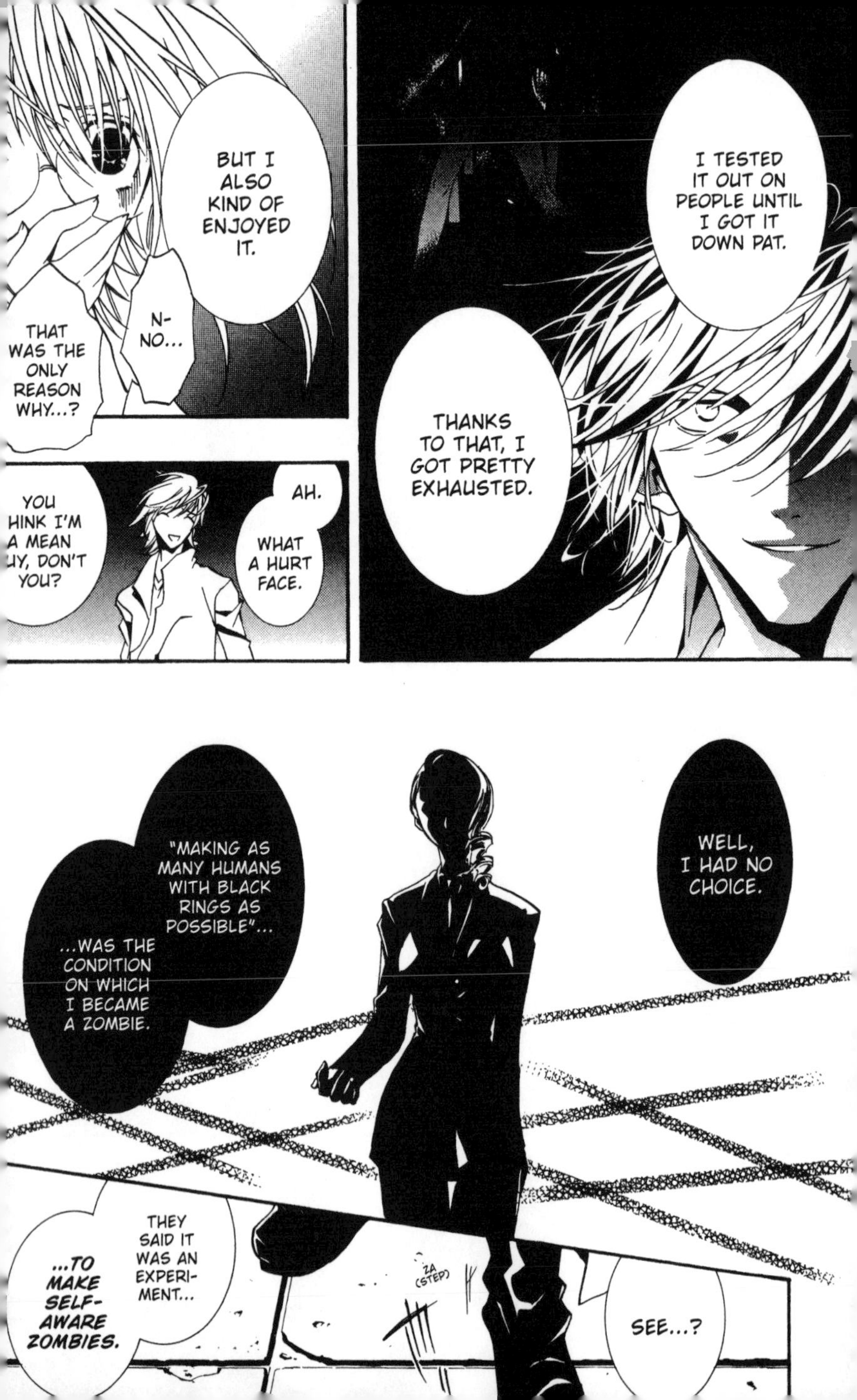
I TESTED IT OUT ON PEOPLE UNTIL I GOT IT DOWN PAT.
THANKS TO THAT, I GOT PRETTY EXHAUSTED.
BUT I ALSO KIND OF ENJOYED IT.
N-NO...
THAT WAS THE ONLY REASON WHY...?
AH.
WHAT A HURT FACE.
YOU HINK I'M A MEAN UY, DON'T YOU?
WELL, I HAD NO CHOICE.
"MAKING AS MANY HUMANS WITH BLACK RINGS AS POSSIBLE"...
...WAS THE CONDITION ON WHICH I BECAME A ZOMBIE.
SEE...?
ZA (STEP)
THEY SAID IT WAS AN EXPERIMENT...
...TO MAKE SELF-AWARE ZOMBIES.

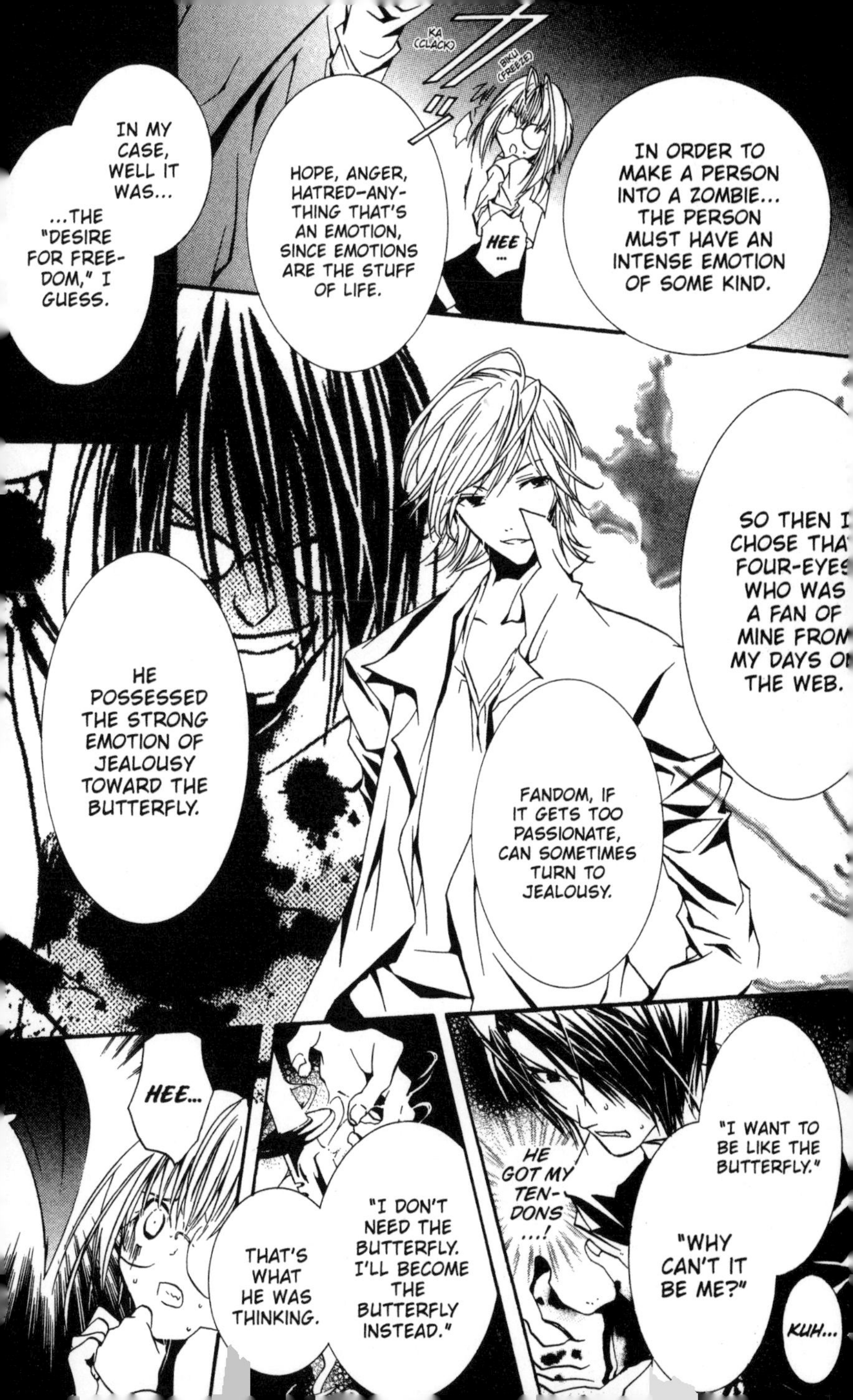

KA (CLACK)
BIKU (FREEZE)
IN ORDER TO MAKE A PERSON INTO A ZOMBIE... THE PERSON MUST HAVE AN INTENSE EMOTION OF SOME KIND.
HEE...
HOPE, ANGER, HATRED—ANYTHING THAT'S AN EMOTION, SINCE EMOTIONS ARE THE STUFF OF LIFE.
IN MY CASE, WELL IT WAS...
...THE "DESIRE FOR FREE-DOM," I GUESS.
SO THEN I CHOSE THAT FOUR-EYES WHO WAS A FAN OF MINE FROM MY DAYS ON THE WEB.
FANDOM, IF IT GETS TOO PASSIONATE, CAN SOMETIMES TURN TO JEALOUSY.
HE POSSESSED THE STRONG EMOTION OF JEALOUSY TOWARD THE BUTTERFLY.
"I WANT TO BE LIKE THE BUTTERFLY."
"WHY CAN'T IT BE ME?"
KUH...
HE GOT MY TEN-DONS...!
"I DON'T NEED THE BUTTERFLY. I'LL BECOME THE BUTTERFLY INSTEAD."
THAT'S WHAT HE WAS THINKING.
HEE...

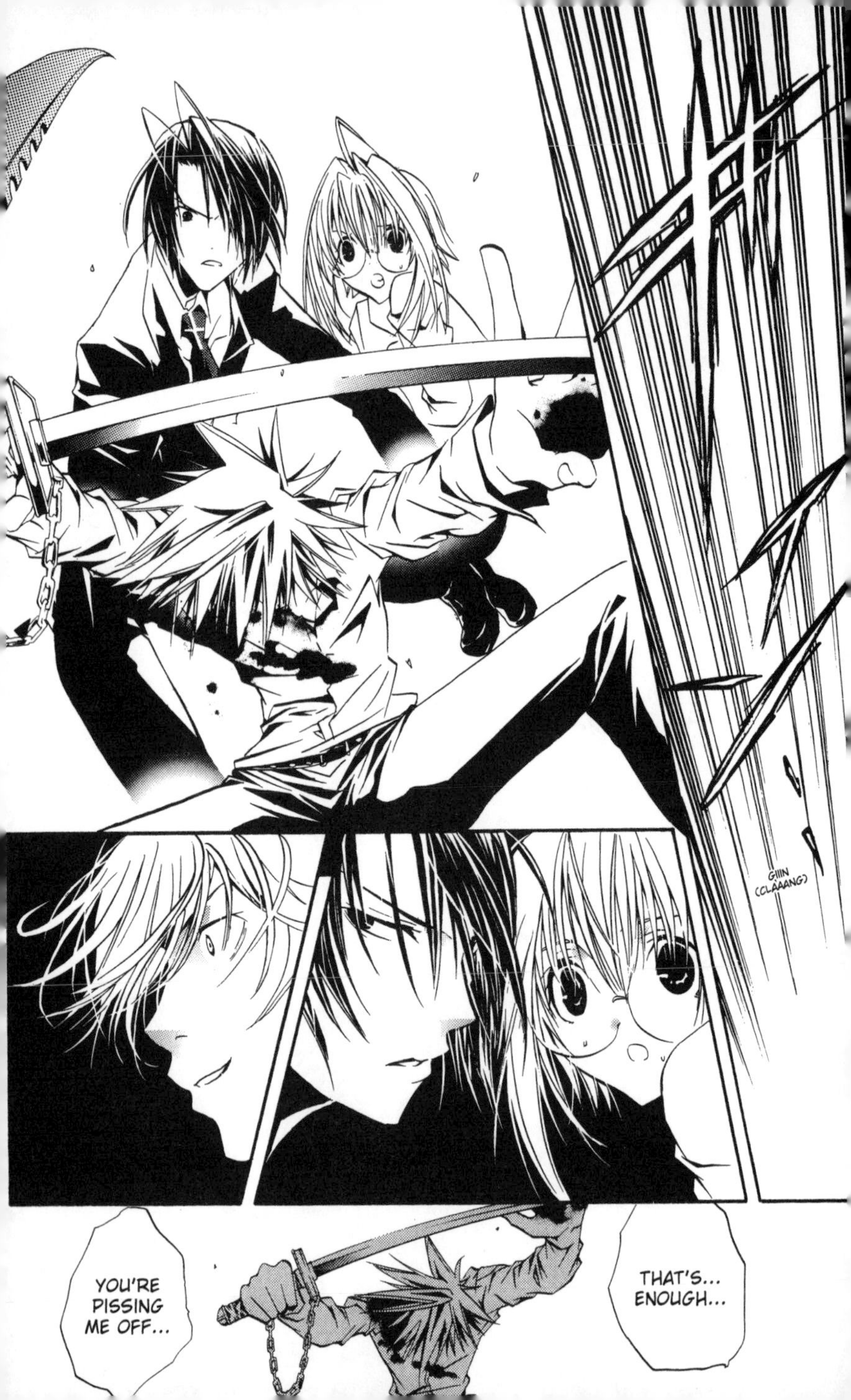
GIIIN
(CLAAANG)
THAT'S... ENOUGH...
YOU'RE PISSING ME OFF...

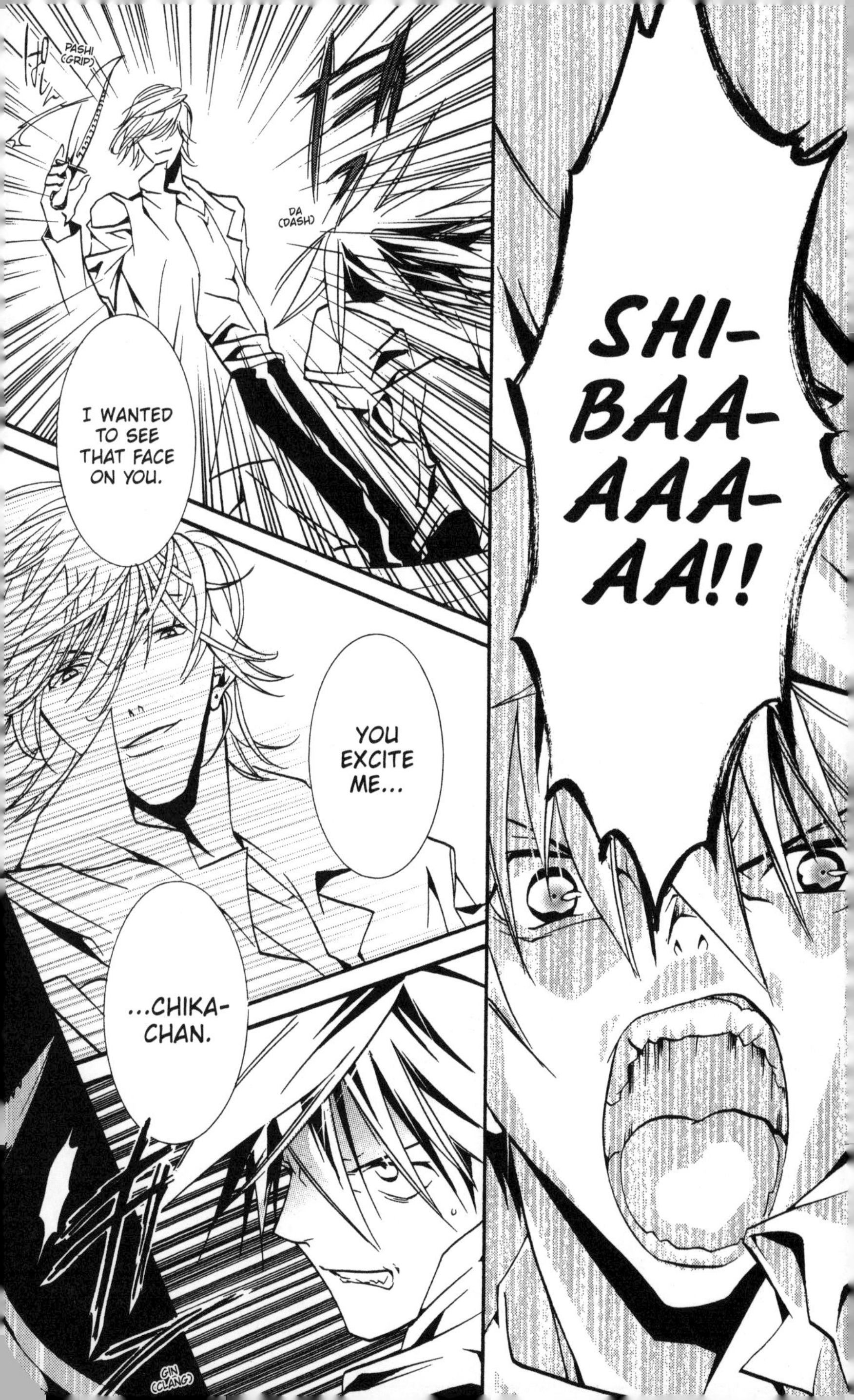
SHI-BAAA-AAAA-AA!!
DA (DASH)
PASHI (GRIP)
I WANTED TO SEE THAT FACE ON YOU.
YOU EXCITE ME...
...CHIKA-CHAN.
GIN (CLANG)

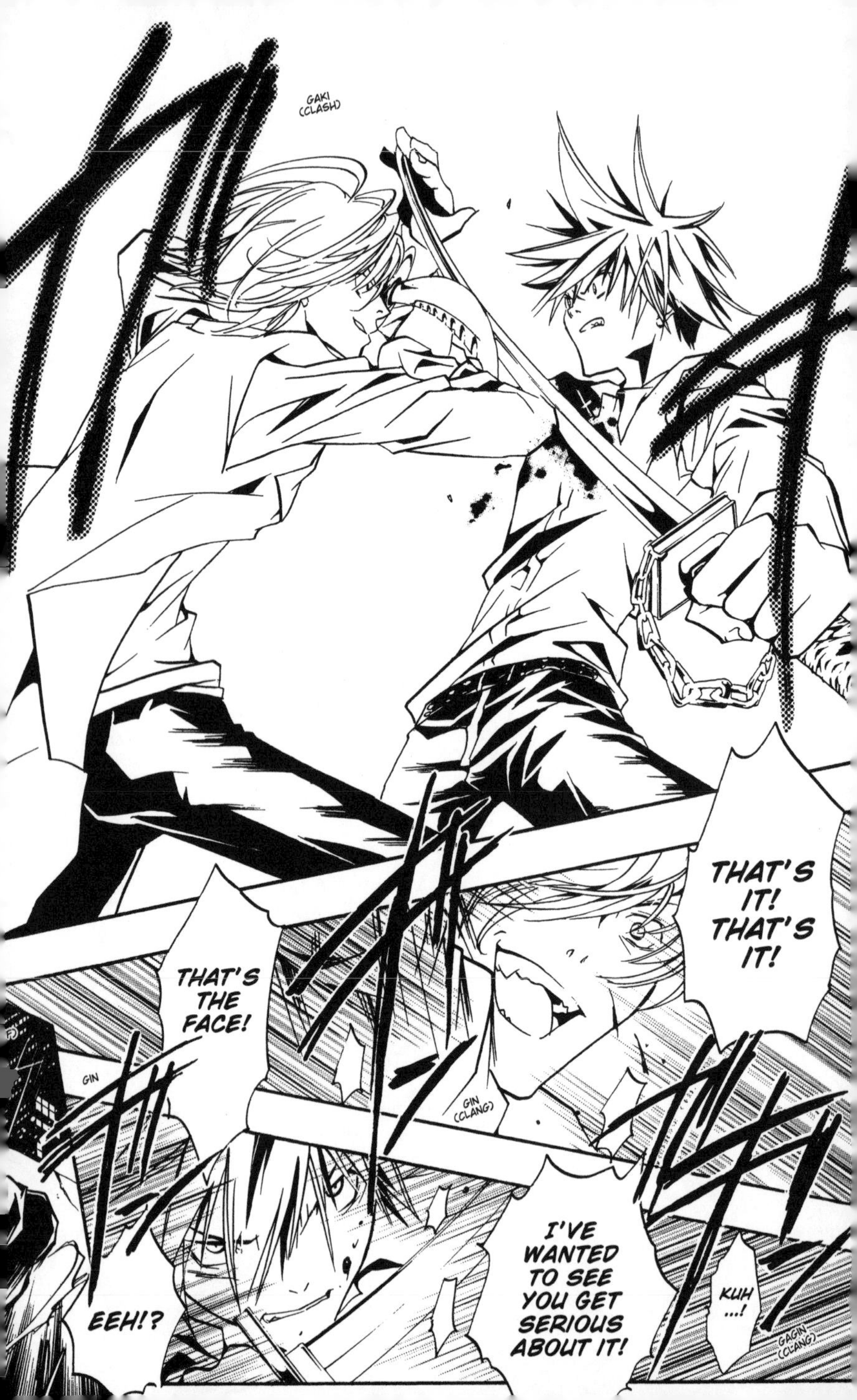
GAKI (CLASH)
THAT'S IT! THAT'S IT!
THAT'S THE FACE!
GIN (CLANG)
GIN
KUH ...!
GAGIN (CLANG)
I'VE WANTED TO SEE YOU GET SERIOUS ABOUT IT!
EEH!?

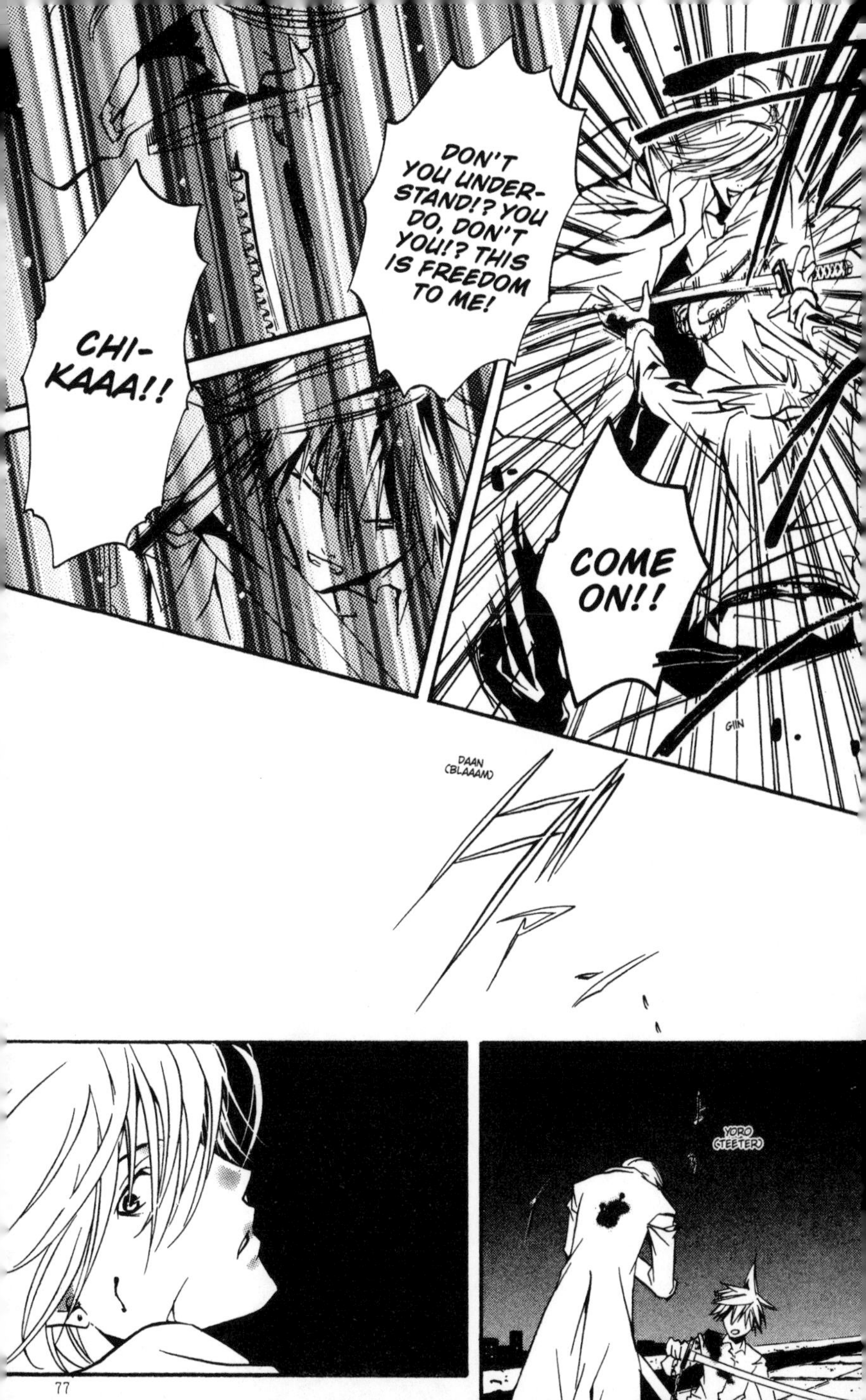
DON'T YOU UNDER-STAND!? YOU DO, DON'T YOU!? THIS IS FREEDOM TO ME!
COME ON!!
GIIN
CHI-KAAA!!
DAAN (BLAAAM)
YORO (TEETER)

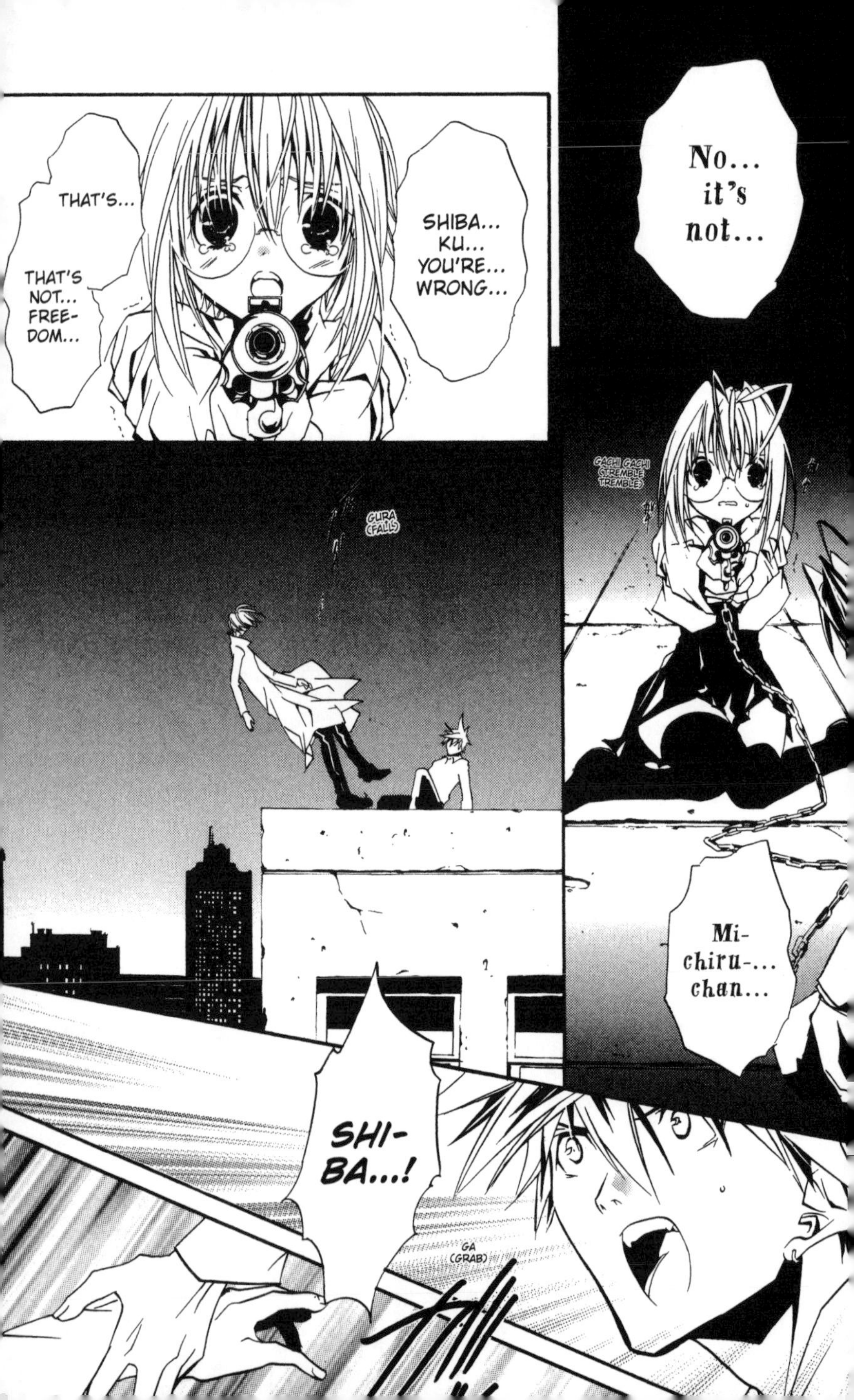
No... it's not...
SHIBA... KU... YOU'RE... WRONG...
THAT'S...
THAT'S NOT... FREE-DOM...
GACHI GACHI (TREMBLE TREMBLE)
GURA (FALLS)
Mi-chiru-... chan...
SHI-BA...!
GA (GRAB)

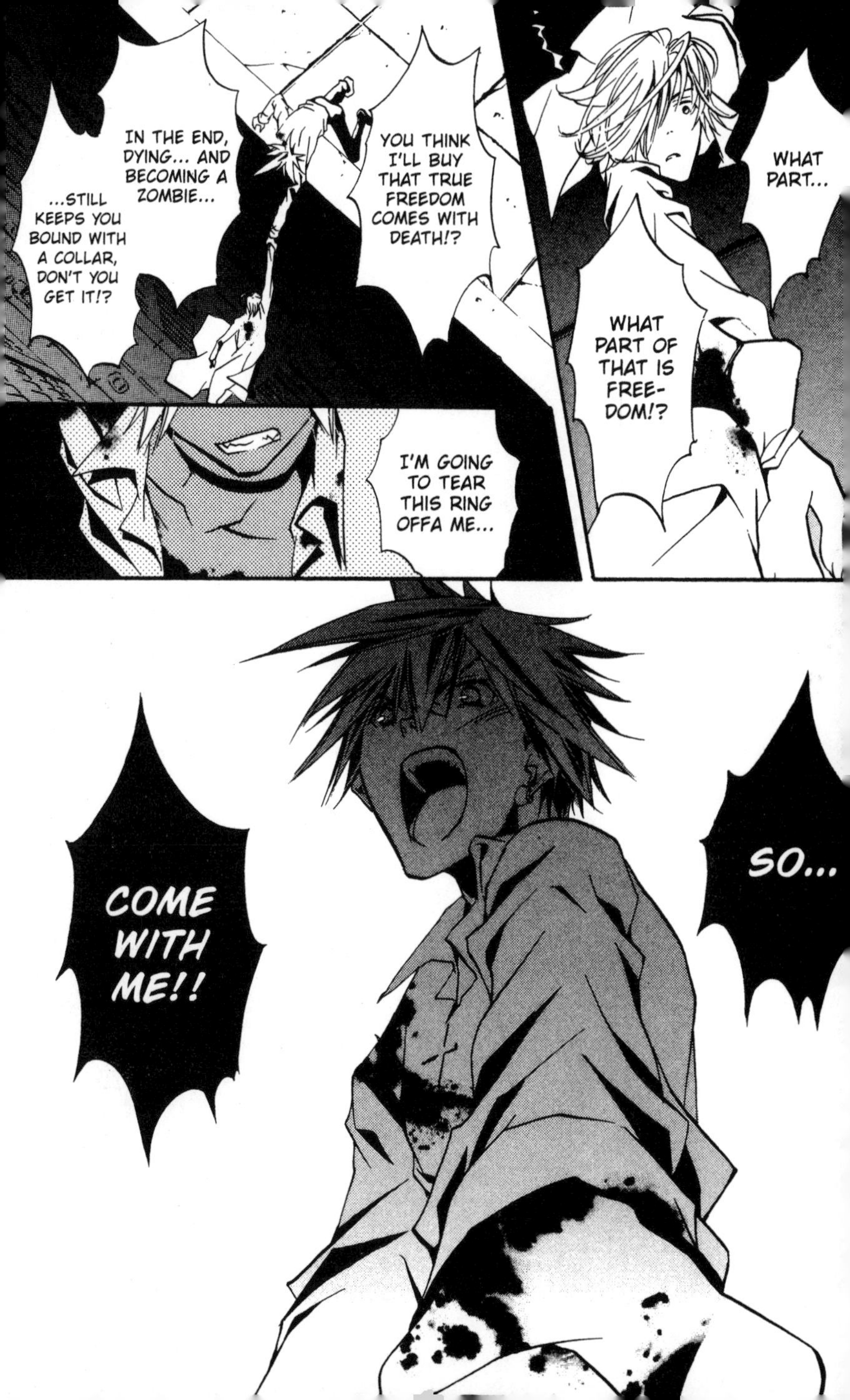
WHAT PART...
WHAT PART OF THAT IS FREE-DOM!?
YOU THINK I'LL BUY THAT TRUE FREEDOM COMES WITH DEATH!?
IN THE END, DYING... AND BECOMING A ZOMBIE...
...STILL KEEPS YOU BOUND WITH A COLLAR, DON'T YOU GET IT!?
I'M GOING TO TEAR THIS RING OFFA ME...
SO...
COME WITH ME!!

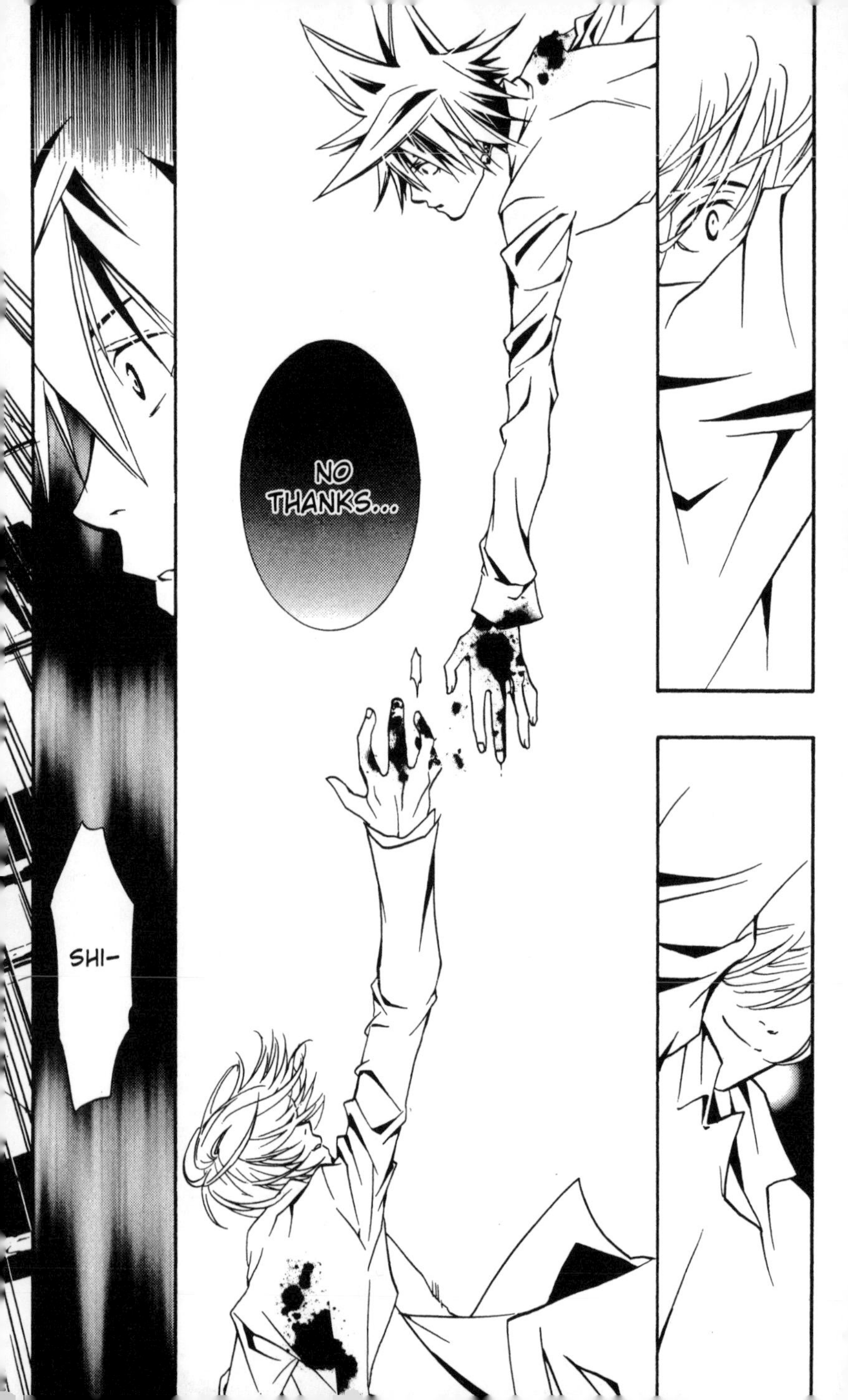
NO THANKS...
SHI-

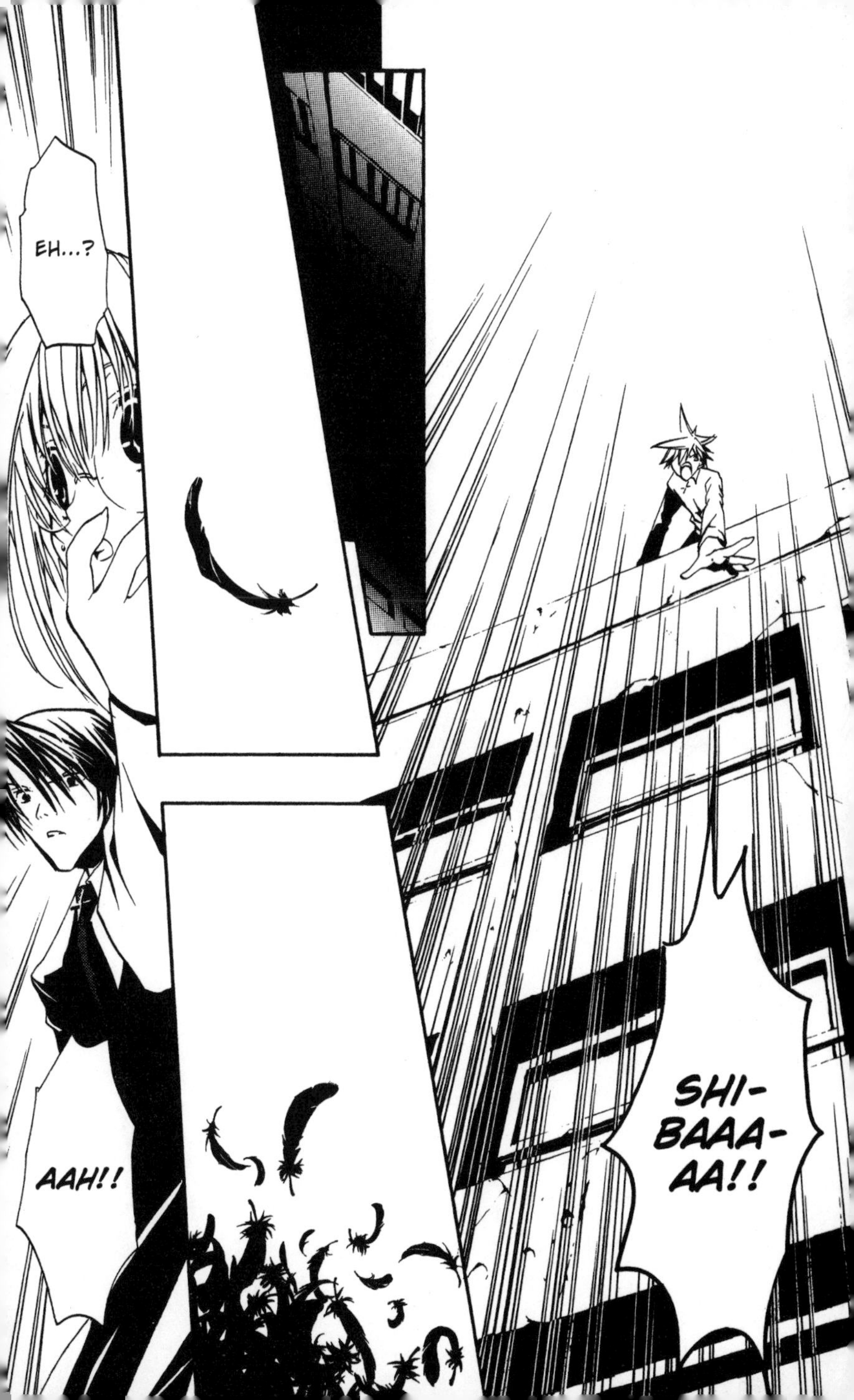
SHI-BAAAA-AA!!
EH...?
AAH!!

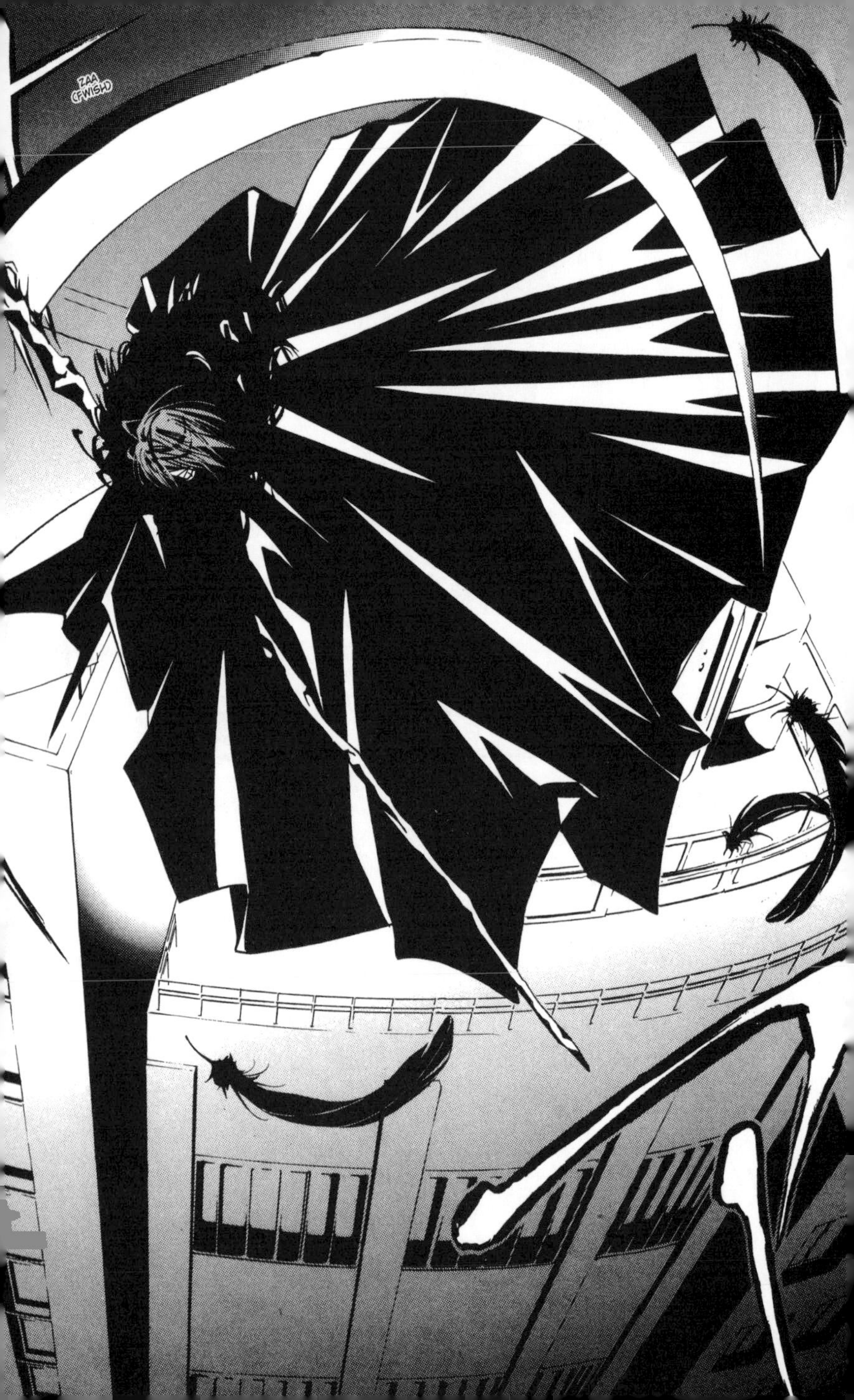
ZAA
(FWISH)

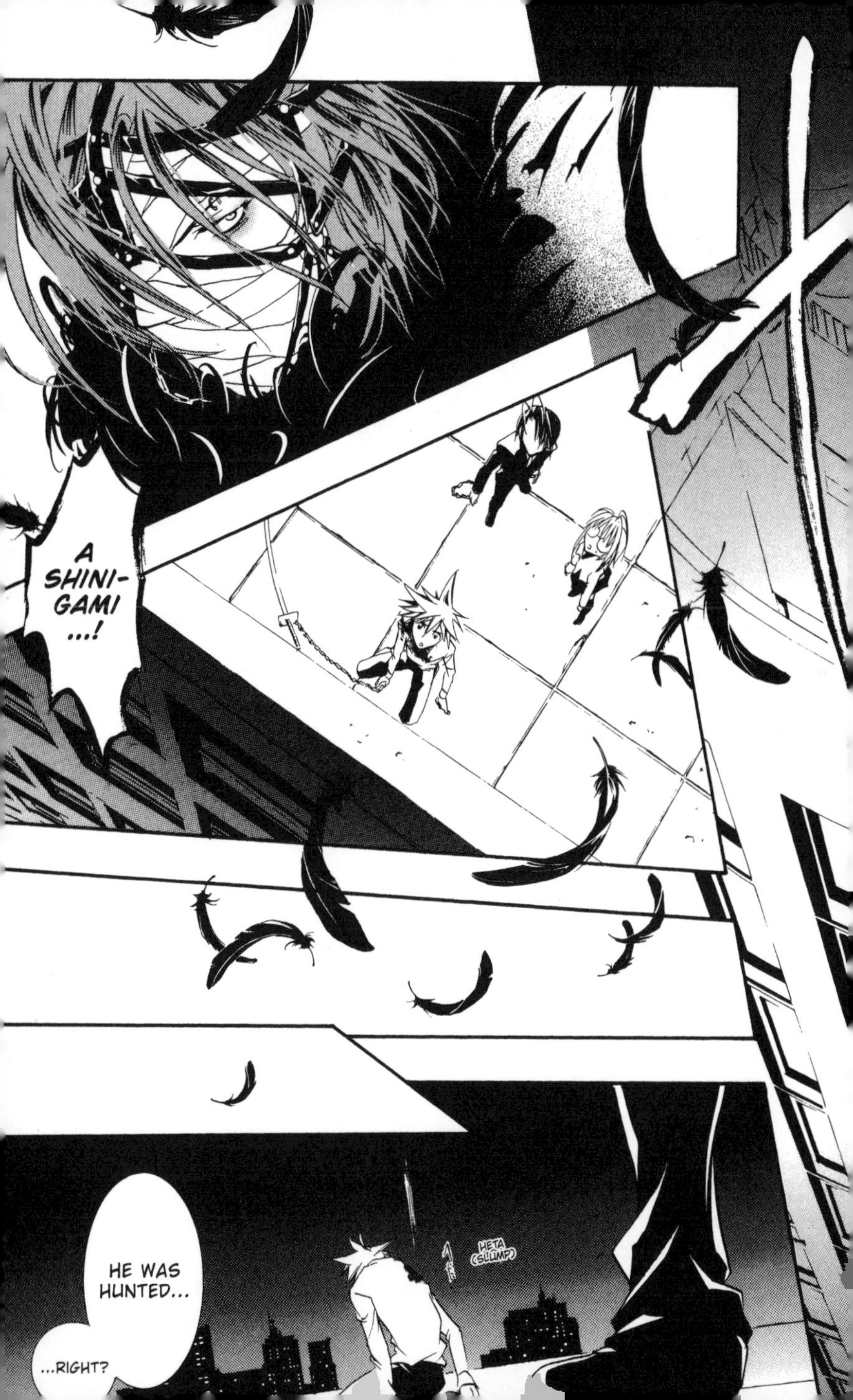
A SHINI-GAMI ...!
HETA (SLUMP)
HE WAS HUNTED...
...RIGHT?

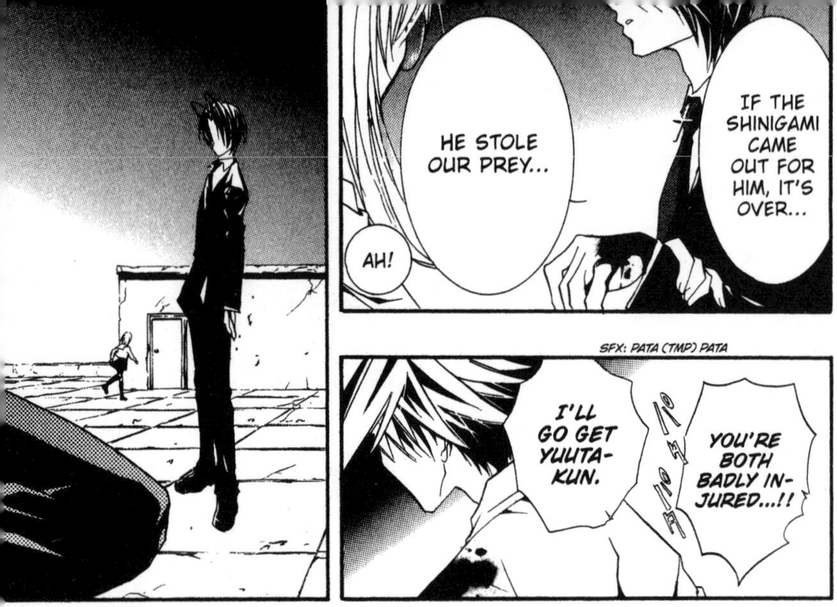
IF THE SHINIGAMI CAME OUT FOR HIM, IT'S OVER...
HE STOLE OUR PREY...
AH!
SFX: PATA (TMP) PATA
YOU'RE BOTH BADLY IN-JURED...!!
I'LL GO GET YUUTA-KUN.

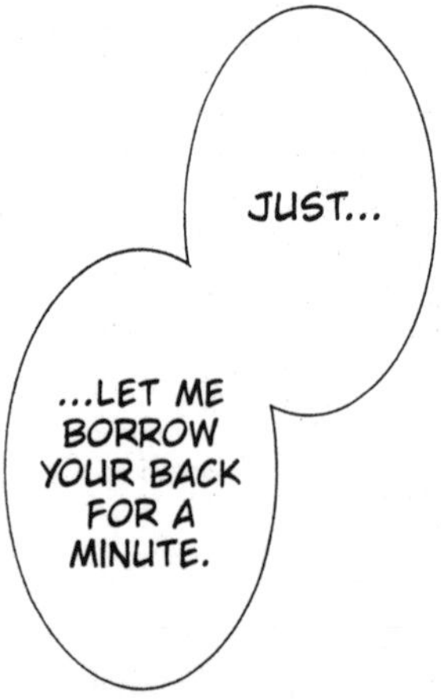
JUST...
...LET ME BORROW YOUR BACK FOR A MINUTE.

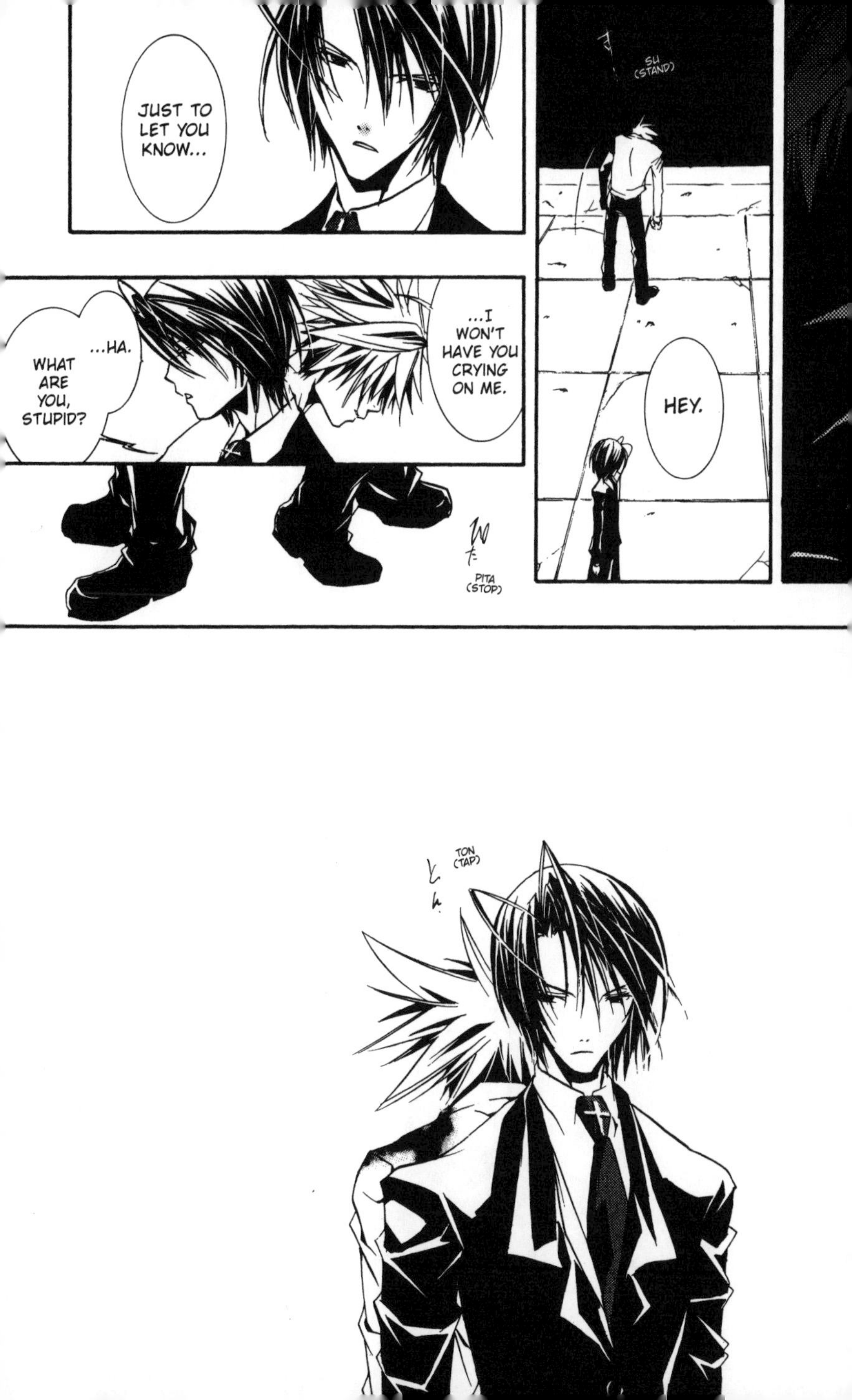
SU (STAND)
HEY.
JUST TO LET YOU KNOW...
...I WON'T HAVE YOU CRYING ON ME.
...HA.
WHAT ARE YOU, STUPID?
PITA (STOP)
TON (TAP)

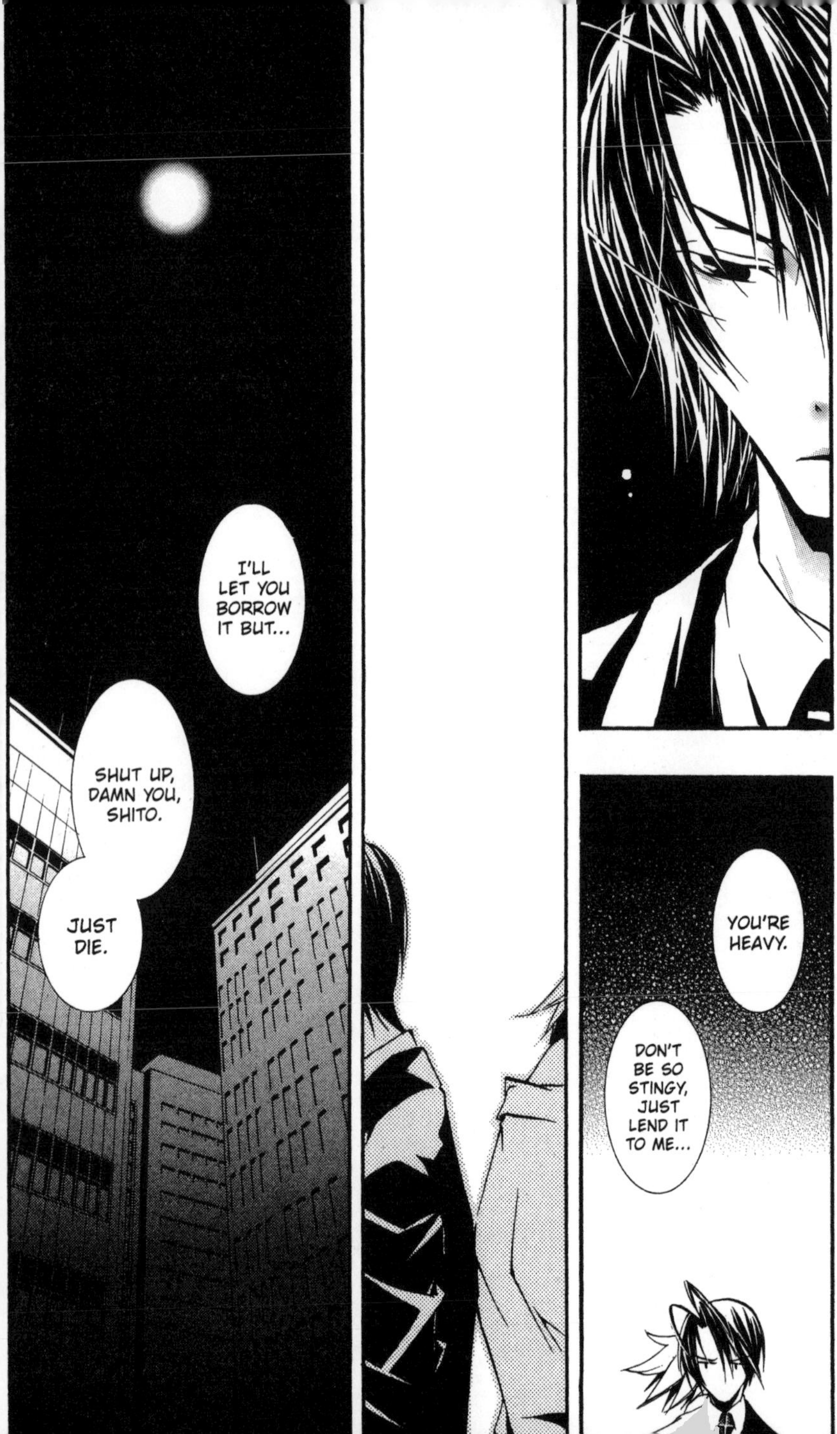
YOU'RE HEAVY.
DON'T BE SO STINGY, JUST LEND IT TO ME...
I'LL LET YOU BORROW IT BUT...
SHUT UP, DAMN YOU, SHITO.
JUST DIE.

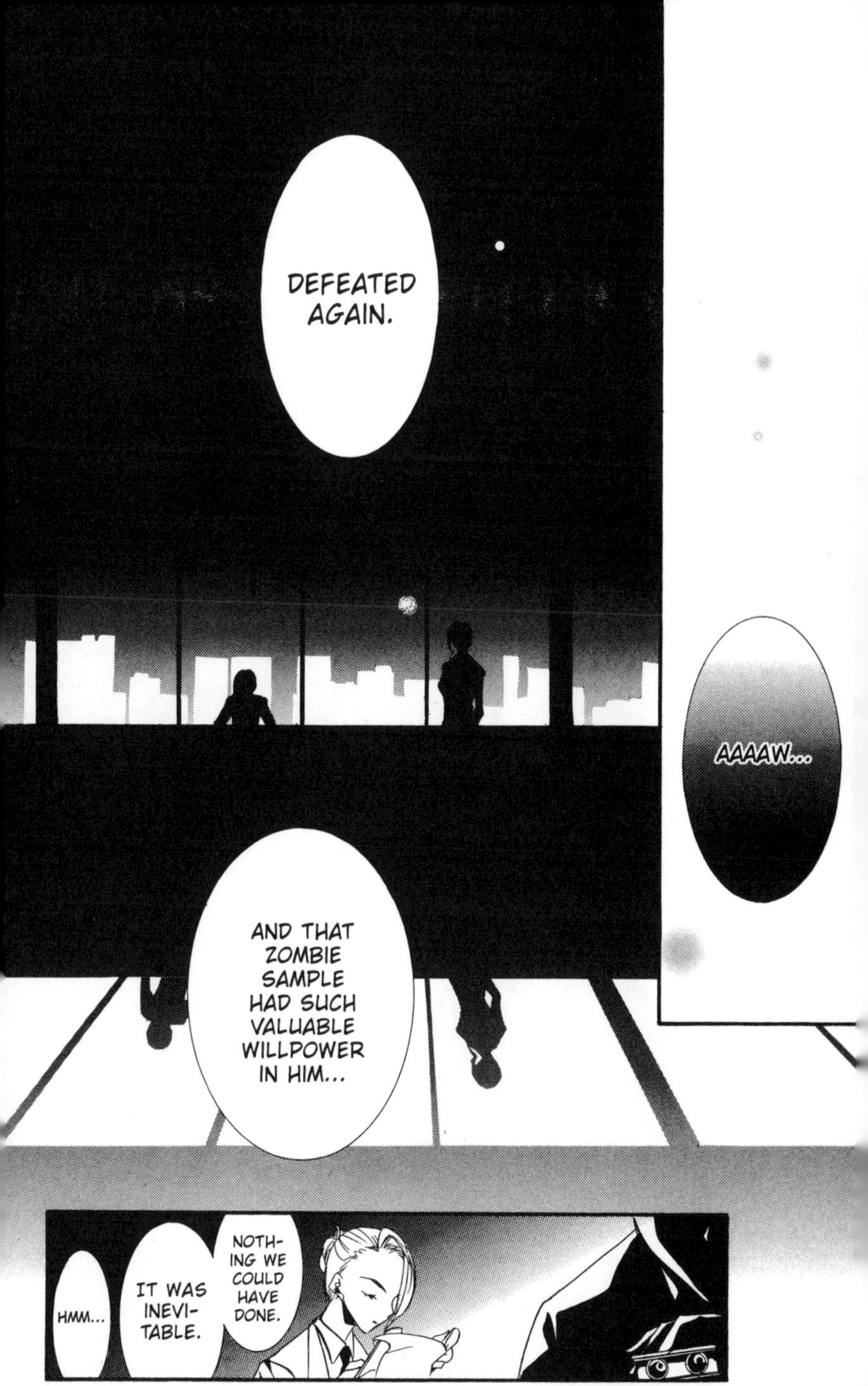
AAAAW...
DEFEATED AGAIN.
AND THAT ZOMBIE SAMPLE HAD SUCH VALUABLE WILLPOWER IN HIM...
NOTH-ING WE COULD HAVE DONE.
IT WAS INEVI-TABLE.
HMM...

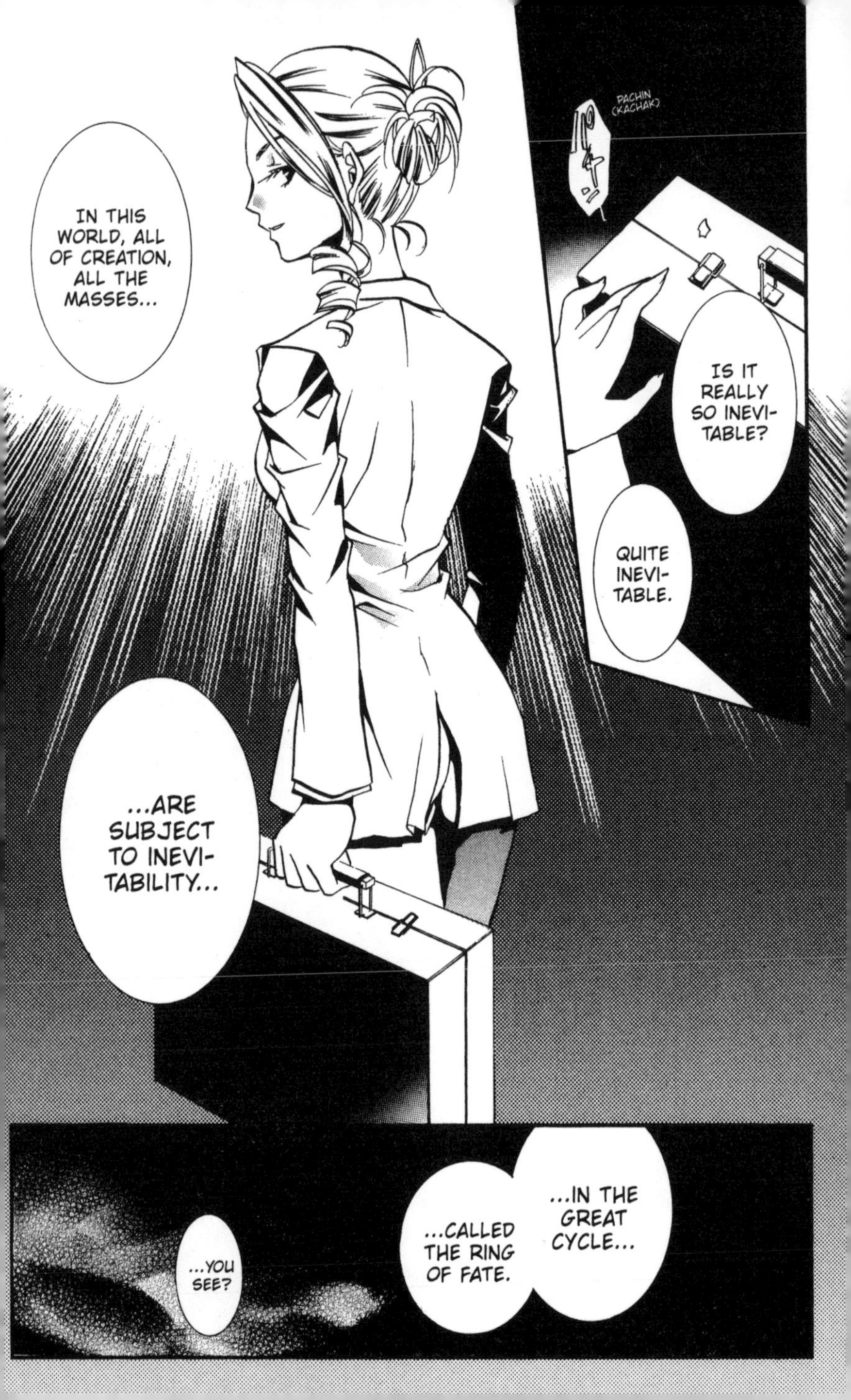
PACHIN (KACHAK)
IS IT REALLY SO INEVITABLE?
QUITE INEVITABLE.
IN THIS WORLD, ALL OF CREATION, ALL THE MASSES...
...ARE SUBJECT TO INEVITABILITY...
...IN THE GREAT CYCLE...
...CALLED THE RING OF FATE.
...YOU SEE?

PAYMENT:17

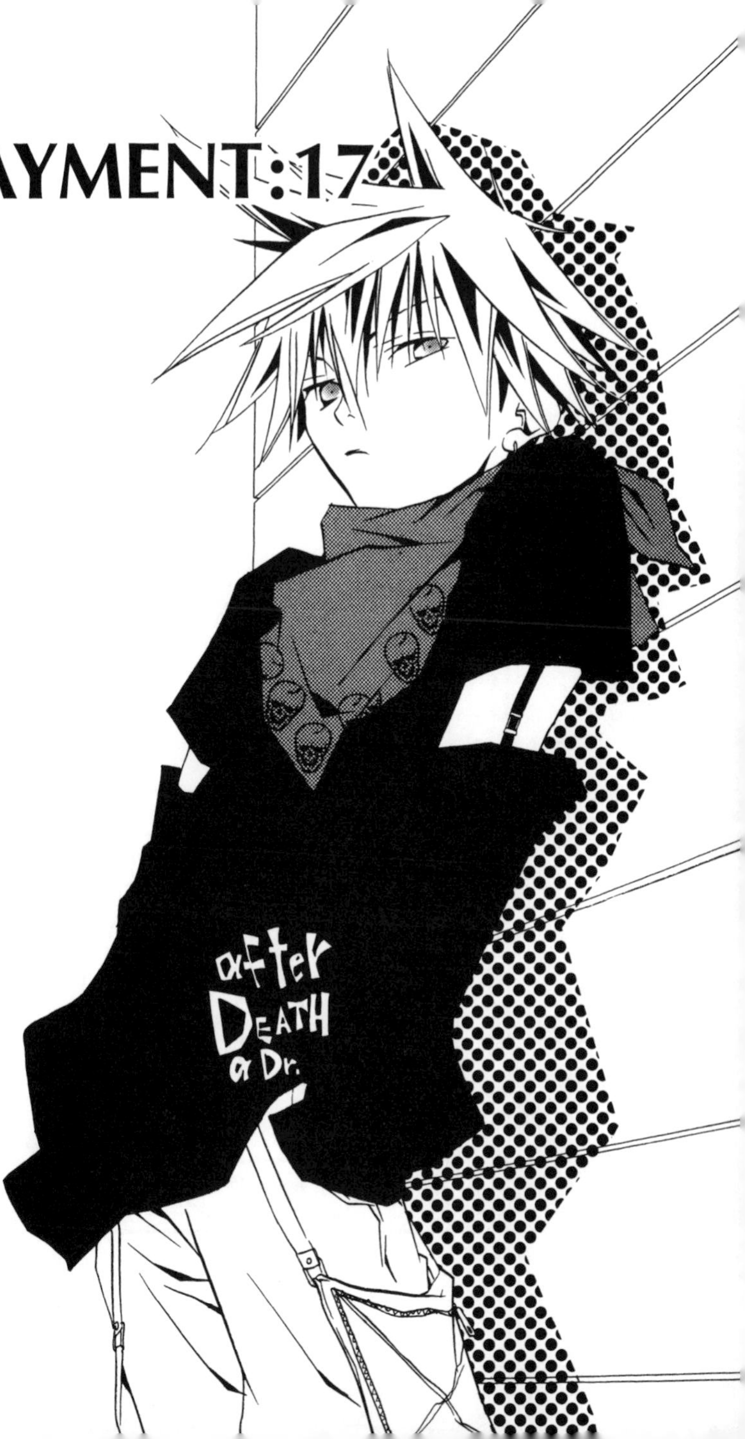
after
DEATH
a Dr.

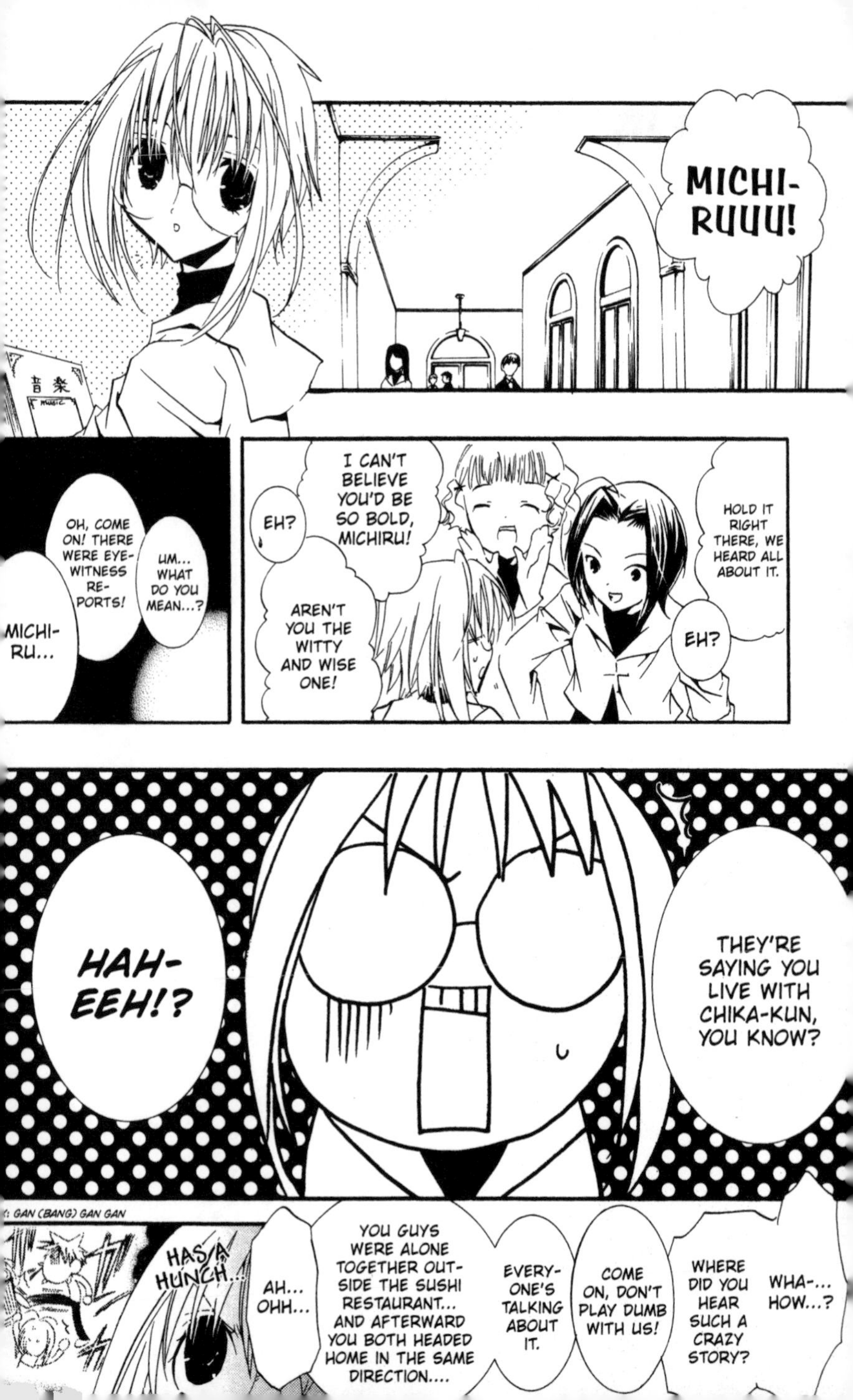
MICHI-RUUU!
音楽
music
HOLD IT RIGHT THERE, WE HEARD ALL ABOUT IT.
EH?
I CAN'T BELIEVE YOU'D BE SO BOLD, MICHIRU!
EH?
AREN'T YOU THE WITTY AND WISE ONE!
UM... WHAT DO YOU MEAN...?
OH, COME ON! THERE WERE EYE-WITNESS REPORTS!
MICHI-RU...
THEY'RE SAYING YOU LIVE WITH CHIKA-KUN, YOU KNOW?
HAH-EEH!?
WHA-... HOW...?
WHERE DID YOU HEAR SUCH A CRAZY STORY?
COME ON, DON'T PLAY DUMB WITH US!
EVERY-ONE'S TALKING ABOUT IT.
YOU GUYS WERE ALONE TOGETHER OUT-SIDE THE SUSHI RESTAURANT... AND AFTERWARD YOU BOTH HEADED HOME IN THE SAME DIRECTION....
AH... OHH...
HAS A HUNCH...
GAN (BANG) GAN GAN

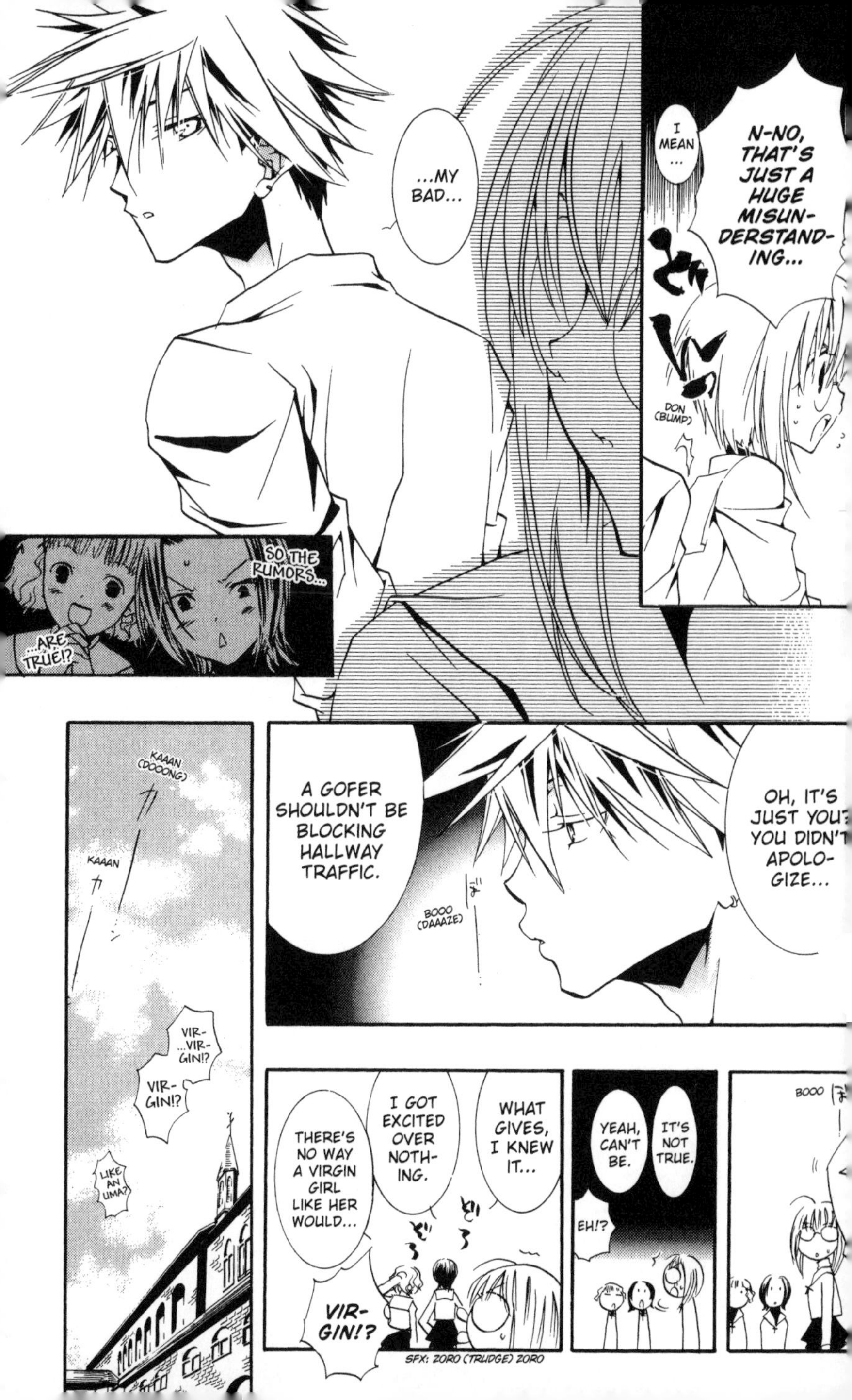
N-NO, THAT'S JUST A HUGE MISUN-DERSTAND-ING...
I MEAN...
DON (BUMP)
...MY BAD...
SO THE RUMORS...
...ARE TRUE!?
OH, IT'S JUST YOU? YOU DIDN'T APOLO-GIZE...
A GOFER SHOULDN'T BE BLOCKING HALLWAY TRAFFIC.
BOOO (DAAAZE)
BOOO
IT'S NOT TRUE.
YEAH, CAN'T BE.
EH!?
WHAT GIVES, I KNEW IT...
I GOT EXCITED OVER NOTH-ING.
THERE'S NO WAY A VIRGIN GIRL LIKE HER WOULD...
VIR-GIN!?
SFX: ZORO (TRUDGE) ZORO
KAAAN (DOOONG)
KAAAN
VIR- ...VIR-GIN!?
VIR-GIN!?
LIKE AN UMA?

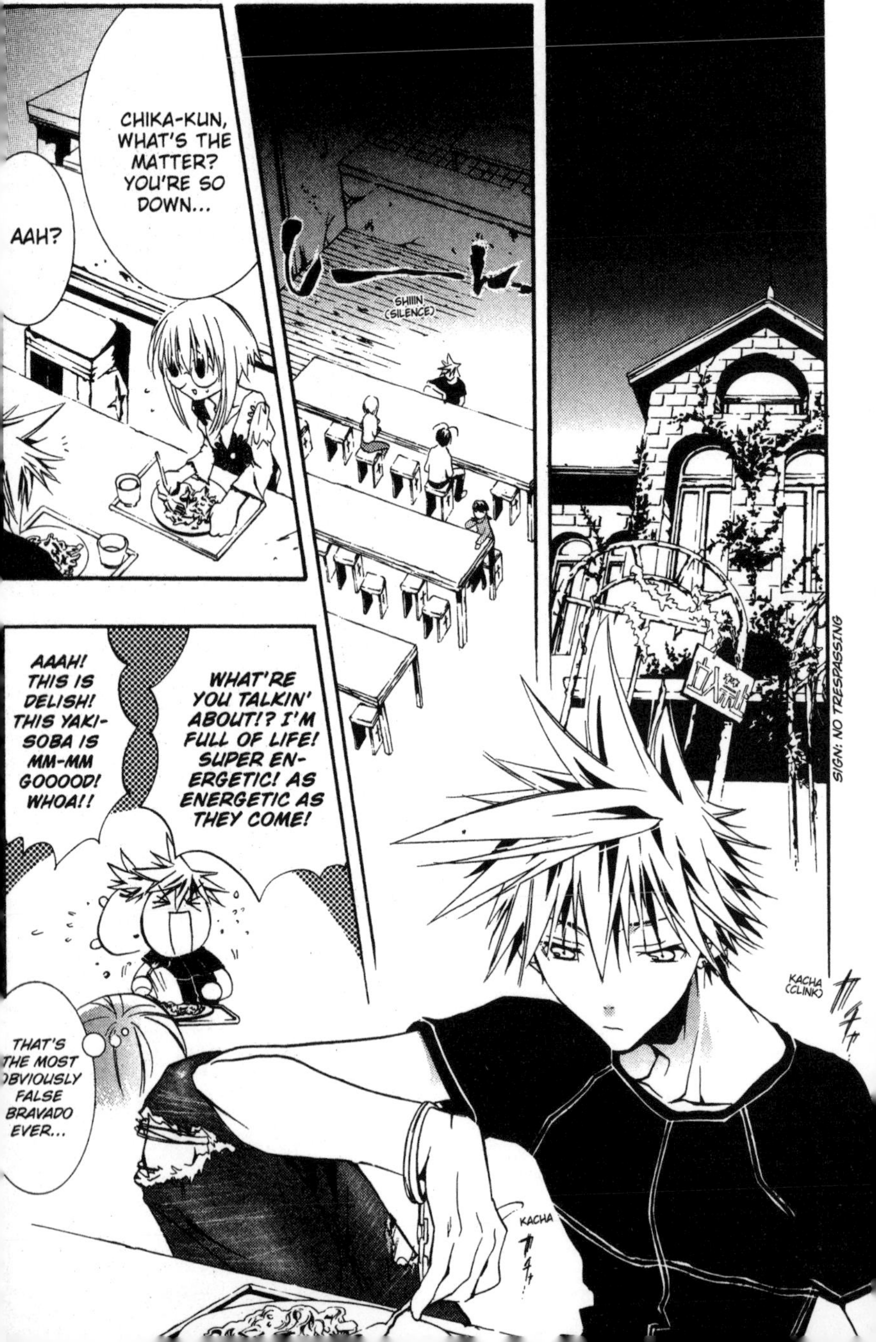
SIGN: NO TRESPASSING
KACHA (CLINK)
KACHA
SHIIIN (SILENCE)
CHIKA-KUN, WHAT'S THE MATTER? YOU'RE SO DOWN...
AAH?
WHAT'RE YOU TALKIN' ABOUT!? I'M FULL OF LIFE! SUPER EN-ERGETIC! AS ENERGETIC AS THEY COME!
AAAH! THIS IS DELISH! THIS YAKI-SOBA IS MM-MM GOOOOD! WHOA!!
THAT'S THE MOST OBVIOUSLY FALSE BRAVADO EVER...

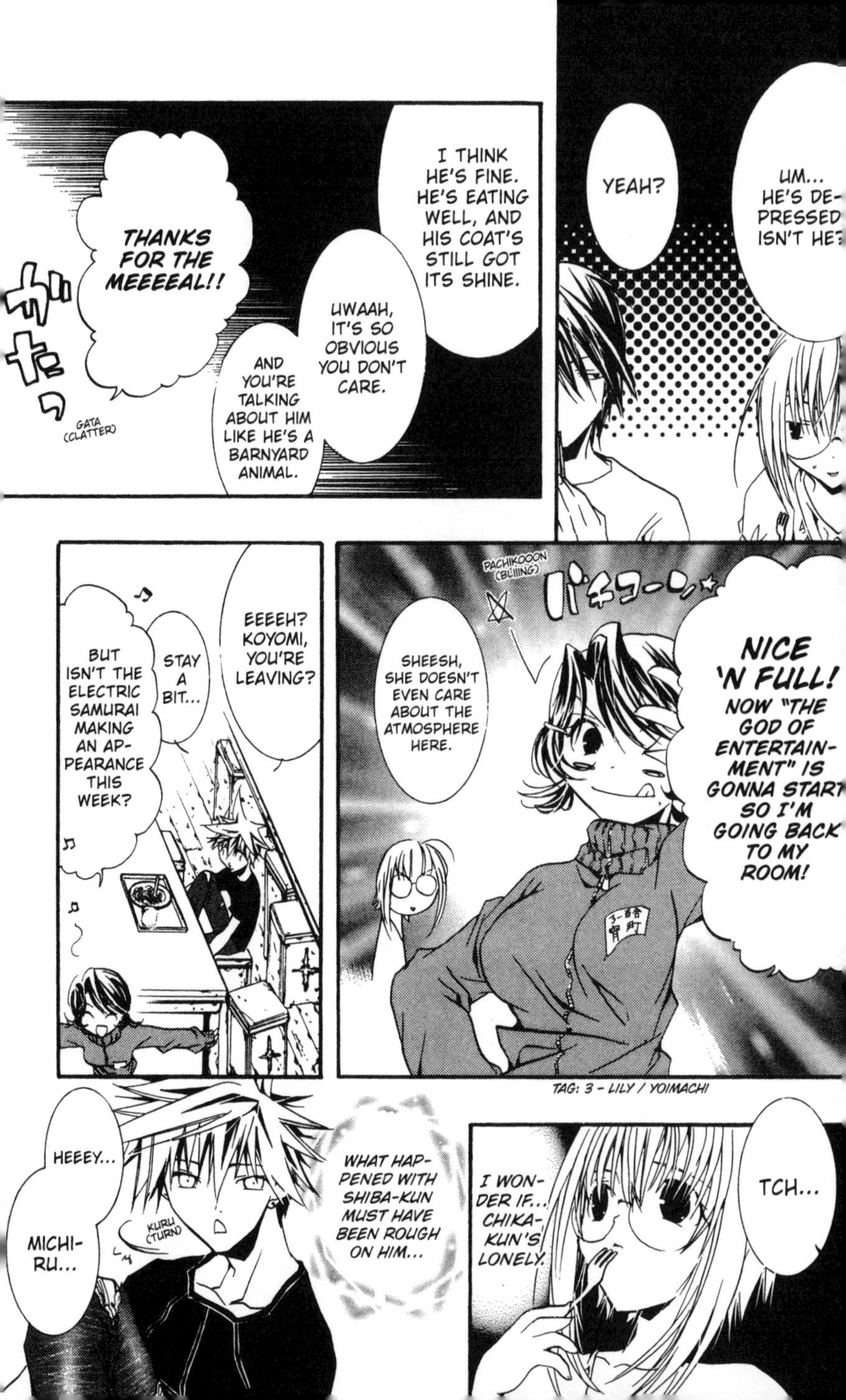
UM... HE'S DE-PRESSED ISN'T HE?
YEAH?
I THINK HE'S FINE. HE'S EATING WELL, AND HIS COAT'S STILL GOT ITS SHINE.
UWAAH, IT'S SO OBVIOUS YOU DON'T CARE.
AND YOU'RE TALKING ABOUT HIM LIKE HE'S A BARNYARD ANIMAL.
THANKS FOR THE MEEEEAL!!
GATA (CLATTER)
PACHIKOOON (BLIIING)
NICE 'N FULL! NOW "THE GOD OF ENTERTAIN-MENT" IS GONNA START SO I'M GOING BACK TO MY ROOM!
SHEESH, SHE DOESN'T EVEN CARE ABOUT THE ATMOSPHERE HERE.
EEEEH? KOYOMI, YOU'RE LEAVING?
STAY A BIT...
BUT ISN'T THE ELECTRIC SAMURAI MAKING AN AP-PEARANCE THIS WEEK?
TAG: 3 - LILY / YOIMACHI
TCH...
I WON-DER IF... CHIKA-KUN'S LONELY.
WHAT HAP-PENED WITH SHIBA-KUN MUST HAVE BEEN ROUGH ON HIM...
HEEEY...
MICHI-RU...
KURU (TURN)

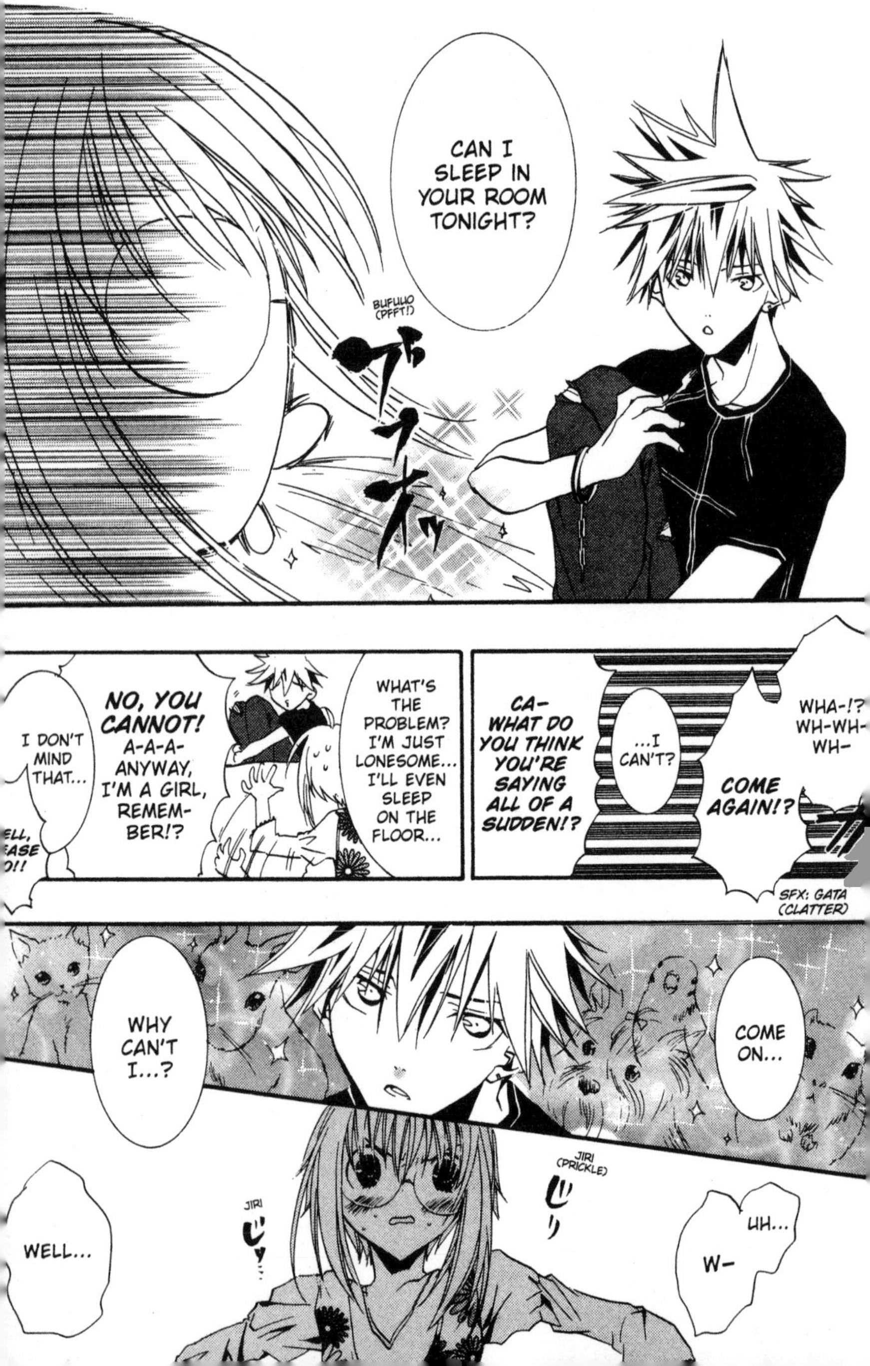
CAN I SLEEP IN YOUR ROOM TONIGHT?
BUFUHO (PFFT!)
WHA-!? WH-WH-WH-
COME AGAIN!?
SFX: GATA (CLATTER)
...I CAN'T?
CA- WHAT DO YOU THINK YOU'RE SAYING ALL OF A SUDDEN!?
WHAT'S THE PROBLEM? I'M JUST LONESOME... I'LL EVEN SLEEP ON THE FLOOR...
NO, YOU CANNOT! A-A-A-ANYWAY, I'M A GIRL, REMEMBER!?
I DON'T MIND THAT...
COME ON...
WHY CAN'T I...?
UH... W-
JIRI (PRICKLE)
JIRI
WELL...

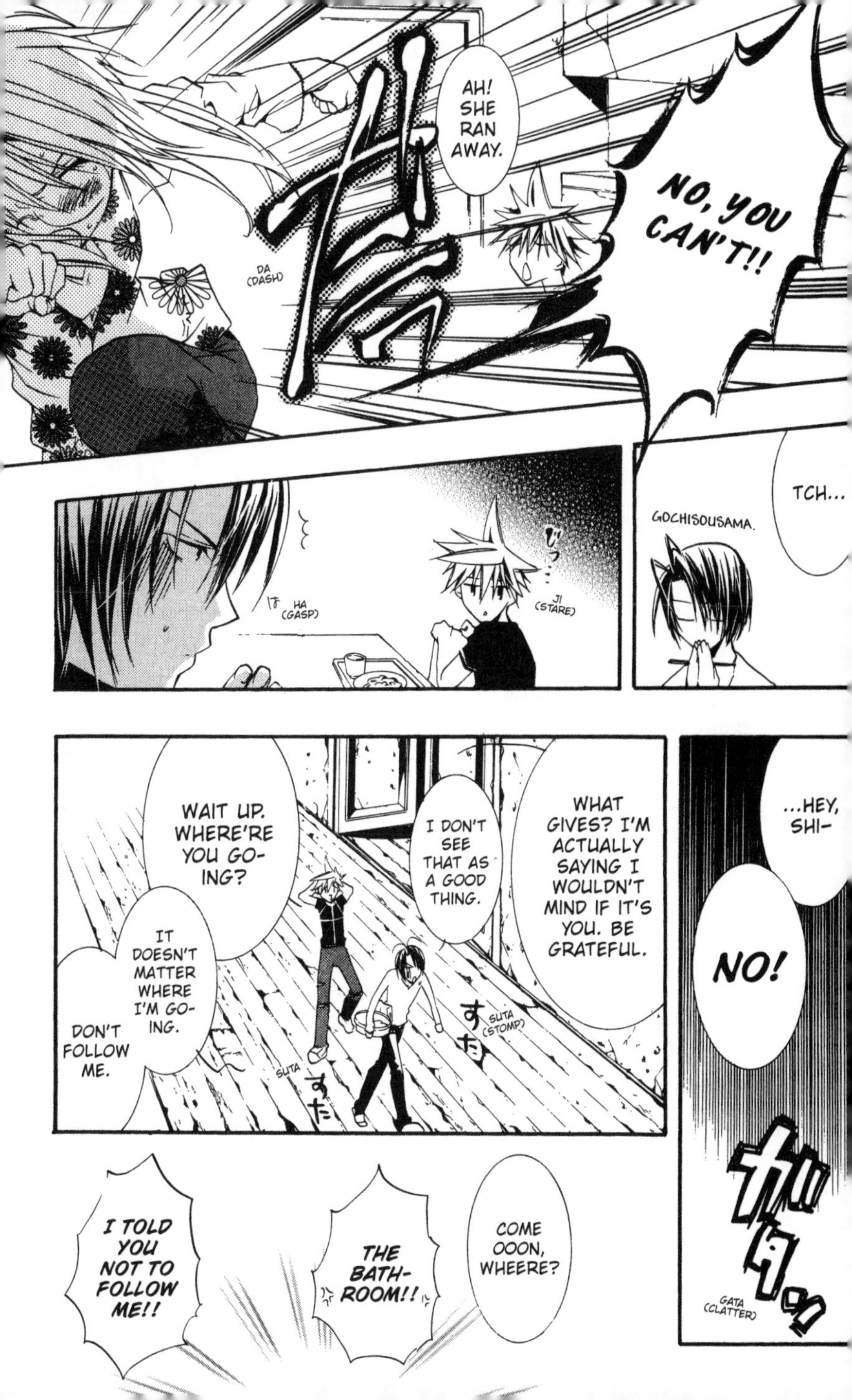
NO, YOU CAN'T!!
AH! SHE RAN AWAY.
DA (DASH)
TCH...
GOCHISOUSAMA.
JI (STARE)
HA (GASP)
...HEY, SHI-
NO!
GATA (CLATTER)
WHAT GIVES? I'M ACTUALLY SAYING I WOULDN'T MIND IF IT'S YOU. BE GRATEFUL.
I DON'T SEE THAT AS A GOOD THING.
WAIT UP. WHERE'RE YOU GO-ING?
SUTA (STOMP)
IT DOESN'T MATTER WHERE I'M GO-ING.
DON'T FOLLOW ME.
SUTA
COME OOON, WHEERE?
THE BATH-ROOM!!
I TOLD YOU NOT TO FOLLOW ME!!

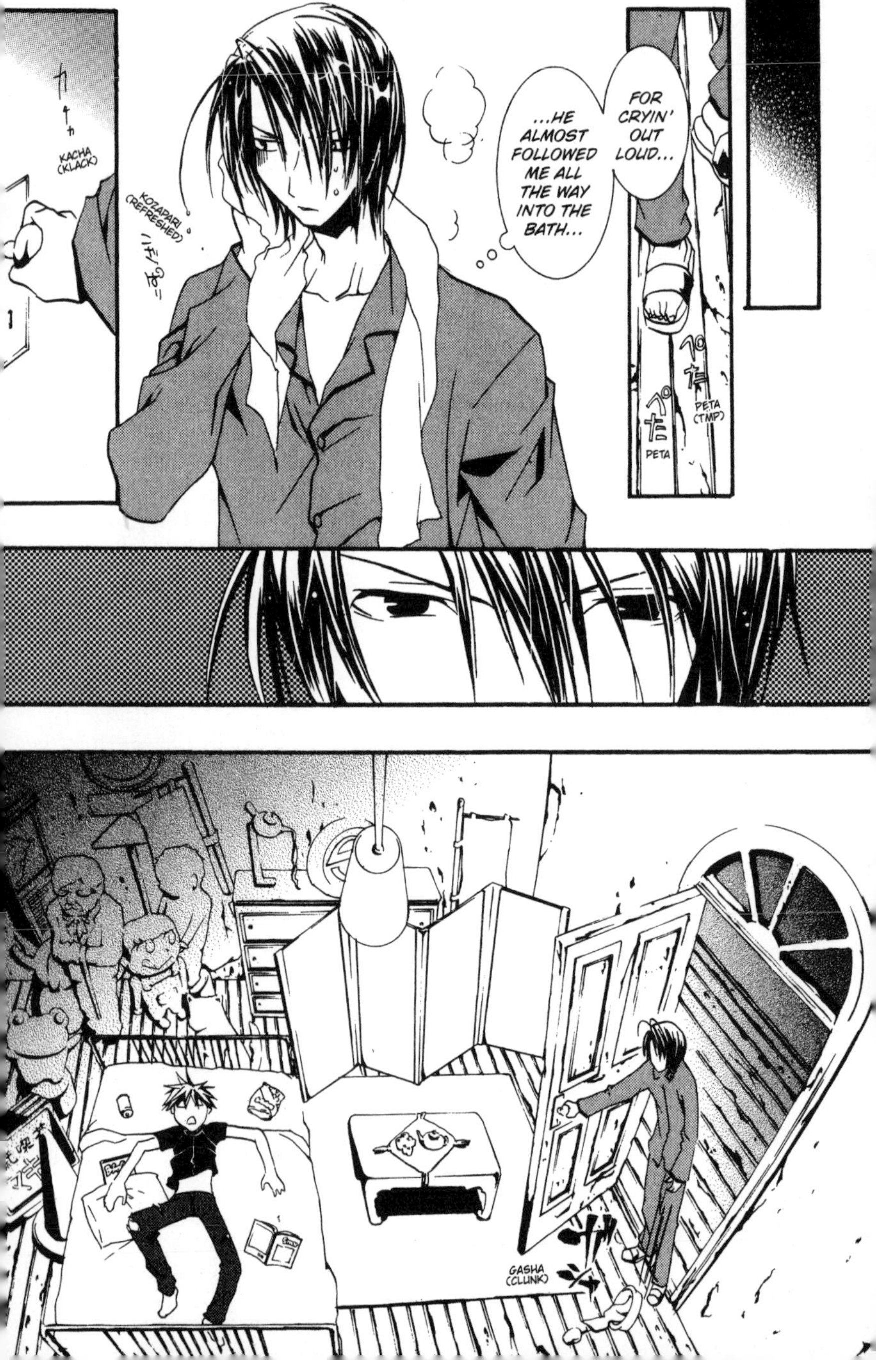
PETA (TMP)
PETA
FOR CRYIN' OUT LOUD...
...HE ALMOST FOLLOWED ME ALL THE WAY INTO THE BATH...
KOZAPARI (REFRESHED)
KACHA (KLACK)
GASHA (CLUNK)

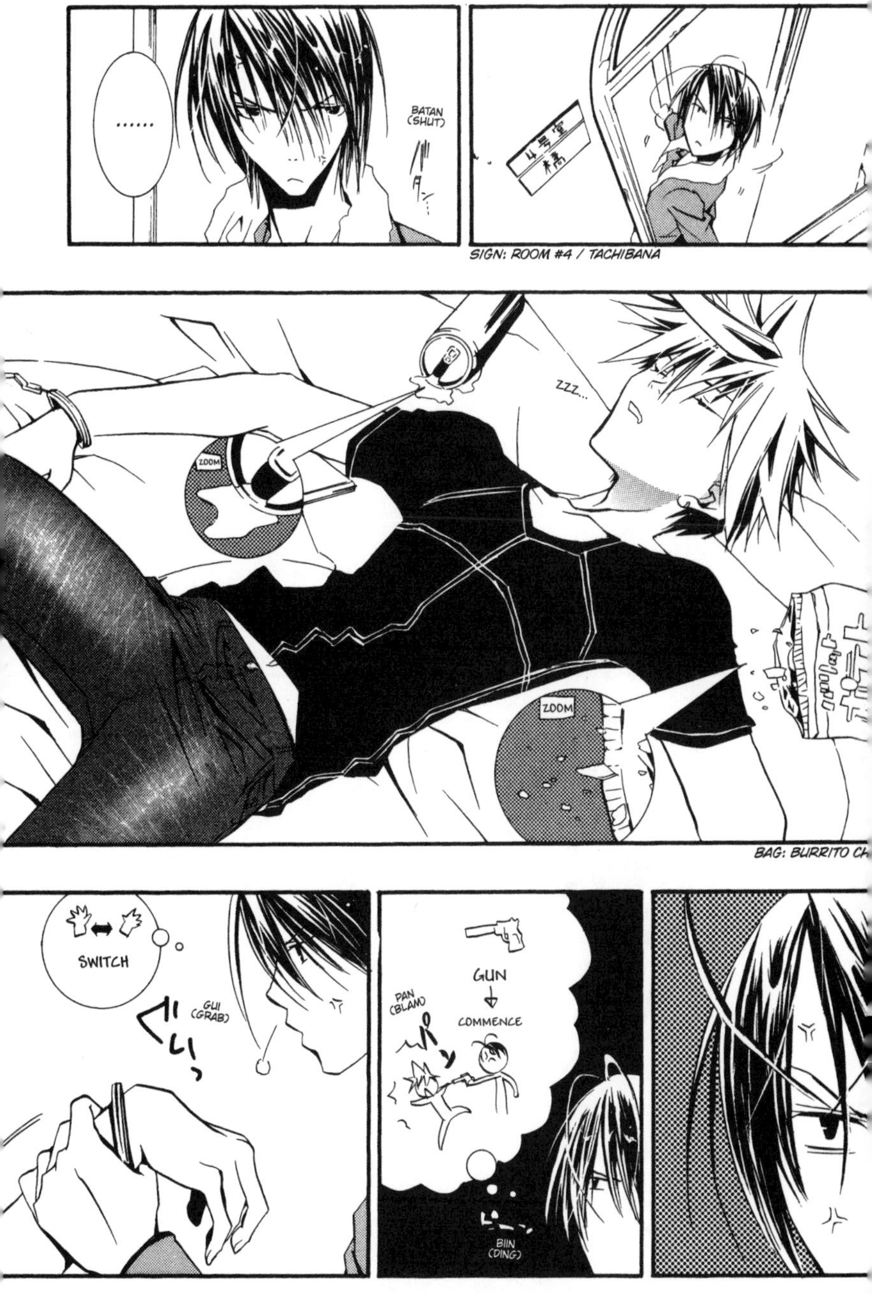
4号室
SIGN: ROOM #4 / TACHIBANA
......
BATAN (SHUT)
ZZZ...
ZOOM
ZOOM
BAG: BURRITO CH
GUN
COMMENCE
PAN (BLAM)
BIIN (DING)
SWITCH
GUI (GRAB)

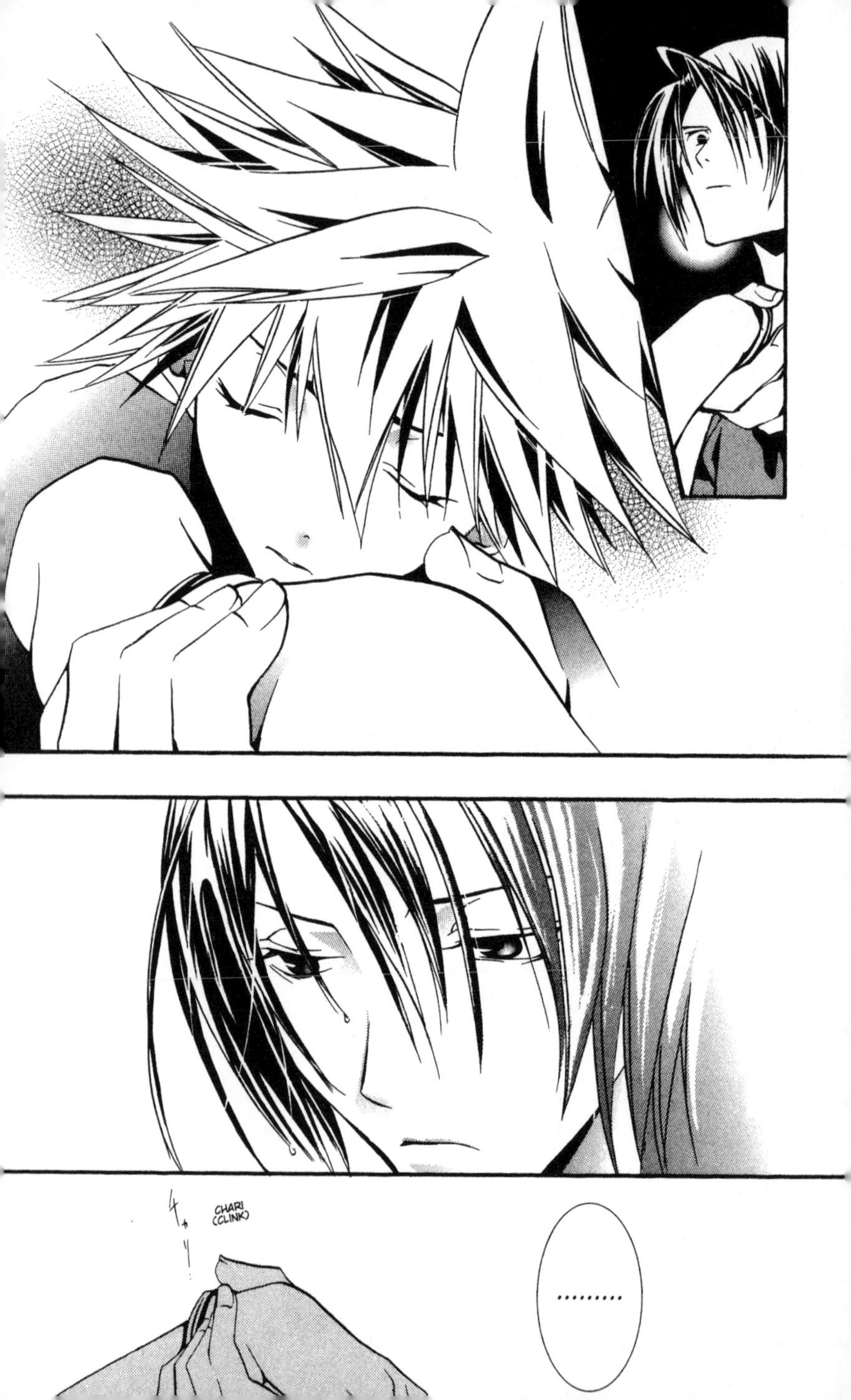
CHARI (CLINK)
....

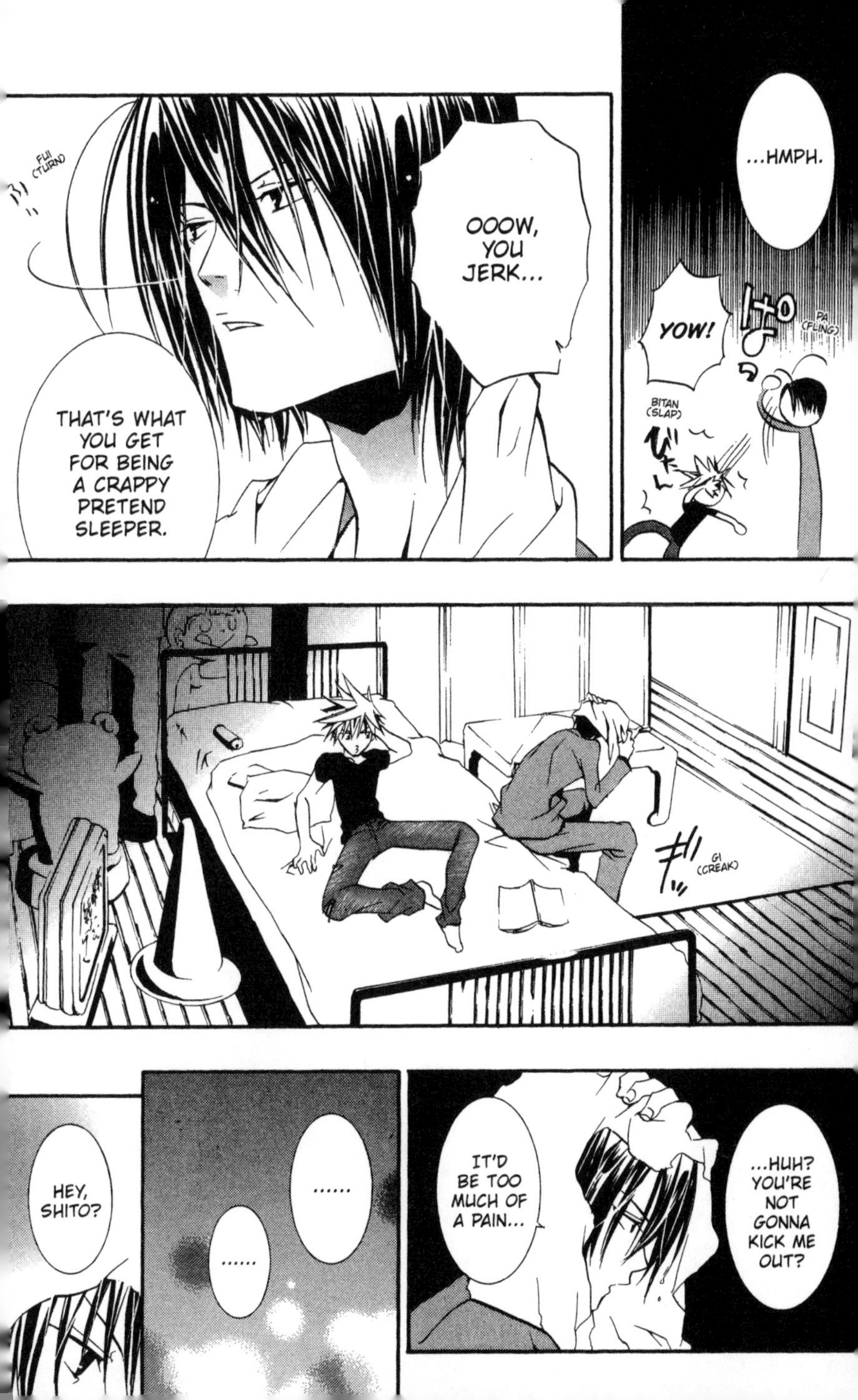
...HMPH.
YOW!
PA (FLING)
BITAN (SLAP)
FUI (TURN)
OOOW, YOU JERK...
THAT'S WHAT YOU GET FOR BEING A CRAPPY PRETEND SLEEPER.
GI (CREAK)
...HUH? YOU'RE NOT GONNA KICK ME OUT?
IT'D BE TOO MUCH OF A PAIN...
......
......
HEY, SHITO?

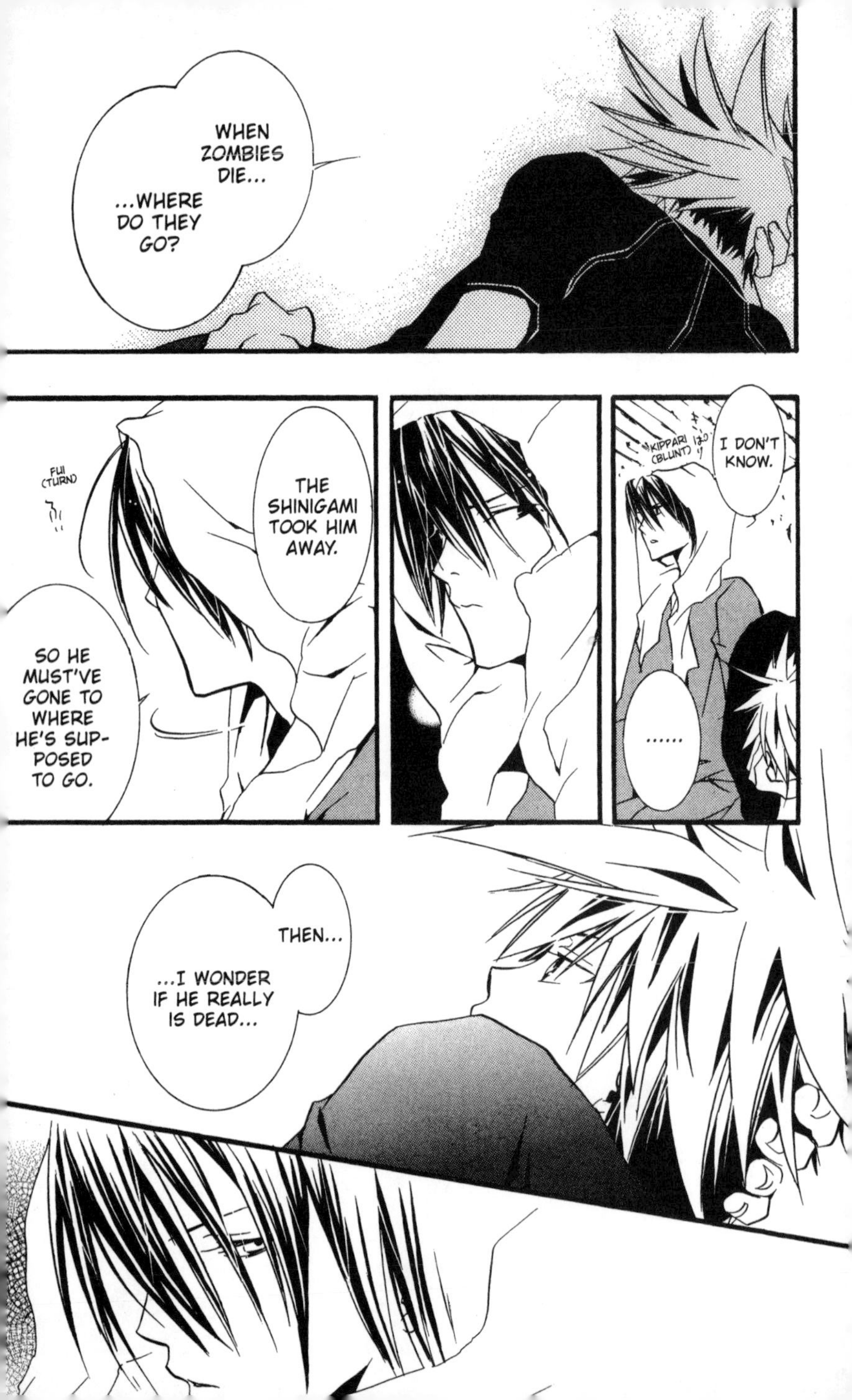
WHEN ZOMBIES DIE...
...WHERE DO THEY GO?
KIPPARI (BLUNT)
I DON'T KNOW.
......
THE SHINIGAMI TOOK HIM AWAY.
FUI (TURN)
SO HE MUST'VE GONE TO WHERE HE'S SUP-POSED TO GO.
THEN...
...I WONDER IF HE REALLY IS DEAD...

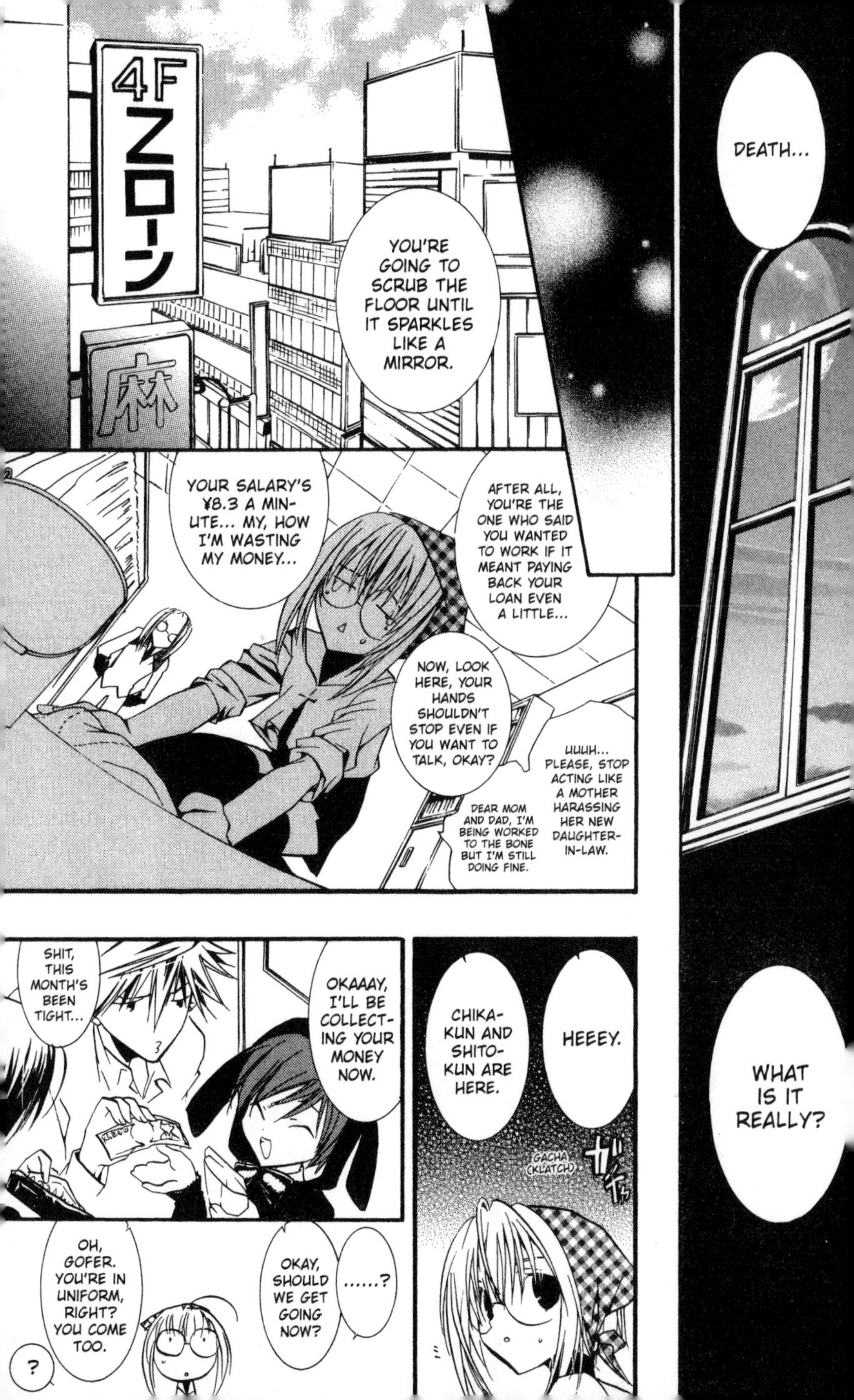
DEATH...
WHAT IS IT REALLY?
4F
Zローン
麻
YOU'RE GOING TO SCRUB THE FLOOR UNTIL IT SPARKLES LIKE A MIRROR.
AFTER ALL, YOU'RE THE ONE WHO SAID YOU WANTED TO WORK IF IT MEANT PAYING BACK YOUR LOAN EVEN A LITTLE...
YOUR SALARY'S ¥8.3 A MIN-UTE... MY, HOW I'M WASTING MY MONEY...
NOW, LOOK HERE, YOUR HANDS SHOULDN'T STOP EVEN IF YOU WANT TO TALK, OKAY?
UUUH... PLEASE, STOP ACTING LIKE A MOTHER HARASSING HER NEW DAUGHTER-IN-LAW.
DEAR MOM AND DAD, I'M BEING WORKED TO THE BONE BUT I'M STILL DOING FINE.
HEEEY.
CHIKA-KUN AND SHITO-KUN ARE HERE.
GACHA (KLATCH)
......?
OKAY, SHOULD WE GET GOING NOW?
OKAAAY, I'LL BE COLLECT-ING YOUR MONEY NOW.
SHIT, THIS MONTH'S BEEN TIGHT...
OH, GOFER. YOU'RE IN UNIFORM, RIGHT? YOU COME TOO.
?

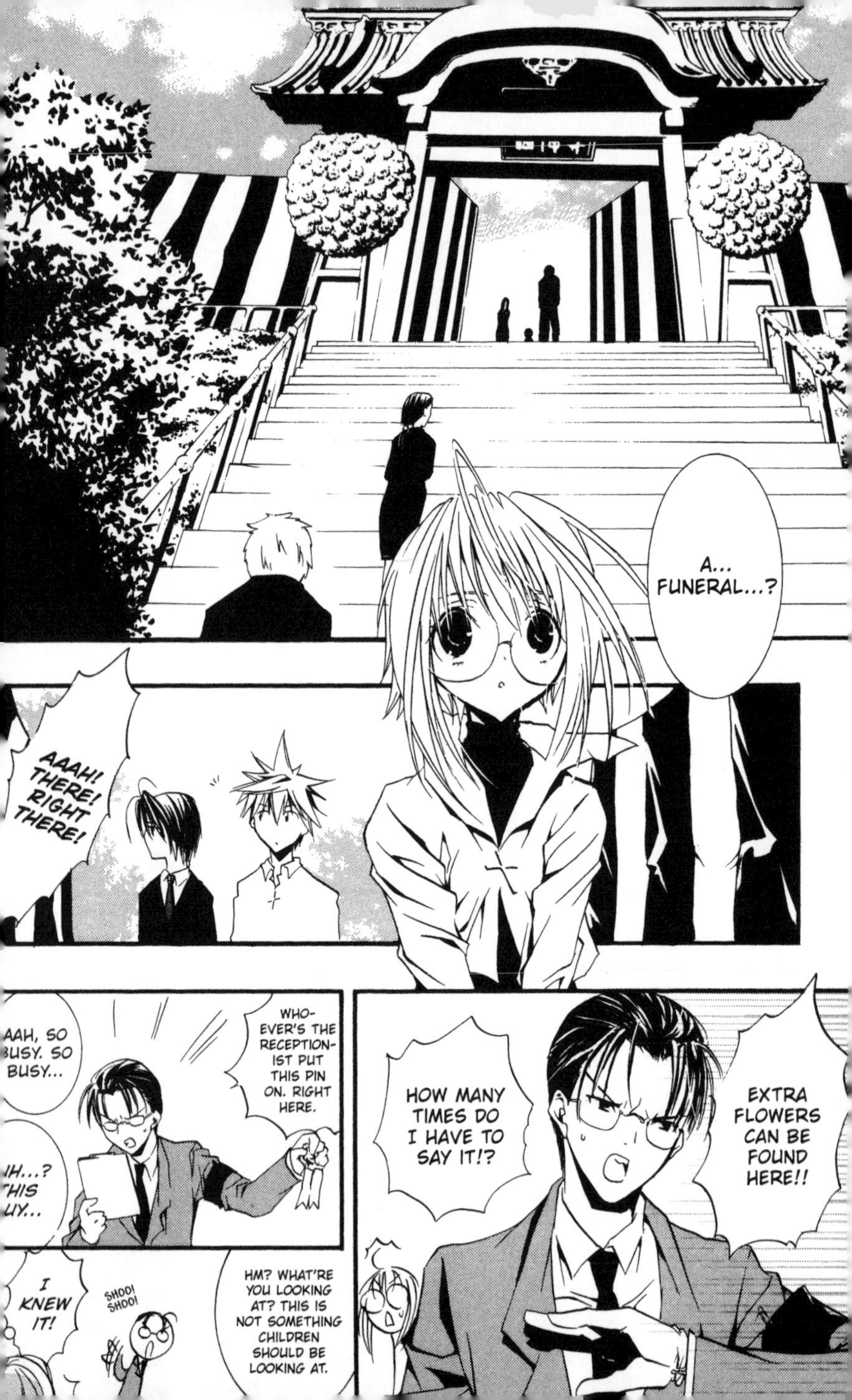
A... FUNERAL...?
AAAH! THERE! RIGHT THERE!
EXTRA FLOWERS CAN BE FOUND HERE!!
HOW MANY TIMES DO I HAVE TO SAY IT!?
WHO-EVER'S THE RECEPTION-IST PUT THIS PIN ON. RIGHT HERE.
AAH, SO BUSY. SO BUSY...
THIS
HM? WHAT'RE YOU LOOKING AT? THIS IS NOT SOMETHING CHILDREN SHOULD BE LOOKING AT.
SHOO! SHOO!
I KNEW IT!

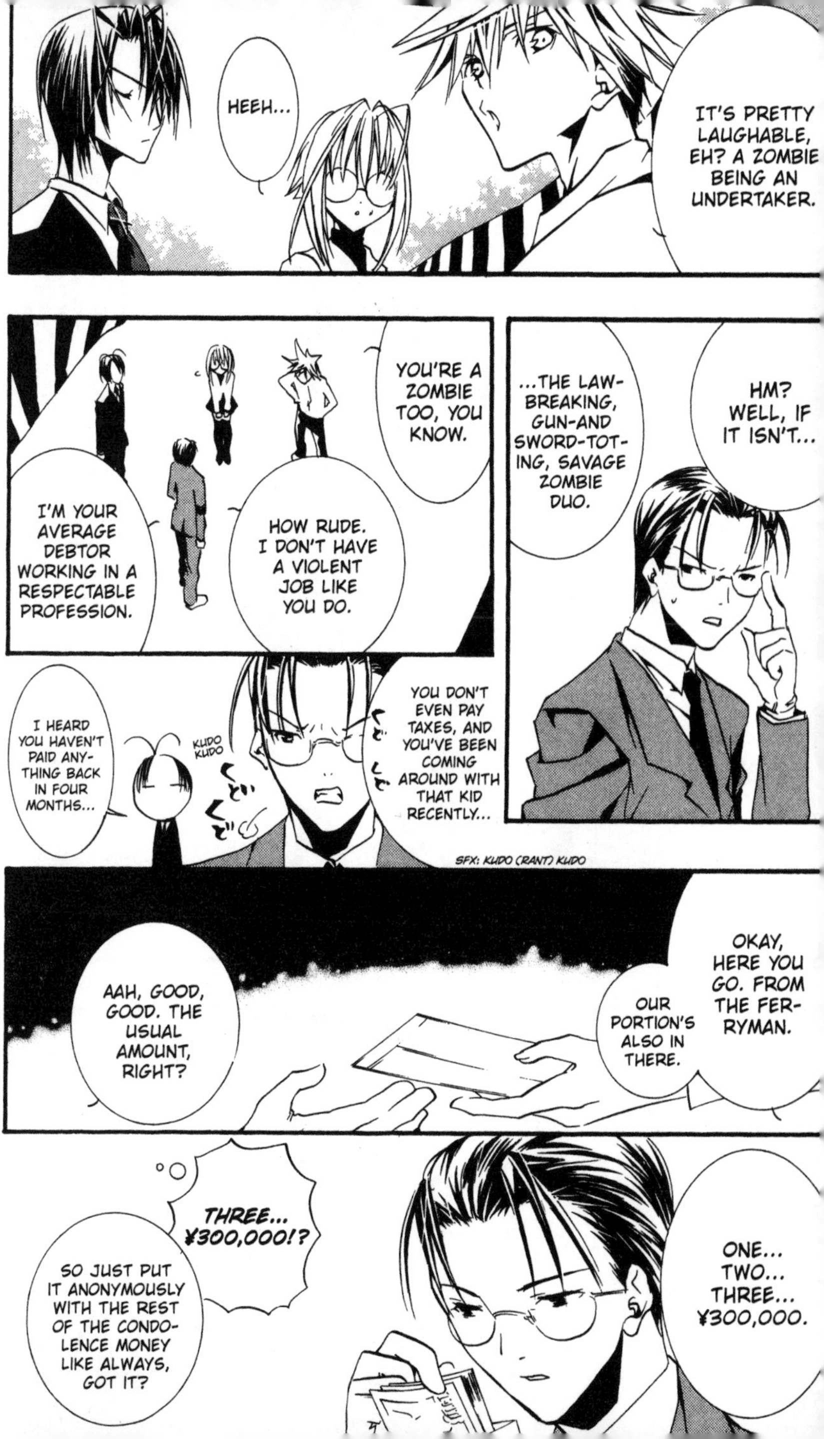
IT'S PRETTY LAUGHABLE, EH? A ZOMBIE BEING AN UNDERTAKER.
HEEH...
HM? WELL, IF IT ISN'T...
...THE LAW-BREAKING, GUN-AND SWORD-TOTING, SAVAGE ZOMBIE DUO.
YOU'RE A ZOMBIE TOO, YOU KNOW.
HOW RUDE. I DON'T HAVE A VIOLENT JOB LIKE YOU DO.
I'M YOUR AVERAGE DEBTOR WORKING IN A RESPECTABLE PROFESSION.
YOU DON'T EVEN PAY TAXES, AND YOU'VE BEEN COMING AROUND WITH THAT KID RECENTLY...
KUDO KUDO
I HEARD YOU HAVEN'T PAID ANYTHING BACK IN FOUR MONTHS...
SFX: KUDO (RANT) KUDO
OKAY, HERE YOU GO. FROM THE FERRYMAN.
OUR PORTION'S ALSO IN THERE.
AAH, GOOD, GOOD. THE USUAL AMOUNT, RIGHT?
ONE... TWO... THREE... ¥300,000.
THREE... ¥300,000!?
SO JUST PUT IT ANONYMOUSLY WITH THE REST OF THE CONDOLENCE MONEY LIKE ALWAYS, GOT IT?

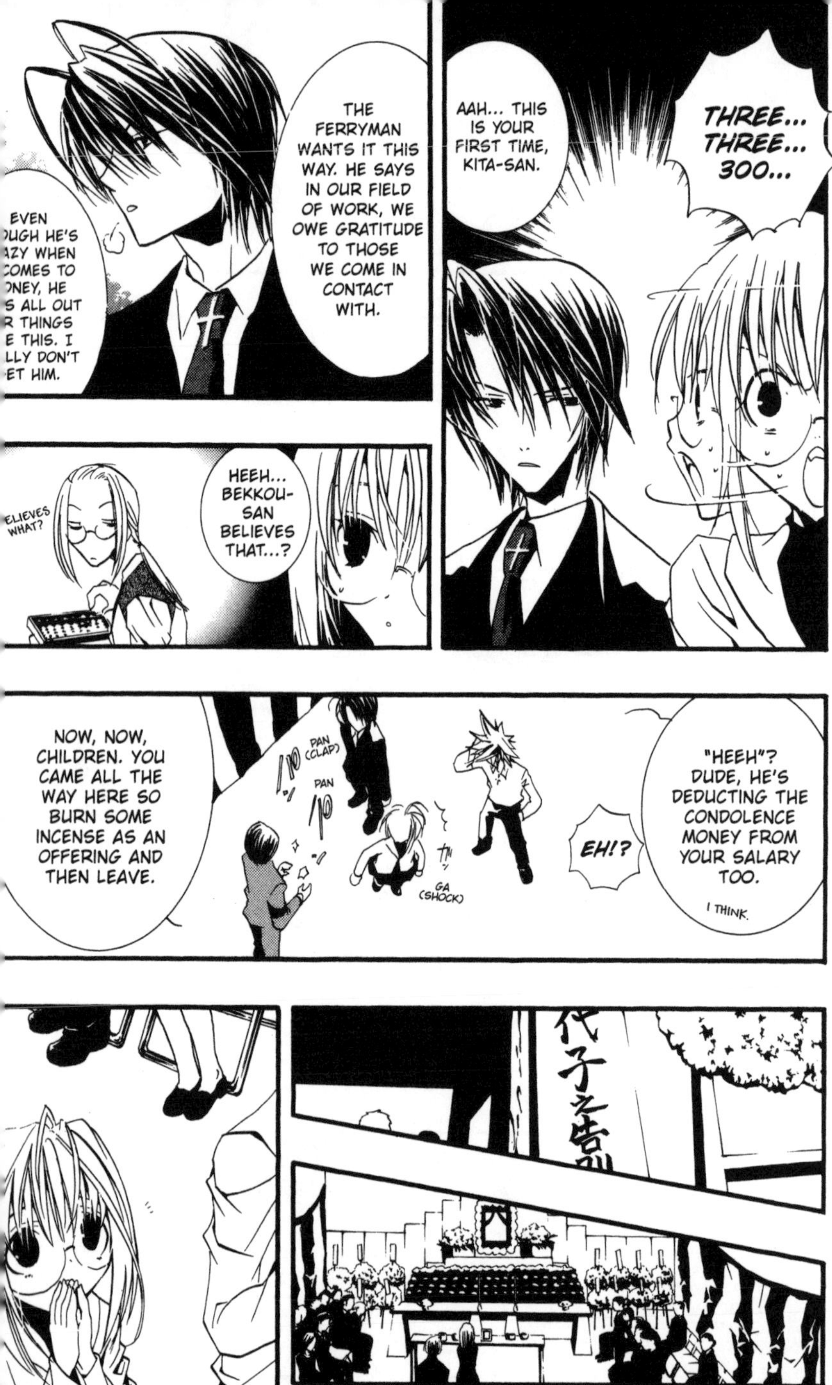
THREE... THREE... 300...
AAH... THIS IS YOUR FIRST TIME, KITA-SAN.
THE FERRYMAN WANTS IT THIS WAY. HE SAYS IN OUR FIELD OF WORK, WE OWE GRATITUDE TO THOSE WE COME IN CONTACT WITH.
EVEN UGH HE'S AZY WHEN COMES TO ONEY, HE S ALL OUT R THINGS E THIS. I LLY DON'T ET HIM.
HEEH... BEKKOU-SAN BELIEVES THAT...?
ELIEVES WHAT?
"HEEH"? DUDE, HE'S DEDUCTING THE CONDOLENCE MONEY FROM YOUR SALARY TOO.
I THINK.
EH!?
GA (SHOCK)
PAN (CLAP)
PAN
NOW, NOW, CHILDREN. YOU CAME ALL THE WAY HERE SO BURN SOME INCENSE AS AN OFFERING AND THEN LEAVE.
代子之告

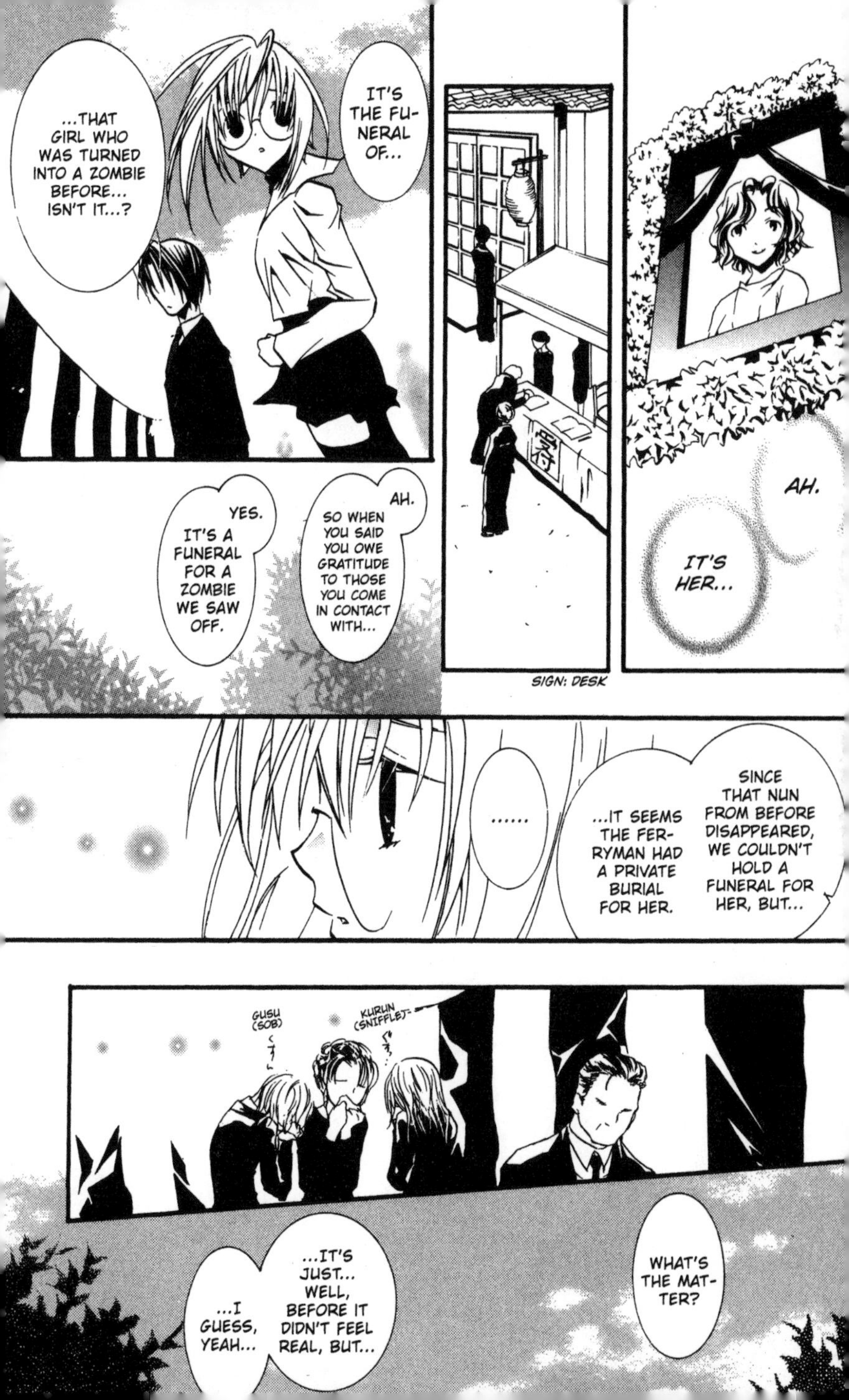
AH.
IT'S HER...
SIGN: DESK
IT'S THE FUNERAL OF...
...THAT GIRL WHO WAS TURNED INTO A ZOMBIE BEFORE... ISN'T IT...?
AH.
SO WHEN YOU SAID YOU OWE GRATITUDE TO THOSE YOU COME IN CONTACT WITH...
YES.
IT'S A FUNERAL FOR A ZOMBIE WE SAW OFF.
SINCE THAT NUN FROM BEFORE DISAPPEARED, WE COULDN'T HOLD A FUNERAL FOR HER, BUT...
...IT SEEMS THE FERRYMAN HAD A PRIVATE BURIAL FOR HER.
......
KURUN (SNIFFLE)
GUSU (SOB)
WHAT'S THE MATTER?
...IT'S JUST... WELL, BEFORE IT DIDN'T FEEL REAL, BUT...
...I GUESS, YEAH...

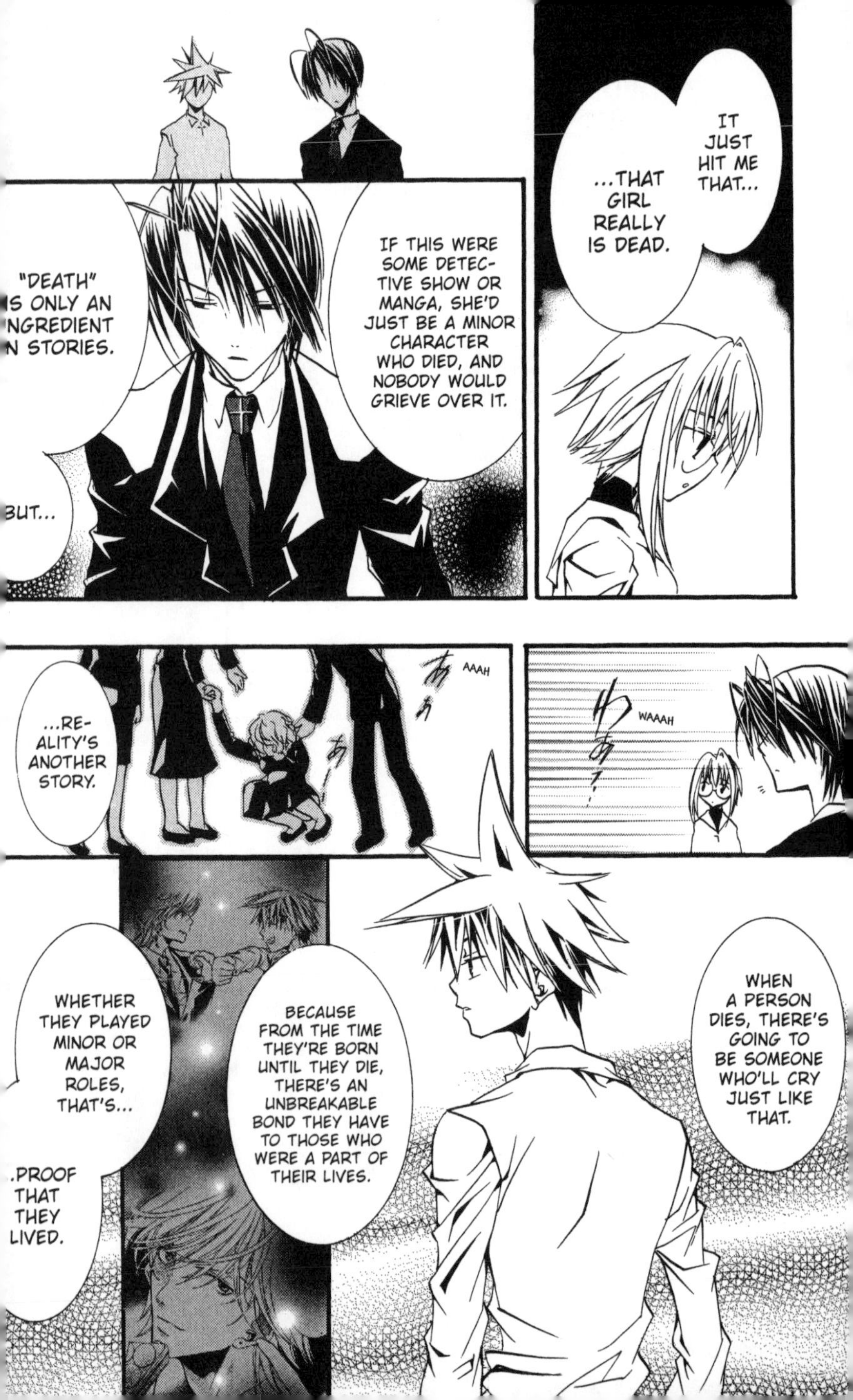
IT JUST HIT ME THAT...
...THAT GIRL REALLY IS DEAD.
IF THIS WERE SOME DETECTIVE SHOW OR MANGA, SHE'D JUST BE A MINOR CHARACTER WHO DIED, AND NOBODY WOULD GRIEVE OVER IT.
"DEATH" IS ONLY AN NGREDIENT N STORIES.
BUT...
WAAAH
AAAH
...REALITY'S ANOTHER STORY.
WHEN A PERSON DIES, THERE'S GOING TO BE SOMEONE WHO'LL CRY JUST LIKE THAT.
BECAUSE FROM THE TIME THEY'RE BORN UNTIL THEY DIE, THERE'S AN UNBREAKABLE BOND THEY HAVE TO THOSE WHO WERE A PART OF THEIR LIVES.
WHETHER THEY PLAYED MINOR OR MAJOR ROLES, THAT'S...
.PROOF THAT THEY LIVED.

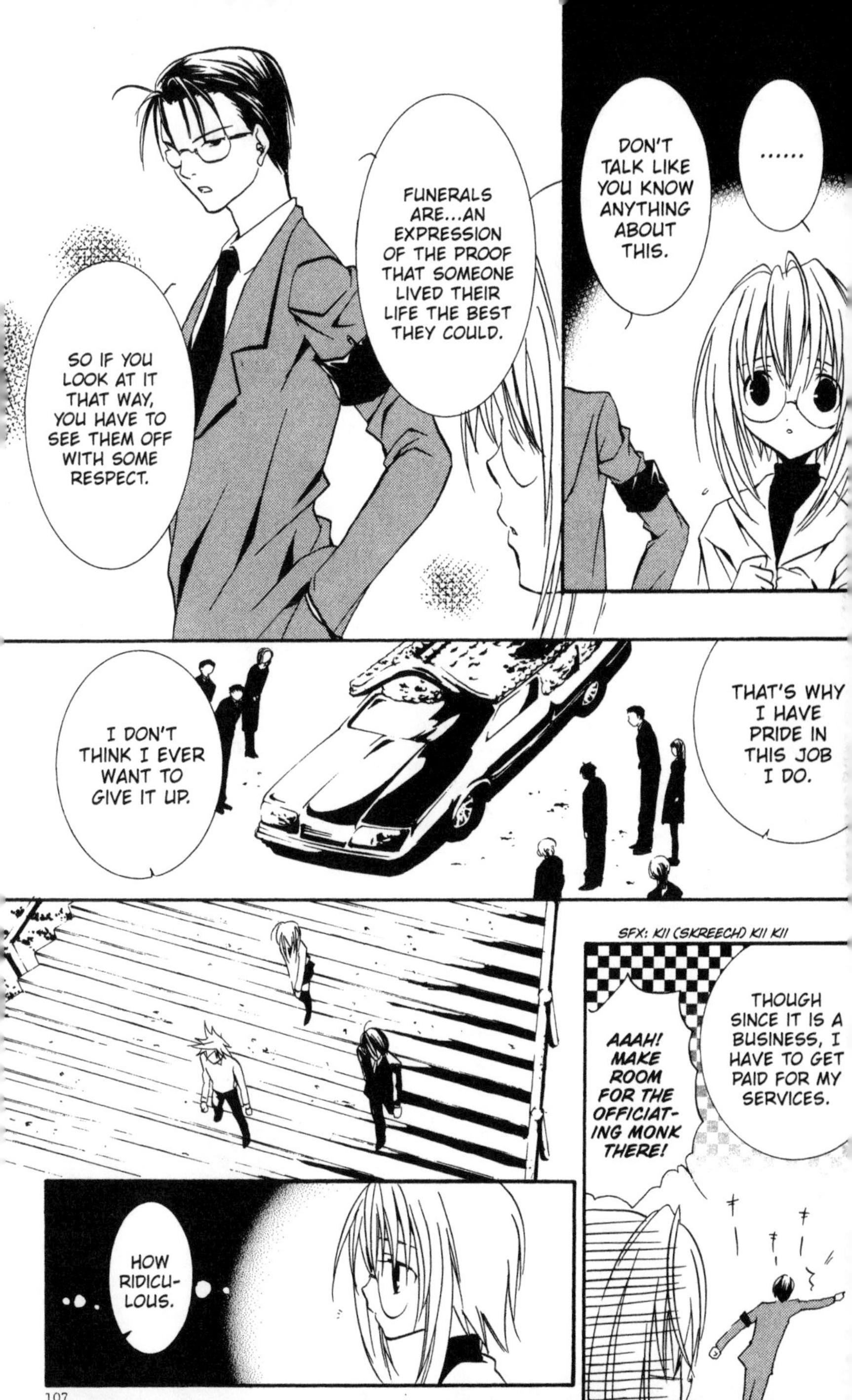
......
DON'T TALK LIKE YOU KNOW ANYTHING ABOUT THIS.
FUNERALS ARE...AN EXPRESSION OF THE PROOF THAT SOMEONE LIVED THEIR LIFE THE BEST THEY COULD.
SO IF YOU LOOK AT IT THAT WAY, YOU HAVE TO SEE THEM OFF WITH SOME RESPECT.
THAT'S WHY I HAVE PRIDE IN THIS JOB I DO.
I DON'T THINK I EVER WANT TO GIVE IT UP.
SFX: KII (SKREECH) KII KII
THOUGH SINCE IT IS A BUSINESS, I HAVE TO GET PAID FOR MY SERVICES.
AAAH! MAKE ROOM FOR THE OFFICIAT-ING MONK THERE!
HOW RIDICU-LOUS.

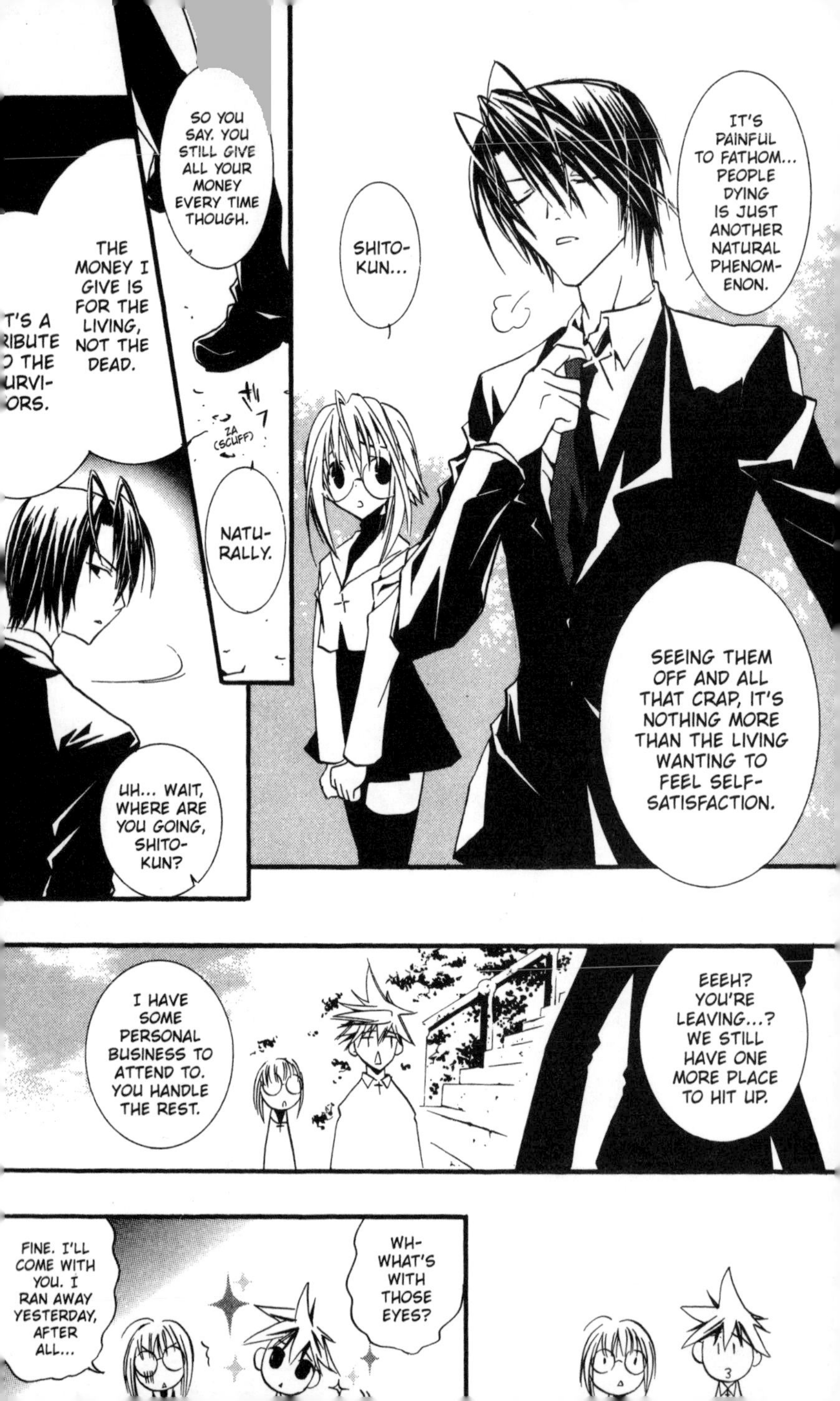
IT'S PAINFUL TO FATHOM... PEOPLE DYING IS JUST ANOTHER NATURAL PHENOMENON.
SHITO-KUN...
SEEING THEM OFF AND ALL THAT CRAP, IT'S NOTHING MORE THAN THE LIVING WANTING TO FEEL SELF-SATISFACTION.
SO YOU SAY. YOU STILL GIVE ALL YOUR MONEY EVERY TIME THOUGH.
ZA (SCUFF)
NATURALLY.
THE MONEY I GIVE IS FOR THE LIVING, NOT THE DEAD.
UH... WAIT, WHERE ARE YOU GOING, SHITO-KUN?
EEEH? YOU'RE LEAVING...? WE STILL HAVE ONE MORE PLACE TO HIT UP.
I HAVE SOME PERSONAL BUSINESS TO ATTEND TO. YOU HANDLE THE REST.
WH- WHAT'S WITH THOSE EYES?
FINE. I'LL COME WITH YOU. I RAN AWAY YESTERDAY, AFTER ALL...

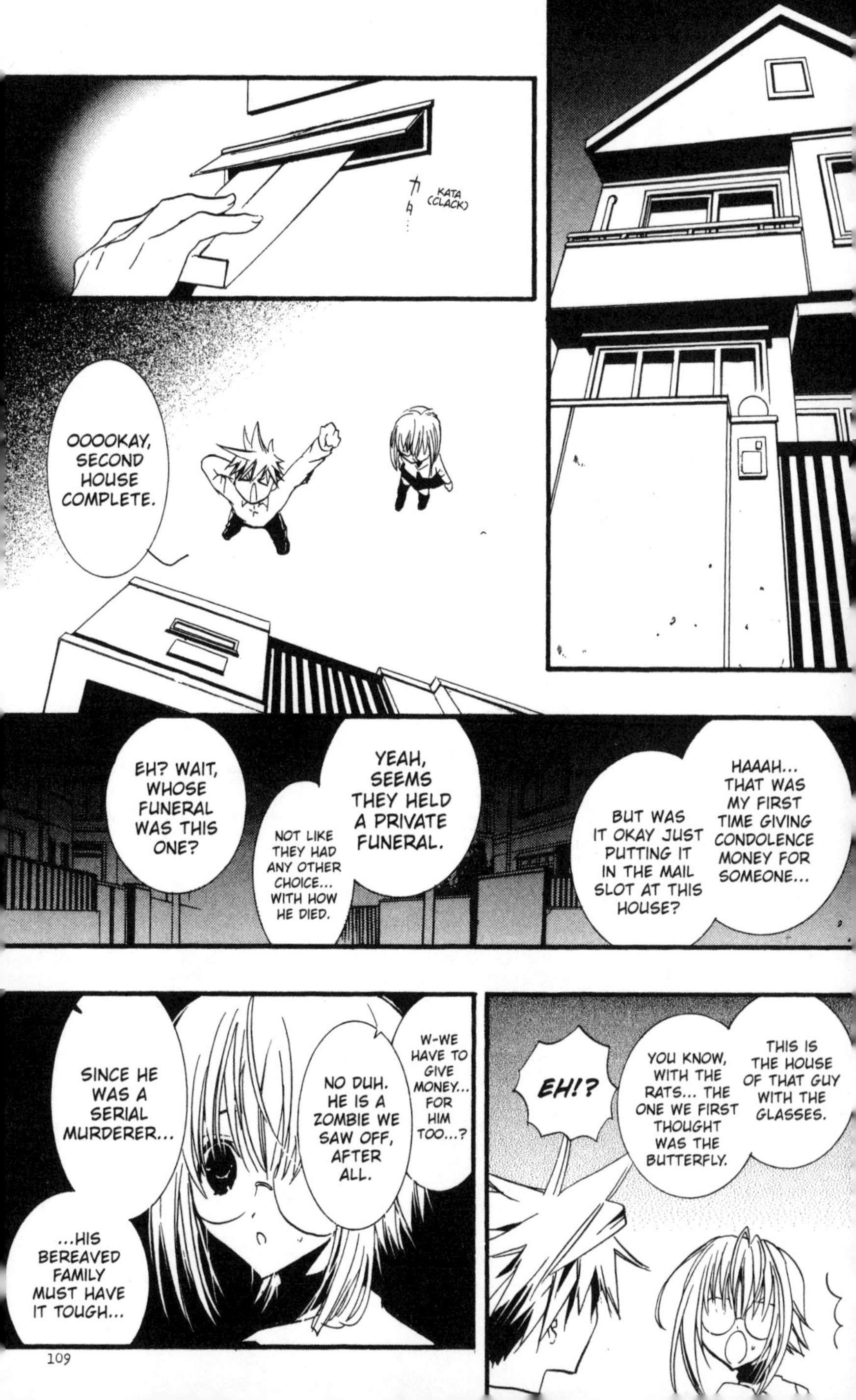
KATA (CLACK)
OOOOKAY, SECOND HOUSE COMPLETE.
HAAAH... THAT WAS MY FIRST TIME GIVING CONDOLENCE MONEY FOR SOMEONE...
BUT WAS IT OKAY JUST PUTTING IT IN THE MAIL SLOT AT THIS HOUSE?
YEAH, SEEMS THEY HELD A PRIVATE FUNERAL.
NOT LIKE THEY HAD ANY OTHER CHOICE... WITH HOW HE DIED.
EH? WAIT, WHOSE FUNERAL WAS THIS ONE?
THIS IS THE HOUSE OF THAT GUY WITH THE GLASSES.
YOU KNOW, WITH THE RATS... THE ONE WE FIRST THOUGHT WAS THE BUTTERFLY.
EH!?
W-WE HAVE TO GIVE MONEY... FOR HIM TOO...?
NO DUH. HE IS A ZOMBIE WE SAW OFF, AFTER ALL.
SINCE HE WAS A SERIAL MURDERER...
...HIS BEREAVED FAMILY MUST HAVE IT TOUGH...

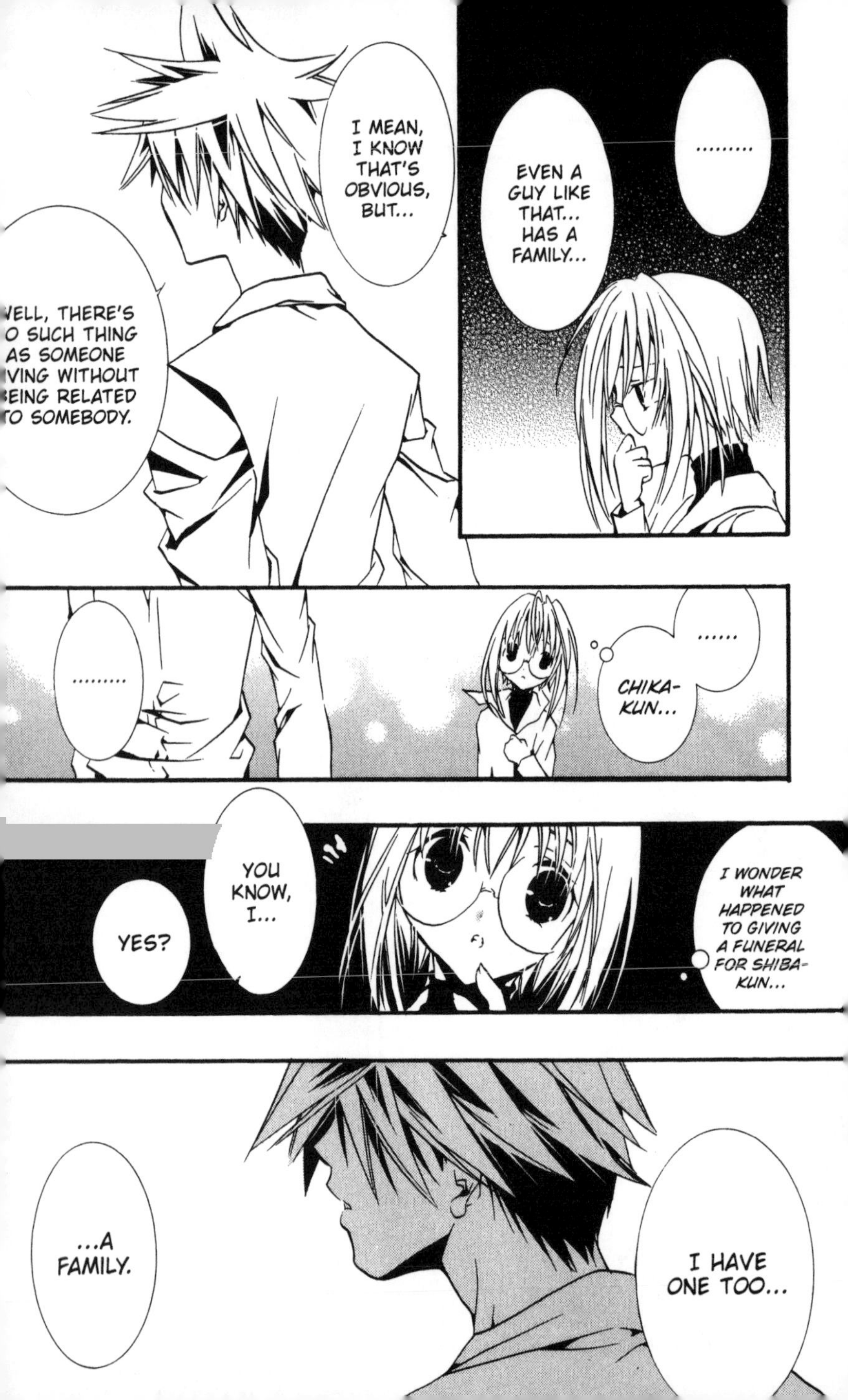
....
EVEN A GUY LIKE THAT... HAS A FAMILY...
I MEAN, I KNOW THAT'S OBVIOUS, BUT...
WELL, THERE'S NO SUCH THING AS SOMEONE LIVING WITHOUT BEING RELATED TO SOMEBODY.
...... CHIKA-KUN...
....
I WONDER WHAT HAPPENED TO GIVING A FUNERAL FOR SHIBA-KUN...
YOU KNOW, I...
YES?
I HAVE ONE TOO...
...A FAMILY.

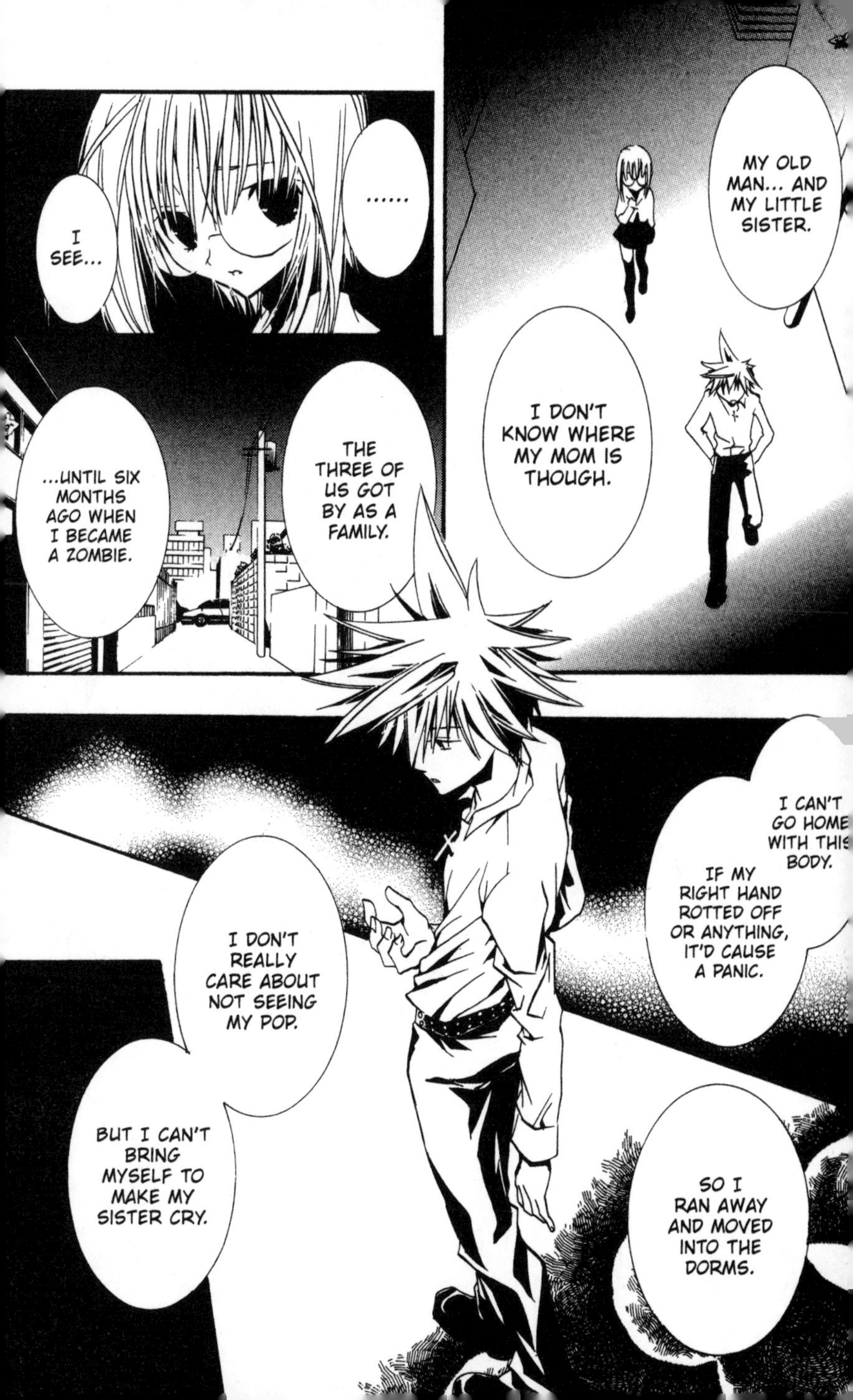
MY OLD MAN... AND MY LITTLE SISTER.
I DON'T KNOW WHERE MY MOM IS THOUGH.
......
I SEE...
THE THREE OF US GOT BY AS A FAMILY.
...UNTIL SIX MONTHS AGO WHEN I BECAME A ZOMBIE.
I CAN'T GO HOME WITH THIS BODY.
IF MY RIGHT HAND ROTTED OFF OR ANYTHING, IT'D CAUSE A PANIC.
SO I RAN AWAY AND MOVED INTO THE DORMS.
I DON'T REALLY CARE ABOUT NOT SEEING MY POP.
BUT I CAN'T BRING MYSELF TO MAKE MY SISTER CRY.

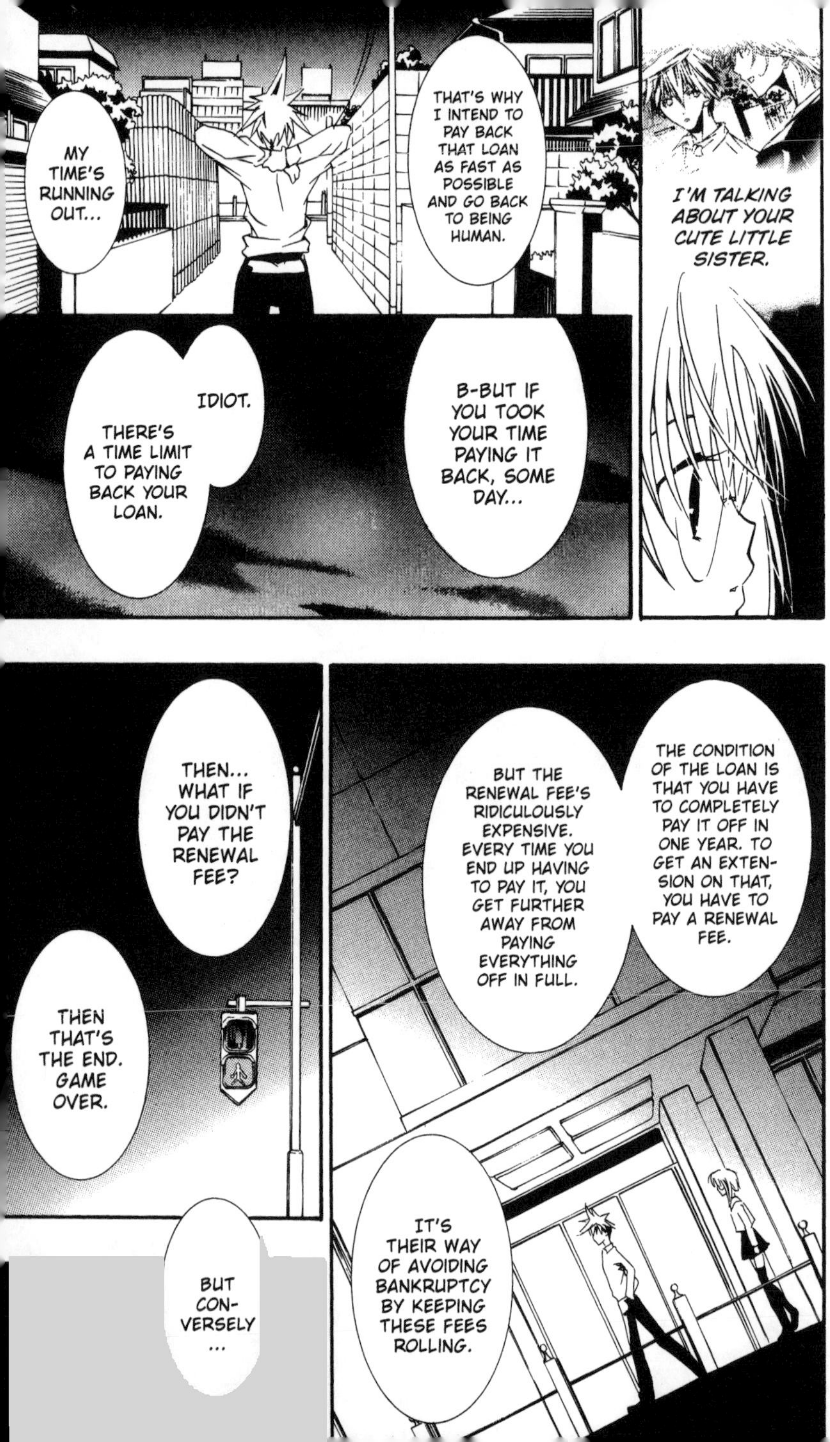
I'M TALKING ABOUT YOUR CUTE LITTLE SISTER.
THAT'S WHY I INTEND TO PAY BACK THAT LOAN AS FAST AS POSSIBLE AND GO BACK TO BEING HUMAN.
MY TIME'S RUNNING OUT...
B-BUT IF YOU TOOK YOUR TIME PAYING IT BACK, SOME DAY...
IDIOT.
THERE'S A TIME LIMIT TO PAYING BACK YOUR LOAN.
THE CONDITION OF THE LOAN IS THAT YOU HAVE TO COMPLETELY PAY IT OFF IN ONE YEAR. TO GET AN EXTENSION ON THAT, YOU HAVE TO PAY A RENEWAL FEE.
BUT THE RENEWAL FEE'S RIDICULOUSLY EXPENSIVE. EVERY TIME YOU END UP HAVING TO PAY IT, YOU GET FURTHER AWAY FROM PAYING EVERYTHING OFF IN FULL.
IT'S THEIR WAY OF AVOIDING BANKRUPTCY BY KEEPING THESE FEES ROLLING.
THEN... WHAT IF YOU DIDN'T PAY THE RENEWAL FEE?
THEN THAT'S THE END. GAME OVER.
BUT CONVERSELY...

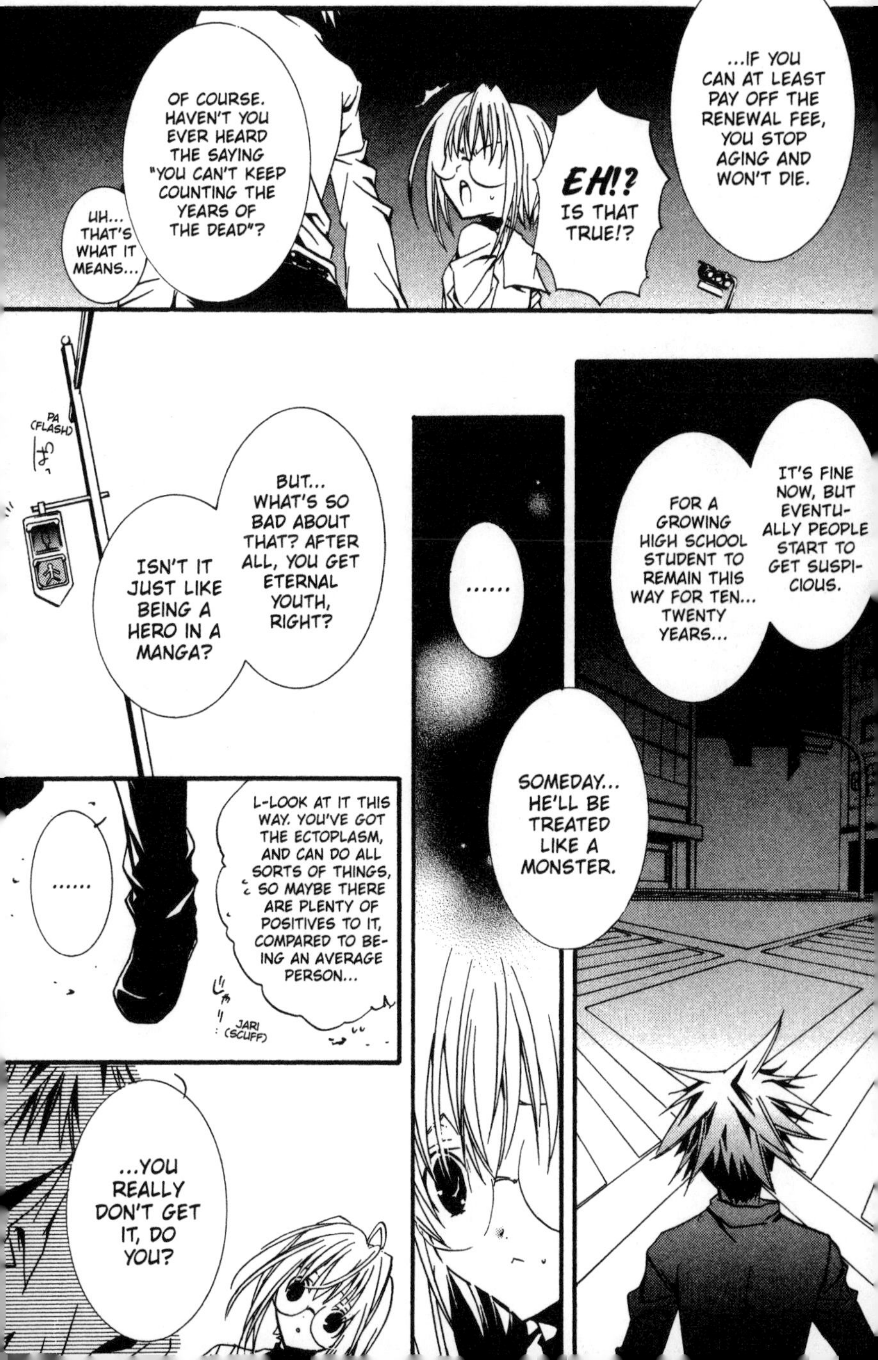
...IF YOU CAN AT LEAST PAY OFF THE RENEWAL FEE, YOU STOP AGING AND WON'T DIE.
EH!? IS THAT TRUE!?
OF COURSE. HAVEN'T YOU EVER HEARD THE SAYING "YOU CAN'T KEEP COUNTING THE YEARS OF THE DEAD"?
UH... THAT'S WHAT IT MEANS...
IT'S FINE NOW, BUT EVENTU-ALLY PEOPLE START TO GET SUSPI-CIOUS.
FOR A GROWING HIGH SCHOOL STUDENT TO REMAIN THIS WAY FOR TEN... TWENTY YEARS...
SOMEDAY... HE'LL BE TREATED LIKE A MONSTER.
......
BUT... WHAT'S SO BAD ABOUT THAT? AFTER ALL, YOU GET ETERNAL YOUTH, RIGHT?
ISN'T IT JUST LIKE BEING A HERO IN A MANGA?
PA (FLASH)
L-LOOK AT IT THIS WAY. YOU'VE GOT THE ECTOPLASM, AND CAN DO ALL SORTS OF THINGS, SO MAYBE THERE ARE PLENTY OF POSITIVES TO IT, COMPARED TO BE-ING AN AVERAGE PERSON...
......
JARI (SCUFF)
...YOU REALLY DON'T GET IT, DO YOU?

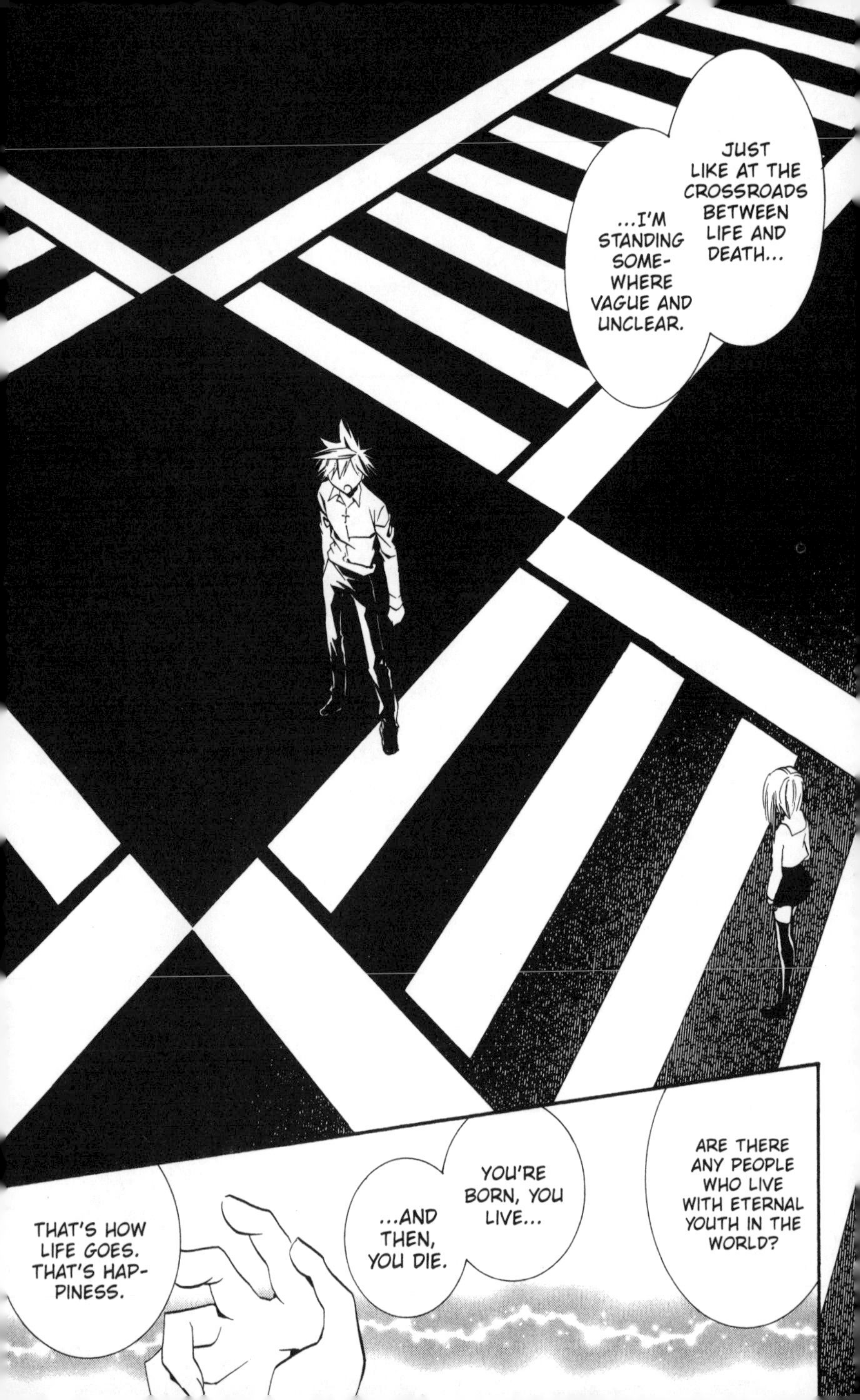
JUST LIKE AT THE CROSSROADS BETWEEN LIFE AND DEATH...
...I'M STANDING SOME-WHERE VAGUE AND UNCLEAR.
ARE THERE ANY PEOPLE WHO LIVE WITH ETERNAL YOUTH IN THE WORLD?
YOU'RE BORN, YOU LIVE...
...AND THEN, YOU DIE.
THAT'S HOW LIFE GOES. THAT'S HAP-PINESS.

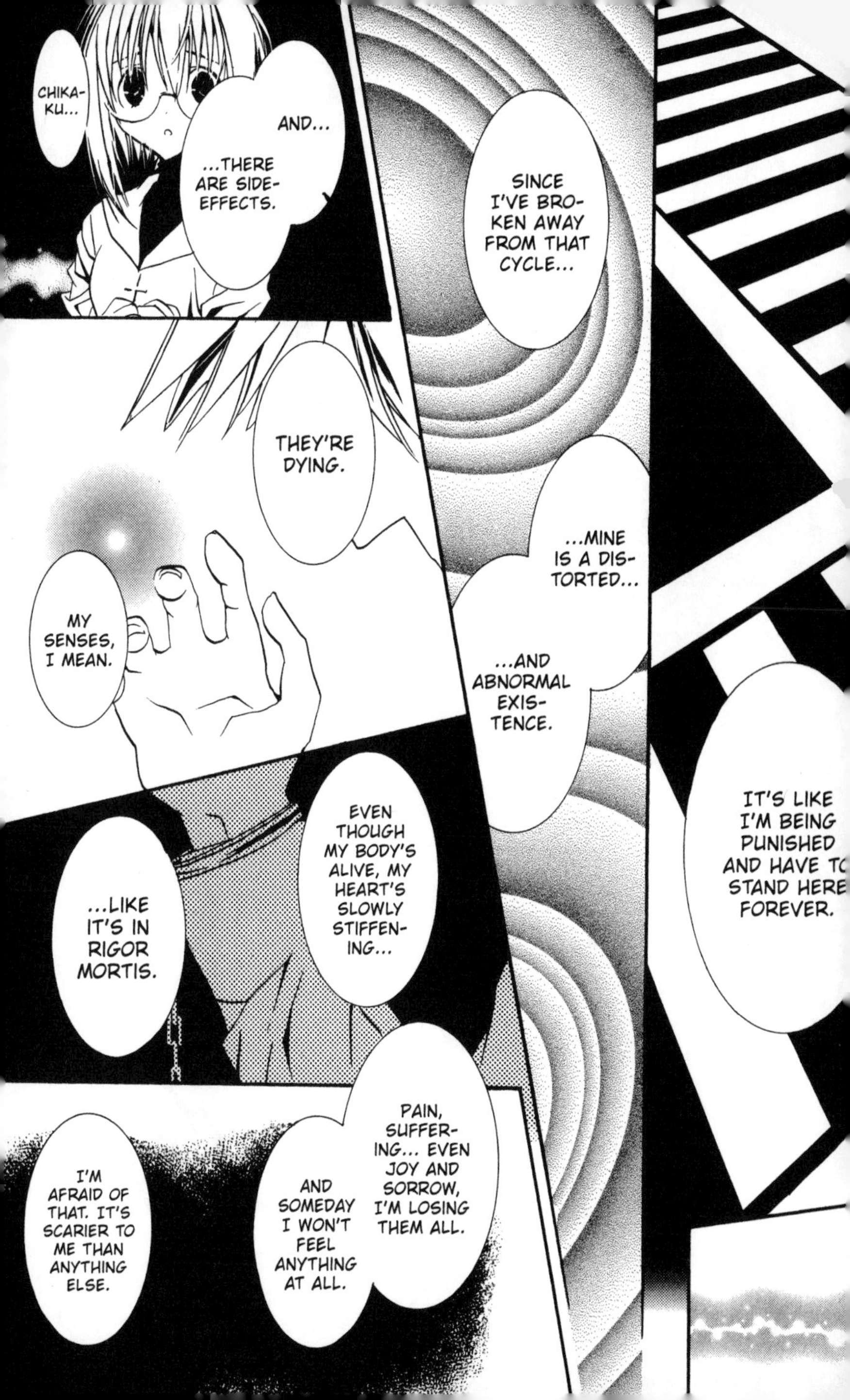
SINCE I'VE BROKEN AWAY FROM THAT CYCLE...
...MINE IS A DISTORTED...
...AND ABNORMAL EXISTENCE.
IT'S LIKE I'M BEING PUNISHED AND HAVE TO STAND HERE FOREVER.
AND...
...THERE ARE SIDE-EFFECTS.
CHIKAKU...
THEY'RE DYING.
MY SENSES, I MEAN.
EVEN THOUGH MY BODY'S ALIVE, MY HEART'S SLOWLY STIFFENING...
...LIKE IT'S IN RIGOR MORTIS.
PAIN, SUFFERING... EVEN JOY AND SORROW, I'M LOSING THEM ALL.
AND SOMEDAY I WON'T FEEL ANYTHING AT ALL.
I'M AFRAID OF THAT. IT'S SCARIER TO ME THAN ANYTHING ELSE.

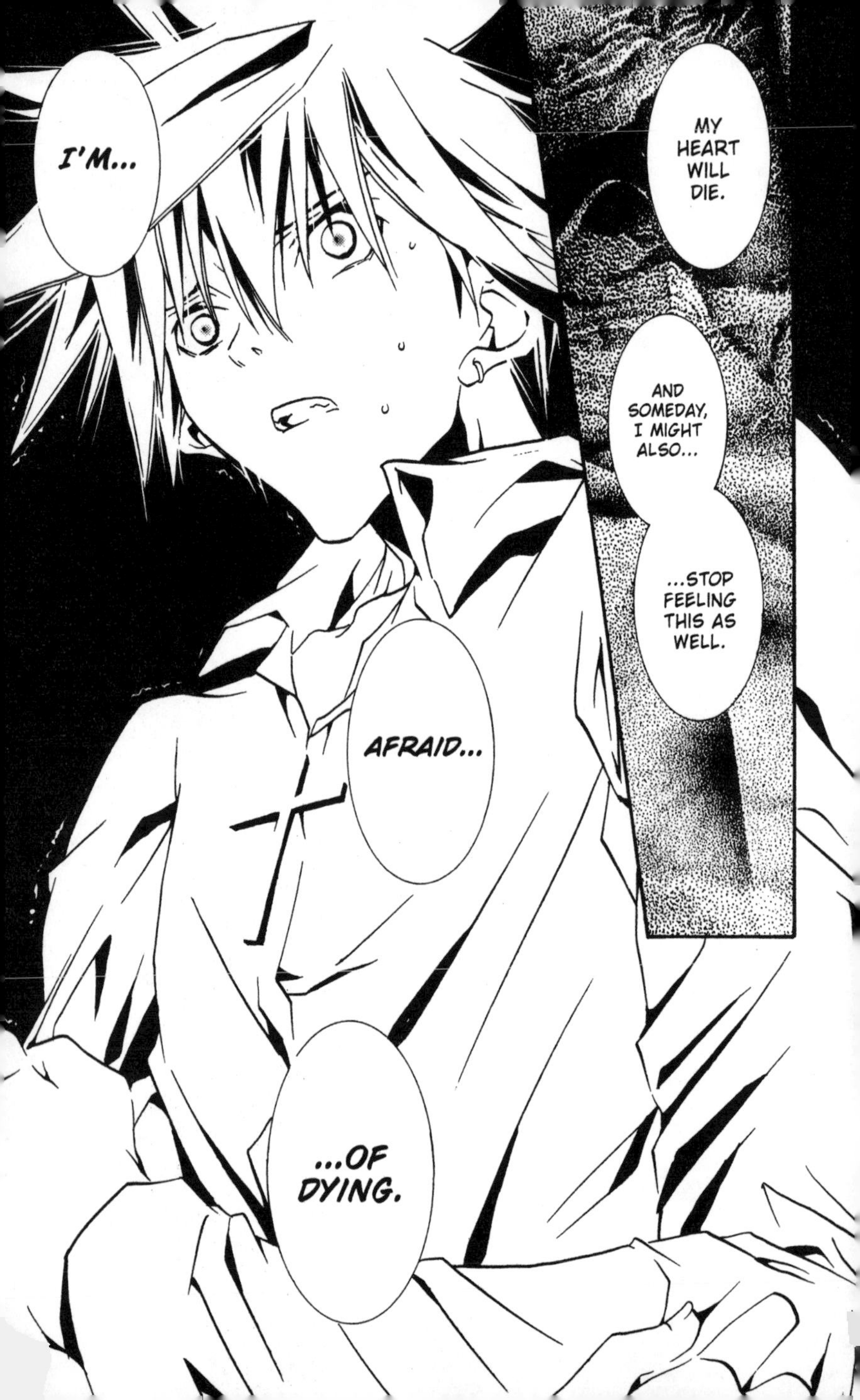
MY HEART WILL DIE.
AND SOMEDAY, I MIGHT ALSO...
...STOP FEELING THIS AS WELL.
I'M...
AFRAID...
...OF DYING.

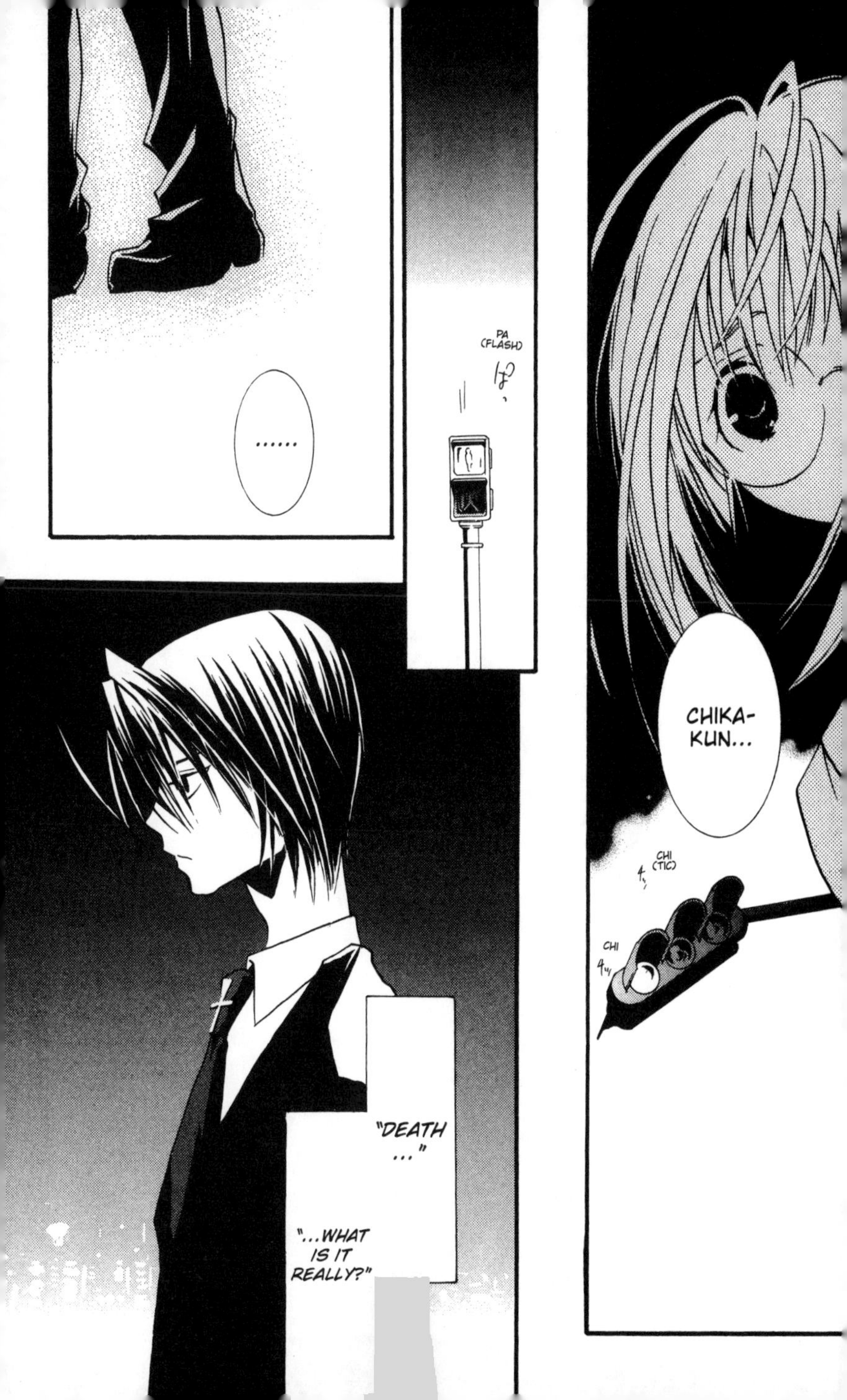
CHIKA-KUN...
CHI (TIC)
CHI
PA (FLASH)
......
"DEATH..."
"...WHAT IS IT REALLY?"

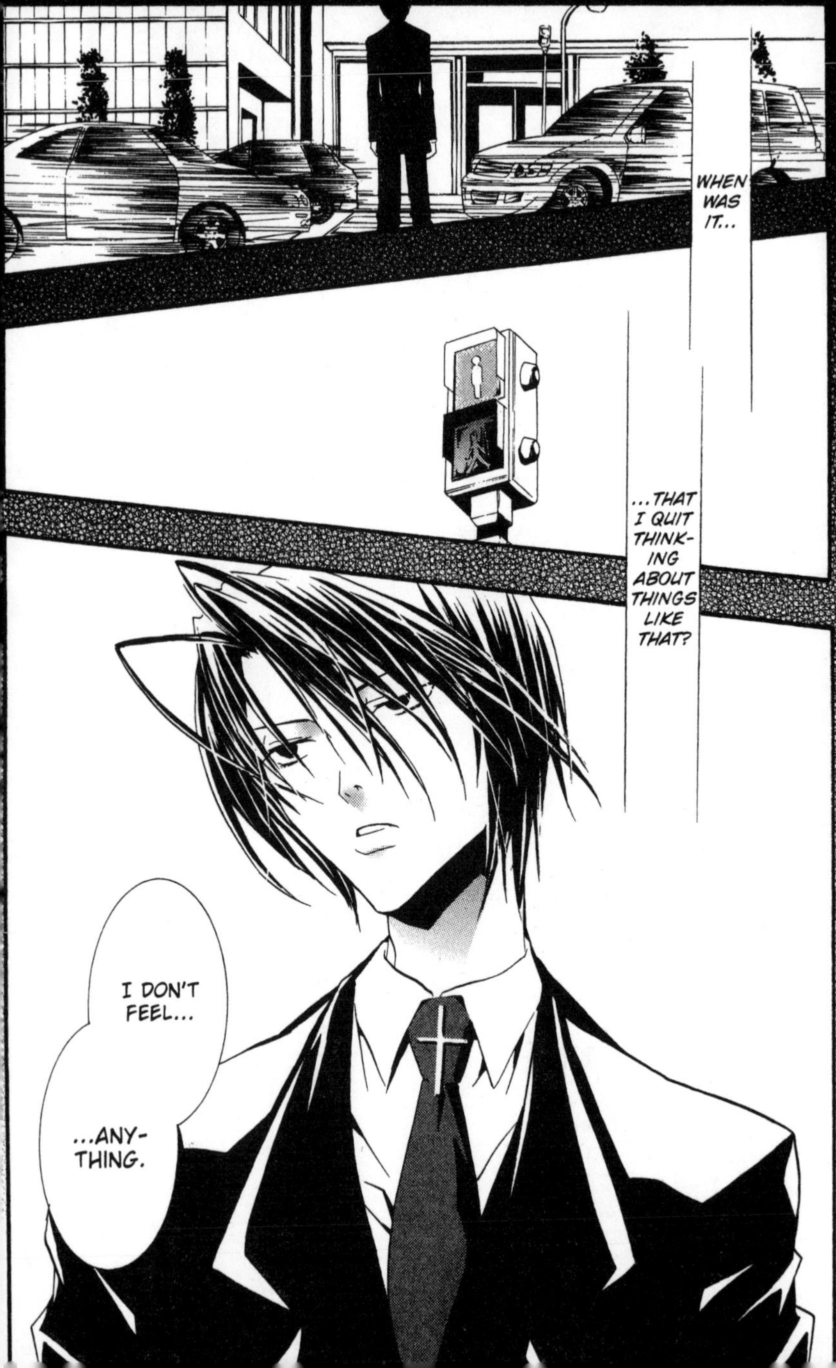
WHEN WAS IT...
...THAT I QUIT THINKING ABOUT THINGS LIKE THAT?
I DON'T FEEL...
...ANYTHING.

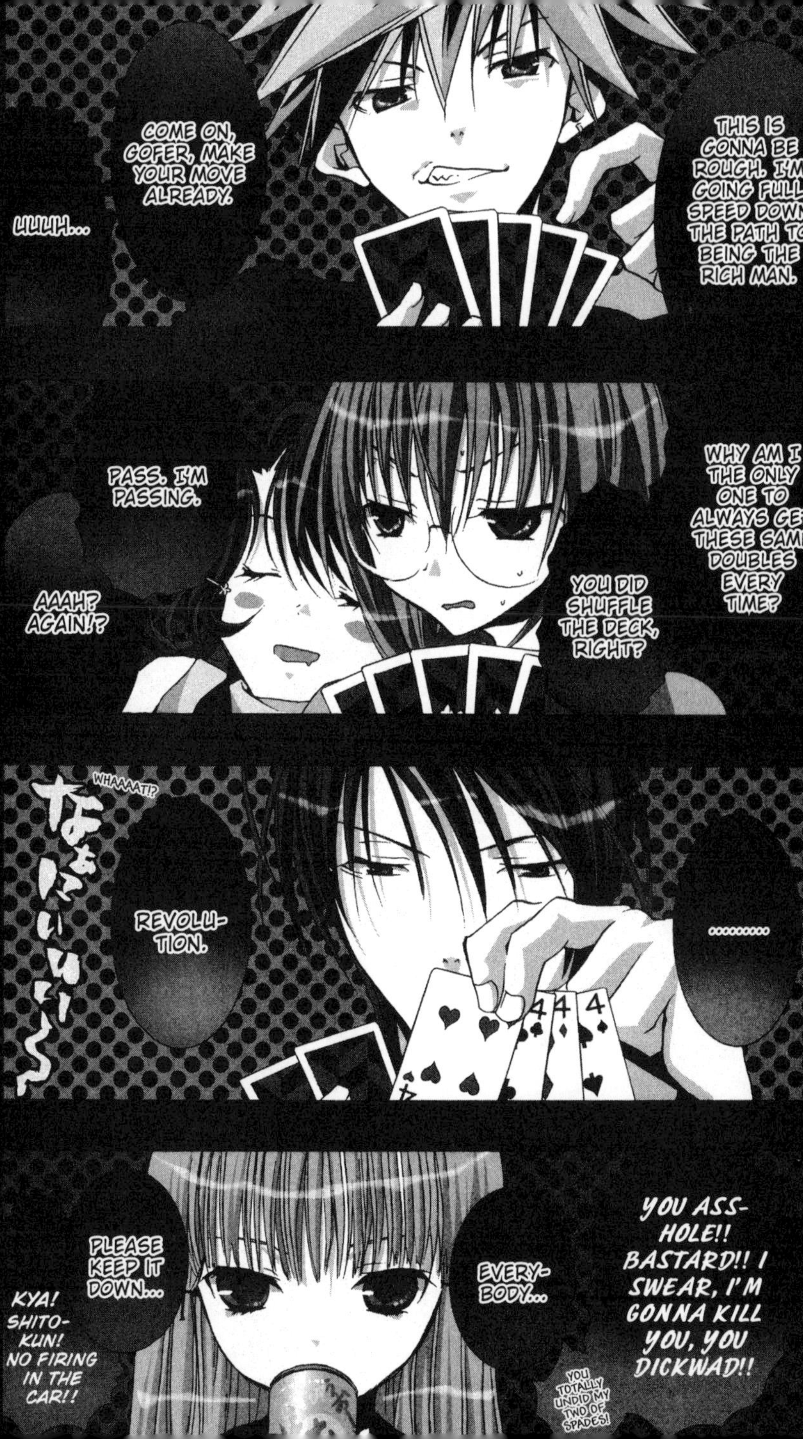
THIS IS GONNA BE ROUGH. I'M GOING FULL SPEED DOWN THE PATH TO BEING THE RICH MAN.
COME ON, GOFER, MAKE YOUR MOVE ALREADY.
UUUH...
WHY AM I THE ONLY ONE TO ALWAYS GET THESE SAME DOUBLES EVERY TIME?
YOU DID SHUFFLE THE DECK, RIGHT?
PASS. I'M PASSING.
AAAH? AGAIN!?
....
REVOLUTION.
WHAAAAT!?
YOU ASS-HOLE!! BASTARD!! I SWEAR, I'M GONNA KILL YOU, YOU DICKWAD!!
YOU TOTALLY UNDID MY TWO OF SPADES!
EVERY-BODY...
PLEASE KEEP IT DOWN...
KYA! SHITO-KUN! NO FIRING IN THE CAR!!

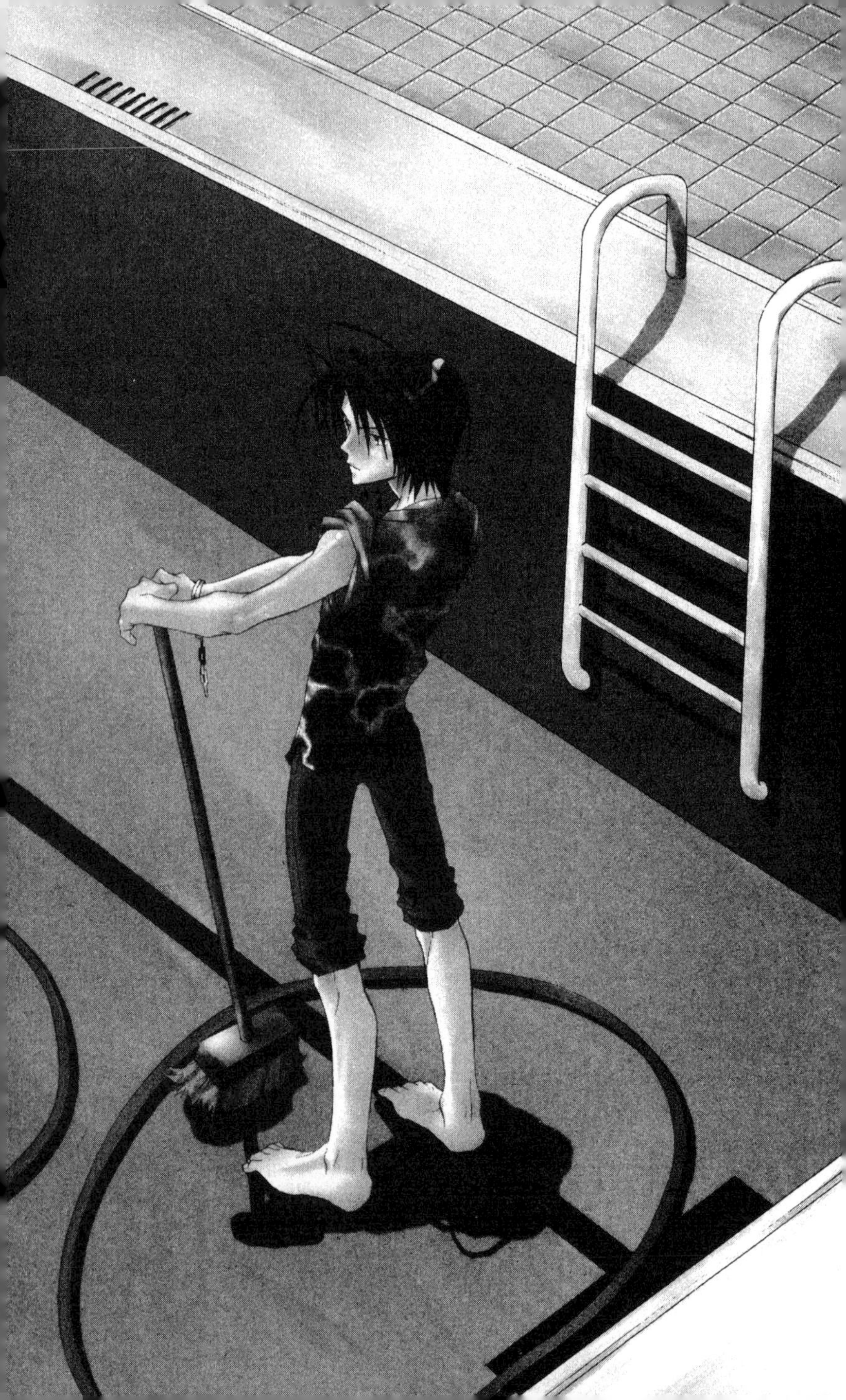

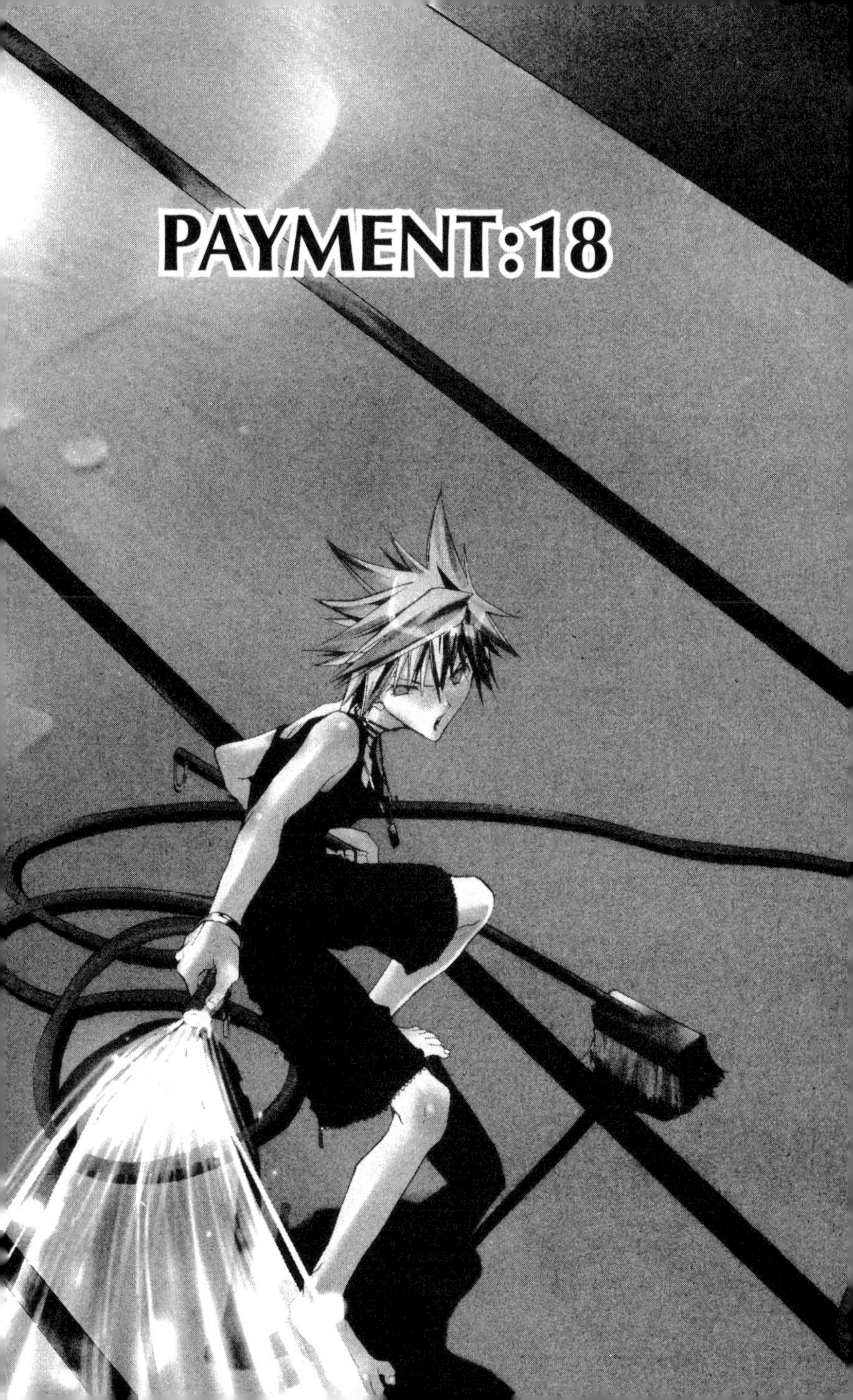
PAYMENT:18

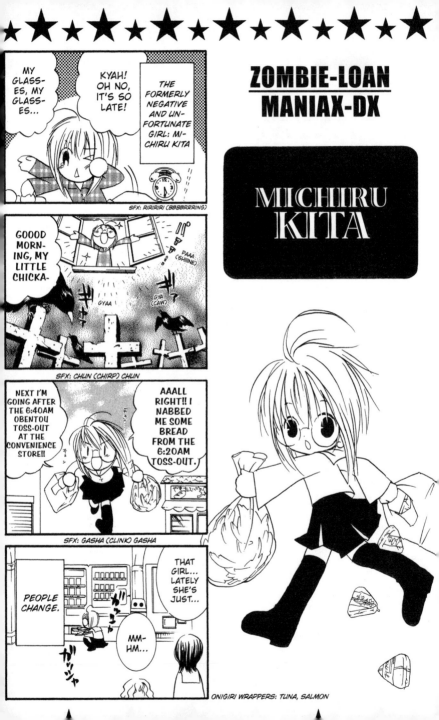

ZOMBIE-LOAN MANIAX-DX

MICHIRU KITA

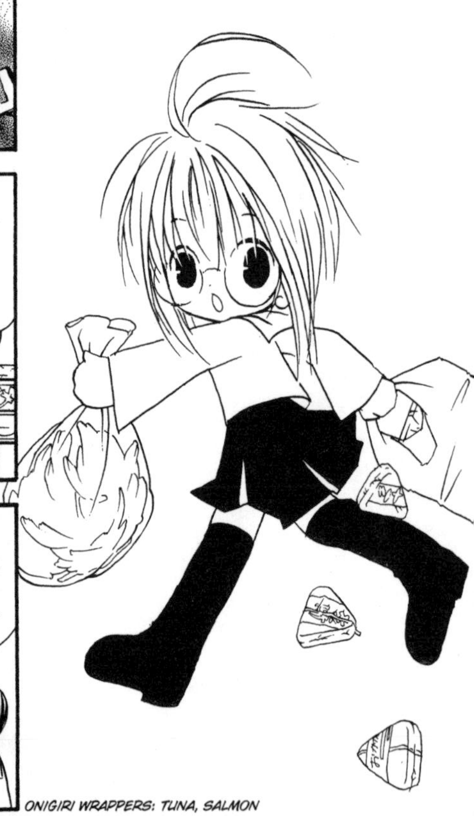

ONIGIRI WRAPPERS: TUNA, SALMON

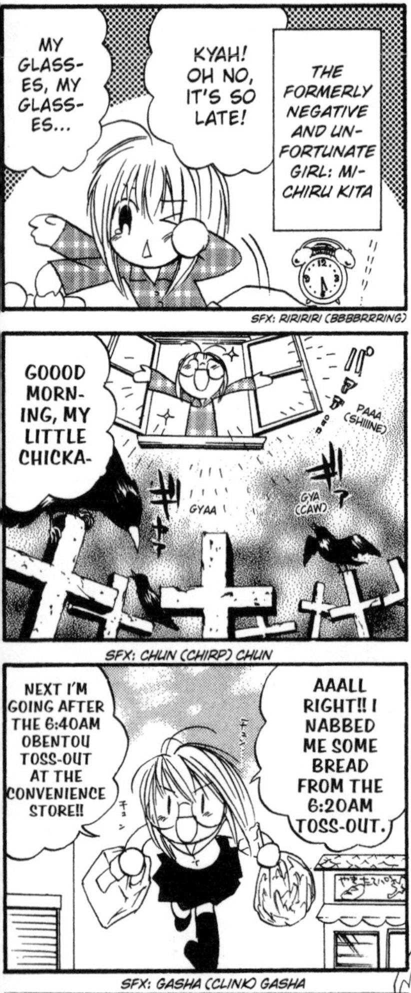

THE FORMERLY NEGATIVE AND UNFORTUNATE GIRL: MICHIRU KITA
KYAH! OH NO, IT'S SO LATE!
MY GLASSES, MY GLASSES...
SFX: RIRIRIRI (BBBBRRRING)
PAAA (SHIIINE)
GYA (CAW)
GYAA
GOOOD MORNING, MY LITTLE CHICKA-
SFX: CHUN (CHIRP) CHUN
AAALL RIGHT!! I NABBED ME SOME BREAD FROM THE 6:20AM TOSS-OUT.
NEXT I'M GOING AFTER THE 6:40AM OBENTOU TOSS-OUT AT THE CONVENIENCE STORE!!
SFX: GASHA (CLINK) GASHA
THAT GIRL... LATELY SHE'S JUST...
MM-HM...
PEOPLE CHANGE.

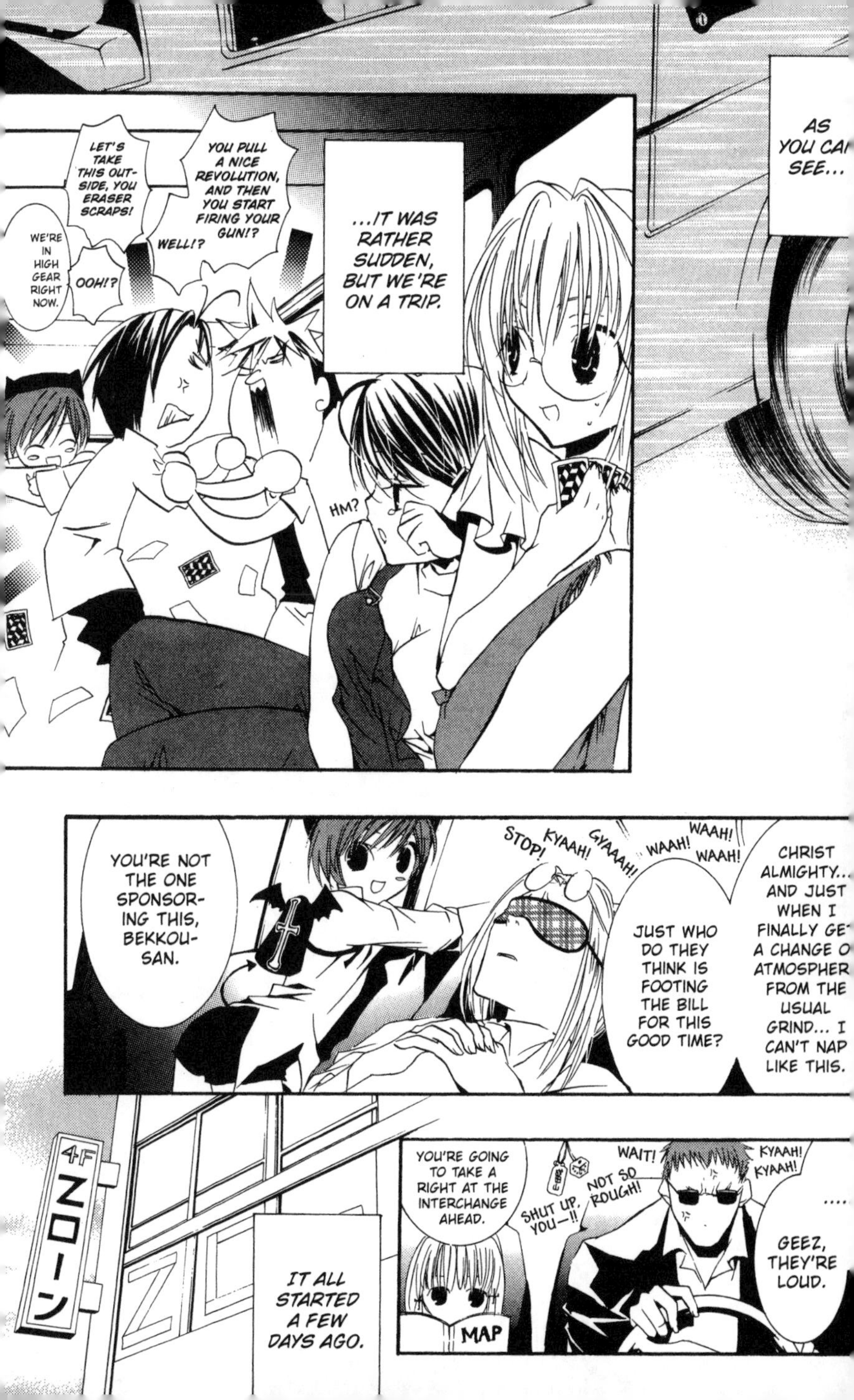
AS YOU CA SEE...
...IT WAS RATHER SUDDEN, BUT WE'RE ON A TRIP.
YOU PULL A NICE REVOLUTION, AND THEN YOU START FIRING YOUR GUN!?
WELL!?
LET'S TAKE THIS OUT-SIDE, YOU ERASER SCRAPS!
OOH!?
WE'RE IN HIGH GEAR RIGHT NOW.
HM?
CHRIST ALMIGHTY... AND JUST WHEN I FINALLY GE A CHANGE O ATMOSPHER FROM THE USUAL GRIND... I CAN'T NAP LIKE THIS.
WAAH! WAAH!
WAAH!
GYAAAAH!
KYAAH!
STOP!
JUST WHO DO THEY THINK IS FOOTING THE BILL FOR THIS GOOD TIME?
YOU'RE NOT THE ONE SPONSORING THIS, BEKKOU-SAN.
KYAAH! KYAAH!
....
GEEZ, THEY'RE LOUD.
WAIT!
NOT SO ROUGH!
SHUT UP, YOU—!!
YOU'RE GOING TO TAKE A RIGHT AT THE INTERCHANGE AHEAD.
MAP
4F
Zローン
IT ALL STARTED A FEW DAYS AGO.

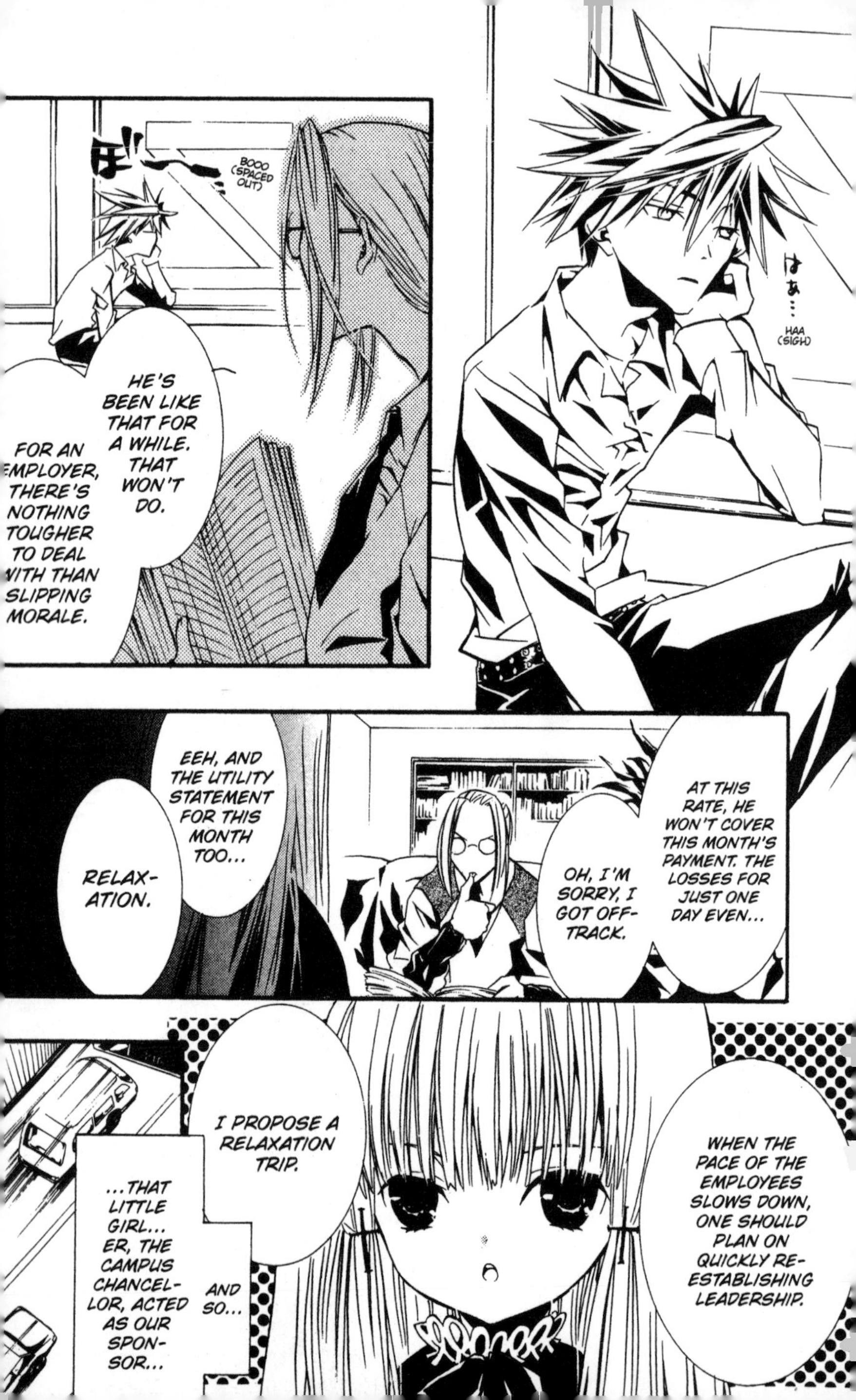
はぁ…
HAA (SIGH)
BOOO (SPACED OUT)
HE'S BEEN LIKE THAT FOR A WHILE. THAT WON'T DO.
FOR AN EMPLOYER, THERE'S NOTHING TOUGHER TO DEAL WITH THAN SLIPPING MORALE.
AT THIS RATE, HE WON'T COVER THIS MONTH'S PAYMENT. THE LOSSES FOR JUST ONE DAY EVEN...
OH, I'M SORRY, I GOT OFF-TRACK.
EEH, AND THE UTILITY STATEMENT FOR THIS MONTH TOO...
RELAX-ATION.
WHEN THE PACE OF THE EMPLOYEES SLOWS DOWN, ONE SHOULD PLAN ON QUICKLY RE-ESTABLISHING LEADERSHIP.
I PROPOSE A RELAXATION TRIP.
AND SO...
...THAT LITTLE GIRL... ER, THE CAMPUS CHANCEL-LOR, ACTED AS OUR SPON-SOR...

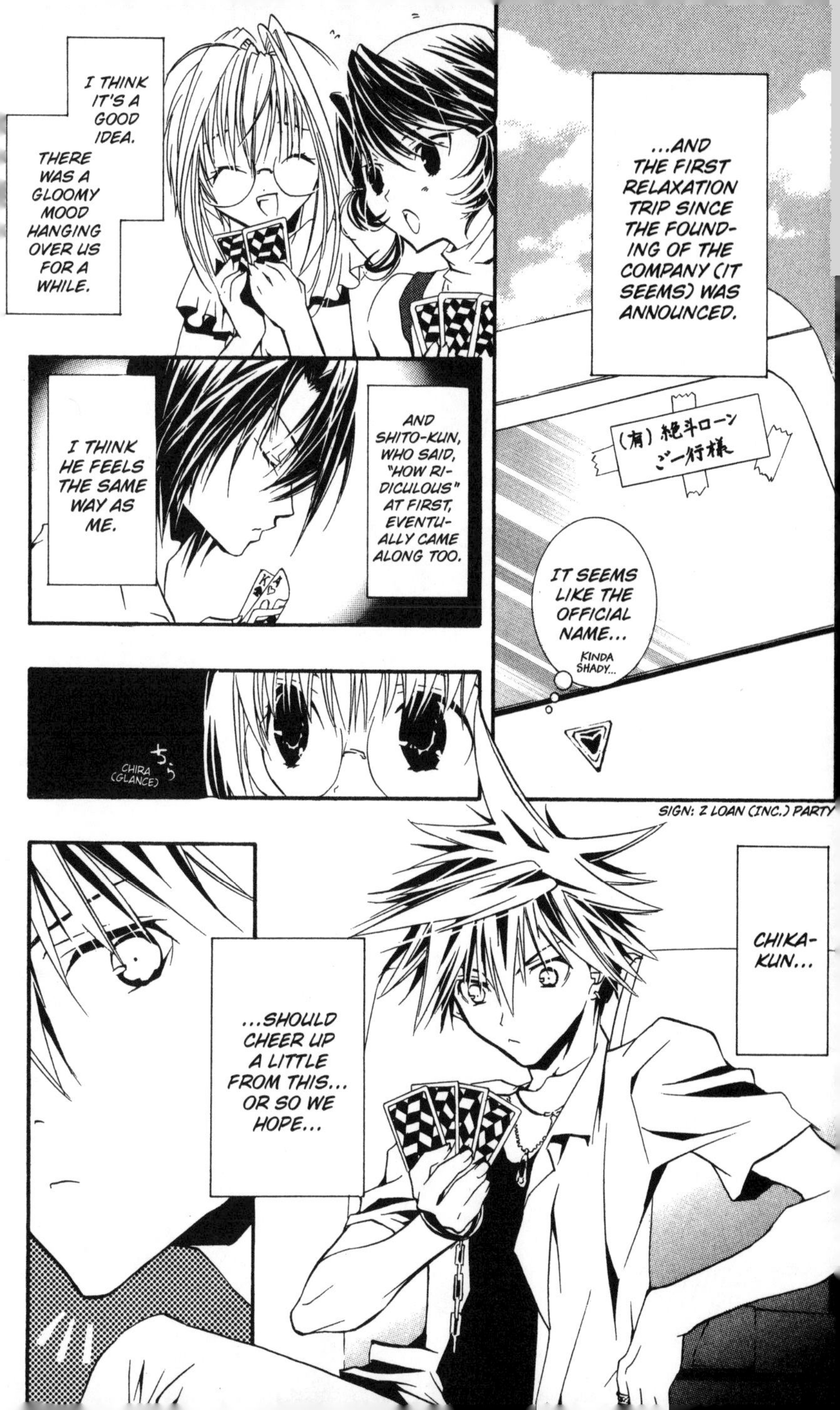
...AND THE FIRST RELAXATION TRIP SINCE THE FOUNDING OF THE COMPANY (IT SEEMS) WAS ANNOUNCED.
(有) 絶斗ローン ご一行様
IT SEEMS LIKE THE OFFICIAL NAME...
KINDA SHADY...
I THINK IT'S A GOOD IDEA.
THERE WAS A GLOOMY MOOD HANGING OVER US FOR A WHILE.
AND SHITO-KUN, WHO SAID, "HOW RIDICULOUS" AT FIRST, EVENTUALLY CAME ALONG TOO.
I THINK HE FEELS THE SAME WAY AS ME.
ちら
CHIRA (GLANCE)
SIGN: Z LOAN (INC.) PARTY
CHIKA-KUN...
...SHOULD CHEER UP A LITTLE FROM THIS... OR SO WE HOPE...

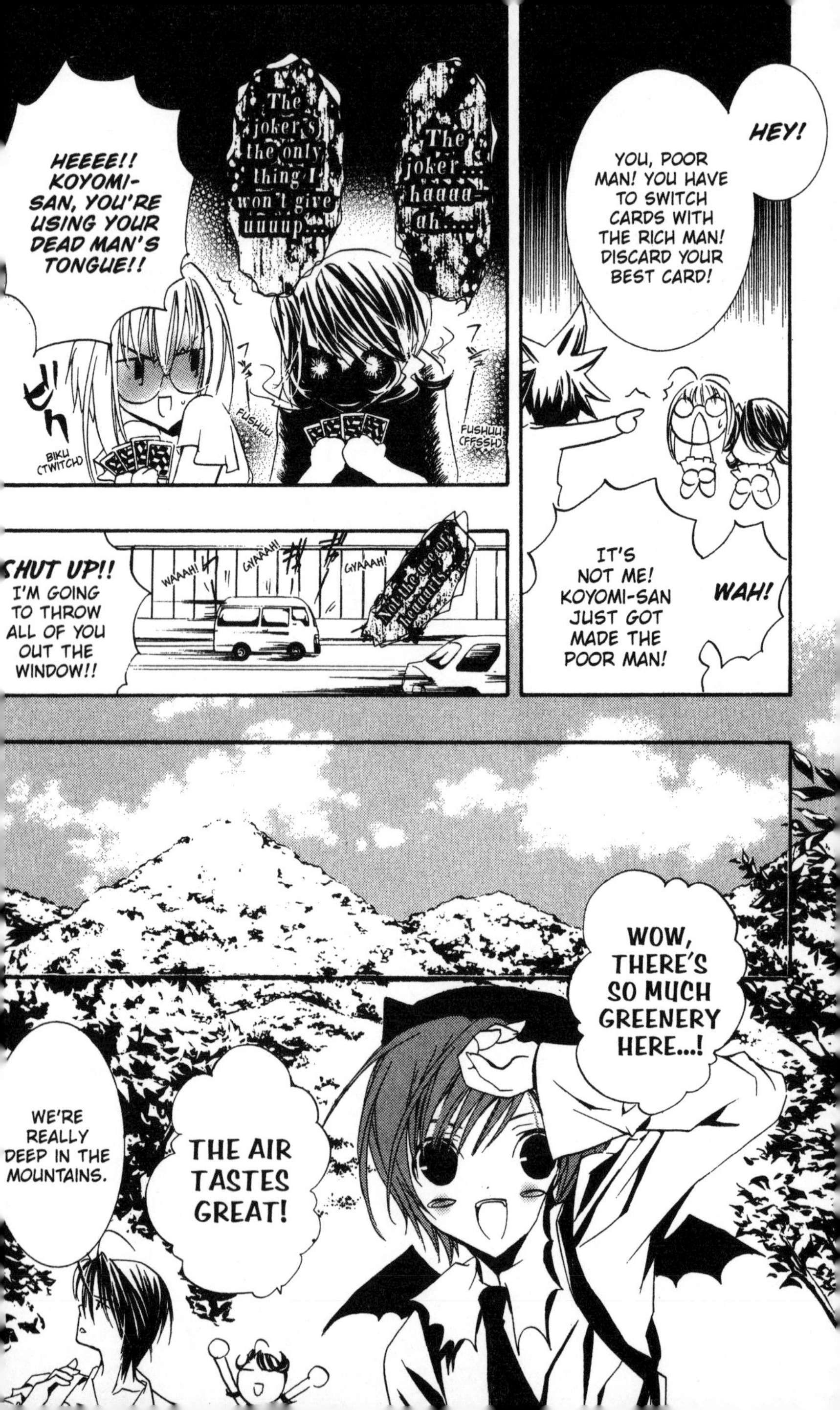

HEY!
YOU, POOR MAN! YOU HAVE TO SWITCH CARDS WITH THE RICH MAN! DISCARD YOUR BEST CARD!
WAH!
IT'S NOT ME! KOYOMI-SAN JUST GOT MADE THE POOR MAN!
The joker... haaaa-ah...
The joker's the only thing I won't give uuuup...
HEEEE!! KOYOMI-SAN, YOU'RE USING YOUR DEAD MAN'S TONGUE!!
FUSHUU (CFFSSH)
FUSHUU
BIKU (TWITCH)
Not the ace of heaaarts...
GYAAAH!
GYAAAH!
WAAAH!
SHUT UP!! I'M GOING TO THROW ALL OF YOU OUT THE WINDOW!!
WOW, THERE'S SO MUCH GREENERY HERE...!
THE AIR TASTES GREAT!
WE'RE REALLY DEEP IN THE MOUNTAINS.

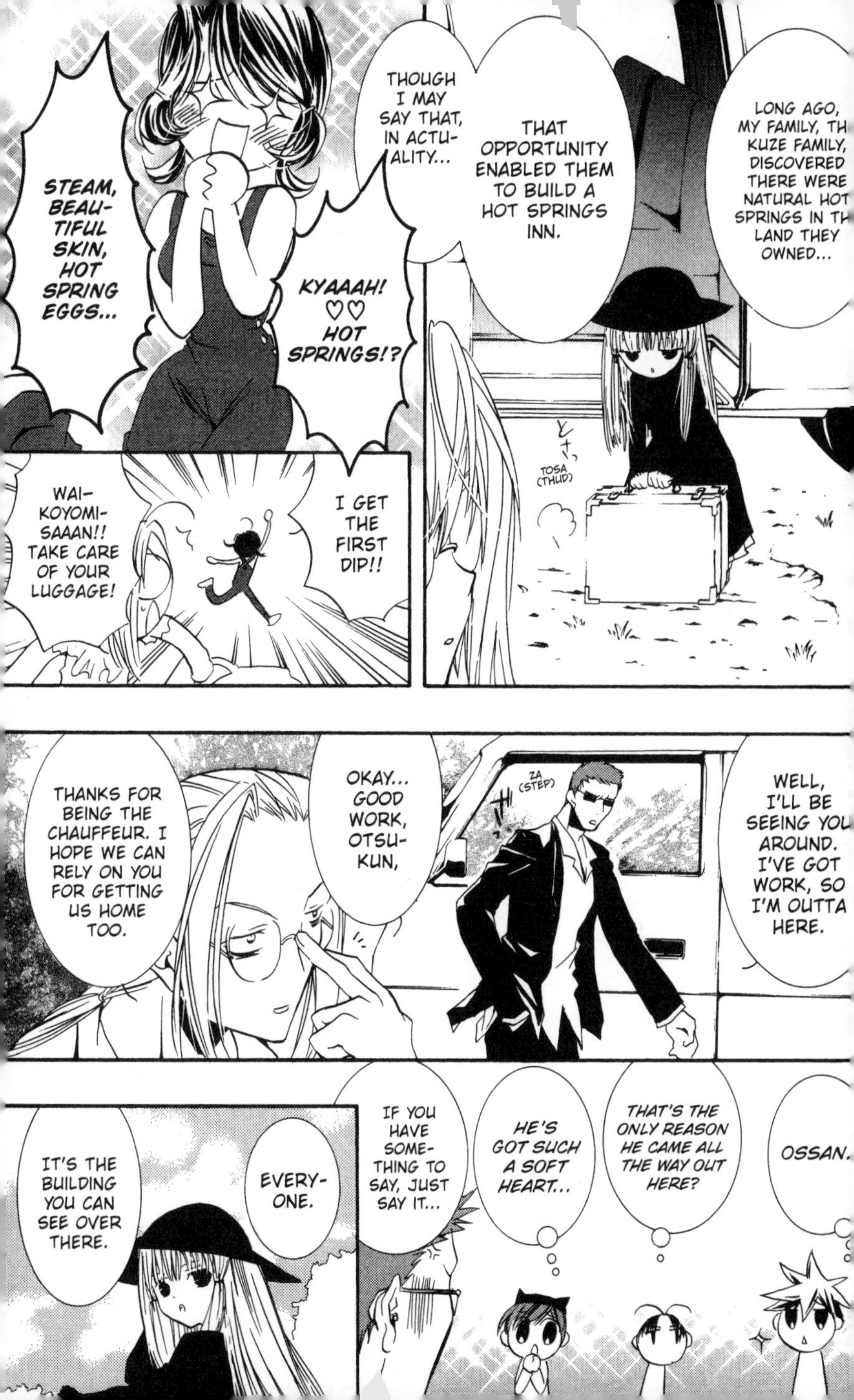
LONG AGO, MY FAMILY, TH KUZE FAMILY, DISCOVERED THERE WERE NATURAL HOT SPRINGS IN TH LAND THEY OWNED...
THAT OPPORTUNITY ENABLED THEM TO BUILD A HOT SPRINGS INN.
THOUGH I MAY SAY THAT, IN ACTU-ALITY...
TOSA (THUD)
KYAAAH! ♡♡ HOT SPRINGS!?
STEAM, BEAU-TIFUL SKIN, HOT SPRING EGGS...
I GET THE FIRST DIP!!
WAI- KOYOMI-SAAAN!! TAKE CARE OF YOUR LUGGAGE!
WELL, I'LL BE SEEING YOU AROUND. I'VE GOT WORK, SO I'M OUTTA HERE.
ZA (STEP)
OKAY... GOOD WORK, OTSU-KUN,
THANKS FOR BEING THE CHAUFFEUR. I HOPE WE CAN RELY ON YOU FOR GETTING US HOME TOO.
OSSAN.
THAT'S THE ONLY REASON HE CAME ALL THE WAY OUT HERE?
HE'S GOT SUCH A SOFT HEART...
IF YOU HAVE SOME-THING TO SAY, JUST SAY IT...
EVERY-ONE.
IT'S THE BUILDING YOU CAN SEE OVER THERE.

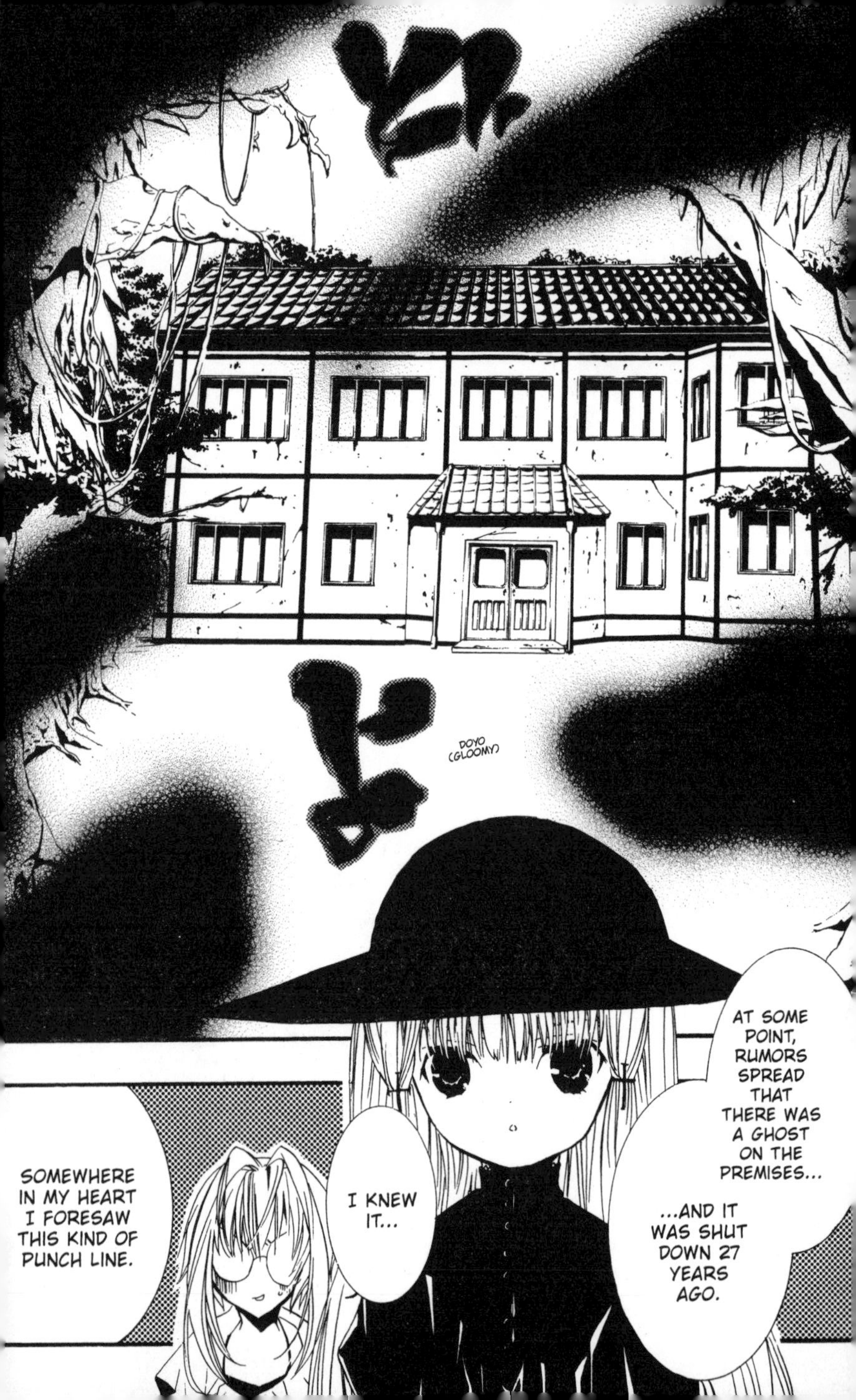
DOYO (GLOOMY)
AT SOME POINT, RUMORS SPREAD THAT THERE WAS A GHOST ON THE PREMISES...
...AND IT WAS SHUT DOWN 27 YEARS AGO.
I KNEW IT...
SOMEWHERE IN MY HEART I FORESAW THIS KIND OF PUNCH LINE.

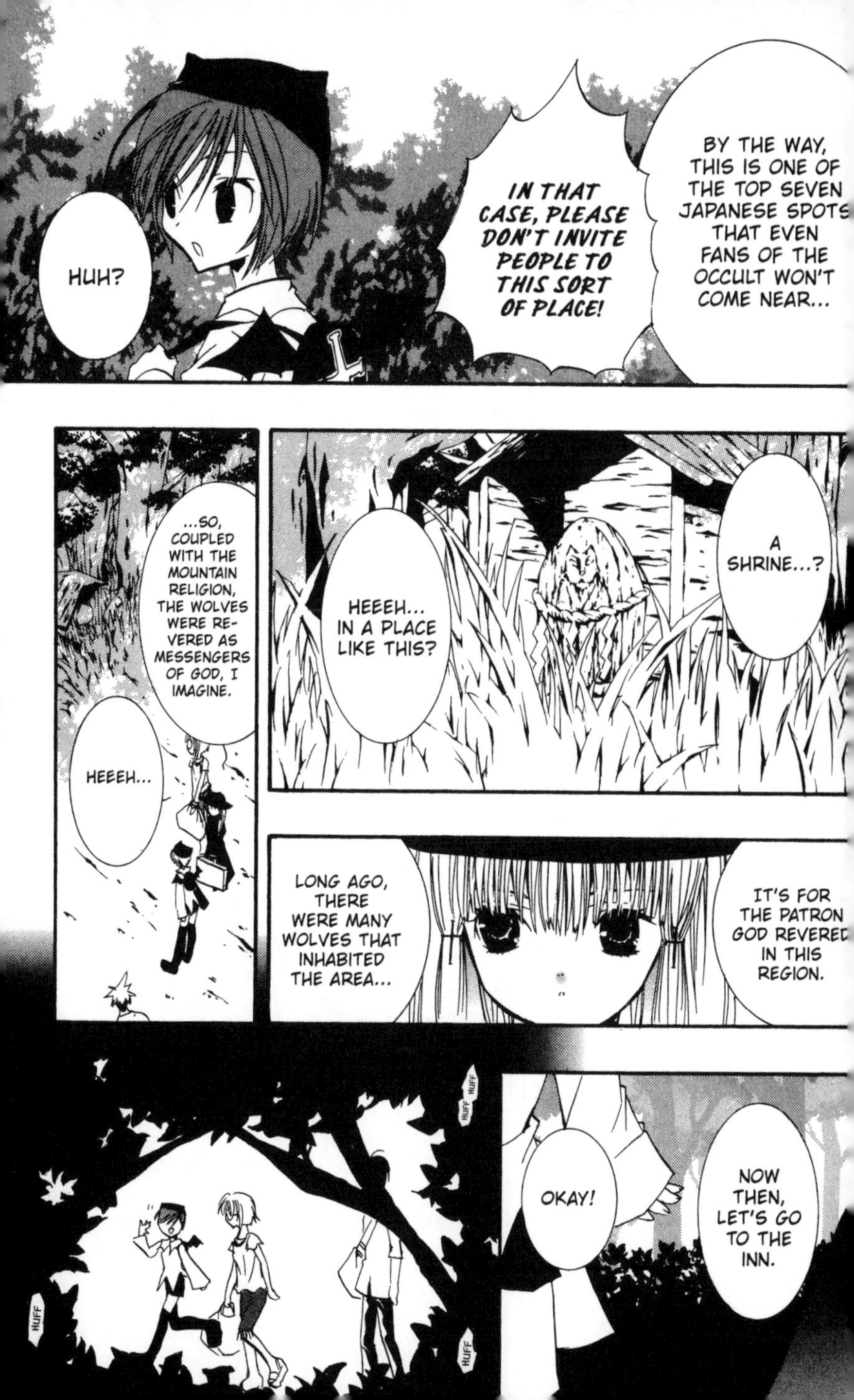
BY THE WAY, THIS IS ONE OF THE TOP SEVEN JAPANESE SPOTS THAT EVEN FANS OF THE OCCULT WON'T COME NEAR...
IN THAT CASE, PLEASE DON'T INVITE PEOPLE TO THIS SORT OF PLACE!
HUH?
A SHRINE...?
HEEEH... IN A PLACE LIKE THIS?
IT'S FOR THE PATRON GOD REVERED IN THIS REGION.
LONG AGO, THERE WERE MANY WOLVES THAT INHABITED THE AREA...
...SO, COUPLED WITH THE MOUNTAIN RELIGION, THE WOLVES WERE RE-VERED AS MESSENGERS OF GOD, I IMAGINE.
HEEEH...
NOW THEN, LET'S GO TO THE INN.
OKAY!
HUFF HUFF
HUFF
HUFF

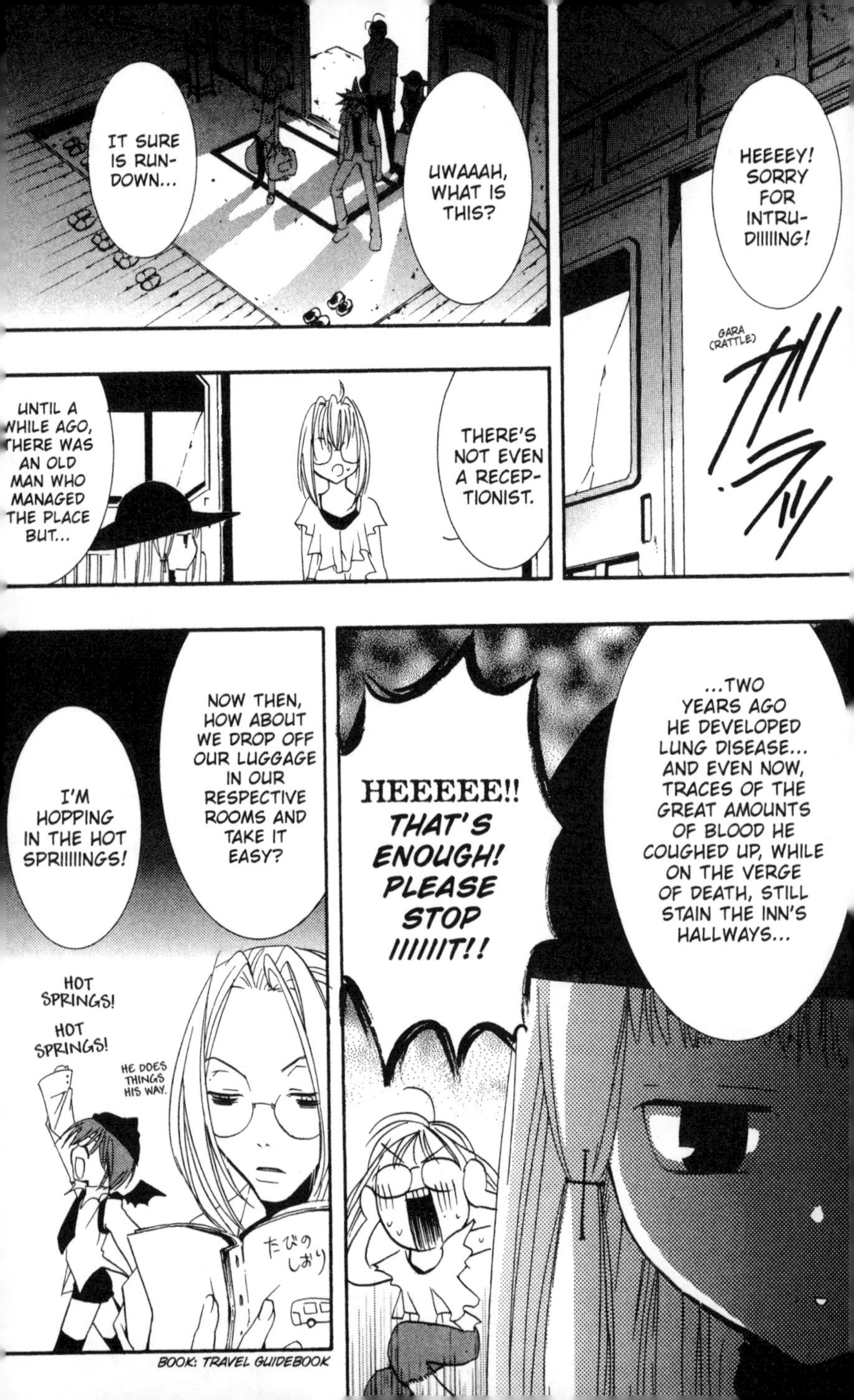
HEEEEY! SORRY FOR INTRU-DIIIIING!
GARA (RATTLE)
UWAAAH, WHAT IS THIS?
IT SURE IS RUN-DOWN...
THERE'S NOT EVEN A RECEPTIONIST.
UNTIL A WHILE AGO, THERE WAS AN OLD MAN WHO MANAGED THE PLACE BUT...
...TWO YEARS AGO HE DEVELOPED LUNG DISEASE... AND EVEN NOW, TRACES OF THE GREAT AMOUNTS OF BLOOD HE COUGHED UP, WHILE ON THE VERGE OF DEATH, STILL STAIN THE INN'S HALLWAYS...
HEEEEEE!! THAT'S ENOUGH! PLEASE STOP IIIIIIT!!
NOW THEN, HOW ABOUT WE DROP OFF OUR LUGGAGE IN OUR RESPECTIVE ROOMS AND TAKE IT EASY?
I'M HOPPING IN THE HOT SPRIIIIINGS!
HOT SPRINGS!
HOT SPRINGS!
HE DOES THINGS HIS WAY.
たびの しおり
BOOK: TRAVEL GUIDEBOOK

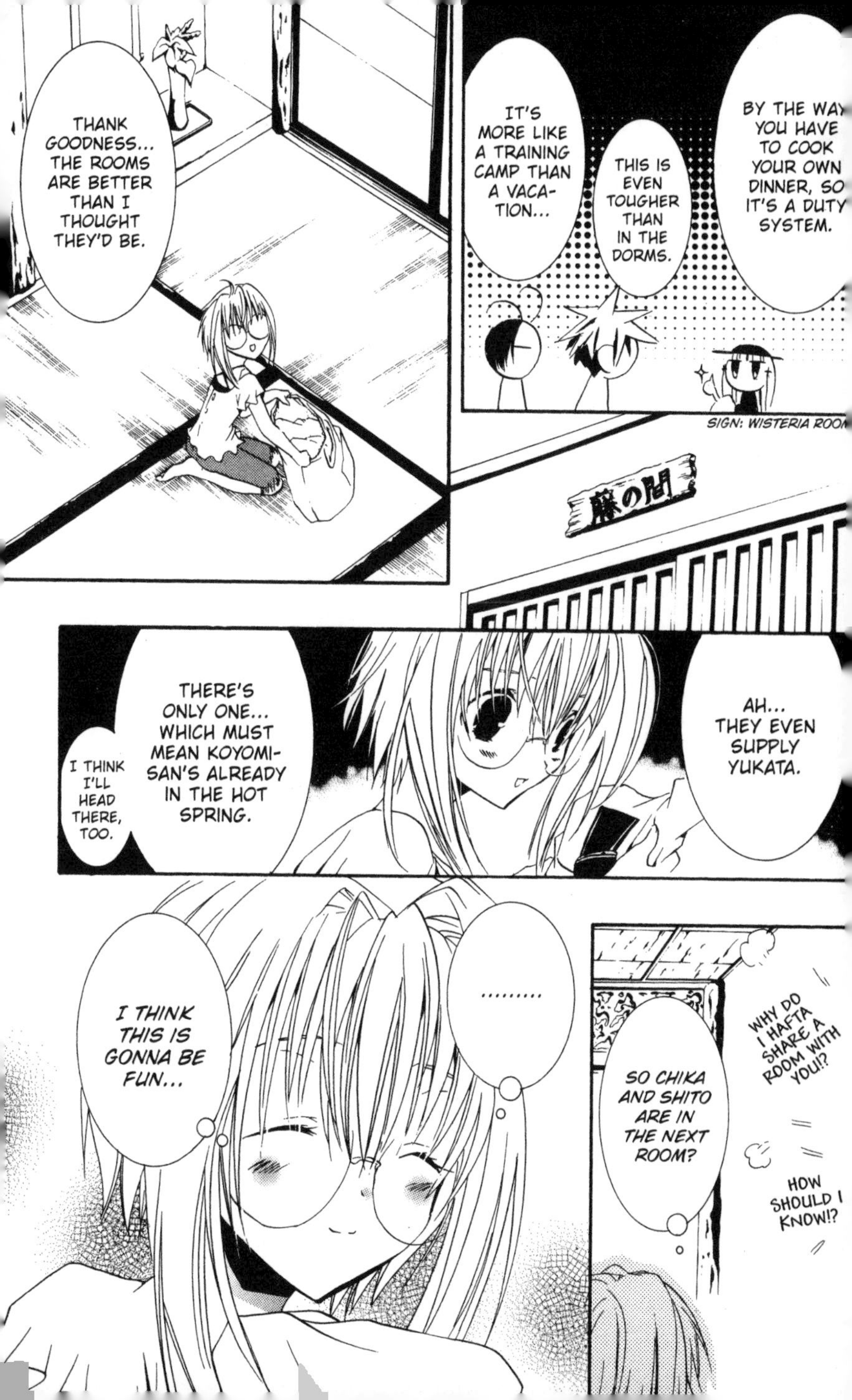
BY THE WAY YOU HAVE TO COOK YOUR OWN DINNER, SO IT'S A DUTY SYSTEM.
THIS IS EVEN TOUGHER THAN IN THE DORMS.
IT'S MORE LIKE A TRAINING CAMP THAN A VACATION...
SIGN: WISTERIA ROO
藤の間
THANK GOODNESS... THE ROOMS ARE BETTER THAN I THOUGHT THEY'D BE.
AH... THEY EVEN SUPPLY YUKATA.
THERE'S ONLY ONE... WHICH MUST MEAN KOYOMI-SAN'S ALREADY IN THE HOT SPRING.
I THINK I'LL HEAD THERE, TOO.
WHY DO I HAFTA SHARE A ROOM WITH YOU!?
HOW SHOULD I KNOW!?
SO CHIKA AND SHITO ARE IN THE NEXT ROOM?
....
I THINK THIS IS GONNA BE FUN...

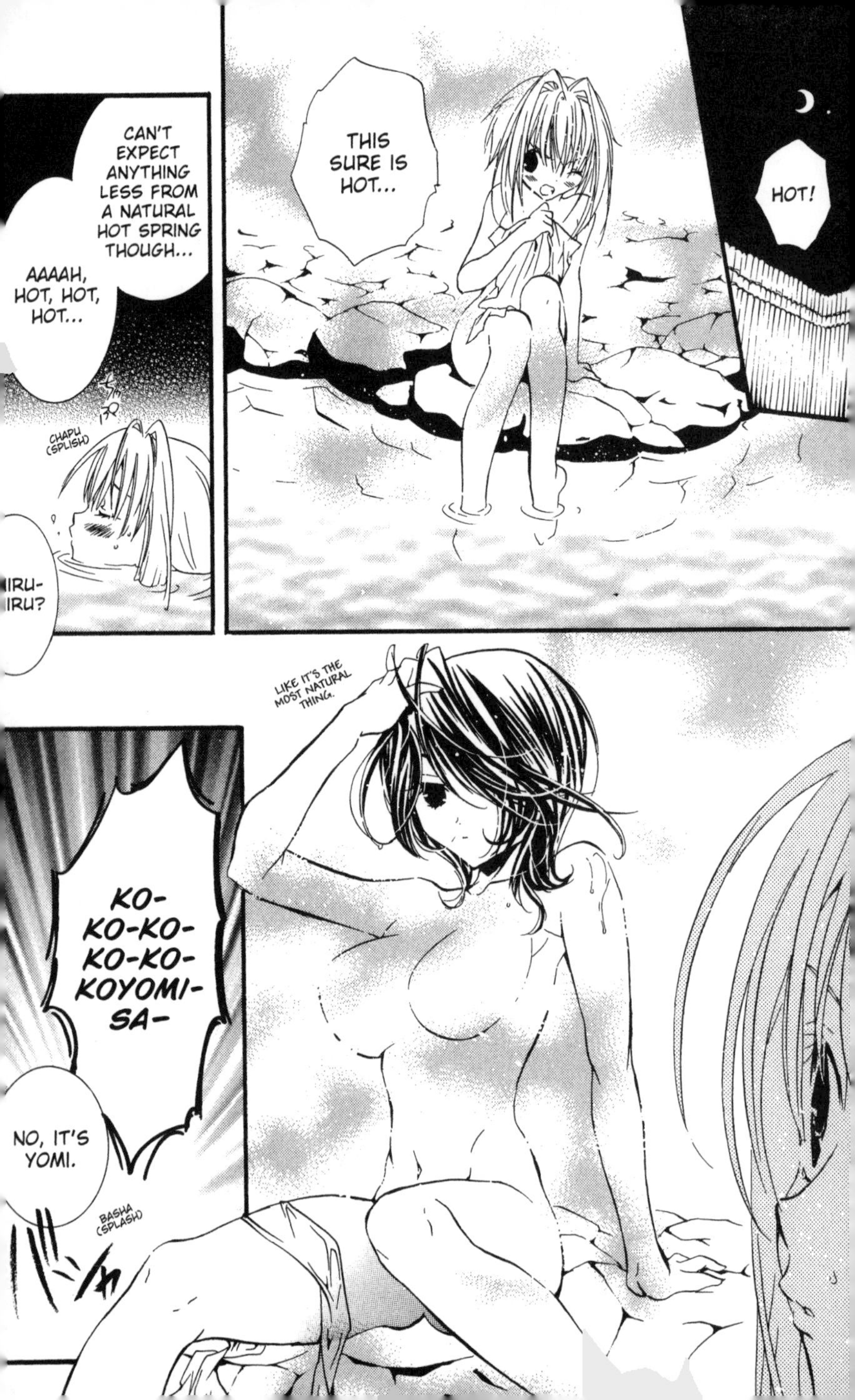

HOT!
THIS SURE IS HOT...
CAN'T EXPECT ANYTHING LESS FROM A NATURAL HOT SPRING THOUGH...
AAAAH, HOT, HOT, HOT...
CHAPU (SPLISH)
IRU-IRU?
LIKE IT'S THE MOST NATURAL THING.
KO-KO-KO-KO-KO-KOYOMI-SA-
NO, IT'S YOMI.
BASHA (SPLASH)

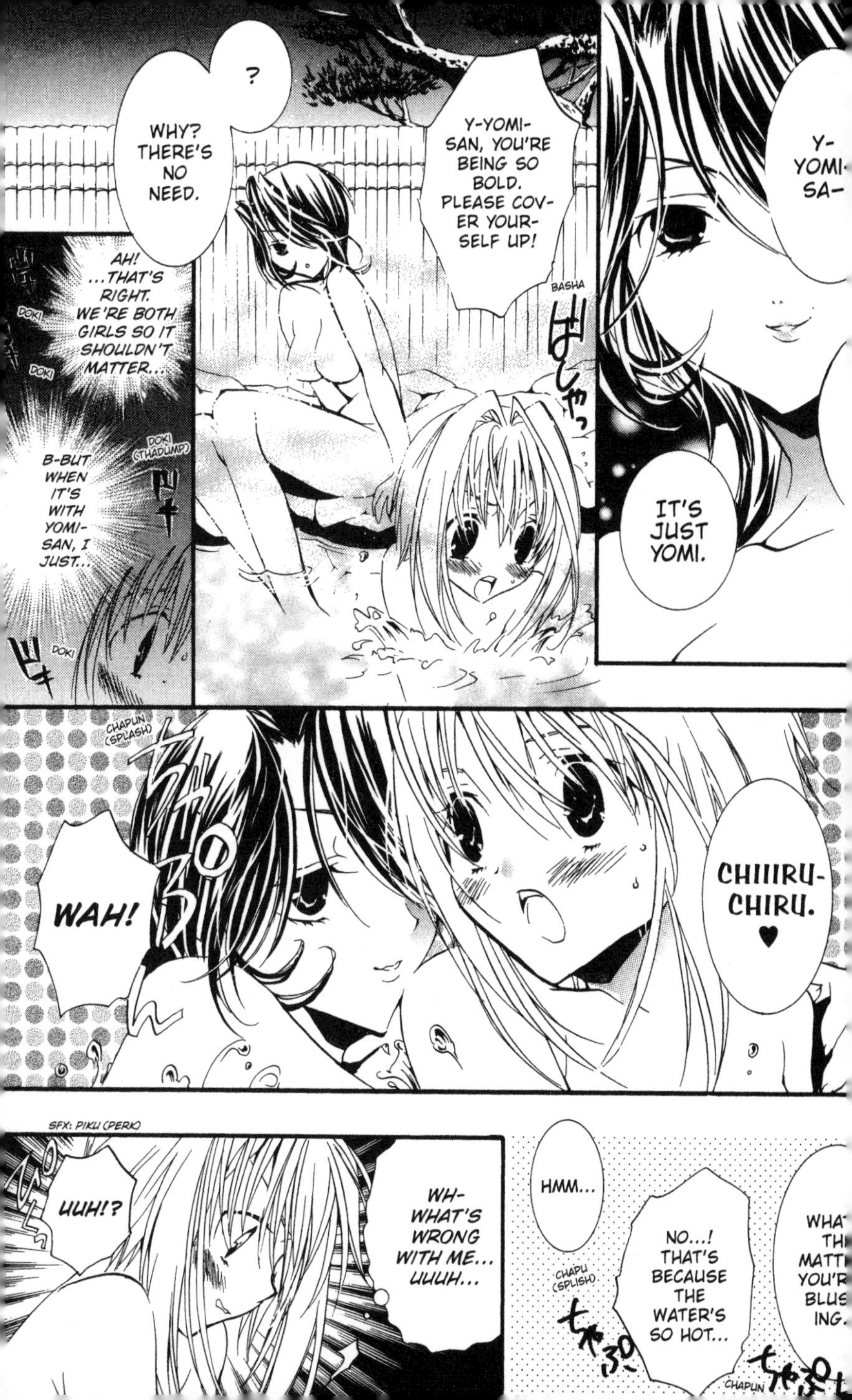
Y-YOMI-SA-
IT'S JUST YOMI.
Y-YOMI-SAN, YOU'RE BEING SO BOLD. PLEASE COVER YOURSELF UP!
BASHA
?
WHY? THERE'S NO NEED.
AH! ...THAT'S RIGHT. WE'RE BOTH GIRLS SO IT SHOULDN'T MATTER...
DOKI
DOKI
DOKI (THADUMP)
B-BUT WHEN IT'S WITH YOMI-SAN, I JUST...
DOKI
CHIIIRU-CHIRU. ♥
WAH!
CHAPUN (SPLASH)
WHA TH MATT YOU'R BLUS ING.
CHAPUN
HMM...
NO...! THAT'S BECAUSE THE WATER'S SO HOT...
CHAPU (SPLISH)
WH-WHAT'S WRONG WITH ME... UUUH...
UUH!?
SFX: PIKU (PERK)

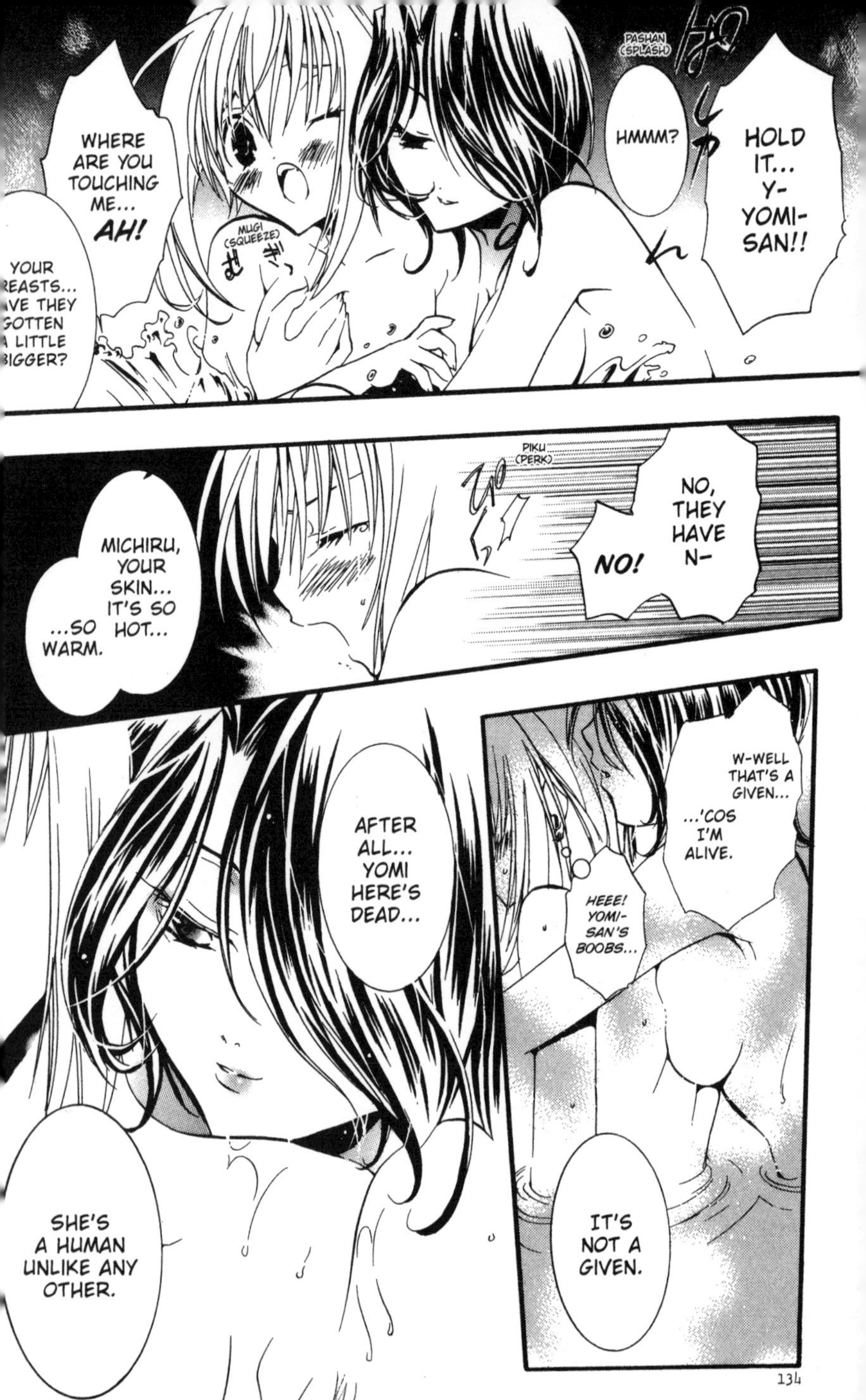
PASHAN (SPLASH)
HOLD IT... Y-YOMI-SAN!!
HMMM?
MUGI (SQUEEZE)
WHERE ARE YOU TOUCHING ME... AH!
YOUR REASTS... AVE THEY GOTTEN A LITTLE BIGGER?
NO, THEY HAVE N- NO!
PIKU (PERK)
MICHIRU, YOUR SKIN... IT'S SO HOT... ...SO WARM.
W-WELL THAT'S A GIVEN...
...'COS I'M ALIVE.
HEEE! YOMI-SAN'S BOOBS...
IT'S NOT A GIVEN.
AFTER ALL... YOMI HERE'S DEAD...
SHE'S A HUMAN UNLIKE ANY OTHER.

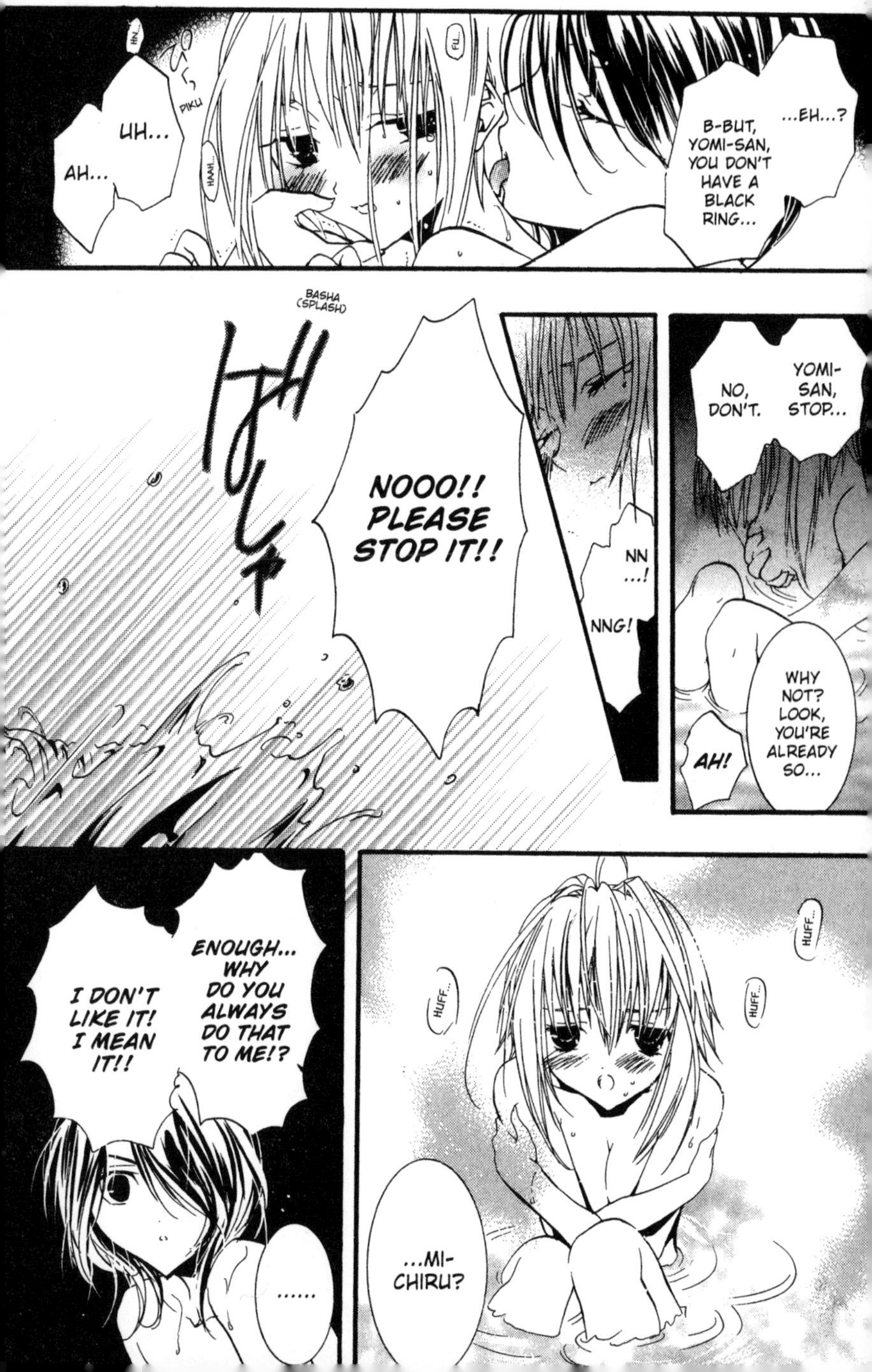

...EH...?
B-BUT, YOMI-SAN, YOU DON'T HAVE A BLACK RING...
FU...
HAAH...
PIKU
UH...
AH...
HN...
YOMI-SAN, STOP...
NO, DON'T.
WHY NOT? LOOK, YOU'RE ALREADY SO...
AH!
NN ...!
NNG!
NOOO!! PLEASE STOP IT!!
BASHA (SPLASH)
HUFF...
HUFF...
HUFF...
...MI-CHIRU?
ENOUGH... WHY DO YOU ALWAYS DO THAT TO ME!?
I DON'T LIKE IT! I MEAN IT!!
......

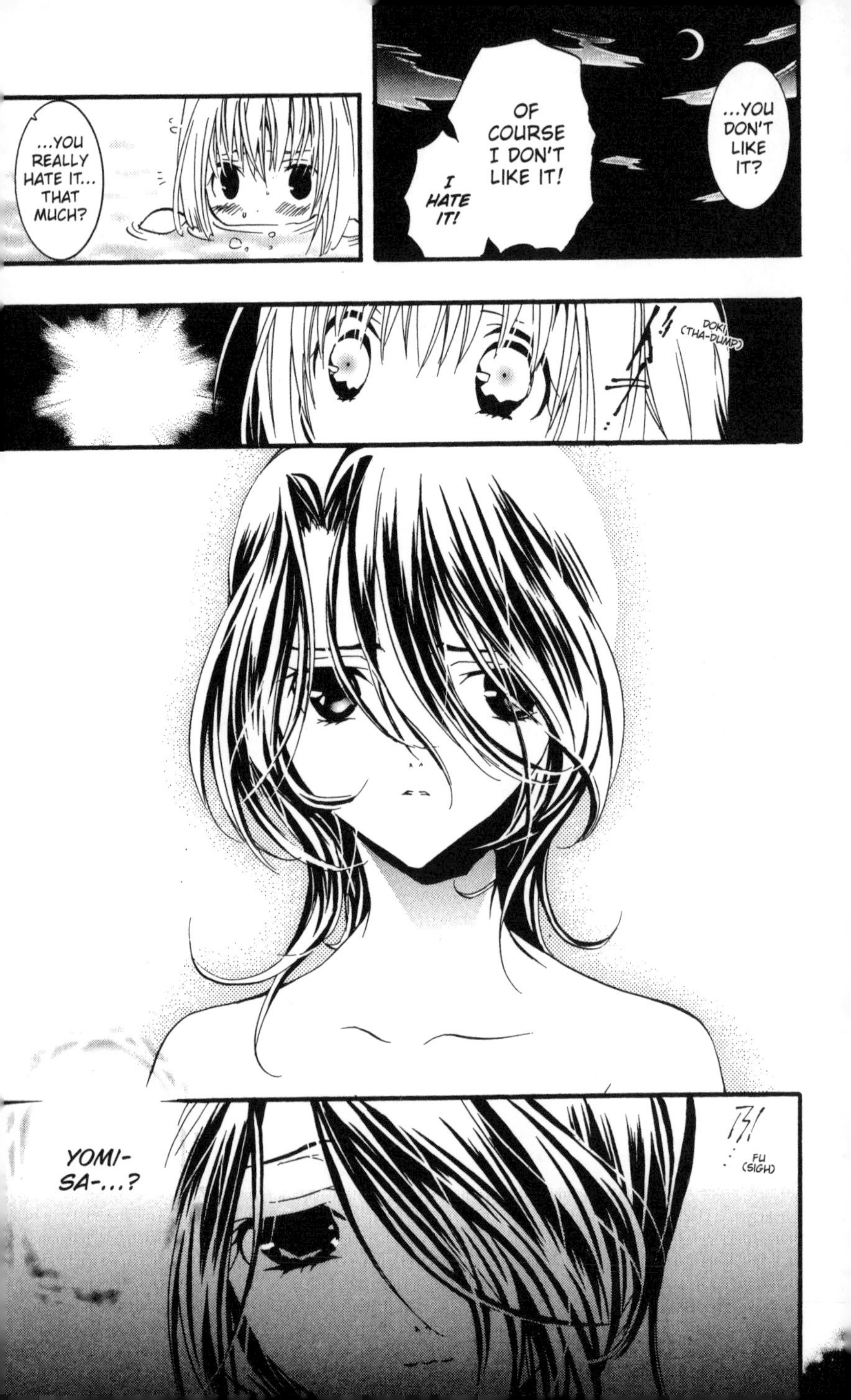
...YOU DON'T LIKE IT?
OF COURSE I DON'T LIKE IT!
I HATE IT!
...YOU REALLY HATE IT... THAT MUCH?
!!
DOKI (THA-DUMP)
FU (SIGH)
YOMI-SA-...?

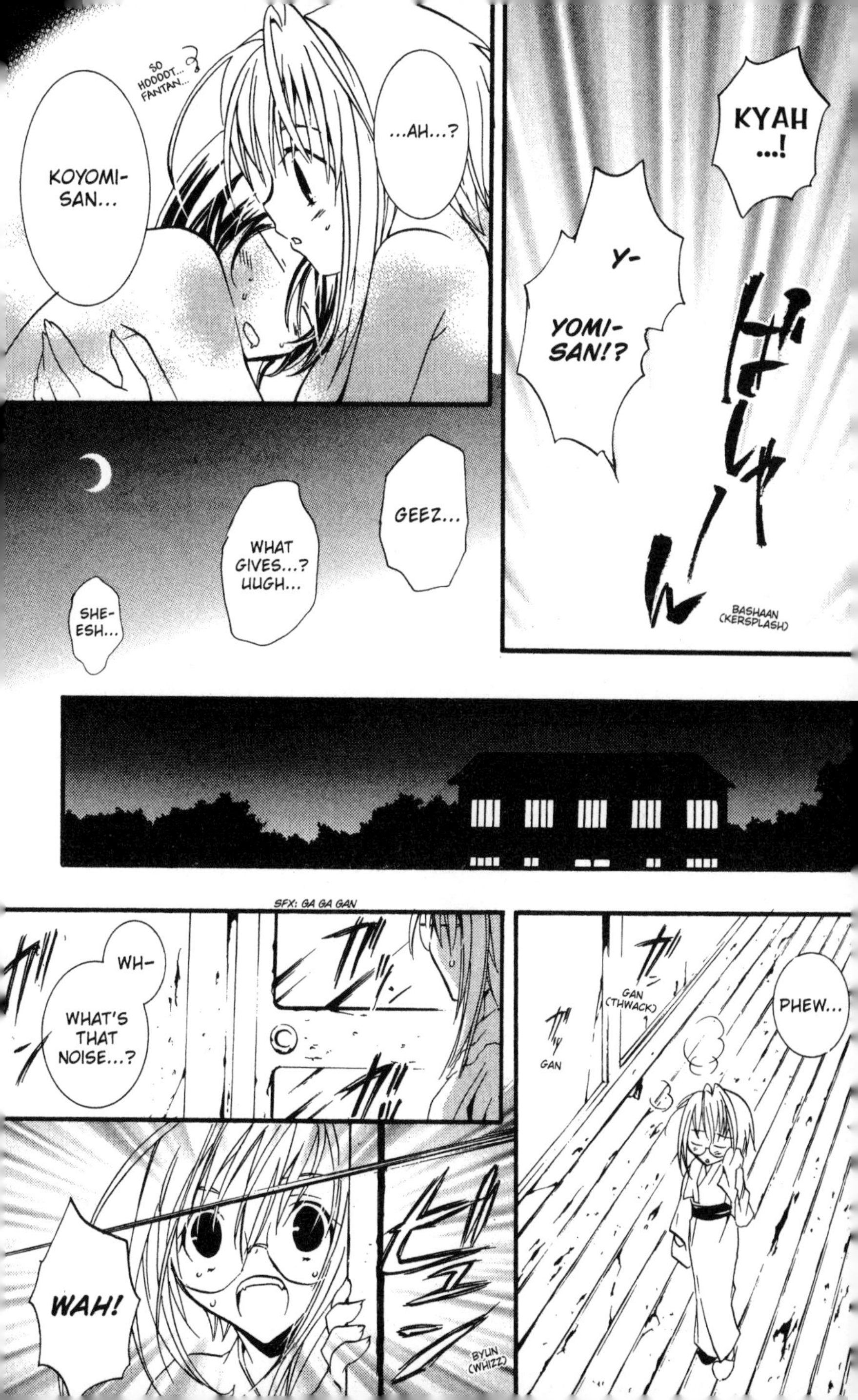
KYAH ...!
Y- YOMI-SAN!?
ばしゃーん
BASHAAN (KERSPLASH)
...AH...?
SO HOOODT... FANTAN...
KOYOMI-SAN...
GEEZ...
WHAT GIVES...? UUGH...
SHE-ESH...
PHEW...
GAN (THWACK)
GAN
SFX: GA GA GAN
WH-
WHAT'S THAT NOISE...?
WAH!
BYUN (WHIZZ)

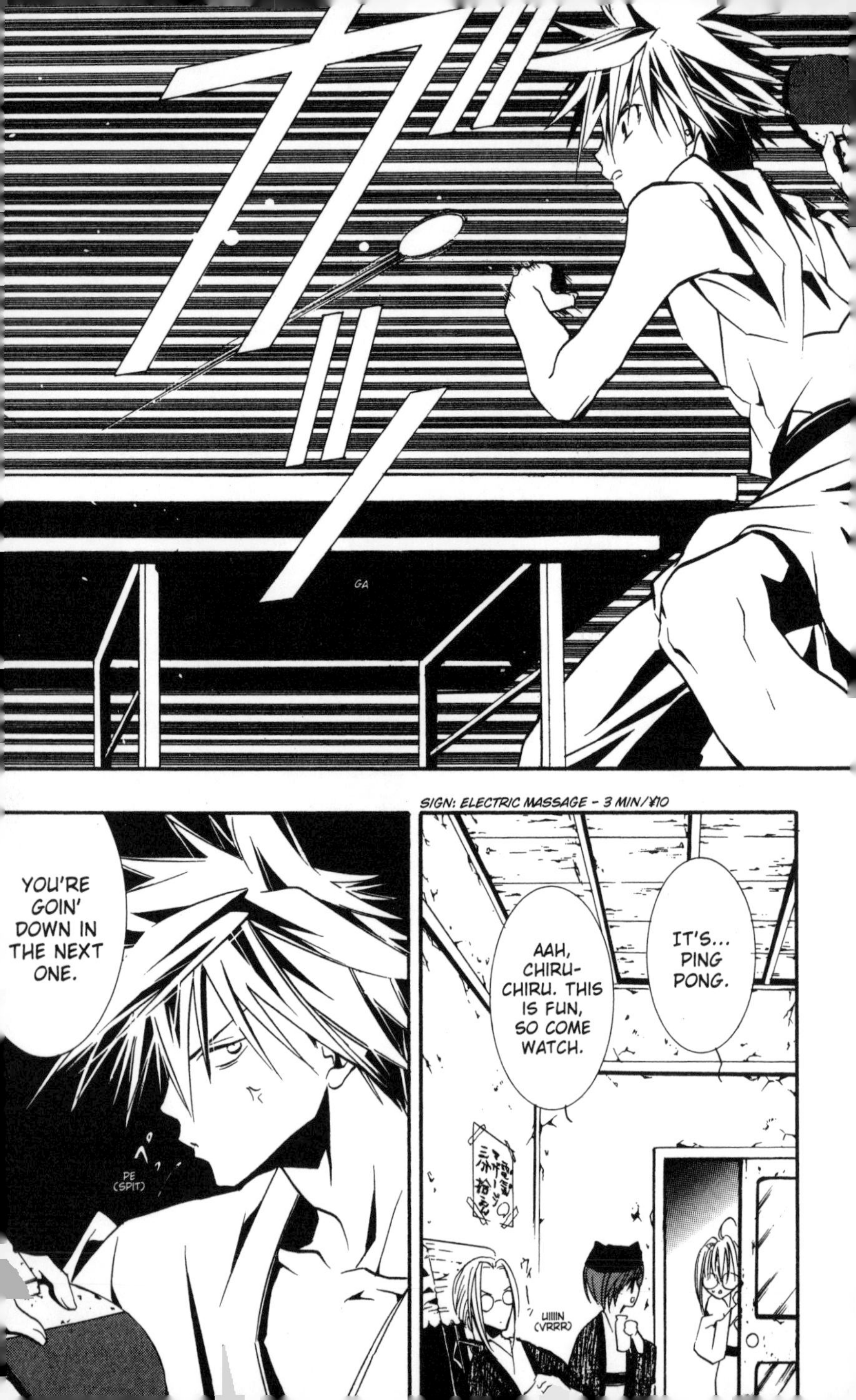
GA
SIGN: ELECTRIC MASSAGE - 3 MIN/¥10
IT'S... PING PONG.
AAH, CHIRU-CHIRU. THIS IS FUN, SO COME WATCH.
UIIIIN (VRRR)
YOU'RE GOIN' DOWN IN THE NEXT ONE.
PE (SPIT)

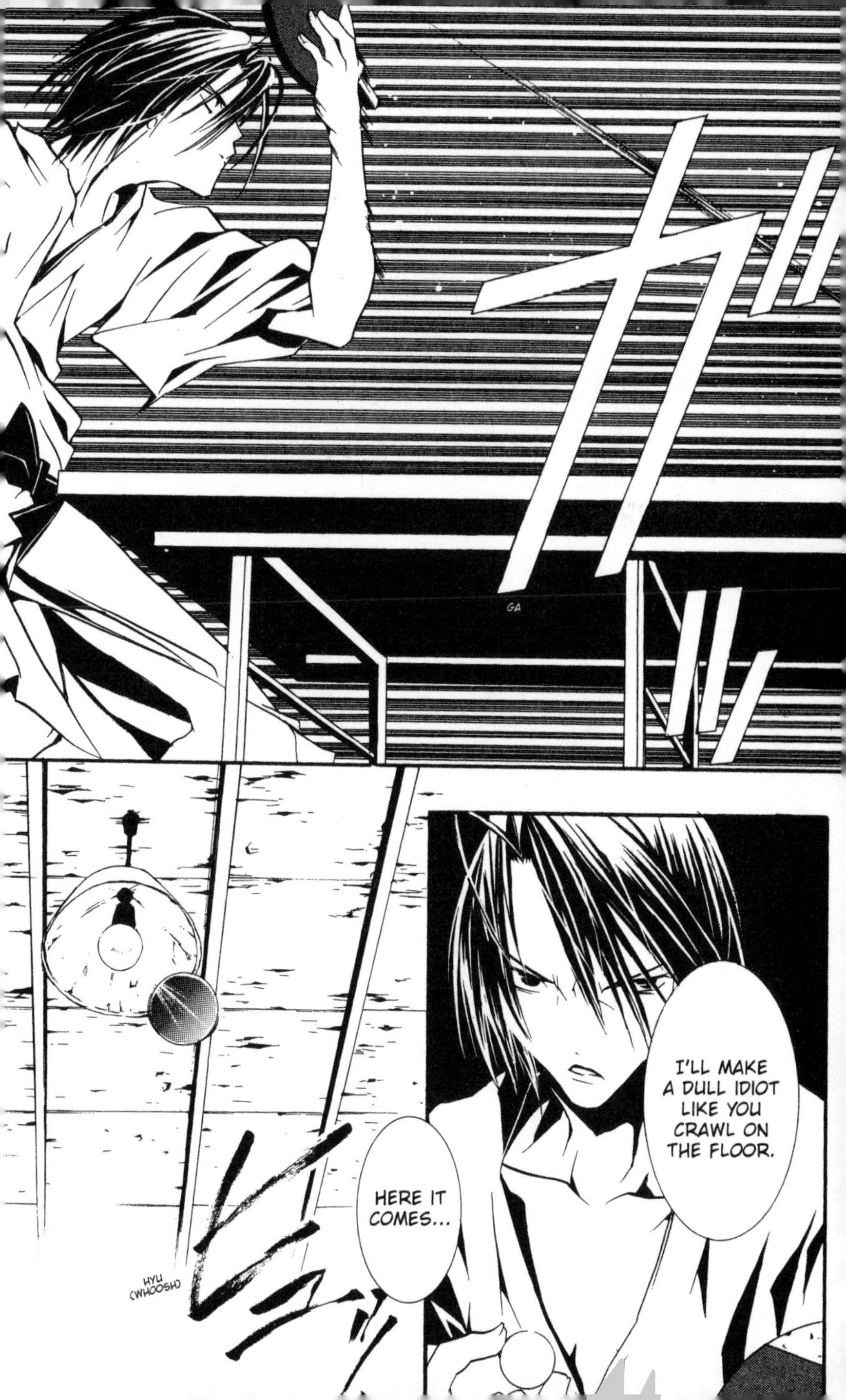
GA
I'LL MAKE A DULL IDIOT LIKE YOU CRAWL ON THE FLOOR.
HERE IT COMES...
HYU (WHOOSH)

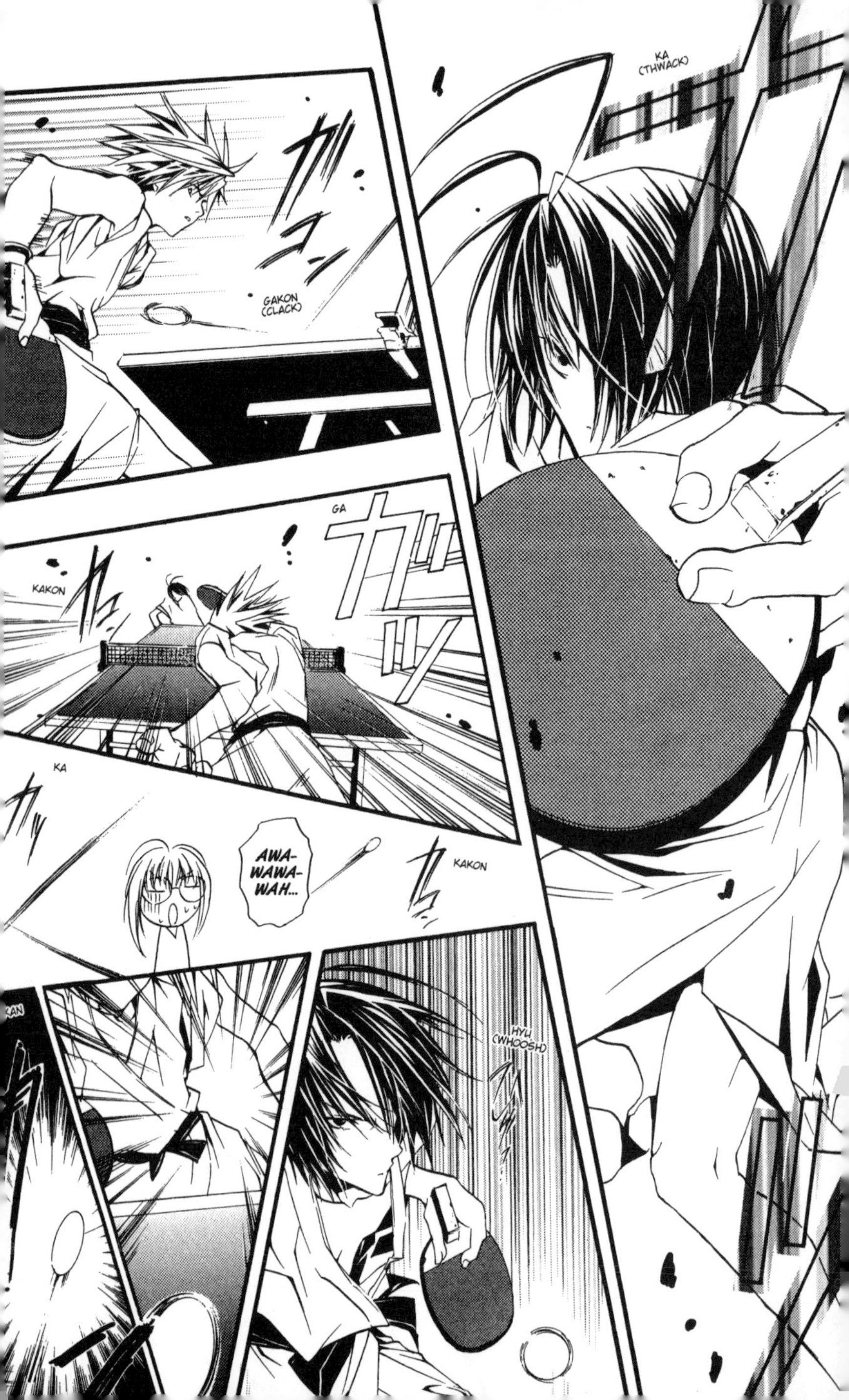
KA (THWACK)
GAKON (CLACK)
GA
KAKON
KAKON
AWA-WAWA-WAWA-WAH...
KA
HYU (WHOOSH)
KAN

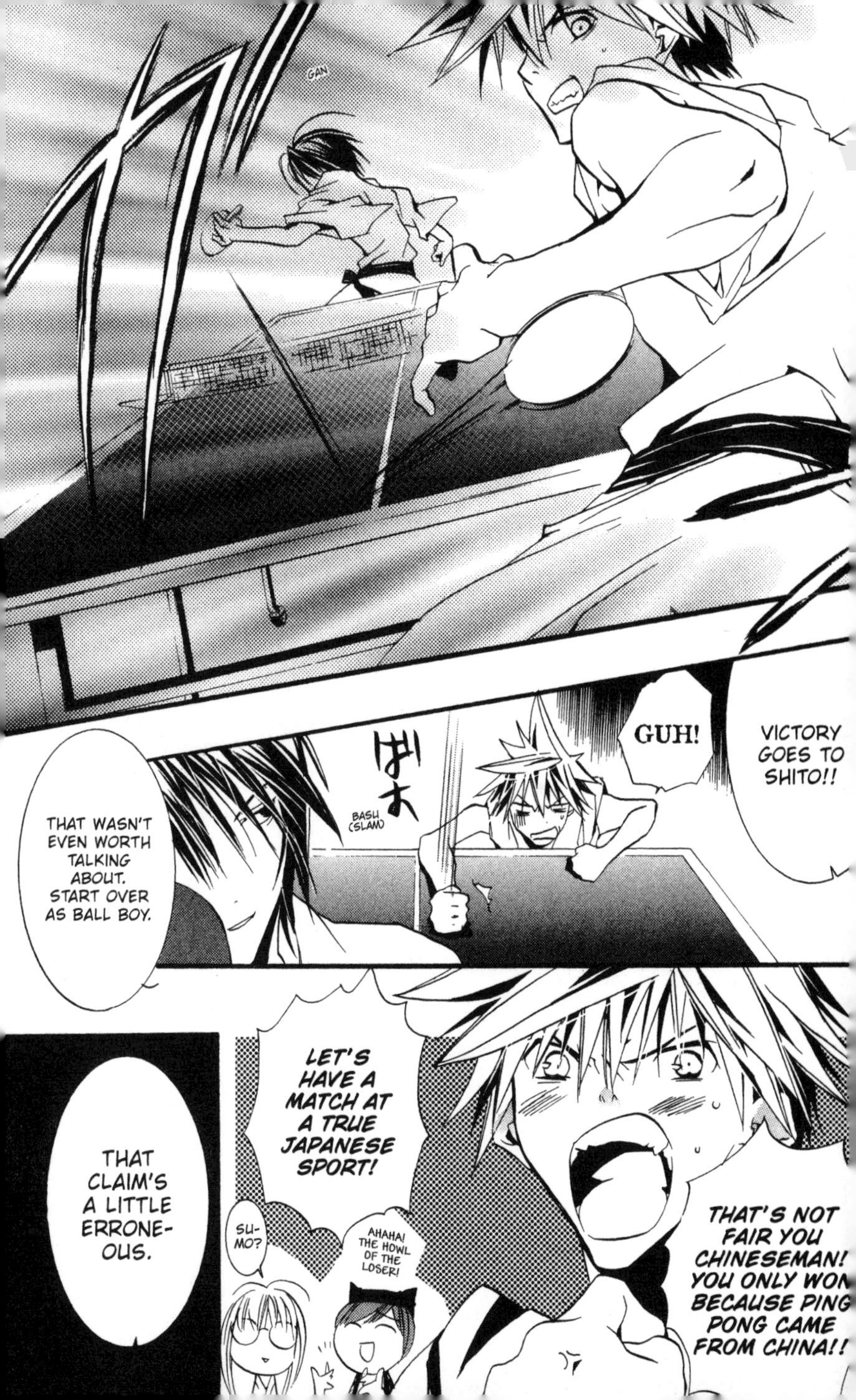
GAN
VICTORY GOES TO SHITO!!
GUH!
BASH (SLAM)
THAT WASN'T EVEN WORTH TALKING ABOUT. START OVER AS BALL BOY.
THAT'S NOT FAIR YOU CHINESEMAN! YOU ONLY WON BECAUSE PING PONG CAME FROM CHINA!!
LET'S HAVE A MATCH AT A TRUE JAPANESE SPORT!
AHAHA! THE HOWL OF THE LOSER!
SU-MO?
THAT CLAIM'S A LITTLE ERRONE-OUS.

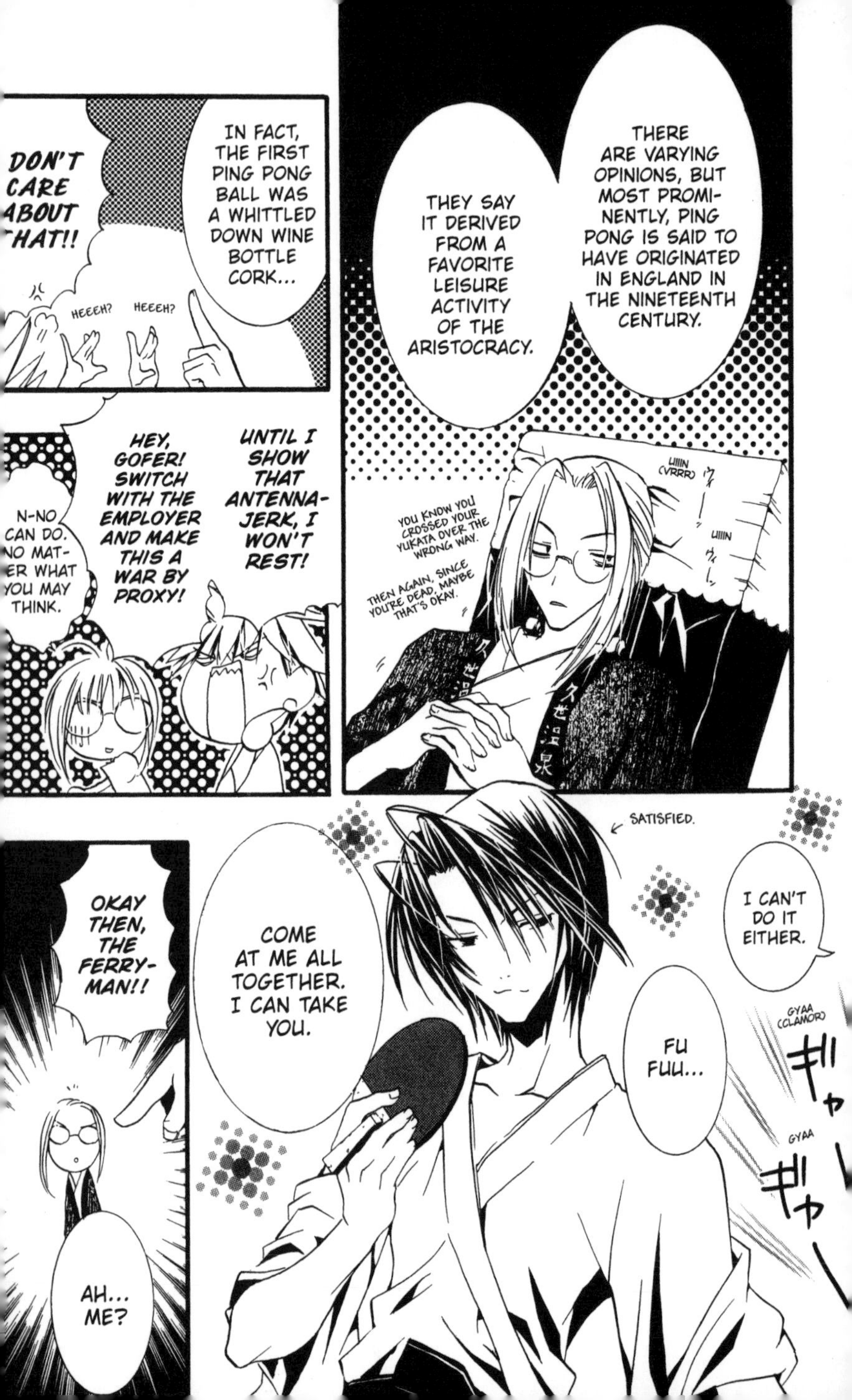
THERE ARE VARYING OPINIONS, BUT MOST PROMINENTLY, PING PONG IS SAID TO HAVE ORIGINATED IN ENGLAND IN THE NINETEENTH CENTURY.
THEY SAY IT DERIVED FROM A FAVORITE LEISURE ACTIVITY OF THE ARISTOCRACY.
UIIIN (VRRR)
UIIIN
YOU KNOW YOU CROSSED YOUR YUKATA OVER THE WRONG WAY.
THEN AGAIN, SINCE YOU'RE DEAD, MAYBE THAT'S OKAY.
IN FACT, THE FIRST PING PONG BALL WAS A WHITTLED DOWN WINE BOTTLE CORK...
DON'T CARE ABOUT HAT!!
HEEEH?
HEEEH?
UNTIL I SHOW THAT ANTENNA-JERK, I WON'T REST!
HEY, GOFER! SWITCH WITH THE EMPLOYER AND MAKE THIS A WAR BY PROXY!
N-NO CAN DO. NO MAT-ER WHAT YOU MAY THINK.
SATISFIED.
I CAN'T DO IT EITHER.
GYAA (CLAMOR)
GYAA
FU FUU...
COME AT ME ALL TOGETHER. I CAN TAKE YOU.
OKAY THEN, THE FERRY-MAN!!
AH... ME?

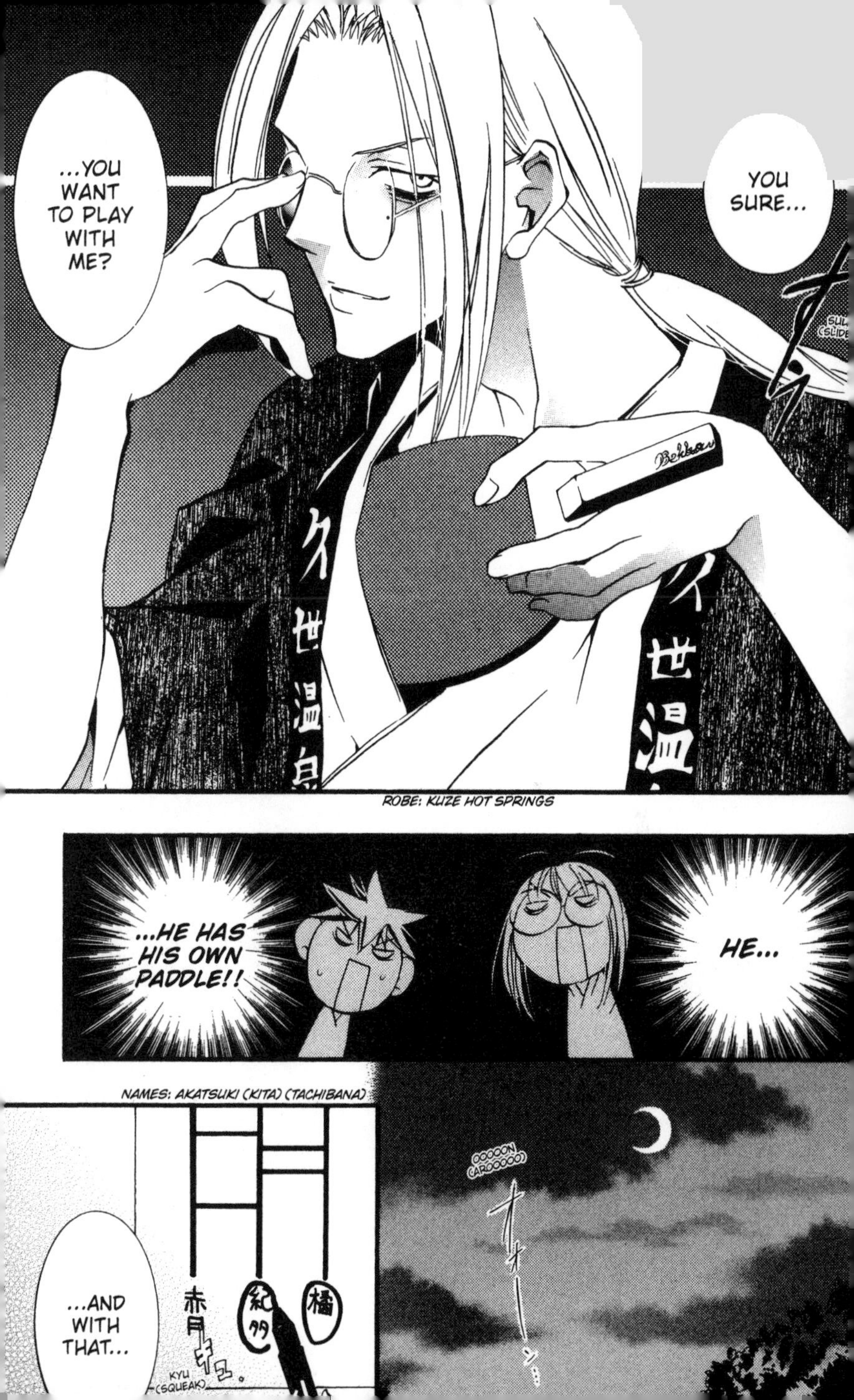
YOU SURE...
...YOU WANT TO PLAY WITH ME?
SUU (SLIDE)
ROBE: KUZE HOT SPRINGS
HE...
...HE HAS HIS OWN PADDLE!!
NAMES: AKATSUKI (KITA) (TACHIBANA)
OOOOON (AROOOOO)
...AND WITH THAT...
KYU (SQUEAK)

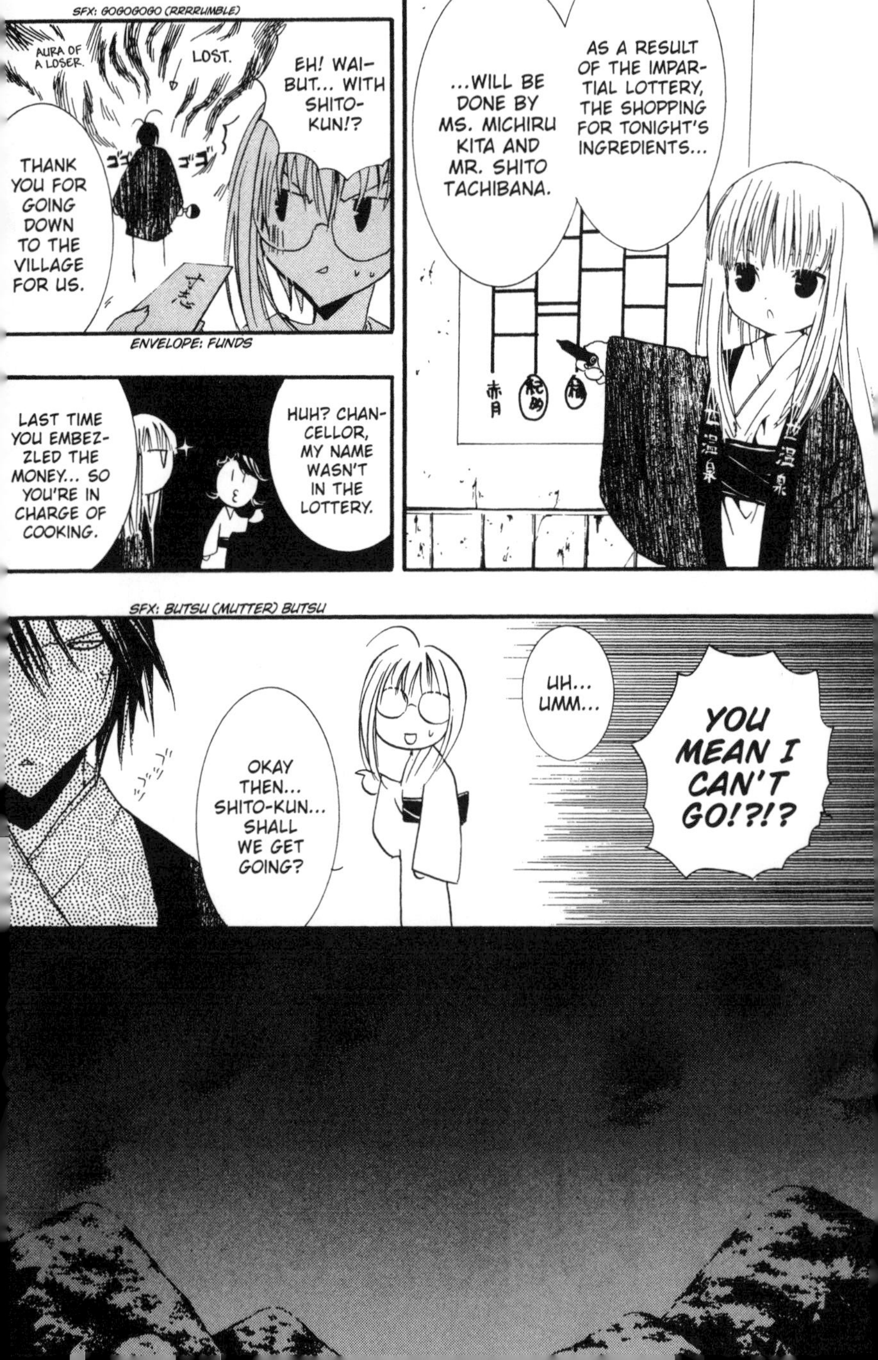
AS A RESULT OF THE IMPAR-TIAL LOTTERY, THE SHOPPING FOR TONIGHT'S INGREDIENTS...
...WILL BE DONE BY MS. MICHIRU KITA AND MR. SHITO TACHIBANA.
SFX: GOGOGOGO (RRRRUMBLE)
EH! WAI- BUT... WITH SHITO-KUN!?
LOST.
AURA OF A LOSER.
THANK YOU FOR GOING DOWN TO THE VILLAGE FOR US.
ENVELOPE: FUNDS
HUH? CHAN-CELLOR, MY NAME WASN'T IN THE LOTTERY.
LAST TIME YOU EMBEZ-ZLED THE MONEY... SO YOU'RE IN CHARGE OF COOKING.
SFX: BUTSU (MUTTER) BUTSU
YOU MEAN I CAN'T GO!?!?
UH... UMM...
OKAY THEN... SHITO-KUN... SHALL WE GET GOING?

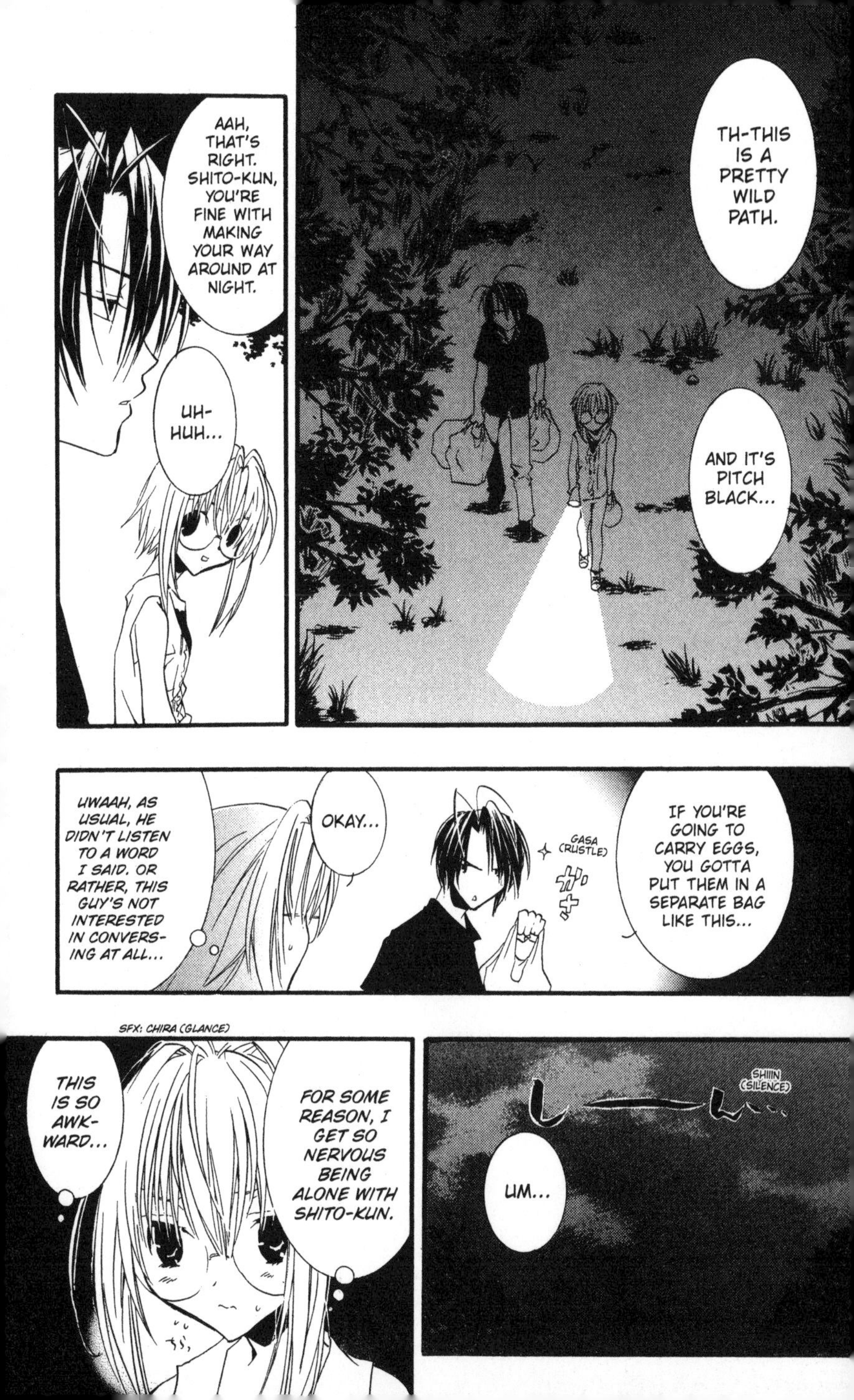
TH-THIS IS A PRETTY WILD PATH.
AND IT'S PITCH BLACK...
AAH, THAT'S RIGHT. SHITO-KUN, YOU'RE FINE WITH MAKING YOUR WAY AROUND AT NIGHT.
UH-HUH...
IF YOU'RE GOING TO CARRY EGGS, YOU GOTTA PUT THEM IN A SEPARATE BAG LIKE THIS...
GASA (RUSTLE)
OKAY...
UWAAH, AS USUAL, HE DIDN'T LISTEN TO A WORD I SAID. OR RATHER, THIS GUY'S NOT INTERESTED IN CONVERSING AT ALL...
SHIIN (SILENCE)
UM...
SFX: CHIRA (GLANCE)
FOR SOME REASON, I GET SO NERVOUS BEING ALONE WITH SHITO-KUN.
THIS IS SO AWKWARD...

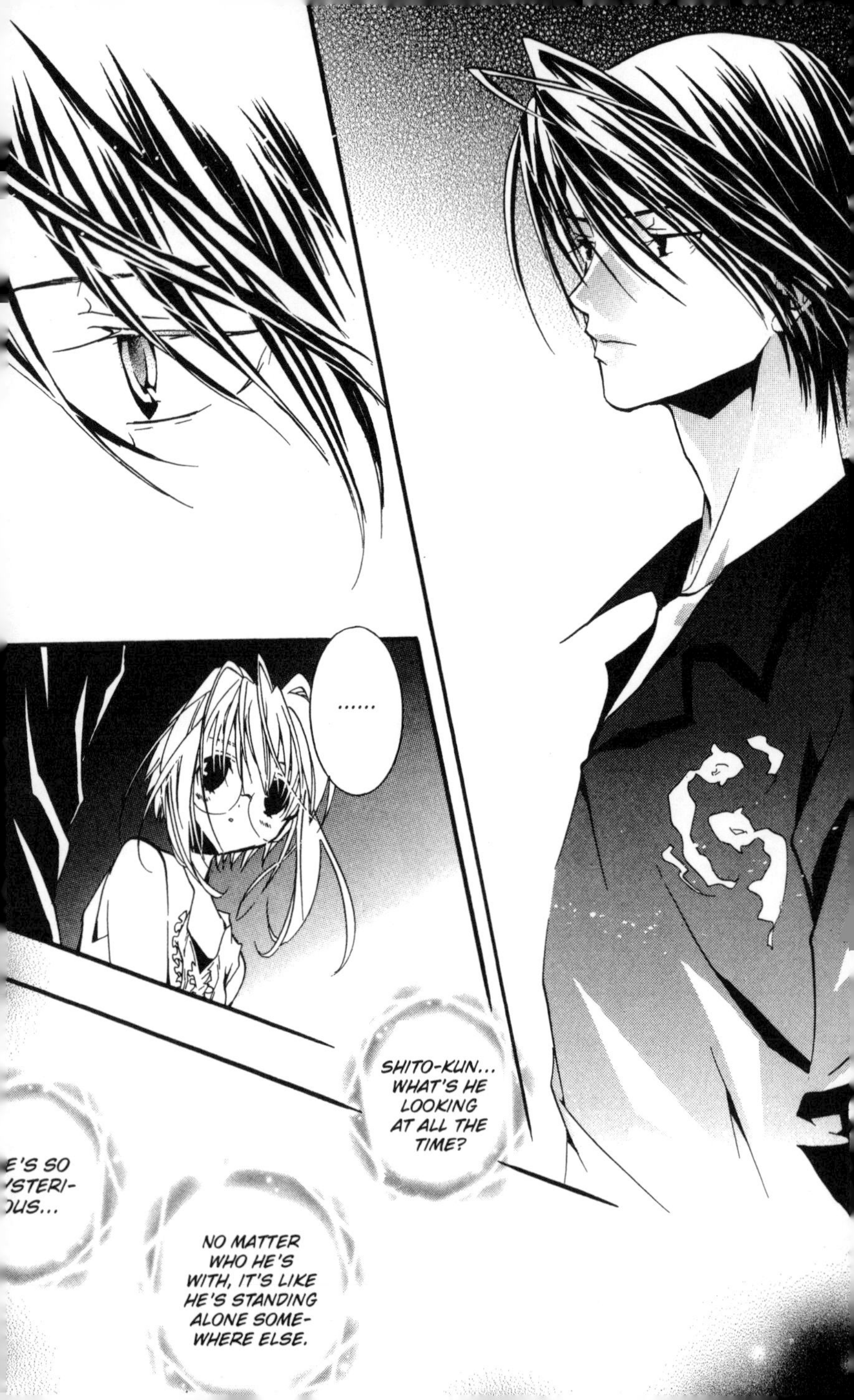
SHITO-KUN... WHAT'S HE LOOKING AT ALL THE TIME?
......
E'S SO YSTERI-OUS...
NO MATTER WHO HE'S WITH, IT'S LIKE HE'S STANDING ALONE SOME-WHERE ELSE.

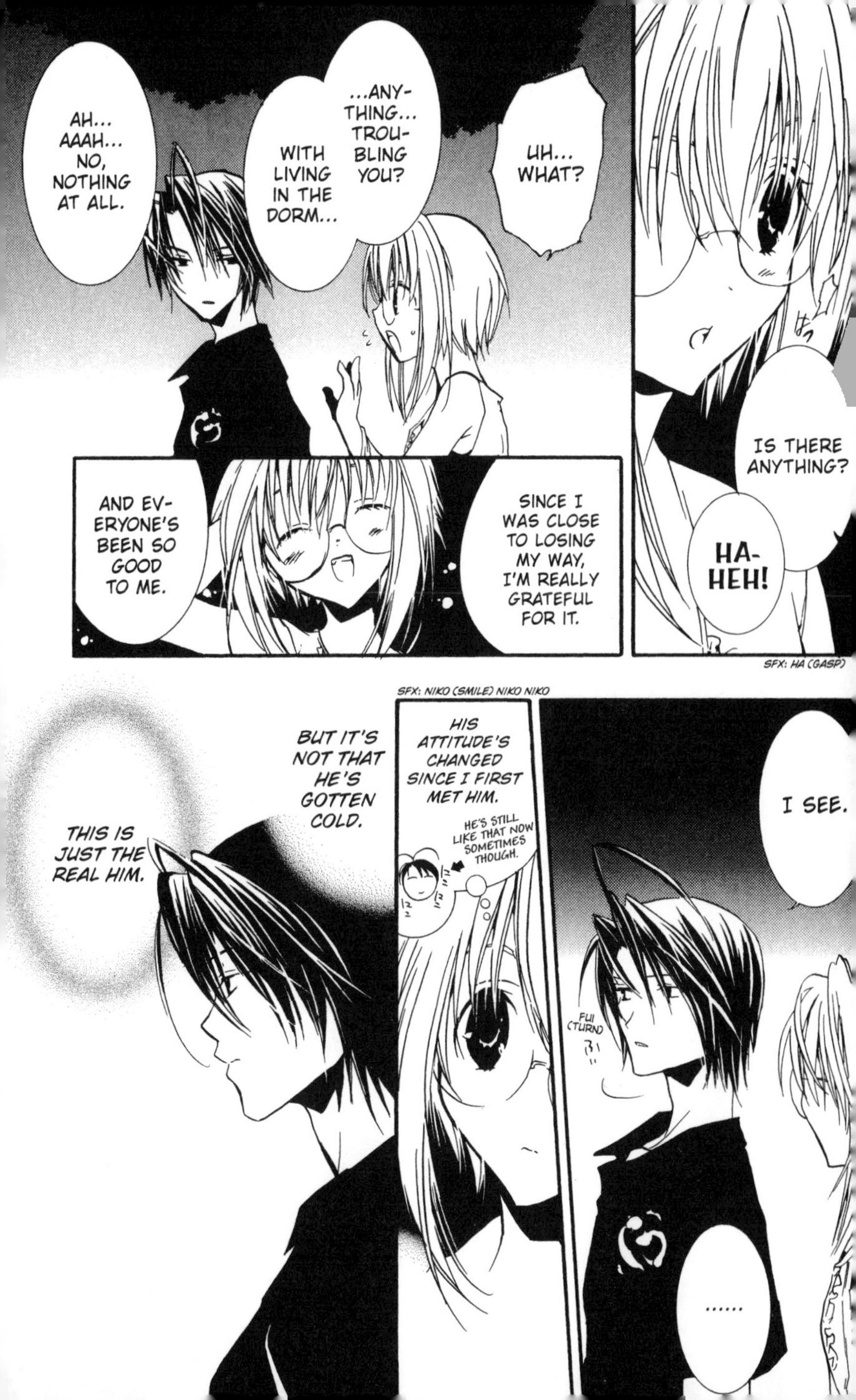
IS THERE ANYTHING?
HA-HEH!
SFX: HA (GASP)
UH... WHAT?
WITH LIVING IN THE DORM... ...ANY-THING... TROU-BLING YOU?
AH... AAAH... NO, NOTHING AT ALL.
SINCE I WAS CLOSE TO LOSING MY WAY, I'M REALLY GRATEFUL FOR IT.
AND EV-ERYONE'S BEEN SO GOOD TO ME.
SFX: NIKO (SMILE) NIKO NIKO
I SEE.
FUI (TURN)
......
HIS ATTITUDE'S CHANGED SINCE I FIRST MET HIM.
HE'S STILL LIKE THAT NOW SOMETIMES THOUGH.
BUT IT'S NOT THAT HE'S GOTTEN COLD.
THIS IS JUST THE REAL HIM.

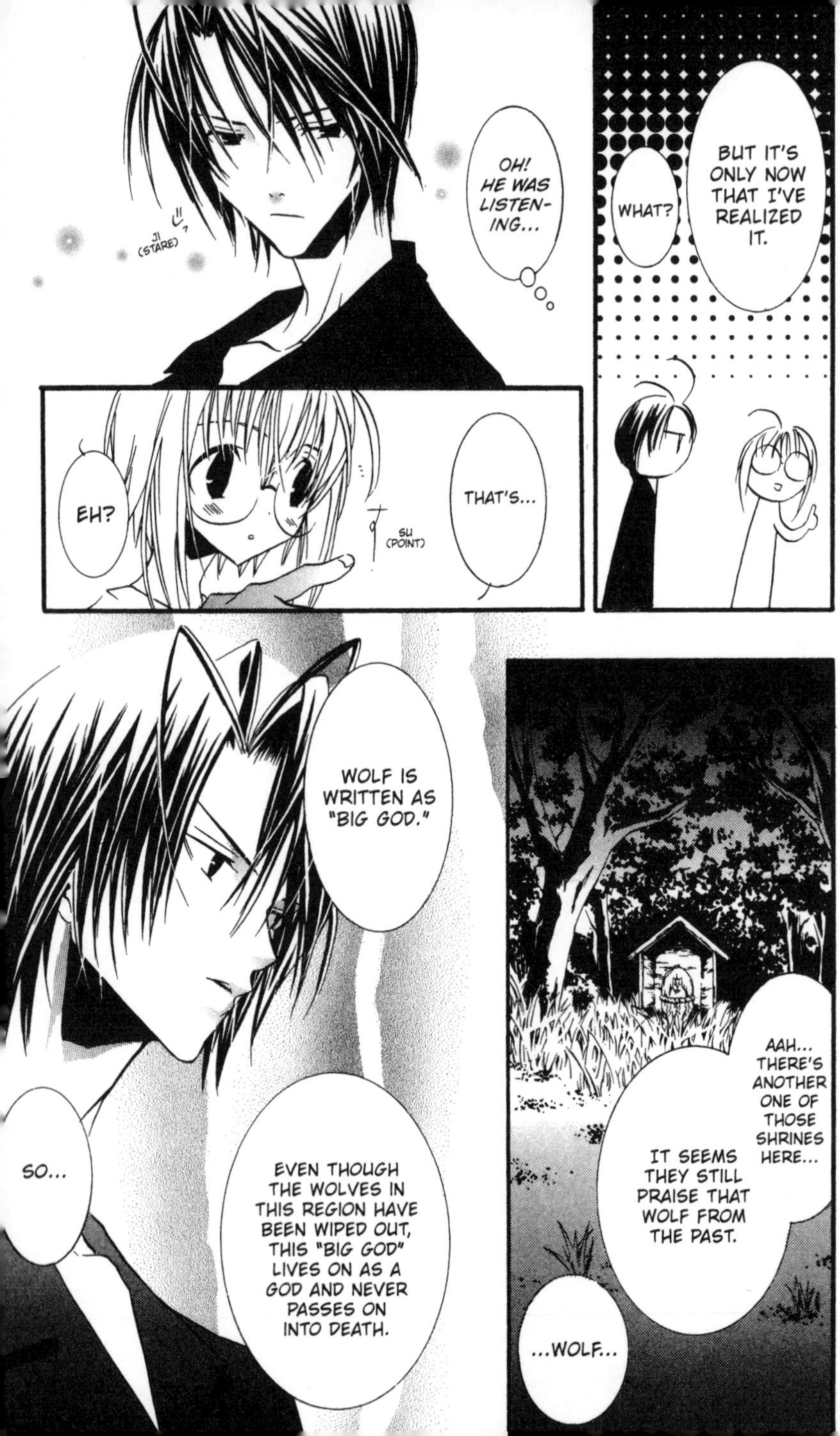
BUT IT'S ONLY NOW THAT I'VE REALIZED IT.
WHAT?
OH! HE WAS LISTENING...
JI (STARE)
THAT'S...
SU (POINT)
EH?
AAH... THERE'S ANOTHER ONE OF THOSE SHRINES HERE...
IT SEEMS THEY STILL PRAISE THAT WOLF FROM THE PAST.
...WOLF...
WOLF IS WRITTEN AS "BIG GOD."
EVEN THOUGH THE WOLVES IN THIS REGION HAVE BEEN WIPED OUT, THIS "BIG GOD" LIVES ON AS A GOD AND NEVER PASSES ON INTO DEATH.
SO...

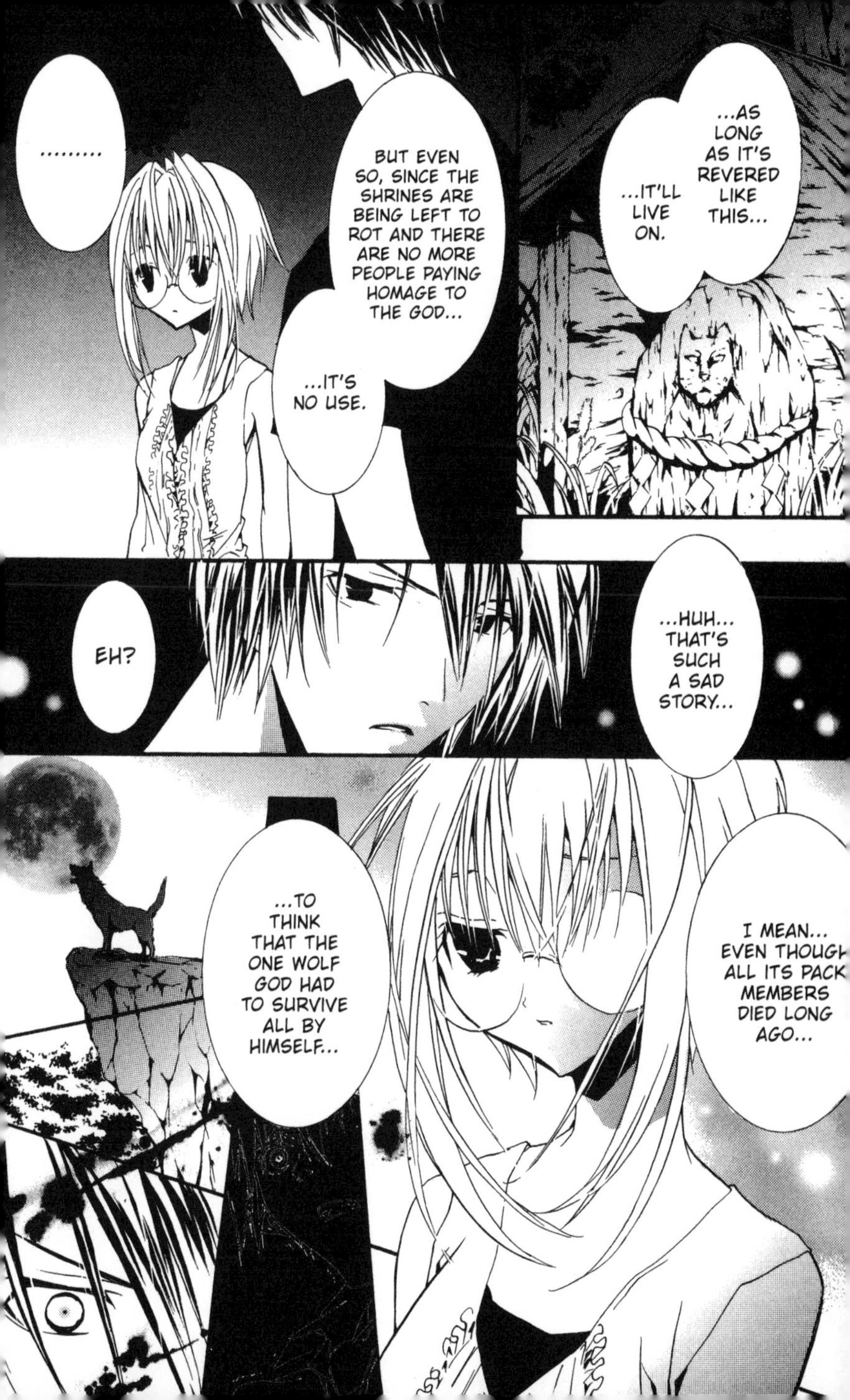
...AS LONG AS IT'S REVERED LIKE THIS...
...IT'LL LIVE ON.
BUT EVEN SO, SINCE THE SHRINES ARE BEING LEFT TO ROT AND THERE ARE NO MORE PEOPLE PAYING HOMAGE TO THE GOD...
...IT'S NO USE.
....
...HUH... THAT'S SUCH A SAD STORY...
EH?
I MEAN... EVEN THOUG ALL ITS PACK MEMBERS DIED LONG AGO...
...TO THINK THAT THE ONE WOLF GOD HAD TO SURVIVE ALL BY HIMSELF...

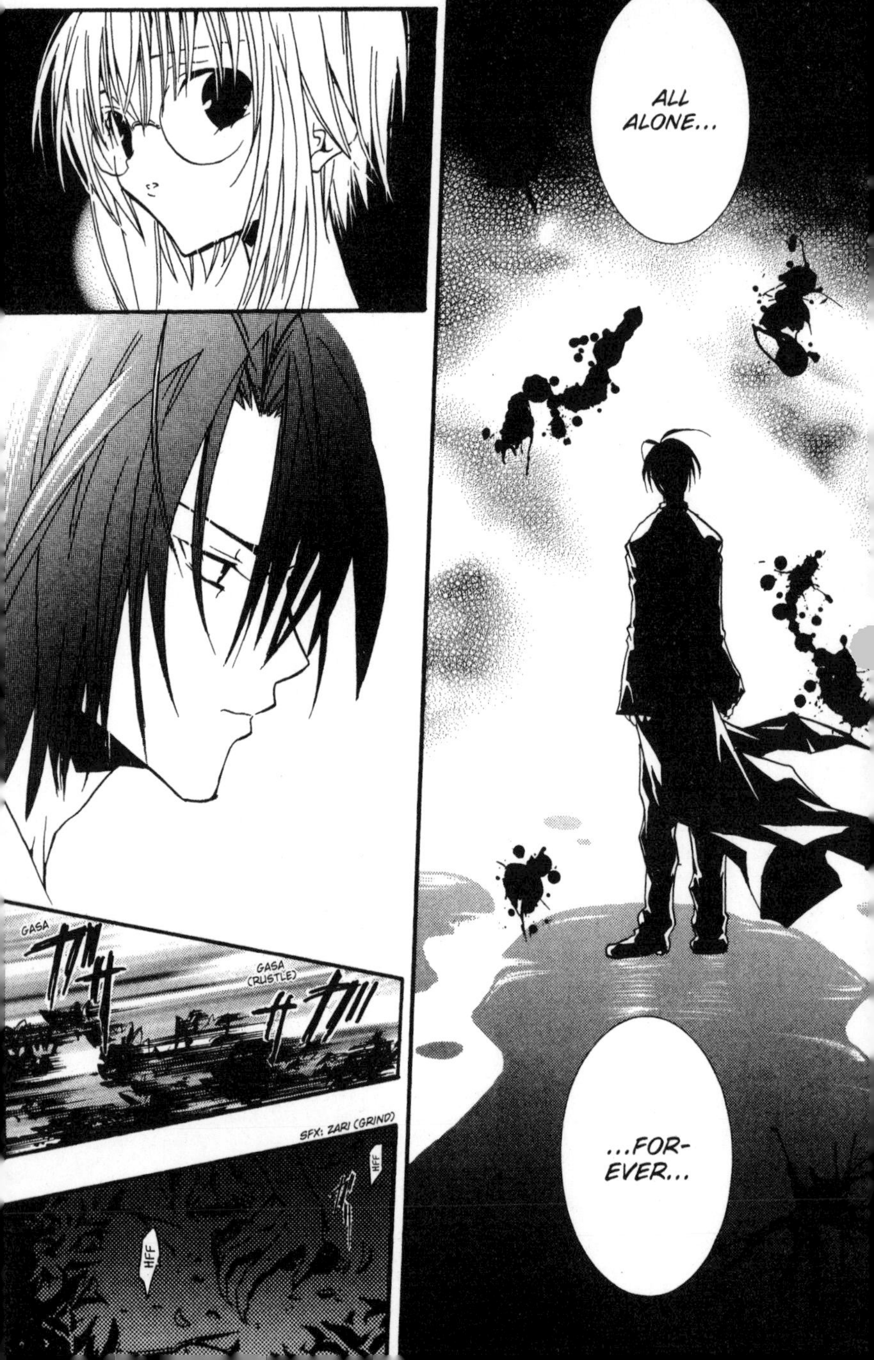
ALL ALONE...
...FOR-EVER...
GASA
GASA (RUSTLE)
SFX: ZARI (GRIND)
HFF
HFF

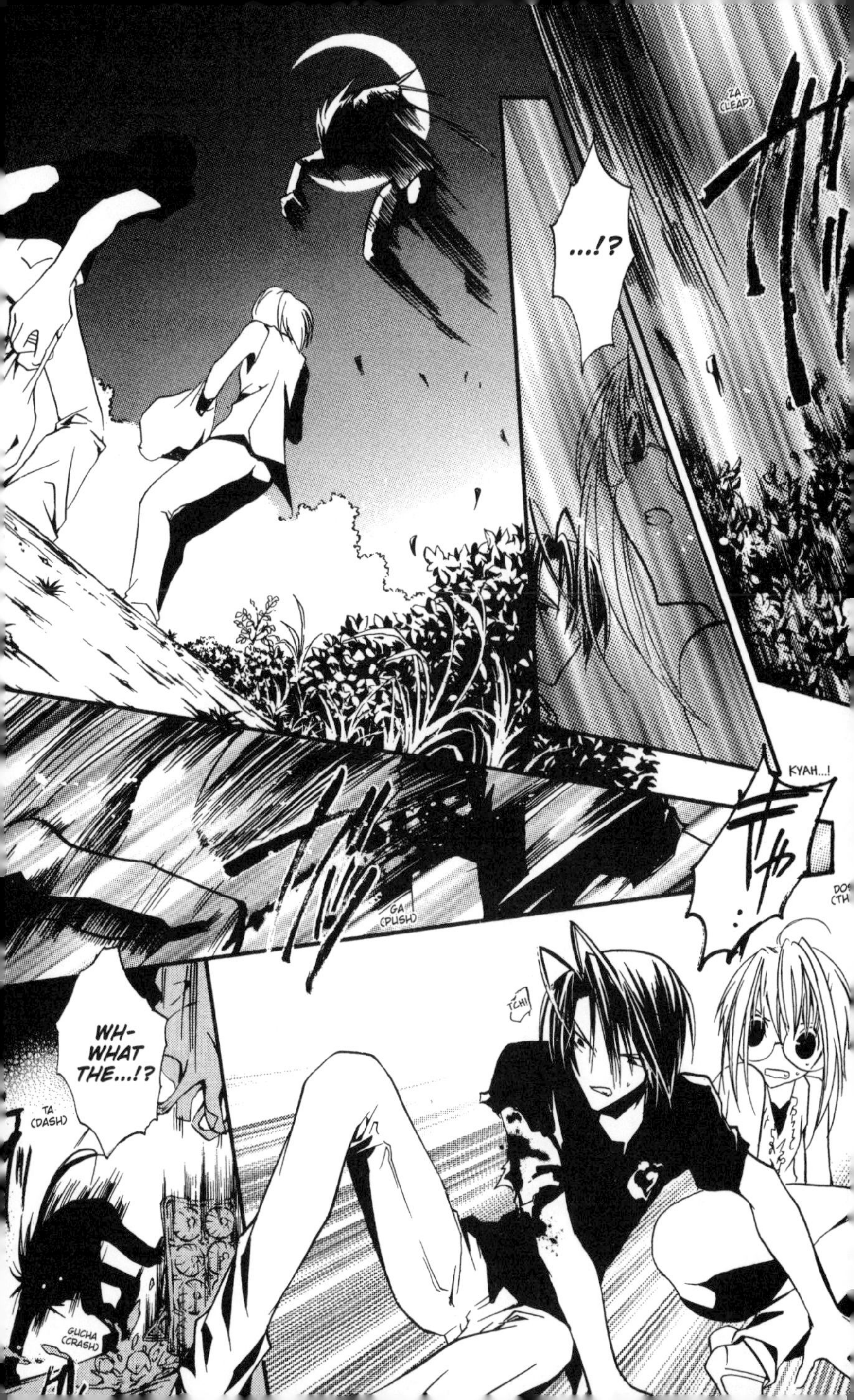
ZA (LEAP)
...!?
KYAH...!
GA (PUSH)
TCH!
WH- WHAT THE...!?
TA (DASH)
GUCHA (CRASH)

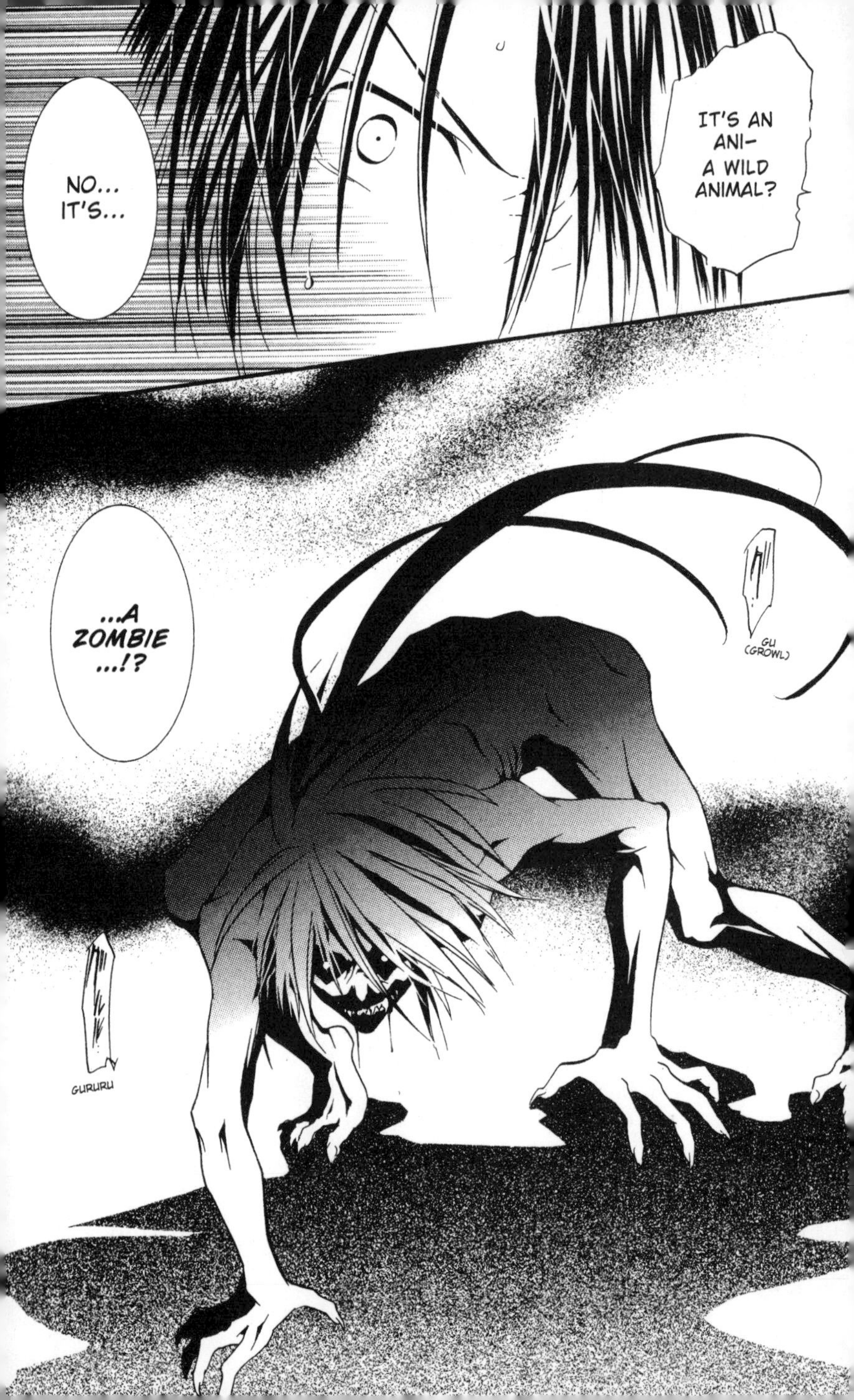
IT'S AN ANI- A WILD ANIMAL?
NO... IT'S...
GU (GROWL)
...A ZOMBIE ...!?
GURURU

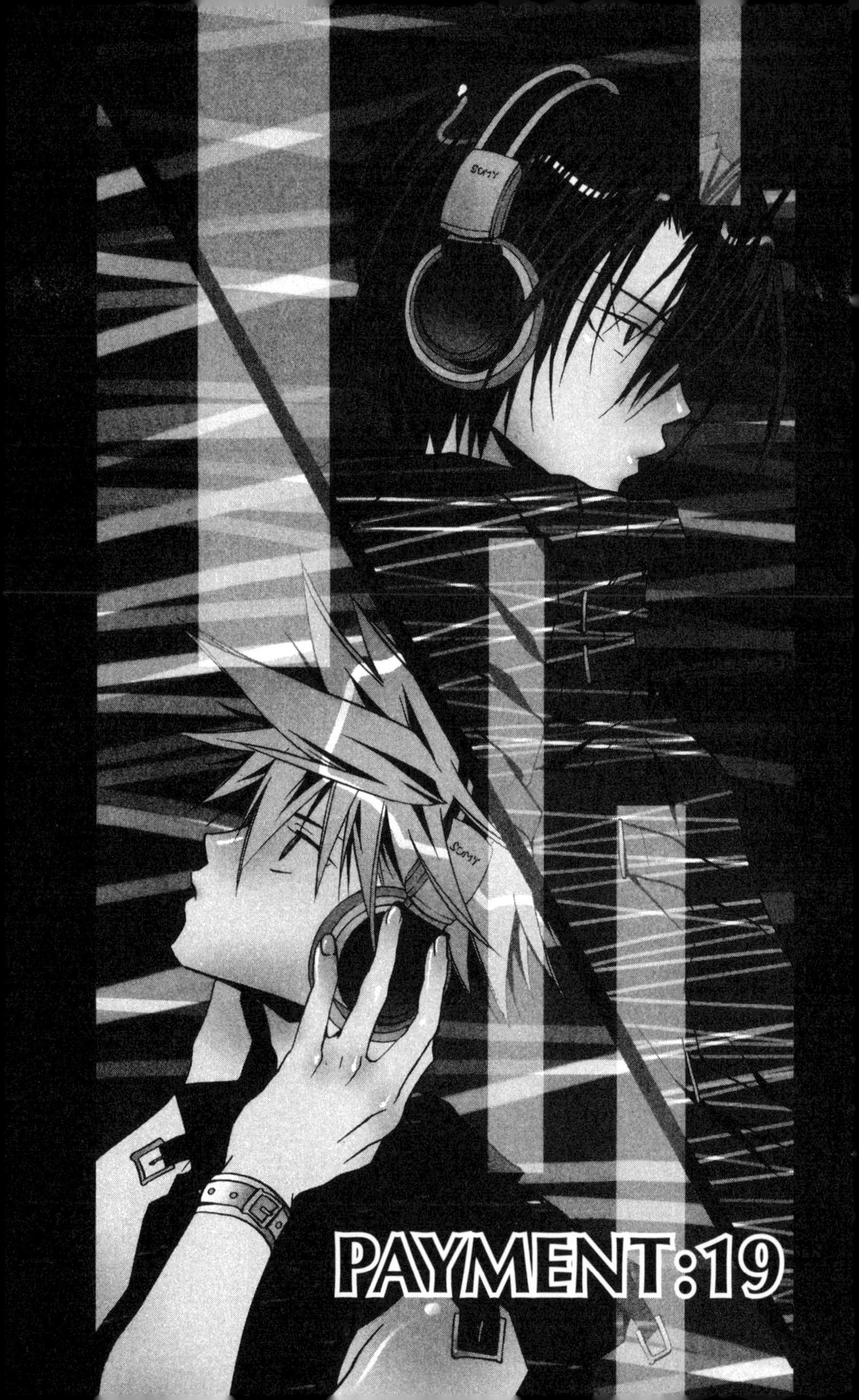
PAYMENT:19

ZOMBIE-LOAN MANIAX-DX

CHIKA AKATSUKI

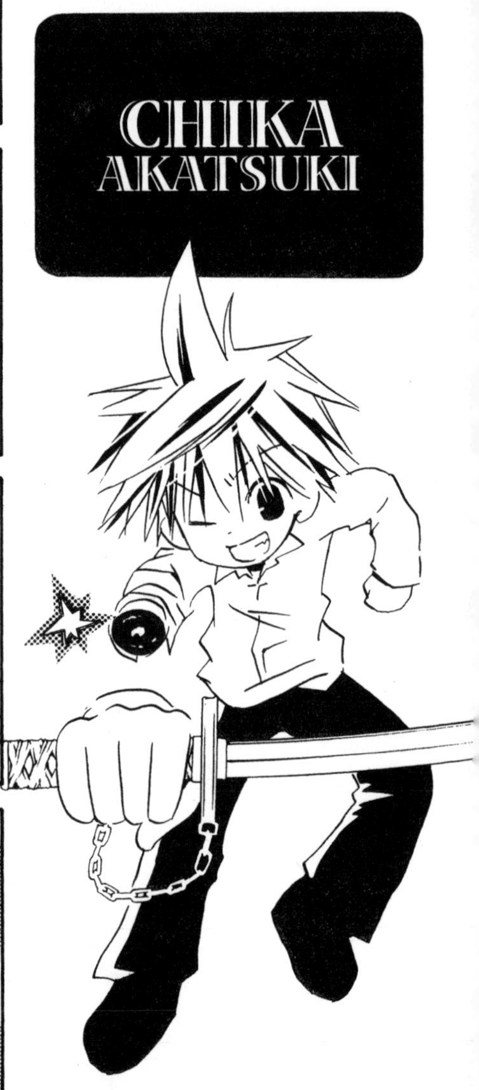

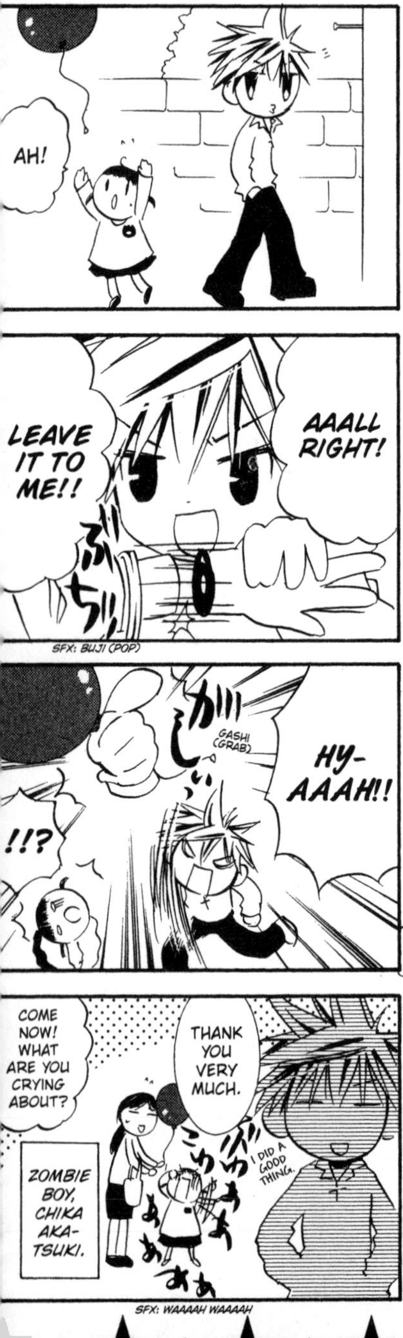
AH!
AAALL RIGHT!
LEAVE IT TO ME!!
SFX: BUJI (POP)
HY-AAAH!!
GASHI (GRAB)
!!?
I DID A GOOD THING.
THANK YOU VERY MUCH.
COME NOW! WHAT ARE YOU CRYING ABOUT?
ZOMBIE BOY, CHIKA AKA-TSUKI.
SFX: WAAAAH WAAAAH

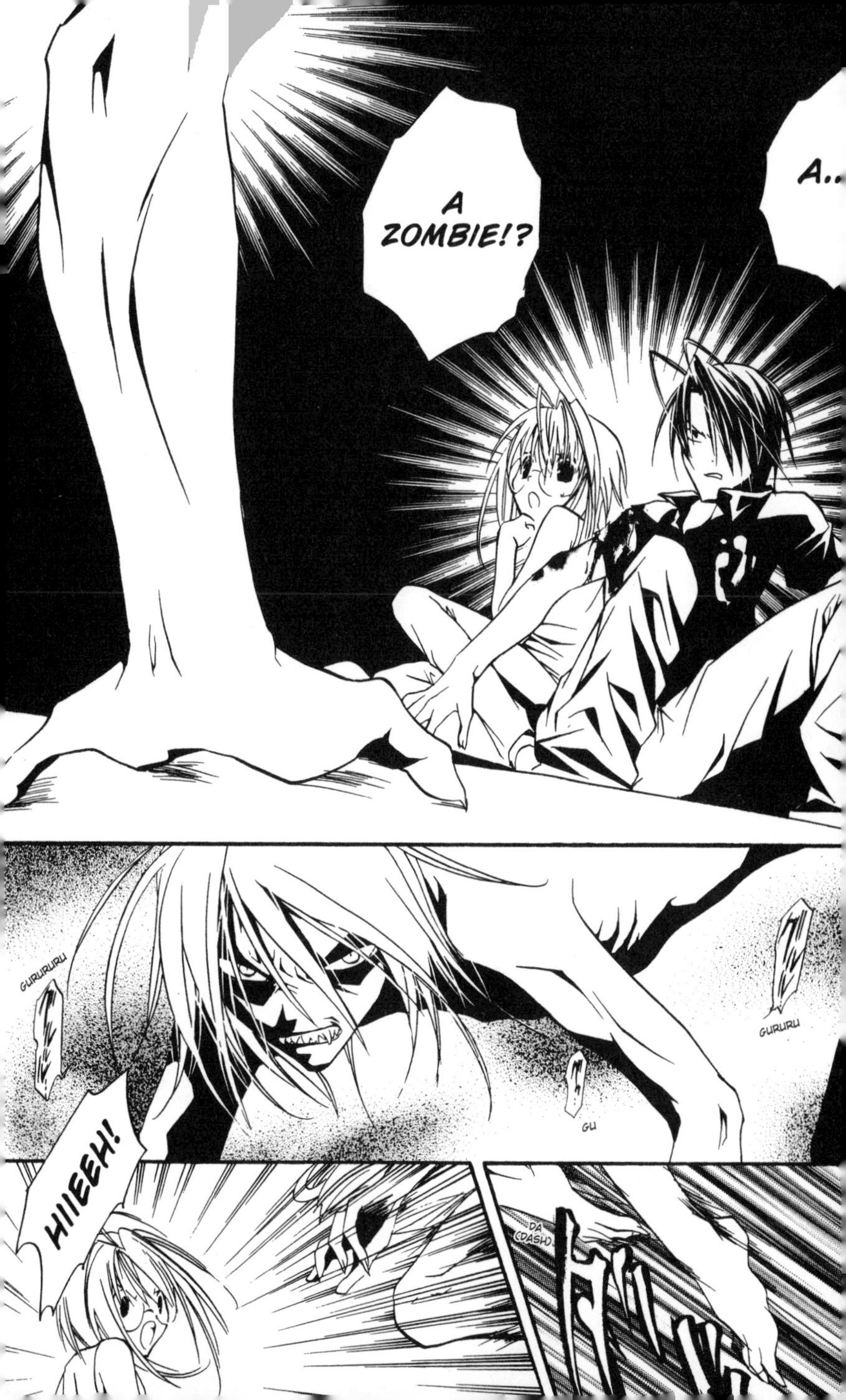
A..
A ZOMBIE!?
GURURU
GU
GURURURU
DA (DASH)
HIIEEH!

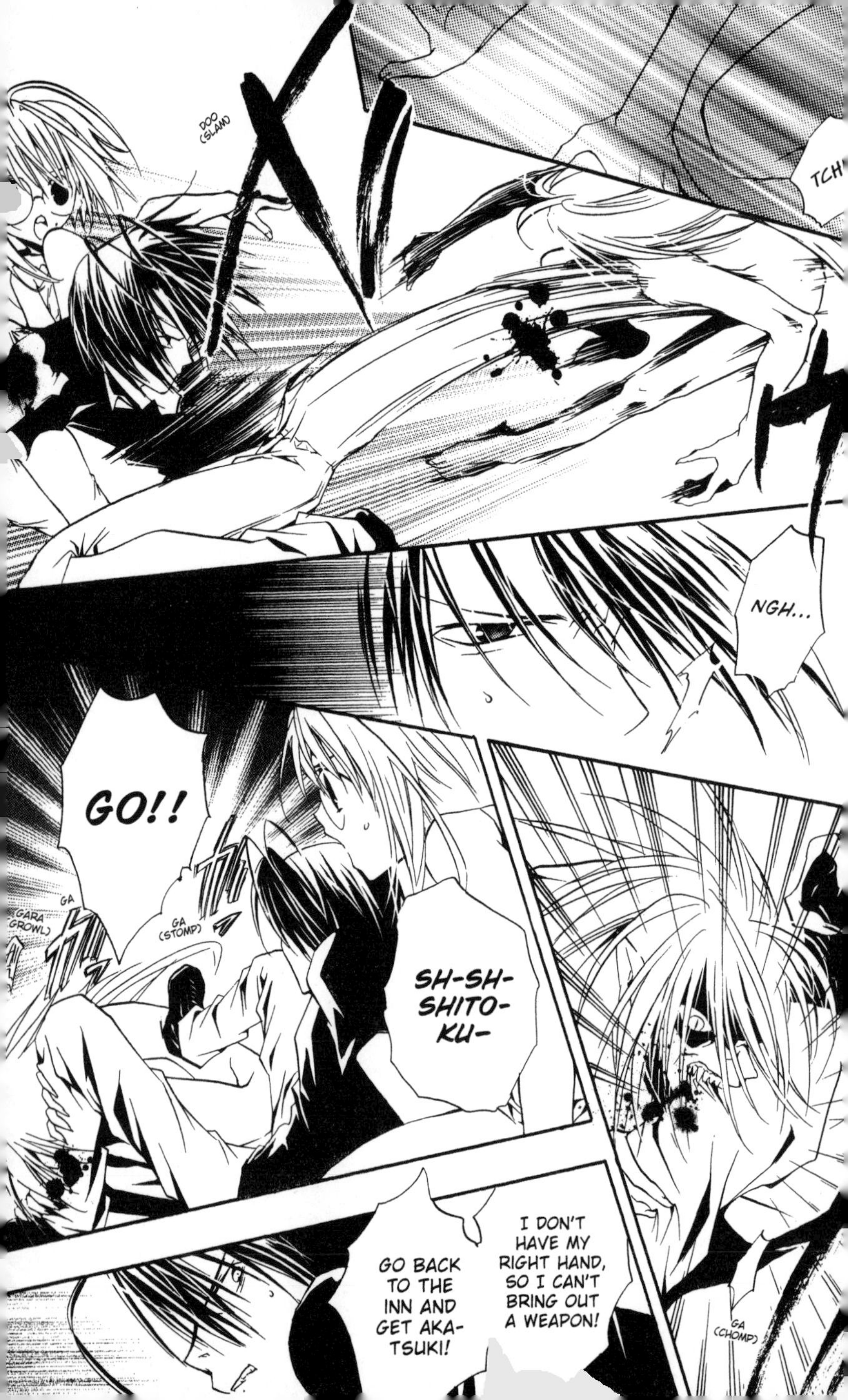
TCH
DOO (SLAM)
NGH...
GA (CHOMP)
SH-SH-SHITOKU-
GO!!
GA (STOMP)
GA (GARA GROWL)
I DON'T HAVE MY RIGHT HAND, SO I CAN'T BRING OUT A WEAPON!
GO BACK TO THE INN AND GET AKATSUKI!

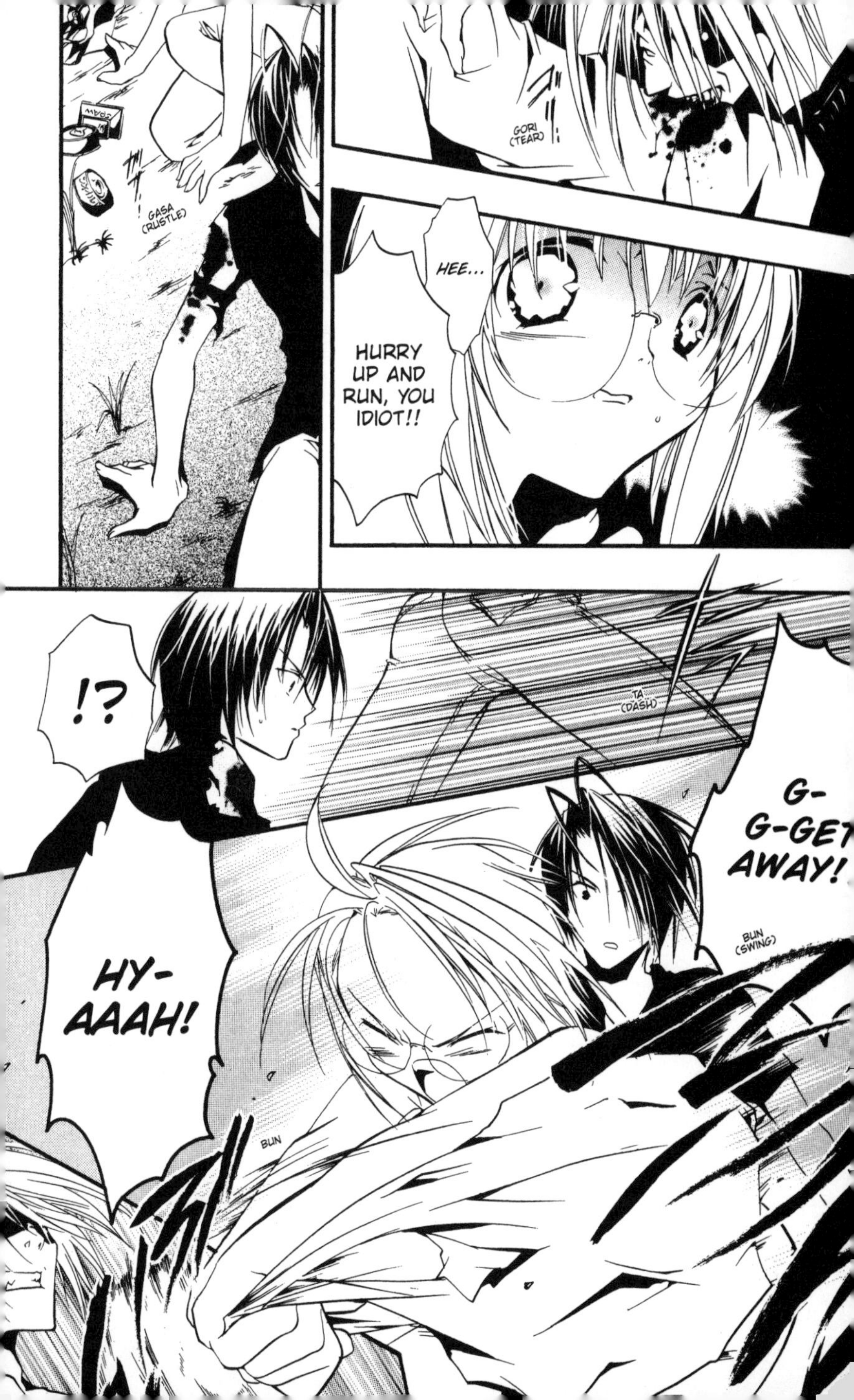
GORI (TEAR)
HEE...
HURRY UP AND RUN, YOU IDIOT!!
GASA (RUSTLE)
G- G-GET AWAY!
TA (DASH)
!?
BUN (SWING)
HY-AAAH!
BUN

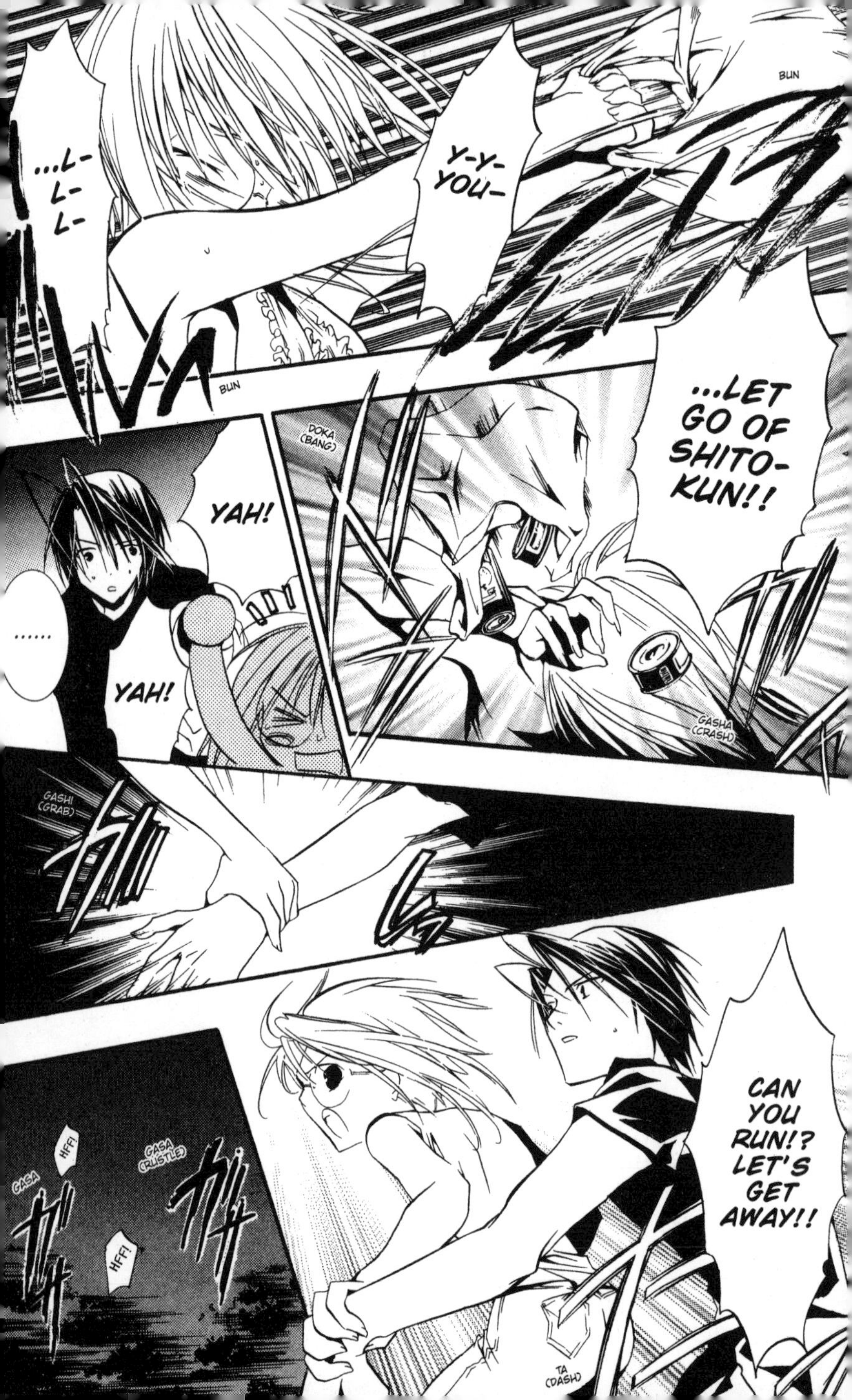
BUN
Y-Y-YOU-
...L-L-L-
BUN
...LET GO OF SHITO-KUN!!
DOKA (BANG)
GASHA (CRASH)
YAH!
......
YAH!
GASHI (GRAB)
CAN YOU RUN!? LET'S GET AWAY!!
GASA (RUSTLE)
HFF!
GASA
HFF!
TA (DASH)

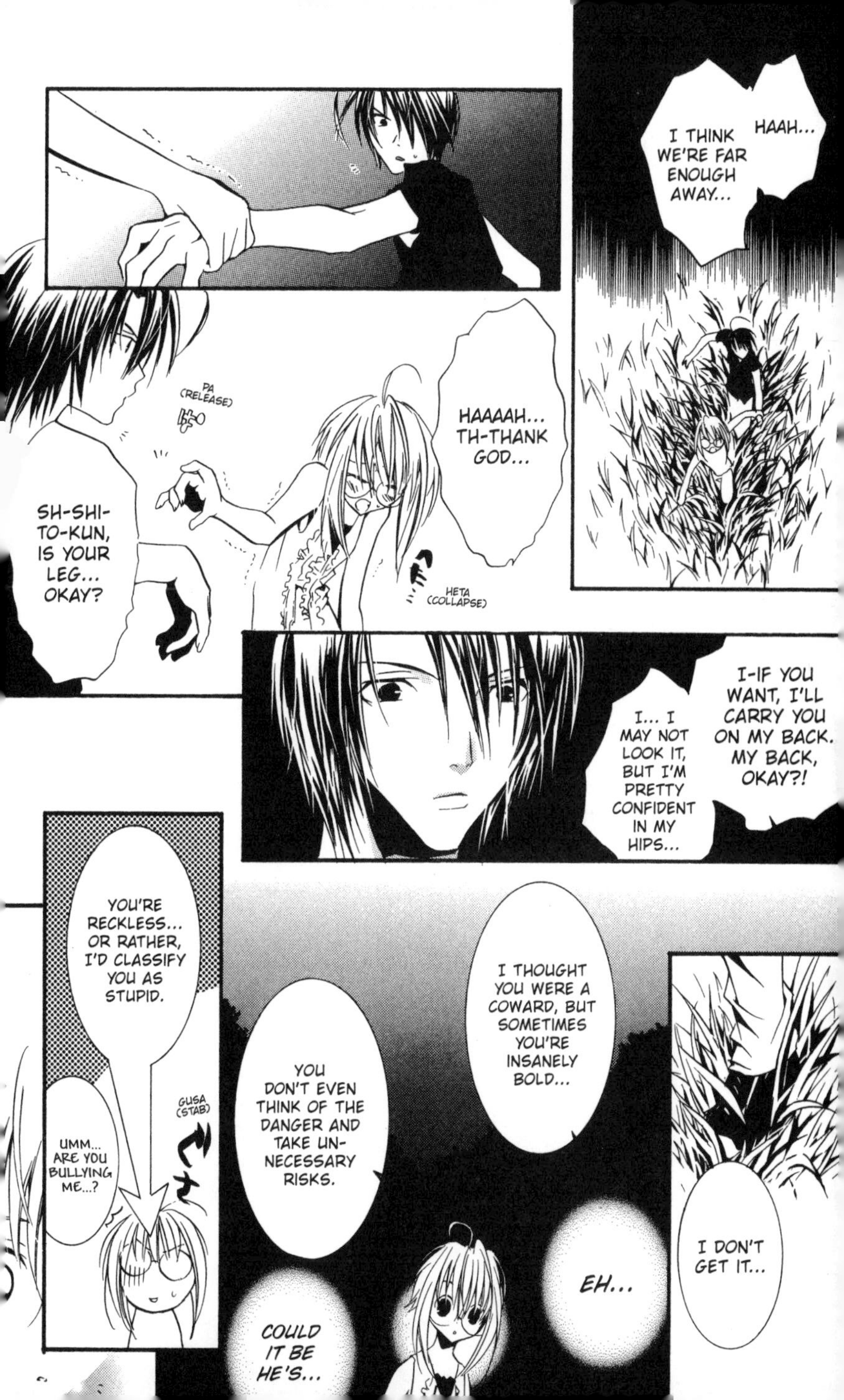
HAAH...
I THINK WE'RE FAR ENOUGH AWAY...
HAAAAH... TH-THANK GOD...
HETA (COLLAPSE)
PA (RELEASE)
SH-SHI-TO-KUN, IS YOUR LEG... OKAY?
I-IF YOU WANT, I'LL CARRY YOU ON MY BACK. MY BACK, OKAY?!
I... I MAY NOT LOOK IT, BUT I'M PRETTY CONFIDENT IN MY HIPS...
I DON'T GET IT...
I THOUGHT YOU WERE A COWARD, BUT SOMETIMES YOU'RE INSANELY BOLD...
EH...
YOU DON'T EVEN THINK OF THE DANGER AND TAKE UN-NECESSARY RISKS.
COULD IT BE HE'S...
YOU'RE RECKLESS... OR RATHER, I'D CLASSIFY YOU AS STUPID.
GUSA (STAB)
UMM... ARE YOU BULLYING ME...?

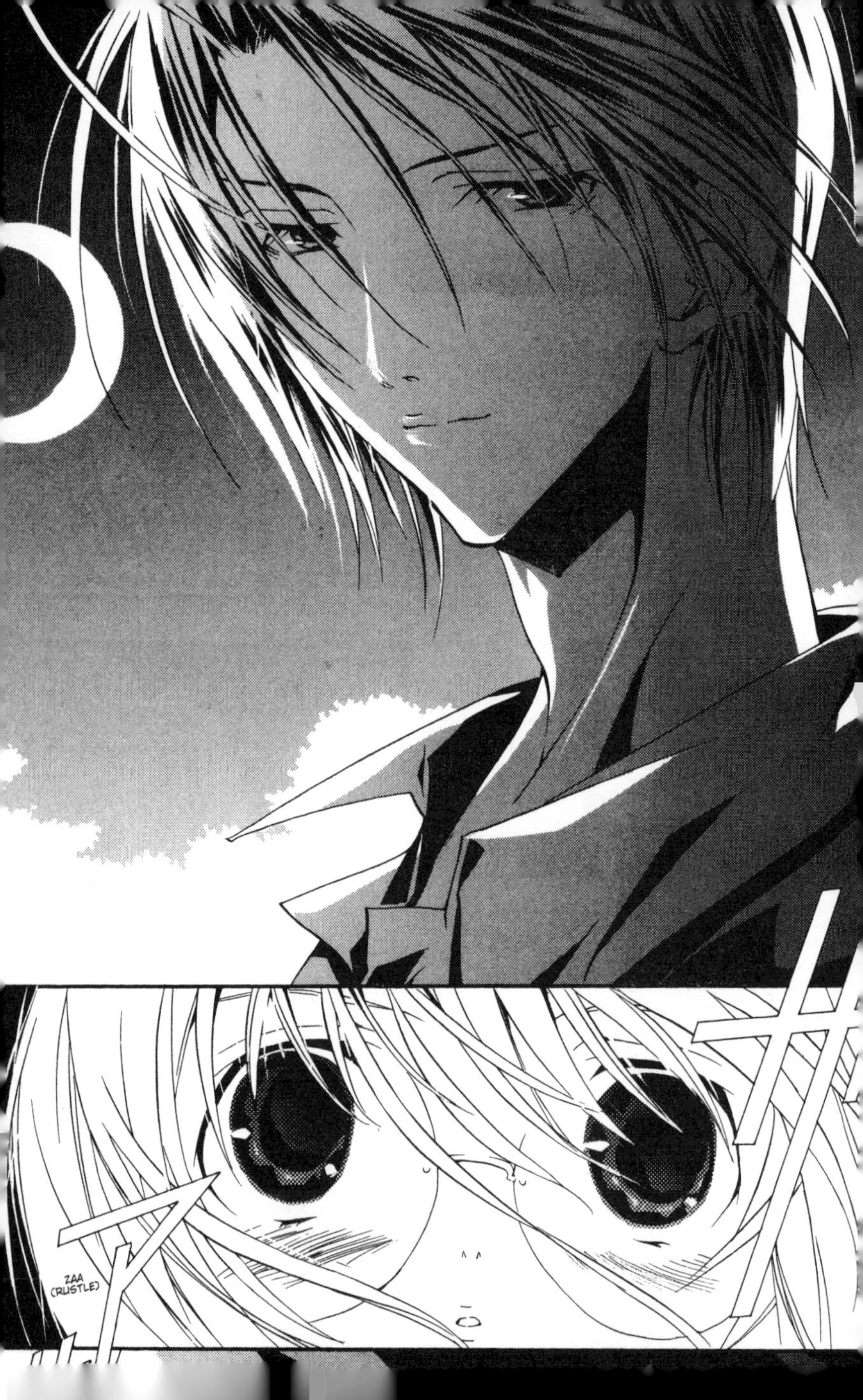
ZAA
(RUSTLE)

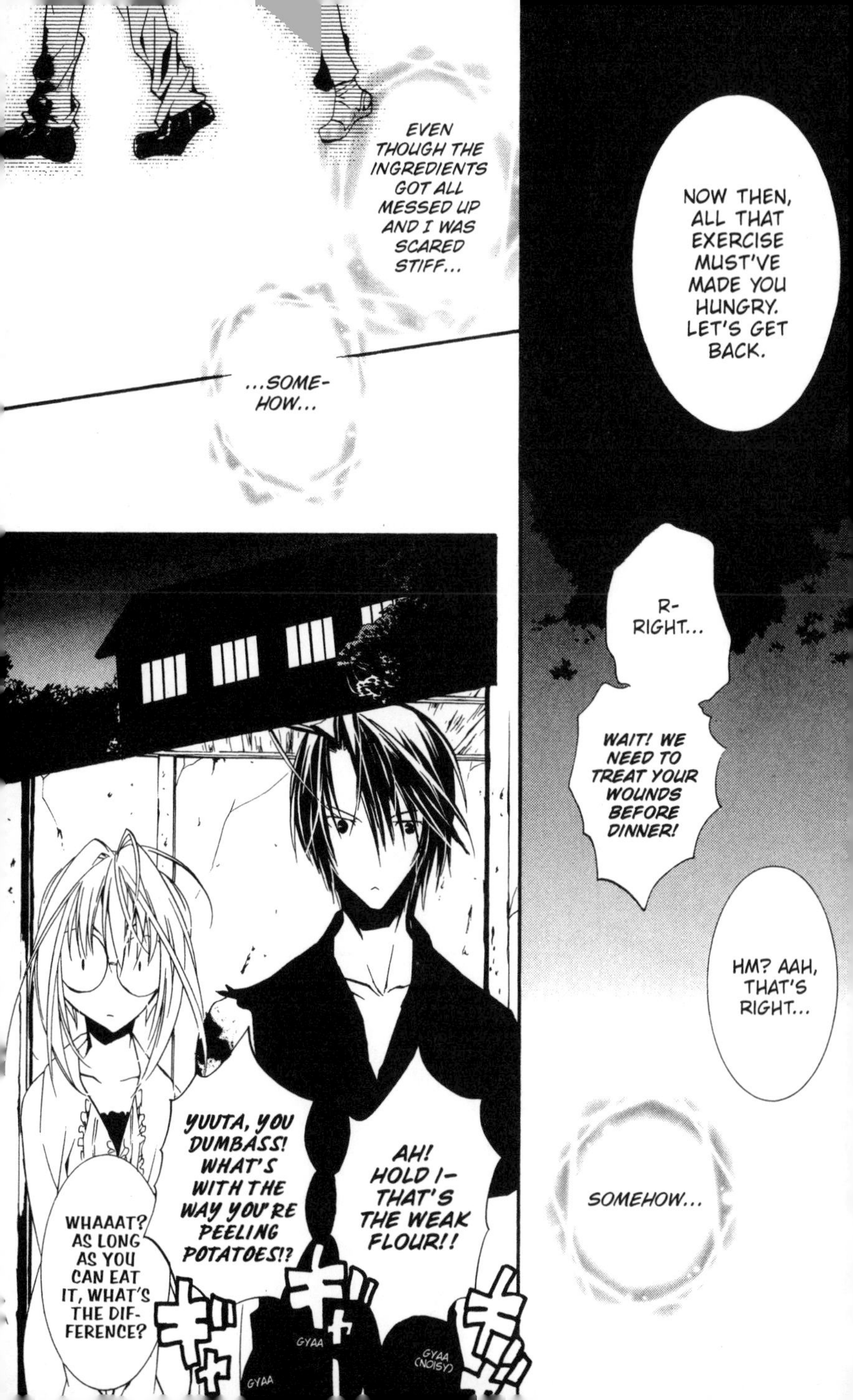
NOW THEN, ALL THAT EXERCISE MUST'VE MADE YOU HUNGRY. LET'S GET BACK.
R-RIGHT...
WAIT! WE NEED TO TREAT YOUR WOUNDS BEFORE DINNER!
HM? AAH, THAT'S RIGHT...
SOMEHOW...
EVEN THOUGH THE INGREDIENTS GOT ALL MESSED UP AND I WAS SCARED STIFF...
...SOME-HOW...
AH! HOLD I- THAT'S THE WEAK FLOUR!!
YUUTA, YOU DUMBASS! WHAT'S WITH THE WAY YOU'RE PEELING POTATOES!?
WHAAAT? AS LONG AS YOU CAN EAT IT, WHAT'S THE DIF-FERENCE?
GYAA (NOISY)
GYAA
GYAA

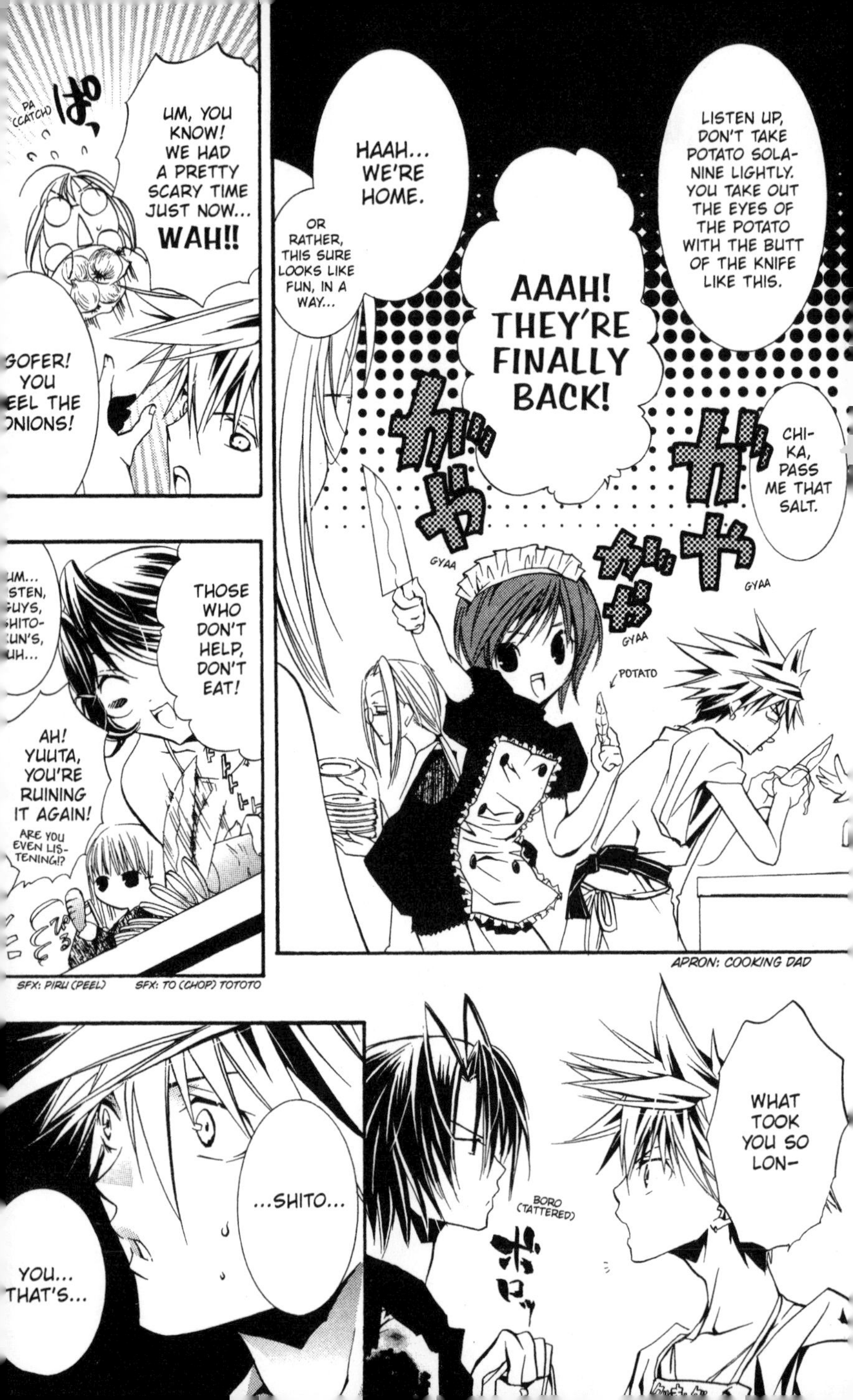

LISTEN UP, DON'T TAKE POTATO SOLANINE LIGHTLY. YOU TAKE OUT THE EYES OF THE POTATO WITH THE BUTT OF THE KNIFE LIKE THIS.
HAAH... WE'RE HOME.
AAAH! THEY'RE FINALLY BACK!
OR RATHER, THIS SURE LOOKS LIKE FUN, IN A WAY...
CHI-KA, PASS ME THAT SALT.
GYAA
GYAA
GYAA
POTATO
APRON: COOKING DAD
PA (CATCH)
UM, YOU KNOW! WE HAD A PRETTY SCARY TIME JUST NOW... WAH!!
GOFER! YOU EEL THE NIONS!
THOSE WHO DON'T HELP, DON'T EAT!
UM... STEN, GUYS, HITO-UN'S, UH...
AH! YUUTA, YOU'RE RUINING IT AGAIN!
ARE YOU EVEN LIS-TENING!?
SFX: PIRU (PEEL)
SFX: TO (CHOP) TOTOTO
WHAT TOOK YOU SO LON-
BORO (TATTERED)
...SHITO...
YOU... THAT'S...

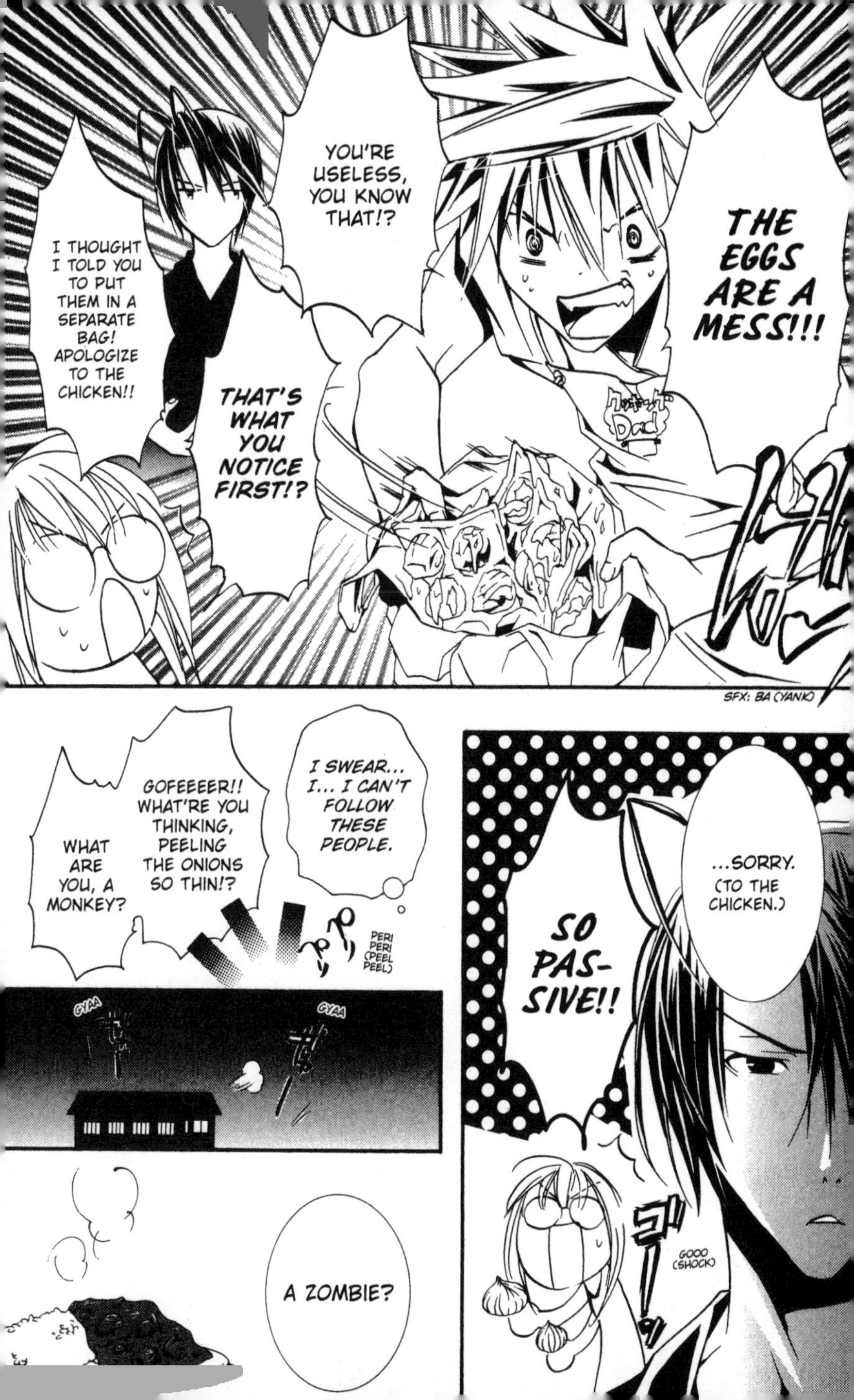
THE EGGS ARE A MESS!!!
YOU'RE USELESS, YOU KNOW THAT!?
THAT'S WHAT YOU NOTICE FIRST!?
I THOUGHT I TOLD YOU TO PUT THEM IN A SEPARATE BAG! APOLOGIZE TO THE CHICKEN!!
SFX: BA (YANK)
...SORRY. (TO THE CHICKEN.)
SO PAS-SIVE!!
GOOO (SHOCK)
I SWEAR... I... I CAN'T FOLLOW THESE PEOPLE.
GOFEEEER!! WHAT'RE YOU THINKING, PEELING THE ONIONS SO THIN!?
WHAT ARE YOU, A MONKEY?
PERI PERI (PEEL PEEL)
GYAA
GYAA
A ZOMBIE?

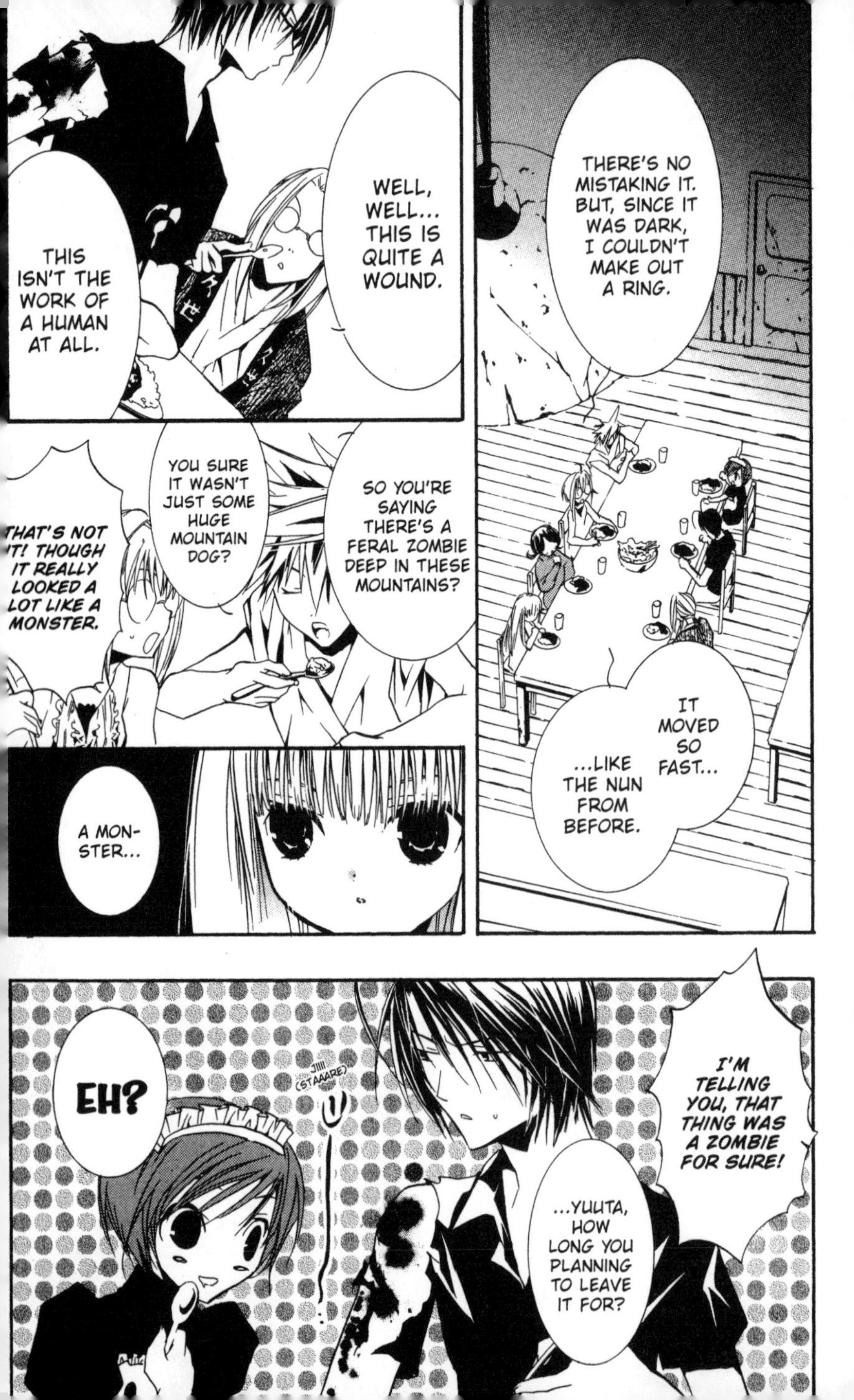
THERE'S NO MISTAKING IT. BUT, SINCE IT WAS DARK, I COULDN'T MAKE OUT A RING.
IT MOVED SO FAST...
...LIKE THE NUN FROM BEFORE.
WELL, WELL... THIS IS QUITE A WOUND.
THIS ISN'T THE WORK OF A HUMAN AT ALL.
SO YOU'RE SAYING THERE'S A FERAL ZOMBIE DEEP IN THESE MOUNTAINS?
YOU SURE IT WASN'T JUST SOME HUGE MOUNTAIN DOG?
THAT'S NOT IT! THOUGH IT REALLY LOOKED A LOT LIKE A MONSTER.
A MON-STER...
I'M TELLING YOU, THAT THING WAS A ZOMBIE FOR SURE!
...YUUTA, HOW LONG YOU PLANNING TO LEAVE IT FOR?
JIIII (STAAARE)
EH?

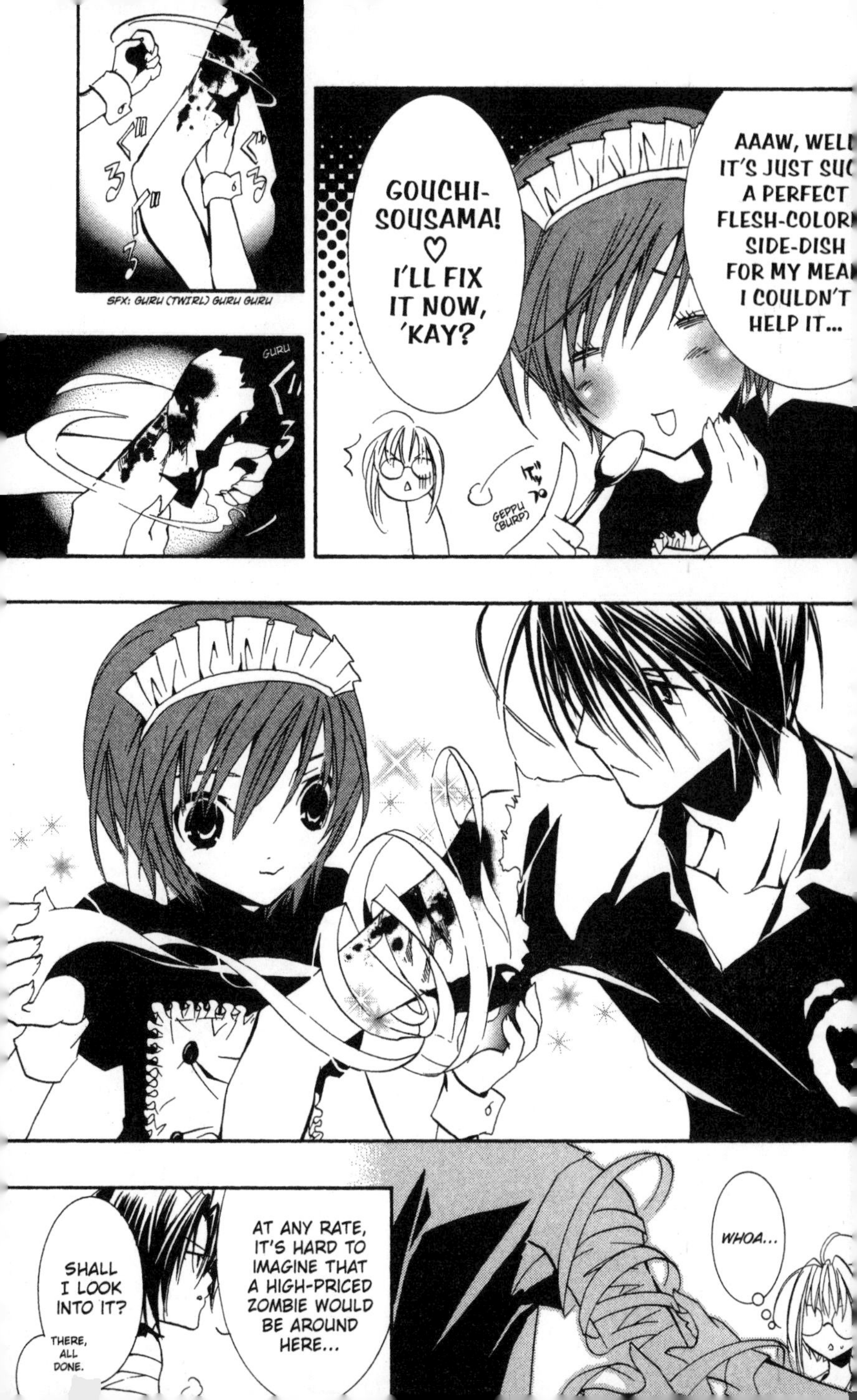
AAAW, WELL IT'S JUST SUC A PERFECT FLESH-COLOR SIDE-DISH FOR MY MEA I COULDN'T HELP IT...
GOUCHI-SOUSAMA! ♡ I'LL FIX IT NOW, 'KAY?
GEPPU (BURP)
SFX: GURU (TWIRL) GURU GURU
GURU
WHOA...
AT ANY RATE, IT'S HARD TO IMAGINE THAT A HIGH-PRICED ZOMBIE WOULD BE AROUND HERE...
SHALL I LOOK INTO IT?
THERE, ALL DONE.

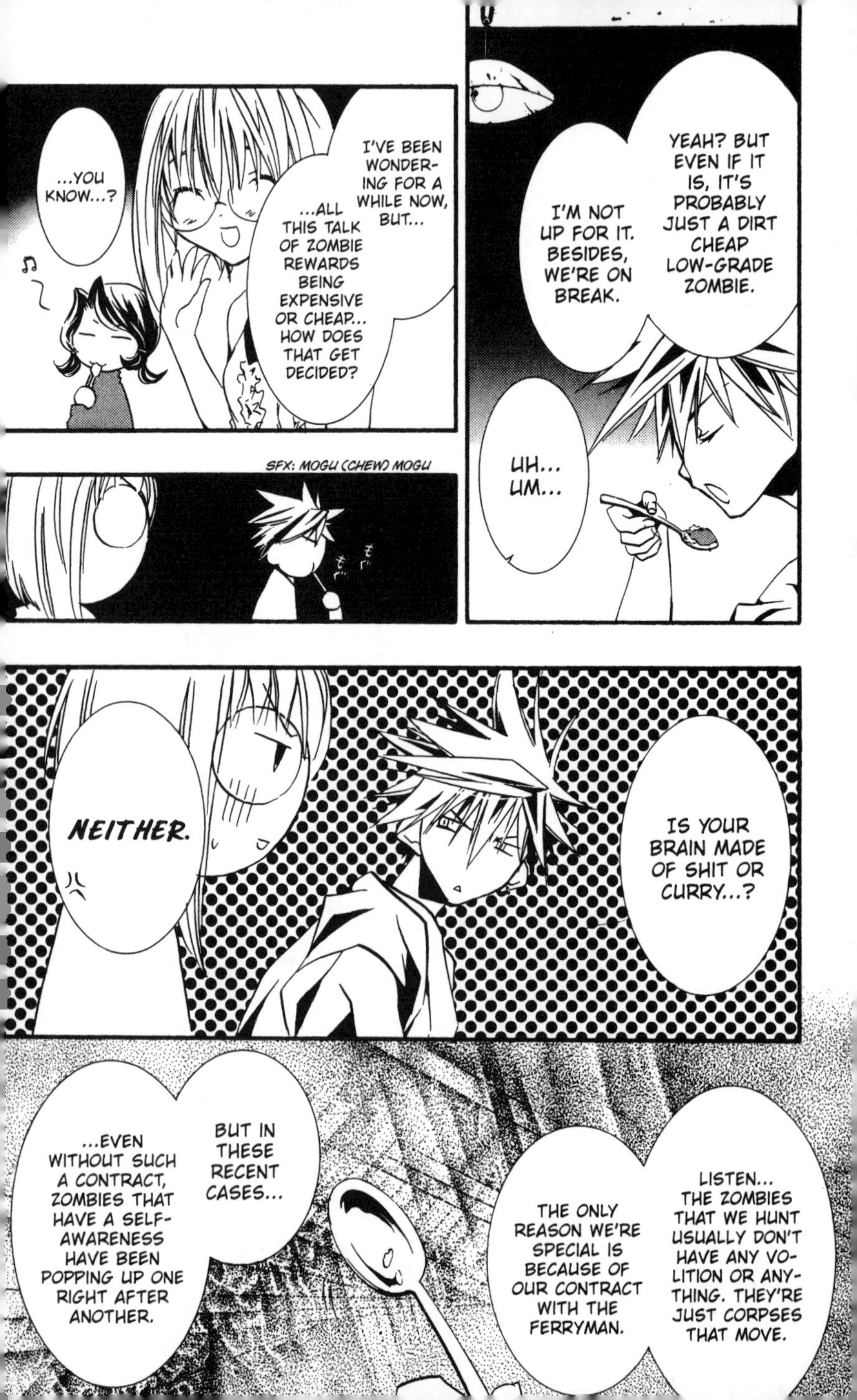
YEAH? BUT EVEN IF IT IS, IT'S PROBABLY JUST A DIRT CHEAP LOW-GRADE ZOMBIE.
I'M NOT UP FOR IT. BESIDES, WE'RE ON BREAK.
UH... UM...
I'VE BEEN WONDERING FOR A WHILE NOW, BUT...
...ALL THIS TALK OF ZOMBIE REWARDS BEING EXPENSIVE OR CHEAP... HOW DOES THAT GET DECIDED?
...YOU KNOW...?
SFX: MOGU (CHEW) MOGU
IS YOUR BRAIN MADE OF SHIT OR CURRY...?
NEITHER.
LISTEN... THE ZOMBIES THAT WE HUNT USUALLY DON'T HAVE ANY VOLITION OR ANYTHING. THEY'RE JUST CORPSES THAT MOVE.
THE ONLY REASON WE'RE SPECIAL IS BECAUSE OF OUR CONTRACT WITH THE FERRYMAN.
BUT IN THESE RECENT CASES...
...EVEN WITHOUT SUCH A CONTRACT, ZOMBIES THAT HAVE A SELF-AWARENESS HAVE BEEN POPPING UP ONE RIGHT AFTER ANOTHER.

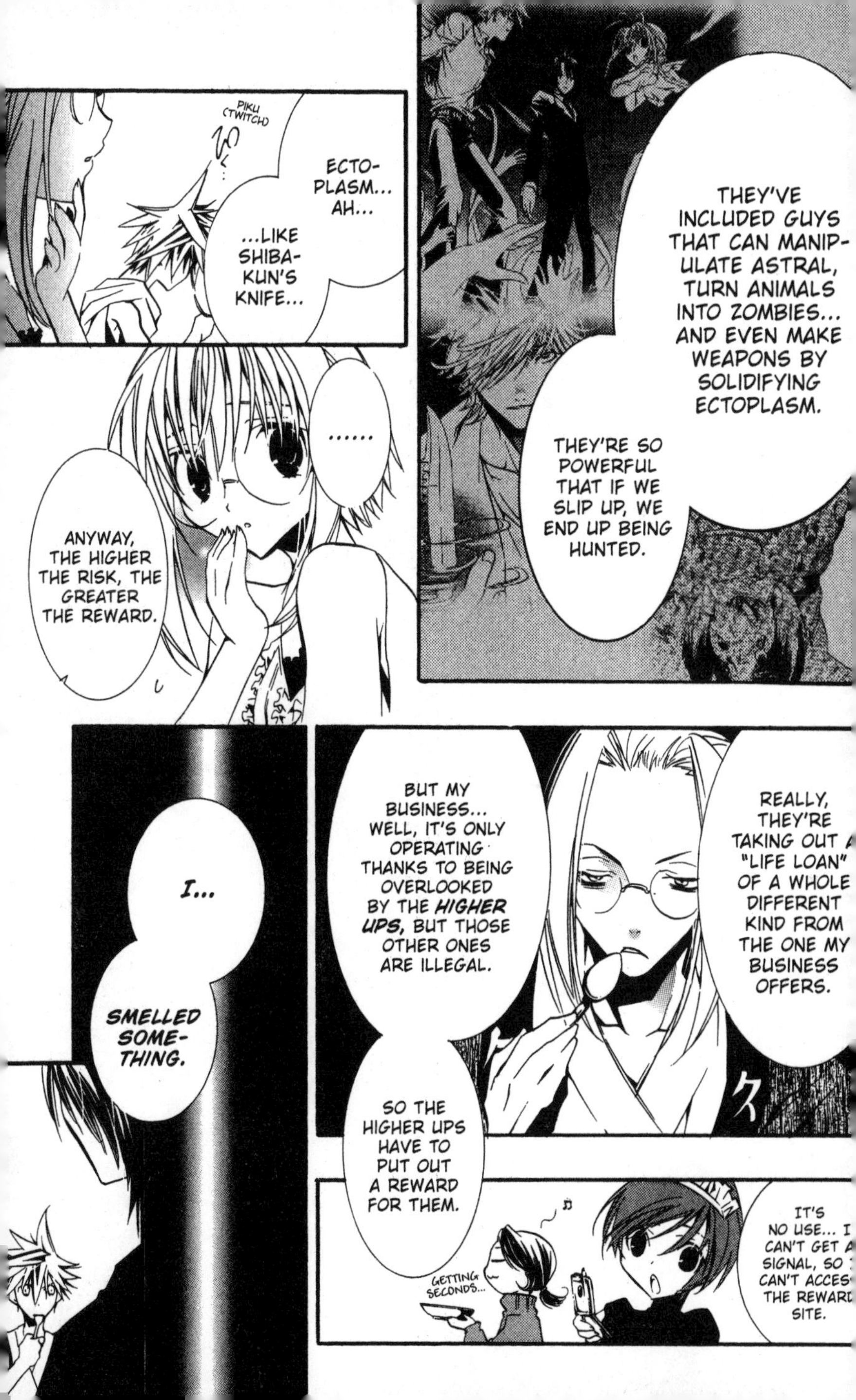

THEY'VE INCLUDED GUYS THAT CAN MANIPULATE ASTRAL, TURN ANIMALS INTO ZOMBIES... AND EVEN MAKE WEAPONS BY SOLIDIFYING ECTOPLASM.
THEY'RE SO POWERFUL THAT IF WE SLIP UP, WE END UP BEING HUNTED.
PIKU (TWITCH)
ECTO-PLASM... AH...
...LIKE SHIBA-KUN'S KNIFE...
......
ANYWAY, THE HIGHER THE RISK, THE GREATER THE REWARD.
REALLY, THEY'RE TAKING OUT A "LIFE LOAN" OF A WHOLE DIFFERENT KIND FROM THE ONE MY BUSINESS OFFERS.
BUT MY BUSINESS... WELL, IT'S ONLY OPERATING THANKS TO BEING OVERLOOKED BY THE ***HIGHER UPS,*** BUT THOSE OTHER ONES ARE ILLEGAL.
SO THE HIGHER UPS HAVE TO PUT OUT A REWARD FOR THEM.
IT'S NO USE... I CAN'T GET A SIGNAL, SO I CAN'T ACCESS THE REWARD SITE.
GETTING SECONDS...
I...
SMELLED SOMETHING.

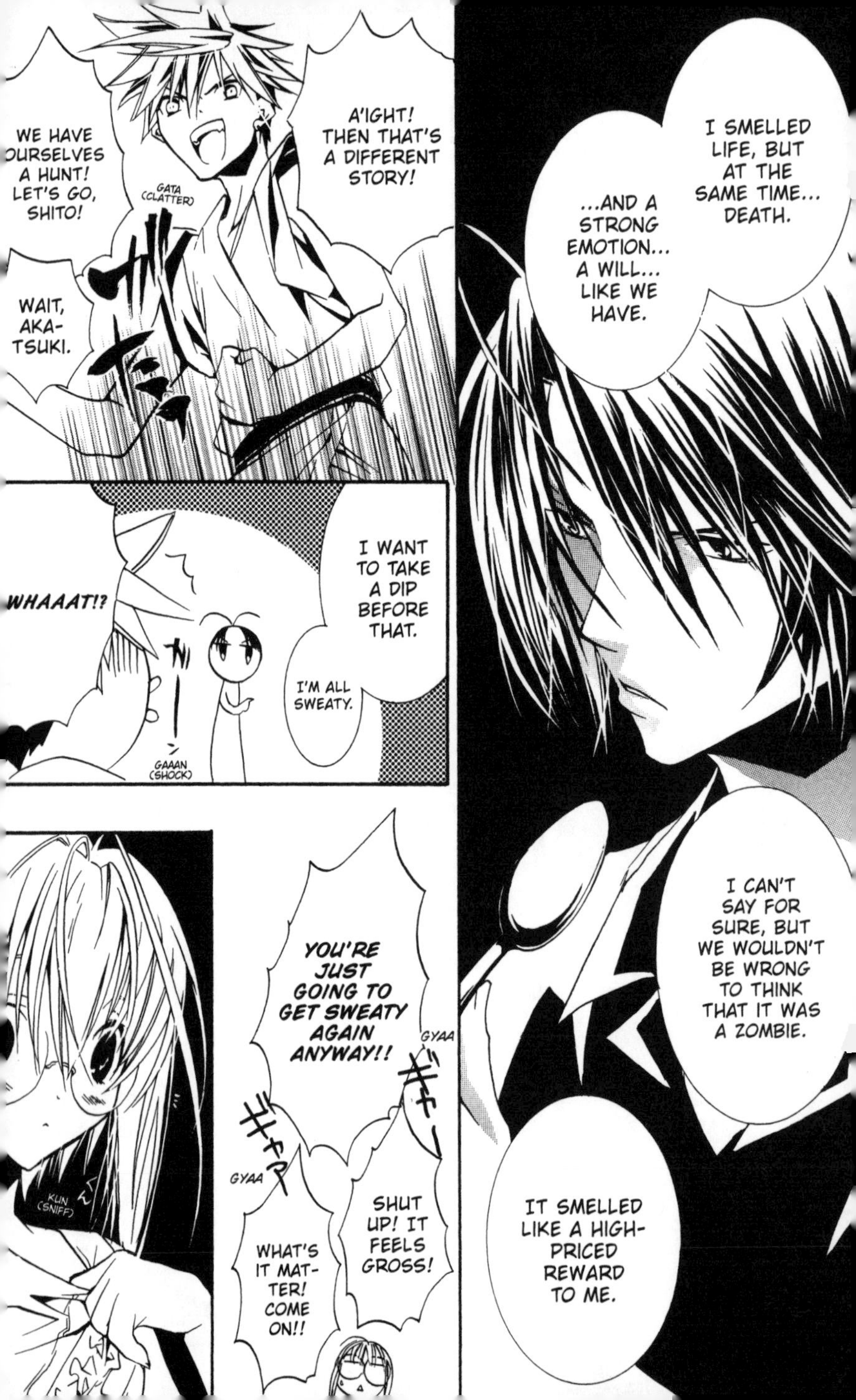
I SMELLED LIFE, BUT AT THE SAME TIME... DEATH.
...AND A STRONG EMOTION... A WILL... LIKE WE HAVE.
I CAN'T SAY FOR SURE, BUT WE WOULDN'T BE WRONG TO THINK THAT IT WAS A ZOMBIE.
IT SMELLED LIKE A HIGH-PRICED REWARD TO ME.
A'IGHT! THEN THAT'S A DIFFERENT STORY!
WE HAVE OURSELVES A HUNT! LET'S GO, SHITO!
GATA (CLATTER)
WAIT, AKA-TSUKI.
I WANT TO TAKE A DIP BEFORE THAT.
I'M ALL SWEATY.
WHAAAT!?
GAAAN (SHOCK)
GYAA
YOU'RE JUST GOING TO GET SWEATY AGAIN ANYWAY!!
GYAA
SHUT UP! IT FEELS GROSS!
WHAT'S IT MATTER! COME ON!!
KUN (SNIFF)

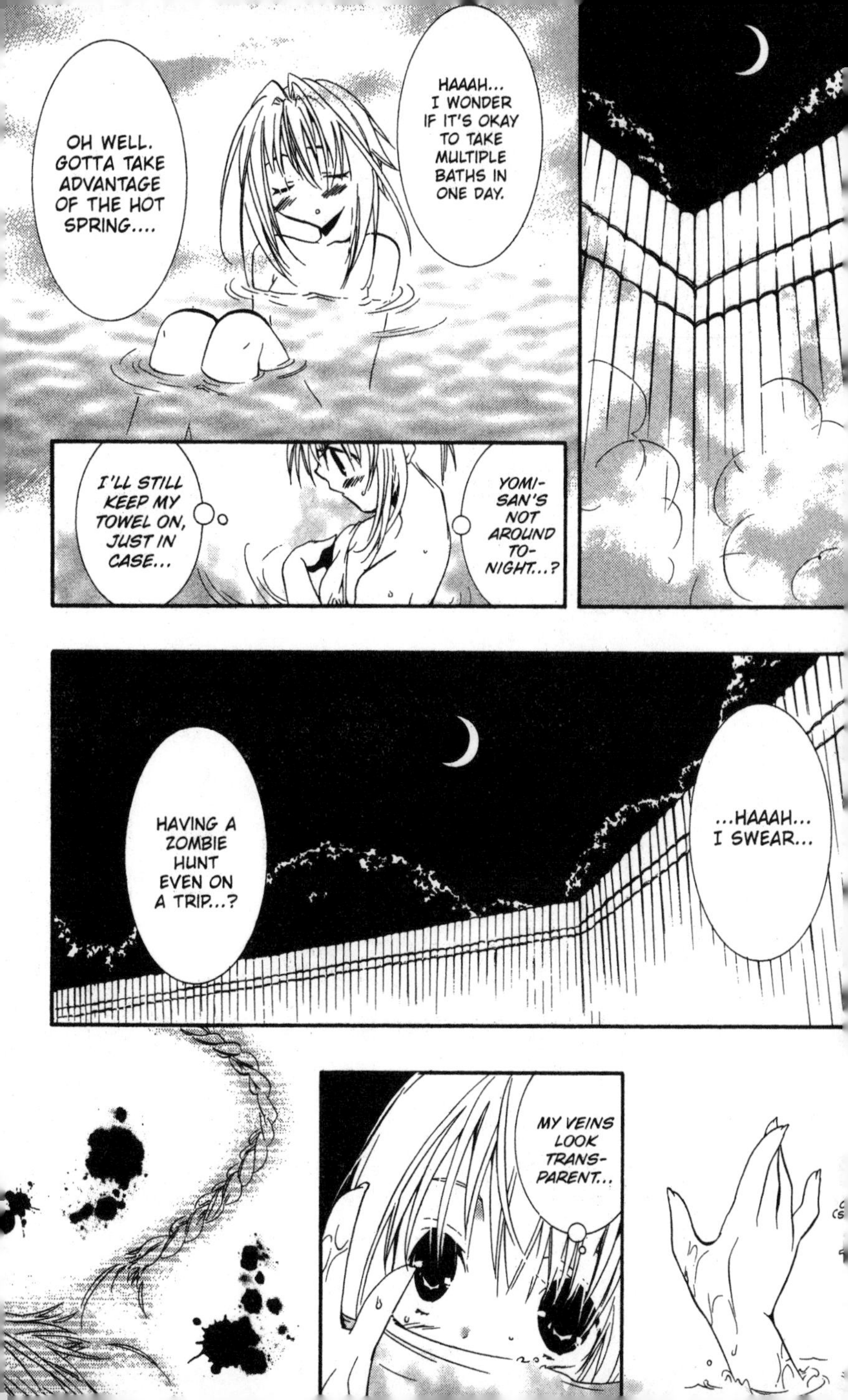
HAAAH... I WONDER IF IT'S OKAY TO TAKE MULTIPLE BATHS IN ONE DAY.
OH WELL. GOTTA TAKE ADVANTAGE OF THE HOT SPRING....
YOMI-SAN'S NOT AROUND TO-NIGHT...?
I'LL STILL KEEP MY TOWEL ON, JUST IN CASE...
...HAAAH... I SWEAR...
HAVING A ZOMBIE HUNT EVEN ON A TRIP...?
MY VEINS LOOK TRANS-PARENT...

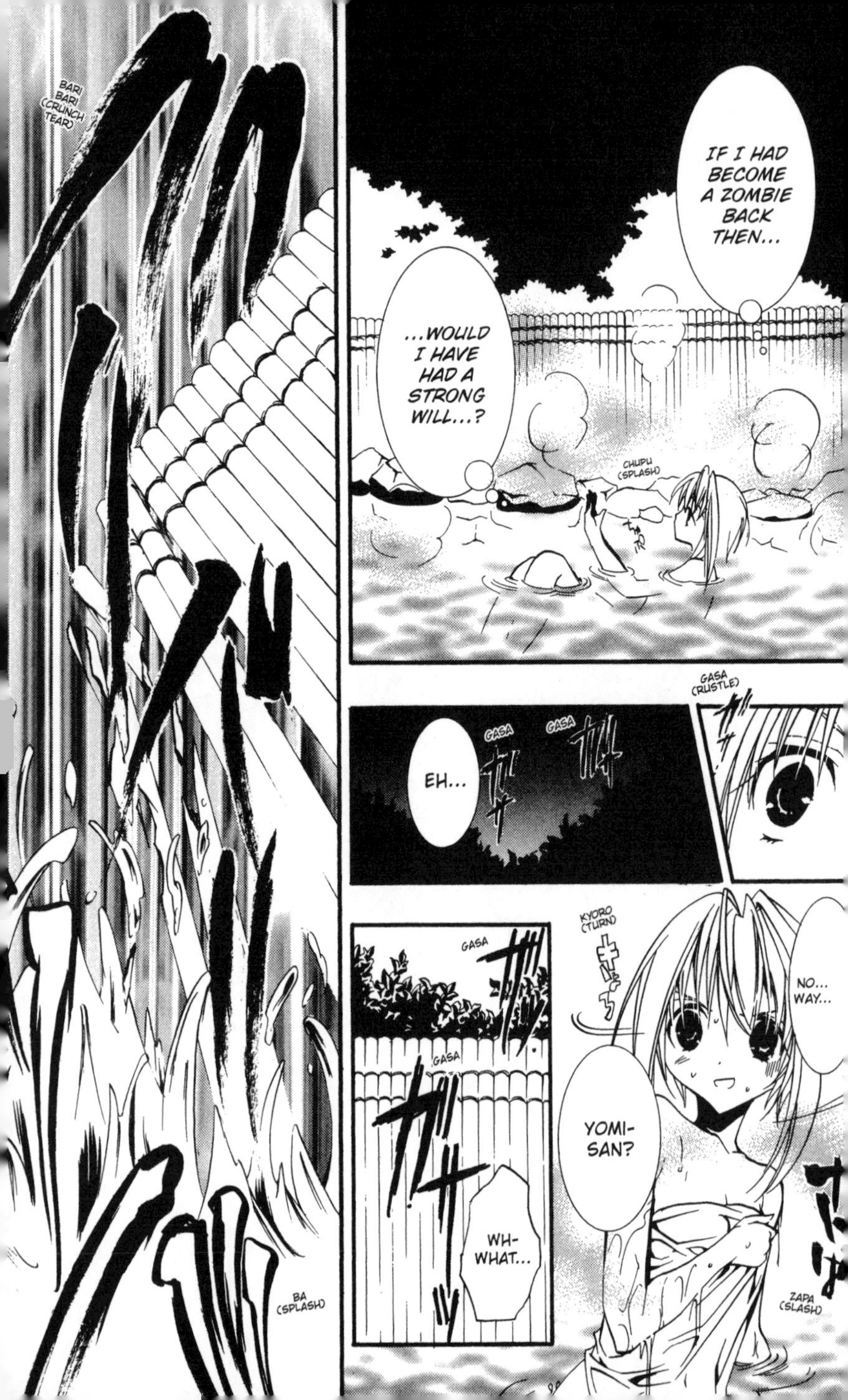
IF I HAD BECOME A ZOMBIE BACK THEN...
...WOULD I HAVE HAD A STRONG WILL...?
CHUPU (SPLASH)
GASA (RUSTLE)
GASA
GASA
EH...
NO... WAY...
KYORO (TURN)
YOMI-SAN?
ZAPA (SLASH)
GASA
GASA
WH-WHAT...
BARI BARI (CRUNCH TEAR)
BA (SPLASH)

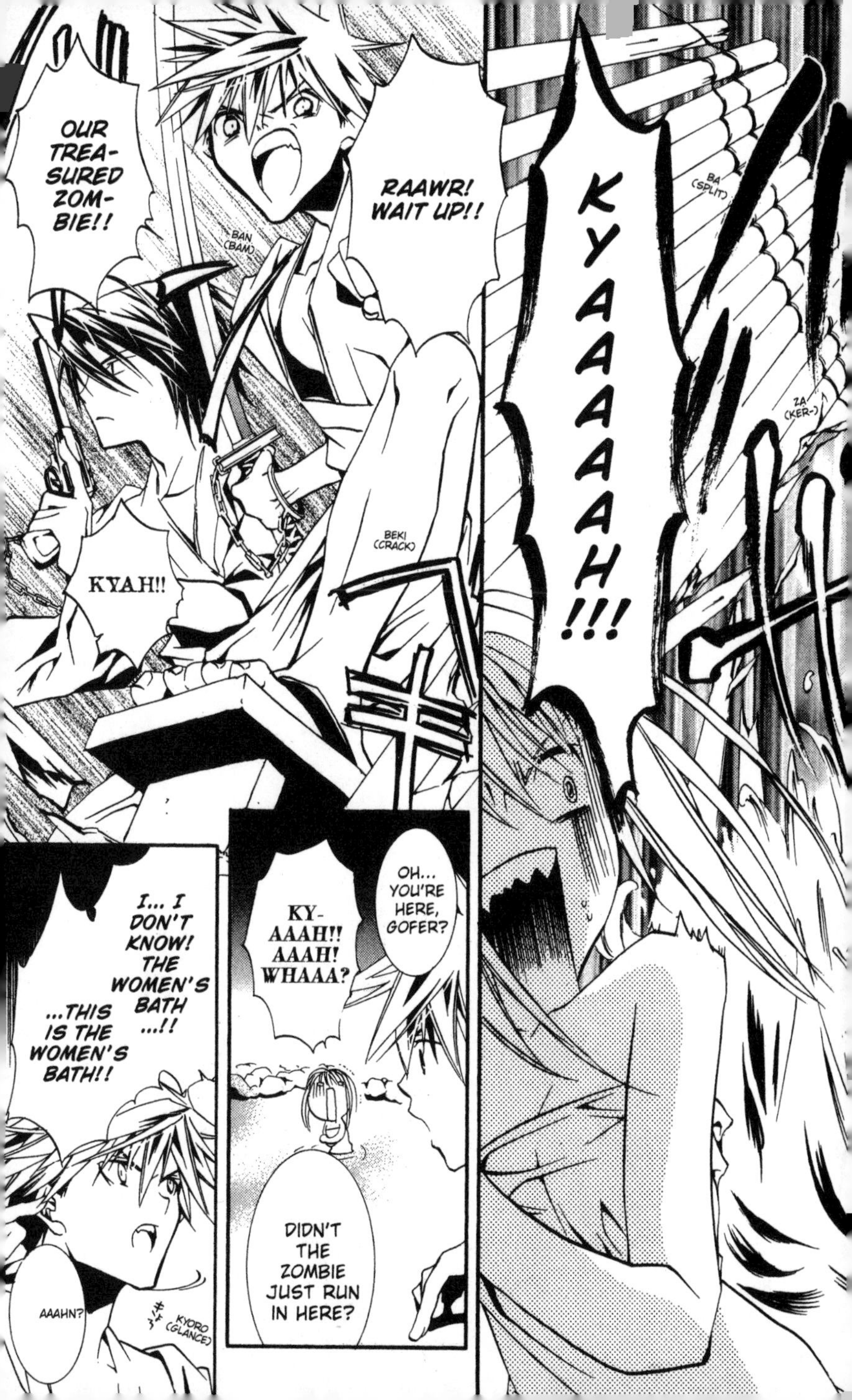
KYAAAAAAH!!!
BA (SPLIT)
ZA (KER-)
RAAWR! WAIT UP!!
OUR TREA-SURED ZOM-BIE!!
BAN (BAM)
BEKI (CRACK)
KYAH!!
OH... YOU'RE HERE, GOFER?
KY-AAAH!! AAAH! WHAAA?
DIDN'T THE ZOMBIE JUST RUN IN HERE?
I... I DON'T KNOW! THE WOMEN'S BATH ...!!
...THIS IS THE WOMEN'S BATH!!
AAAHN?
KYORO (GLANCE)

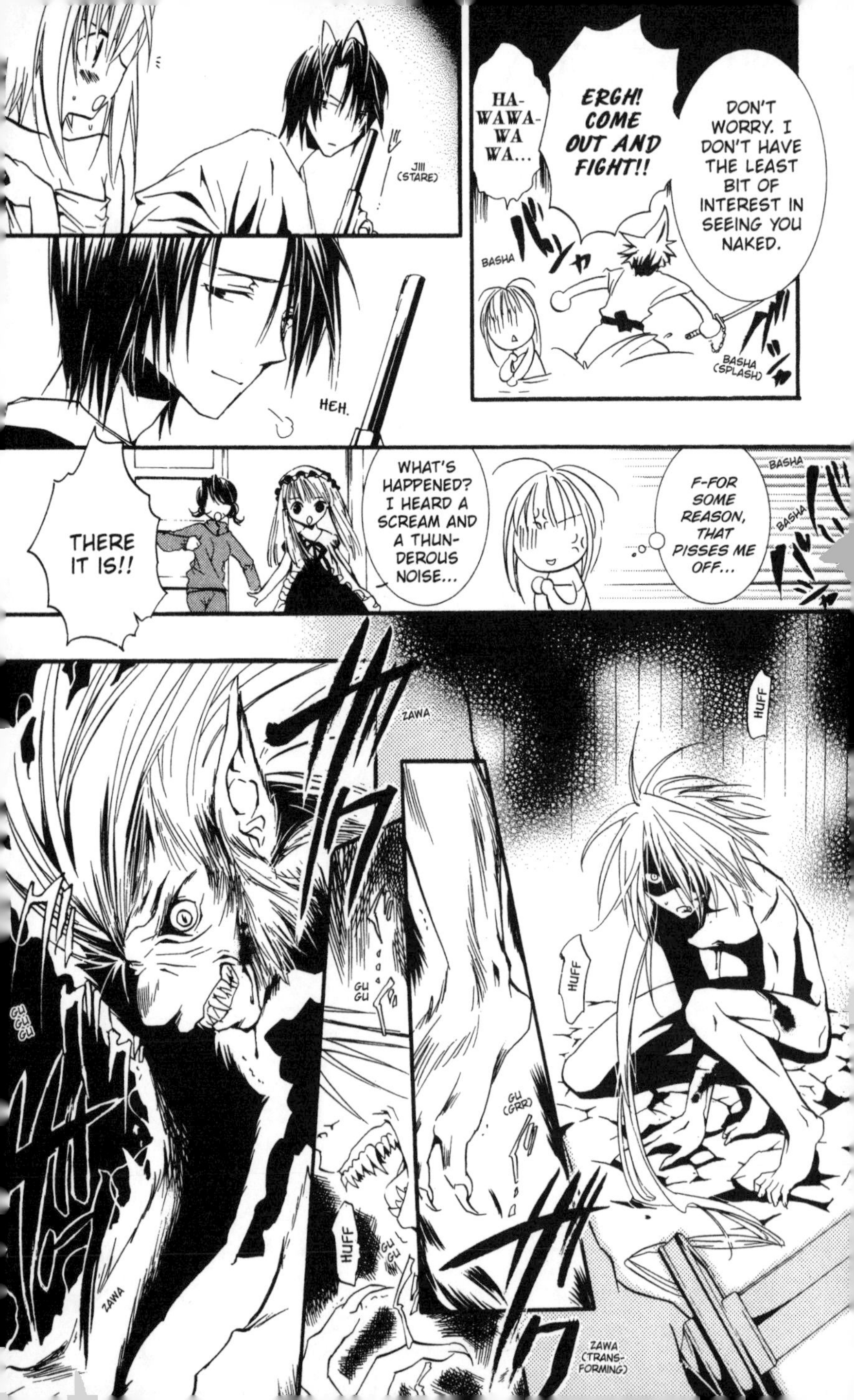
DON'T WORRY. I DON'T HAVE THE LEAST BIT OF INTEREST IN SEEING YOU NAKED.
ERGH! COME OUT AND FIGHT!!
HA-WAWA-WA WA...
BASHA
BASHA (SPLASH)
JIII (STARE)
HEH.
BASHA
BASHA
F-FOR SOME REASON, THAT PISSES ME OFF...
WHAT'S HAPPENED? I HEARD A SCREAM AND A THUNDEROUS NOISE...
THERE IT IS!!
HUFF
ZAWA
HUFF
GU GU
GU (GRR)
ZAWA (TRANSFORMING)
HUFF
GU GU
GU GU GU
ZAWA

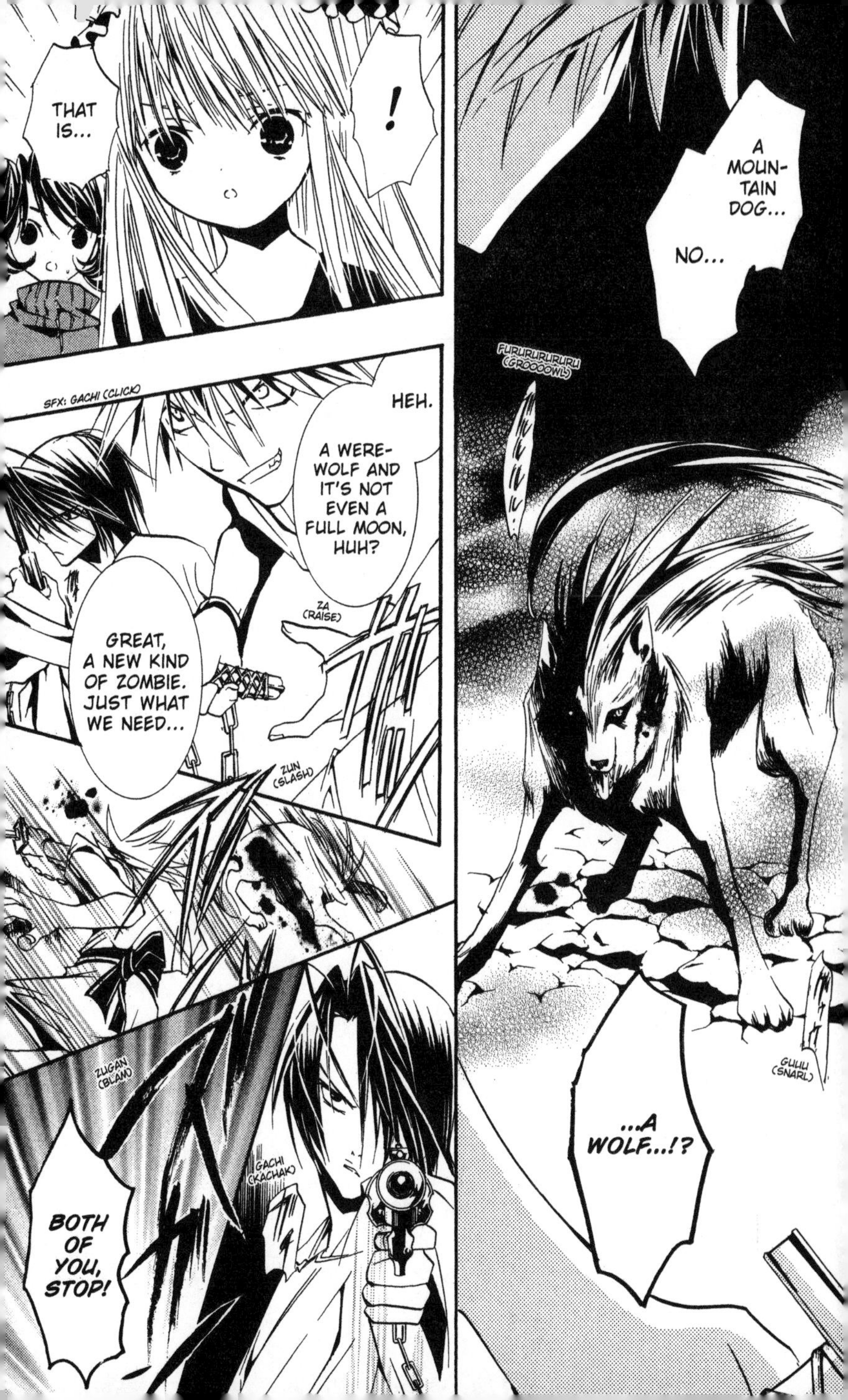
A MOUNTAIN DOG...
NO...
FURURURURURU (GROOOOWL)
GUUU (SNARL)
...A WOLF...!?
!
THAT IS...
SFX: GACHI (CLICK)
HEH.
A WEREWOLF AND IT'S NOT EVEN A FULL MOON, HUH?
ZA (RAISE)
GREAT, A NEW KIND OF ZOMBIE. JUST WHAT WE NEED...
ZUN (SLASH)
GACHI (KACHAK)
ZUGAN (BLAM)
BOTH OF YOU, STOP!

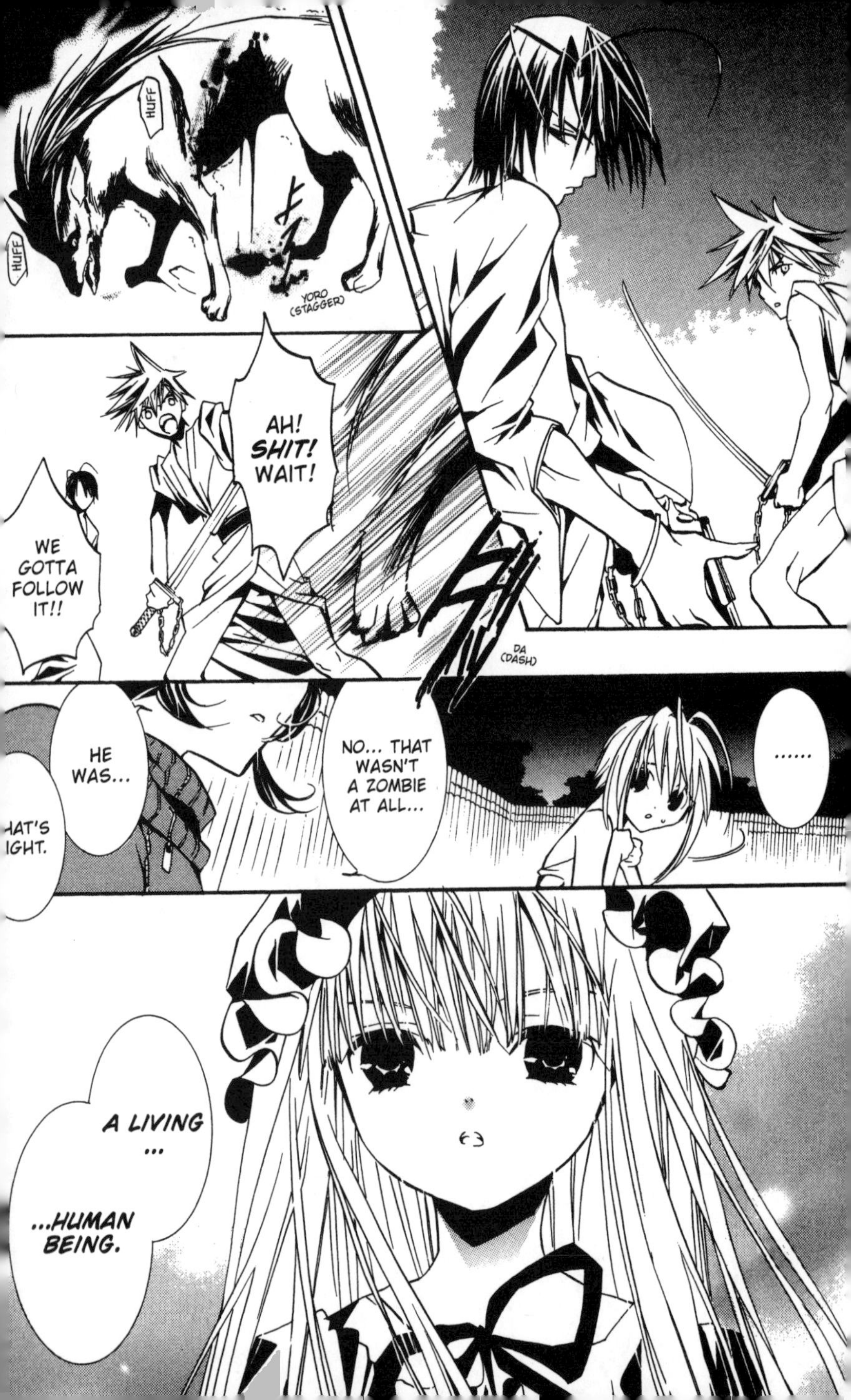
DA (DASH)
HUFF
HUFF
YORO (STAGGER)
AH! SHIT! WAIT!
WE GOTTA FOLLOW IT!!
......
NO... THAT WASN'T A ZOMBIE AT ALL...
HE WAS...
HAT'S IGHT.
A LIVING ...
...HUMAN BEING.

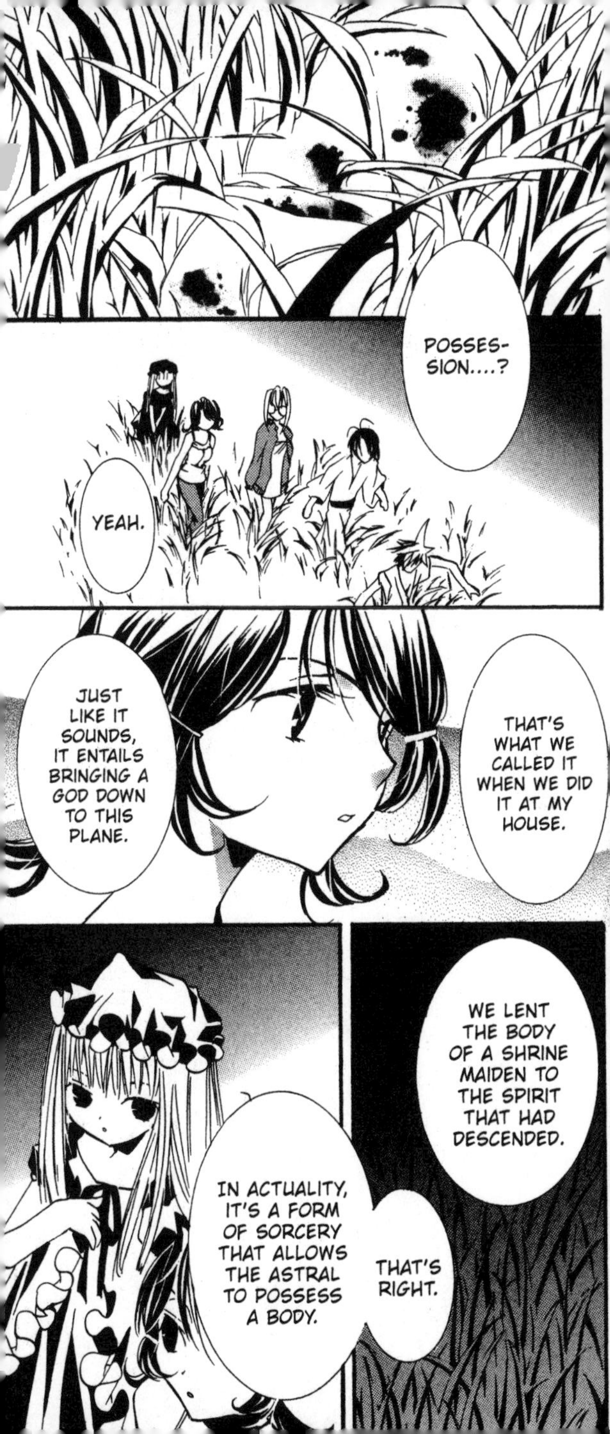
POSSES-SION....?
YEAH.
THAT'S WHAT WE CALLED IT WHEN WE DID IT AT MY HOUSE.
JUST LIKE IT SOUNDS, IT ENTAILS BRINGING A GOD DOWN TO THIS PLANE.
WE LENT THE BODY OF A SHRINE MAIDEN TO THE SPIRIT THAT HAD DESCENDED.
THAT'S RIGHT.
IN ACTUALITY, IT'S A FORM OF SORCERY THAT ALLOWS THE ASTRAL TO POSSESS A BODY.

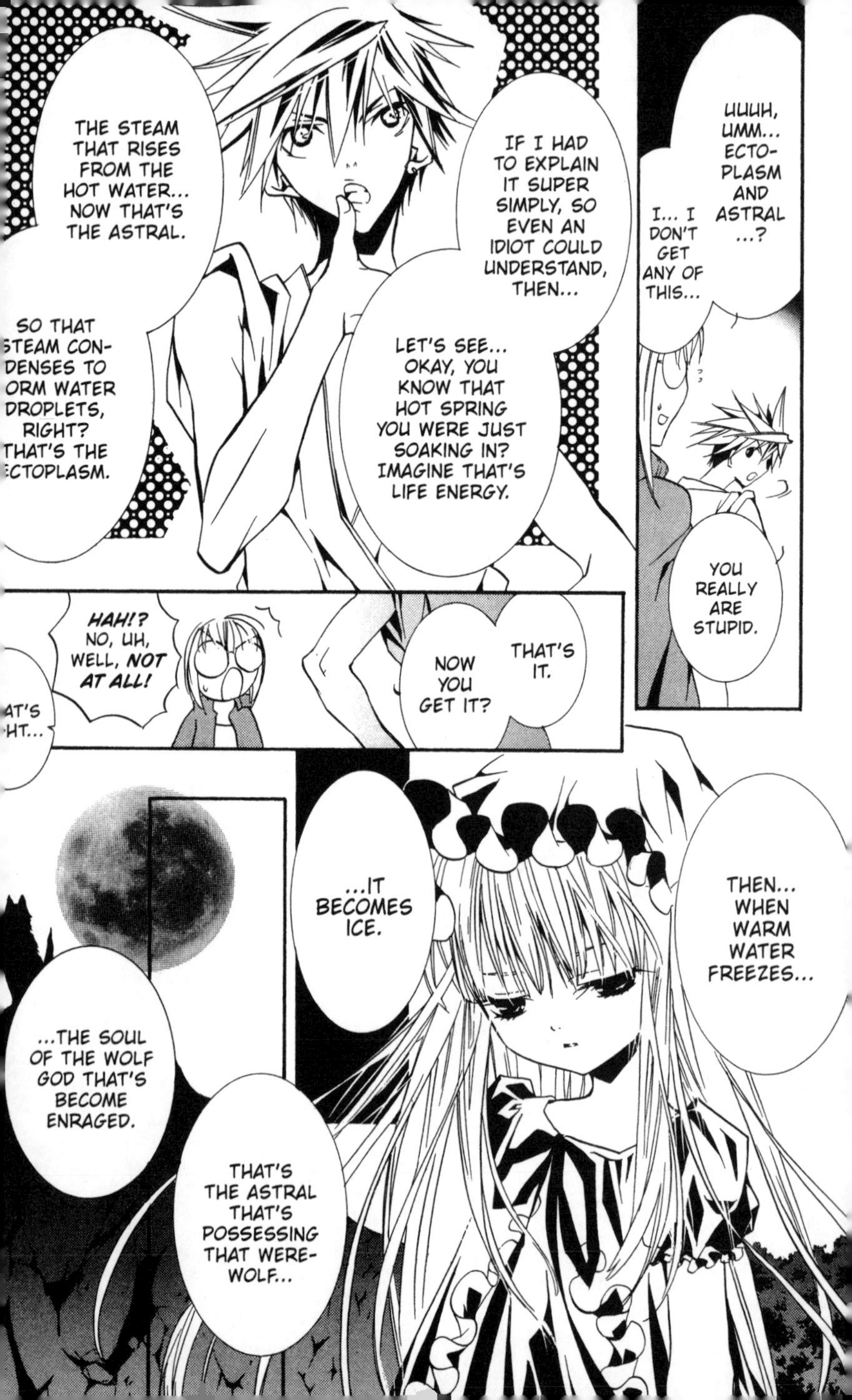
UUUH, UMM... ECTO-PLASM AND ASTRAL ...?
I... I DON'T GET ANY OF THIS...
YOU REALLY ARE STUPID.
IF I HAD TO EXPLAIN IT SUPER SIMPLY, SO EVEN AN IDIOT COULD UNDERSTAND, THEN...
LET'S SEE... OKAY, YOU KNOW THAT HOT SPRING YOU WERE JUST SOAKING IN? IMAGINE THAT'S LIFE ENERGY.
THE STEAM THAT RISES FROM THE HOT WATER... NOW THAT'S THE ASTRAL.
SO THAT STEAM CON-DENSES TO ORM WATER DROPLETS, RIGHT? THAT'S THE ECTOPLASM.
THAT'S IT.
NOW YOU GET IT?
HAH!? NO, UH, WELL, NOT AT ALL!
AT'S HT...
THEN... WHEN WARM WATER FREEZES...
...IT BECOMES ICE.
THAT'S THE ASTRAL THAT'S POSSESSING THAT WERE-WOLF...
...THE SOUL OF THE WOLF GOD THAT'S BECOME ENRAGED.

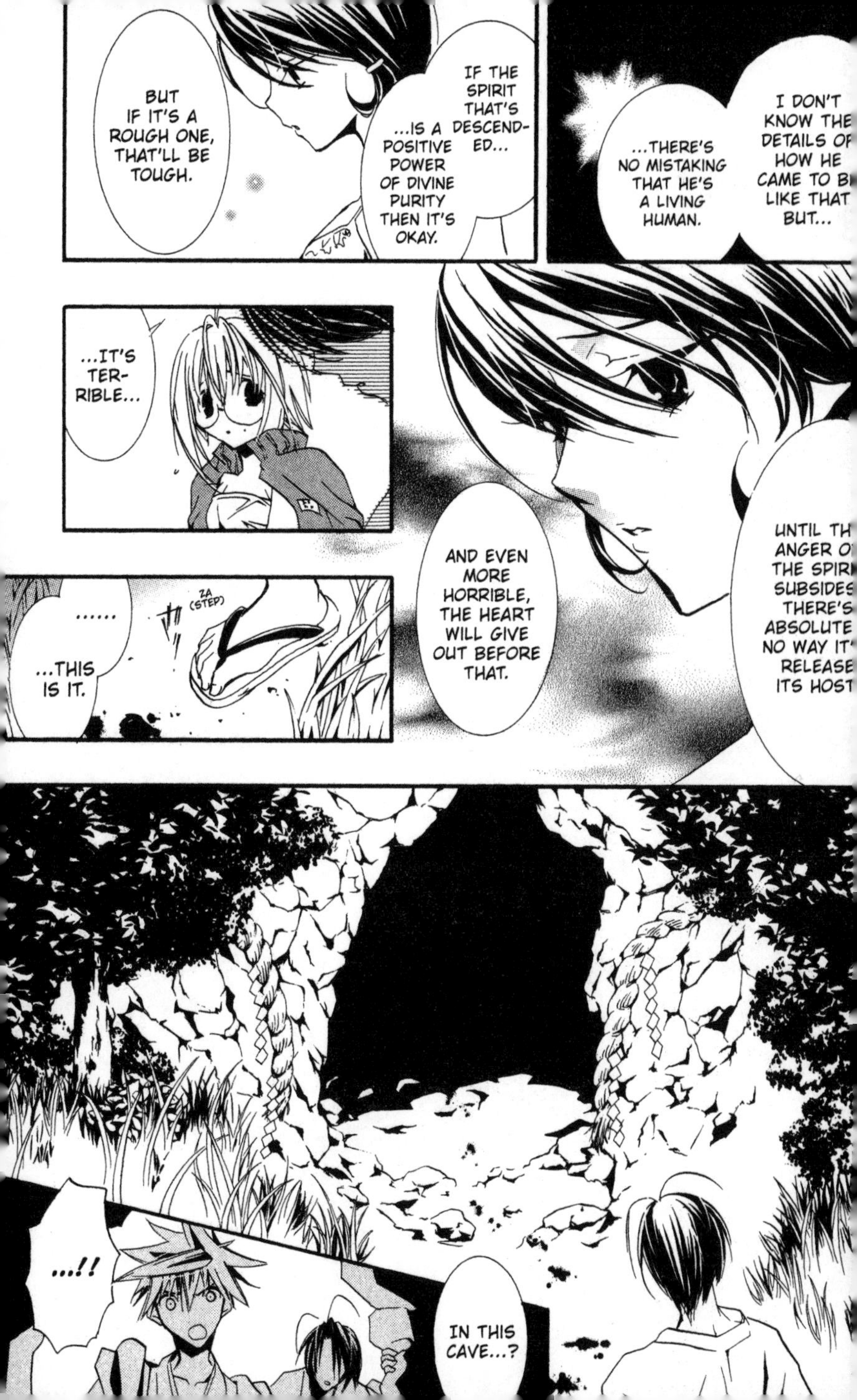
I DON'T KNOW THE DETAILS OF HOW HE CAME TO B LIKE THAT BUT...
...THERE'S NO MISTAKING THAT HE'S A LIVING HUMAN.
IF THE SPIRIT THAT'S DESCEND-ED...
...IS A POSITIVE POWER OF DIVINE PURITY THEN IT'S OKAY.
BUT IF IT'S A ROUGH ONE, THAT'LL BE TOUGH.
UNTIL TH ANGER O THE SPIRI SUBSIDES THERE'S ABSOLUTE NO WAY IT' RELEASE ITS HOST
AND EVEN MORE HORRIBLE, THE HEART WILL GIVE OUT BEFORE THAT.
...IT'S TER-RIBLE...
ZA (STEP)
......
...THIS IS IT.
IN THIS CAVE...?
...!!

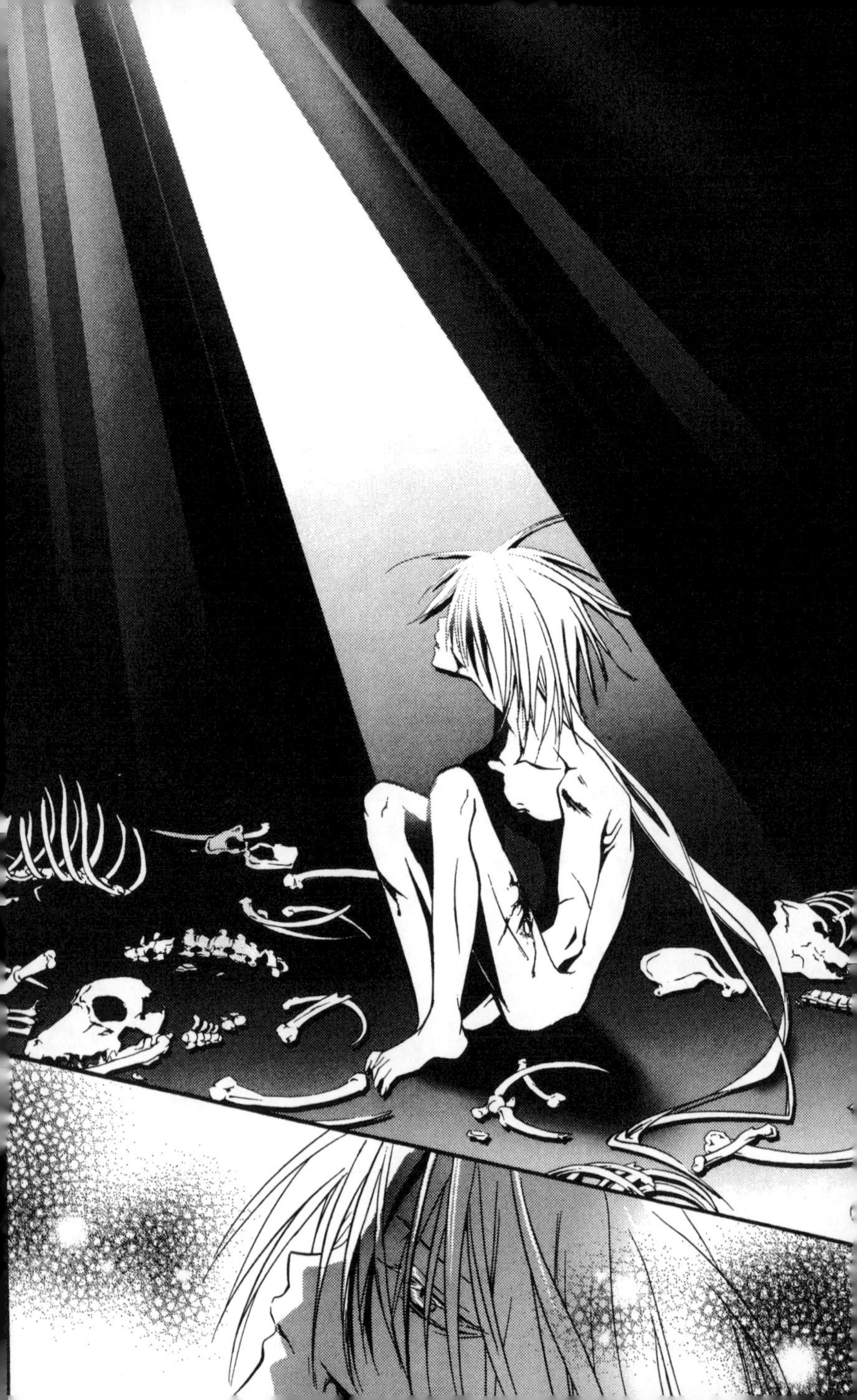

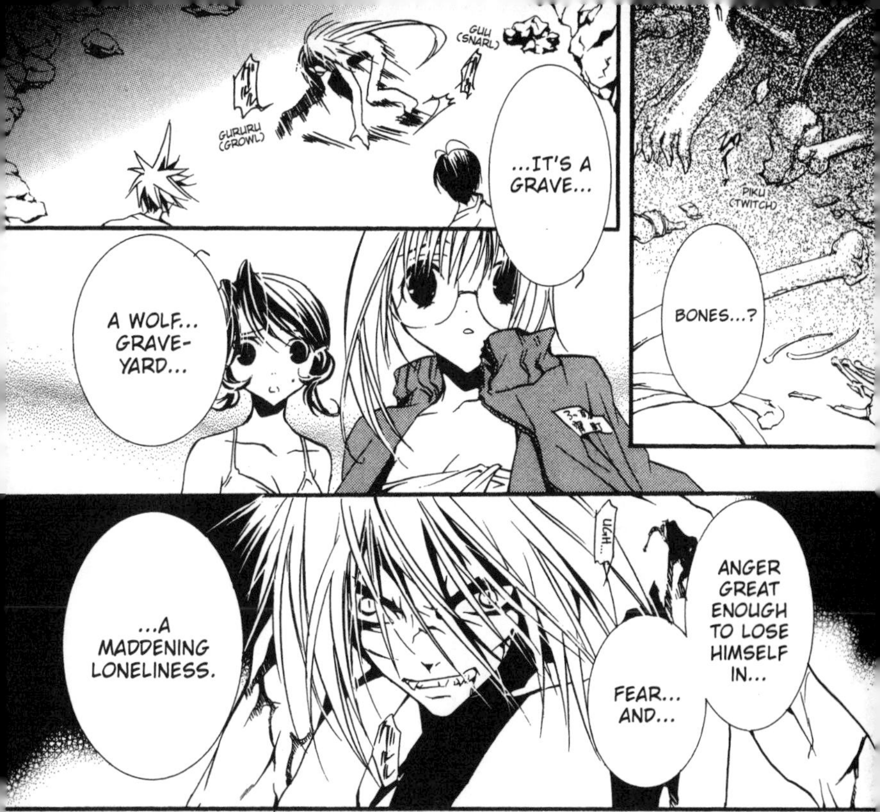
PIKU (TWITCH)
BONES...?
GUU (SNARL)
GURURU (GROWL)
...IT'S A GRAVE...
A WOLF... GRAVEYARD...
ANGER GREAT ENOUGH TO LOSE HIMSELF IN...
FEAR... AND...
UGH...
...A MADDENING LONELINESS.

SFX: GURURU

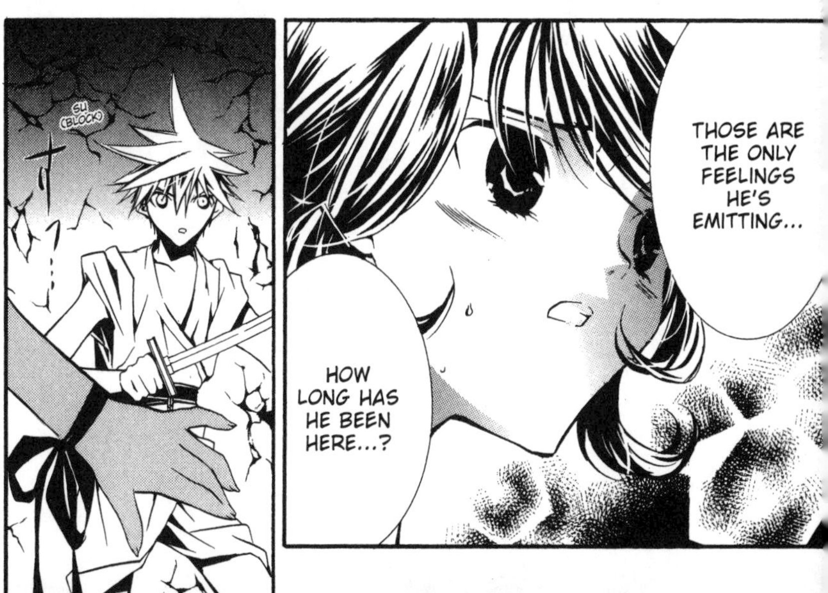
THOSE ARE THE ONLY FEELINGS HE'S EMITTING...
HOW LONG HAS HE BEEN HERE...?
SU (BLOCK)

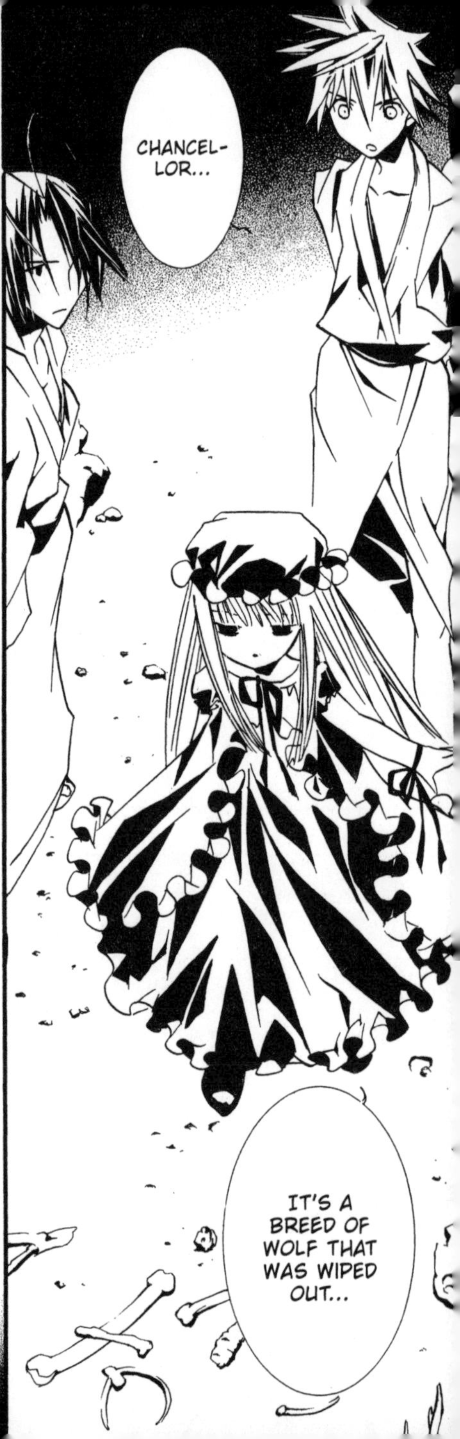
CHANCEL-LOR...
IT'S A BREED OF WOLF THAT WAS WIPED OUT...

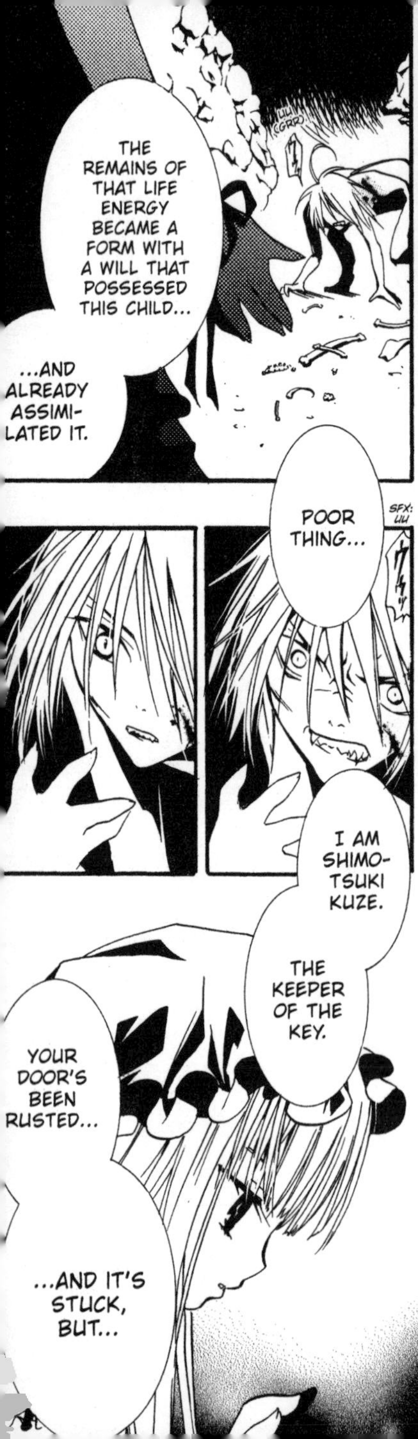
UU (GRR)
THE REMAINS OF THAT LIFE ENERGY BECAME A FORM WITH A WILL THAT POSSESSED THIS CHILD...
...AND ALREADY ASSIMILATED IT.
SFX: UU
POOR THING...
I AM SHIMOTSUKI KUZE.
THE KEEPER OF THE KEY.
YOUR DOOR'S BEEN RUSTED...
...AND IT'S STUCK, BUT...

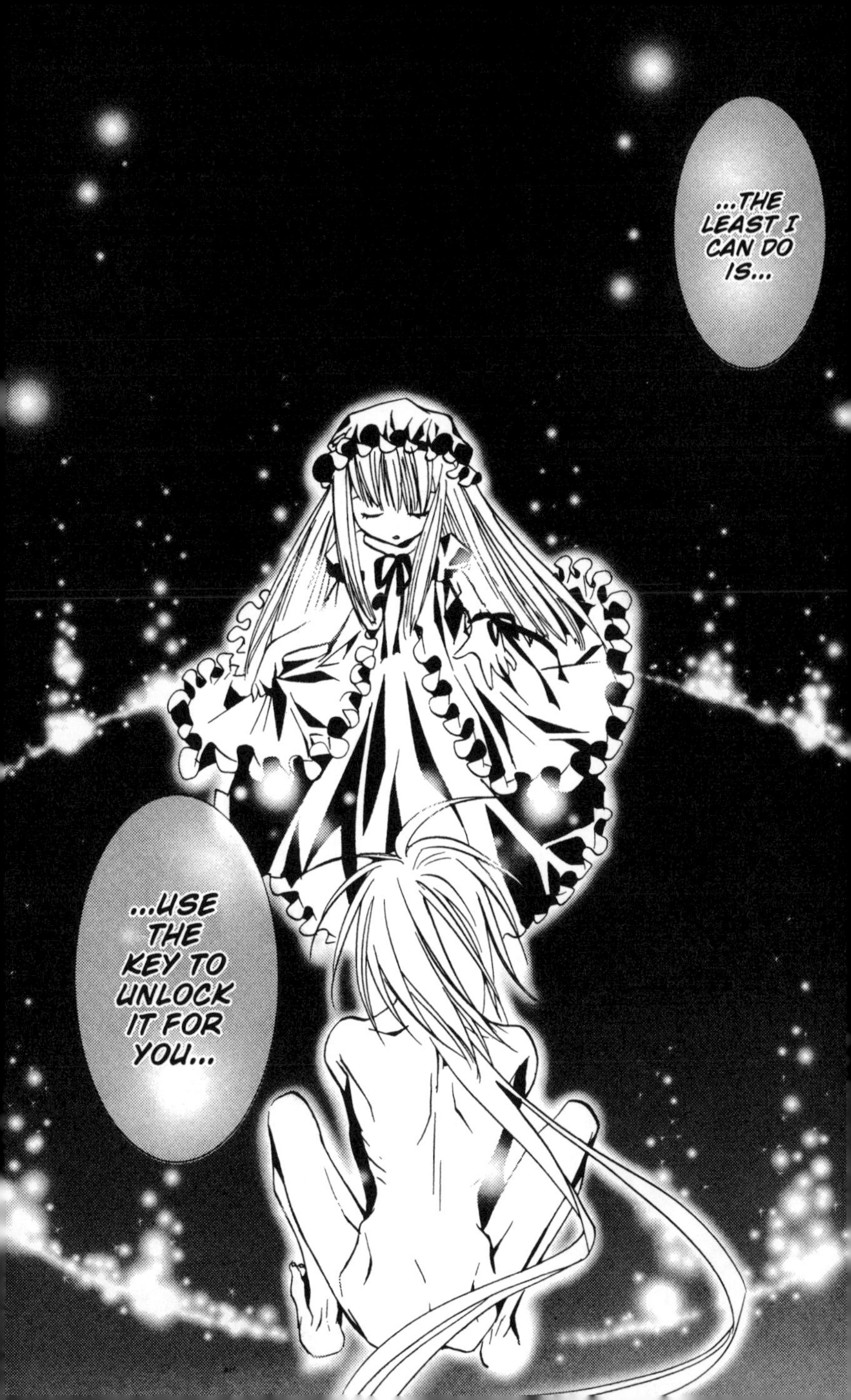
...THE LEAST I CAN DO IS...
...USE THE KEY TO UNLOCK IT FOR YOU...

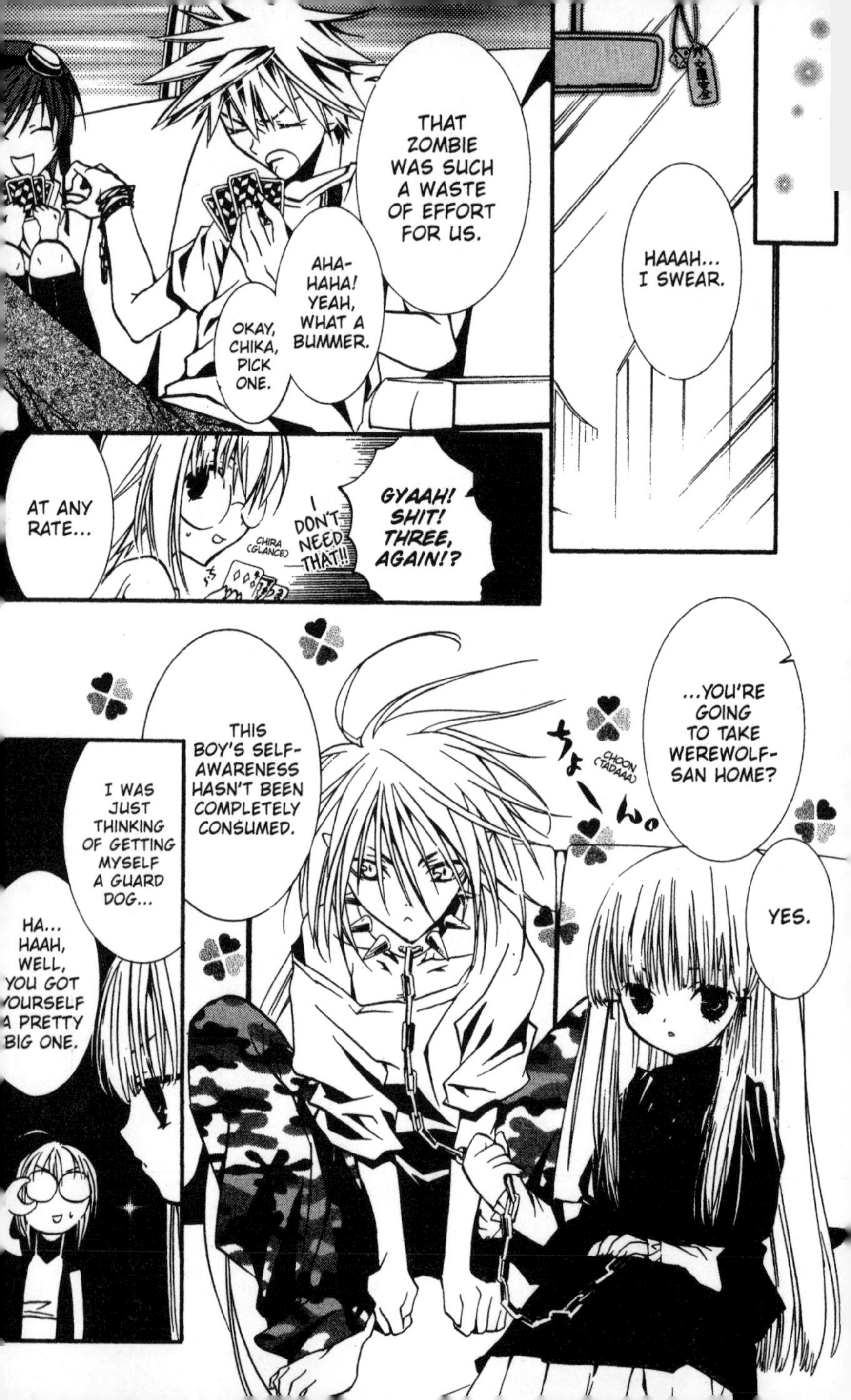
HAAAH... I SWEAR.
THAT ZOMBIE WAS SUCH A WASTE OF EFFORT FOR US.
AHA-HAHA! YEAH, WHAT A BUMMER.
OKAY, CHIKA, PICK ONE.
GYAAH! SHIT! THREE, AGAIN!?
I DON'T NEED THAT!!
CHIRA (GLANCE)
AT ANY RATE...
...YOU'RE GOING TO TAKE WEREWOLF-SAN HOME?
YES.
CHOON (TADAAA)
THIS BOY'S SELF-AWARENESS HASN'T BEEN COMPLETELY CONSUMED.
I WAS JUST THINKING OF GETTING MYSELF A GUARD DOG...
HA... HAAAH, WELL, YOU GOT YOURSELF A PRETTY BIG ONE.

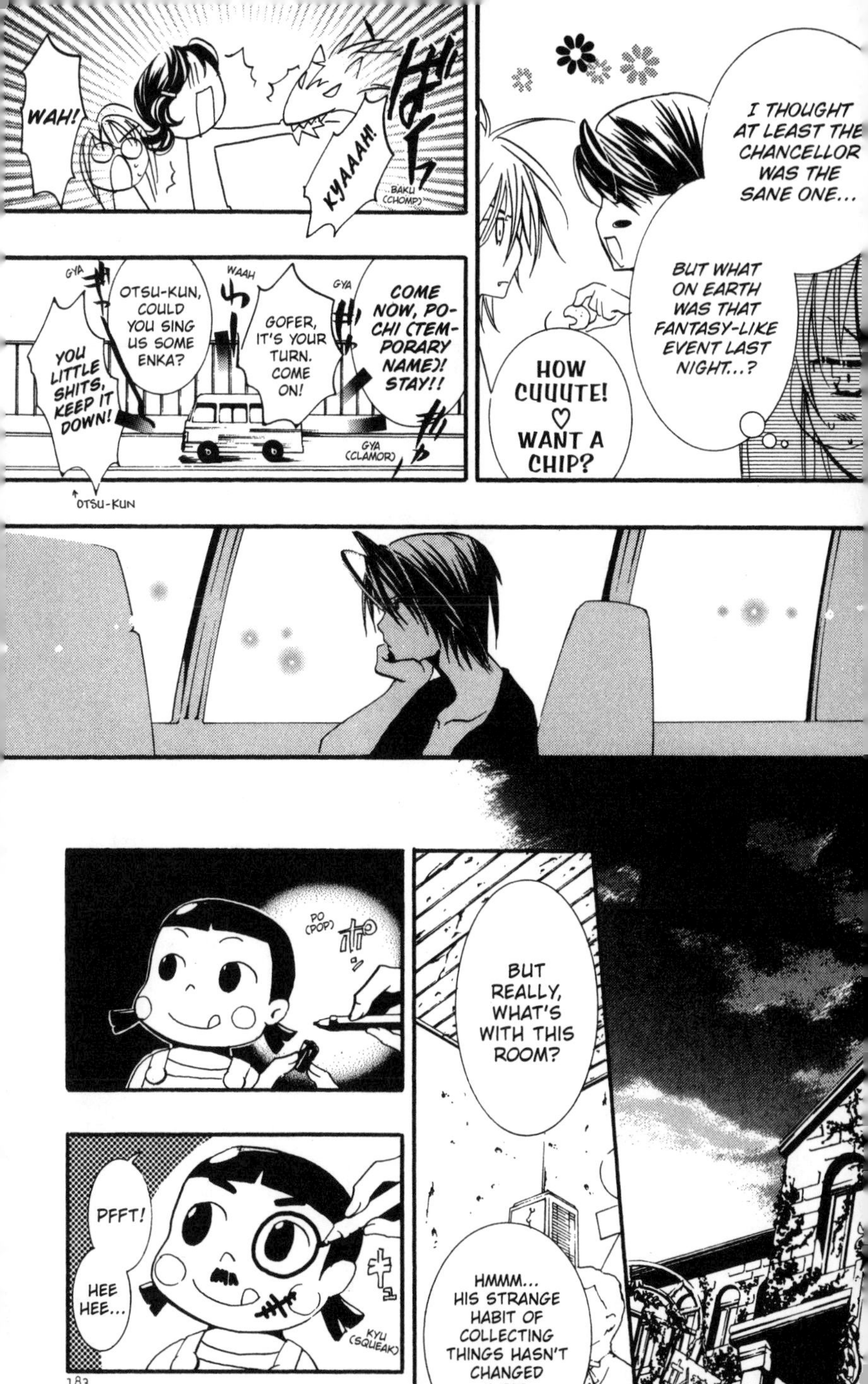

I THOUGHT AT LEAST THE CHANCELLOR WAS THE SANE ONE...
BUT WHAT ON EARTH WAS THAT FANTASY-LIKE EVENT LAST NIGHT...?
HOW CUUUTE! ♡ WANT A CHIP?
BAKU (CHOMP)
KYAAAH!
WAH!
GYA
COME NOW, PO-CHI (TEMPORARY NAME)! STAY!!
GYA (CLAMOR)
GOFER, IT'S YOUR TURN. COME ON!
WAAH
OTSU-KUN, COULD YOU SING US SOME ENKA?
GYA
YOU LITTLE SHITS, KEEP IT DOWN!
OTSU-KUN
BUT REALLY, WHAT'S WITH THIS ROOM?
HMMM... HIS STRANGE HABIT OF COLLECTING THINGS HASN'T CHANGED A BIT.
PO (POP)
KYU (SQUEAK)
PFFT!
HEE HEE...

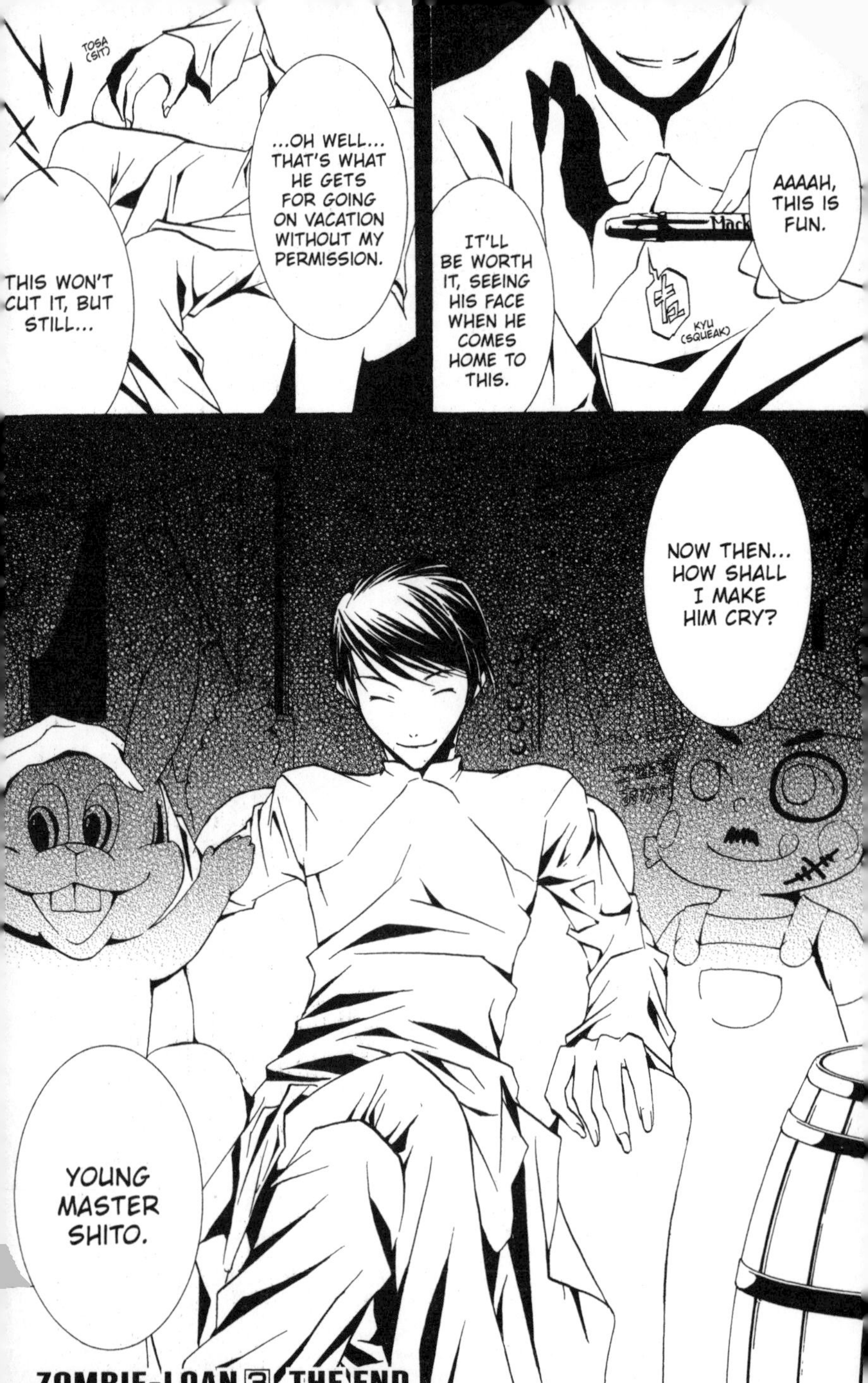
AAAAH, THIS IS FUN.
KYU (SQUEAK)
IT'LL BE WORTH IT, SEEING HIS FACE WHEN HE COMES HOME TO THIS.
TOSA (SIT)
...OH WELL... THAT'S WHAT HE GETS FOR GOING ON VACATION WITHOUT MY PERMISSION.
THIS WON'T CUT IT, BUT STILL...
NOW THEN... HOW SHALL I MAKE HIM CRY?
YOUNG MASTER SHITO.

ZOMBIE-LOAN 3 THE END

ZOMBIE-LOAN

all produced by
PEACH-PIT
Banri Sendou : Shibuko Ebara

staff
Nao
Zaki
Chie
Kinomin
Tama
Takako
Mimu

special thanks
A.Kitamura

...and your reading

tO be cOntinued vOl. 4

ZOMBIE-LOAN MANIAX-DX

YUUTA

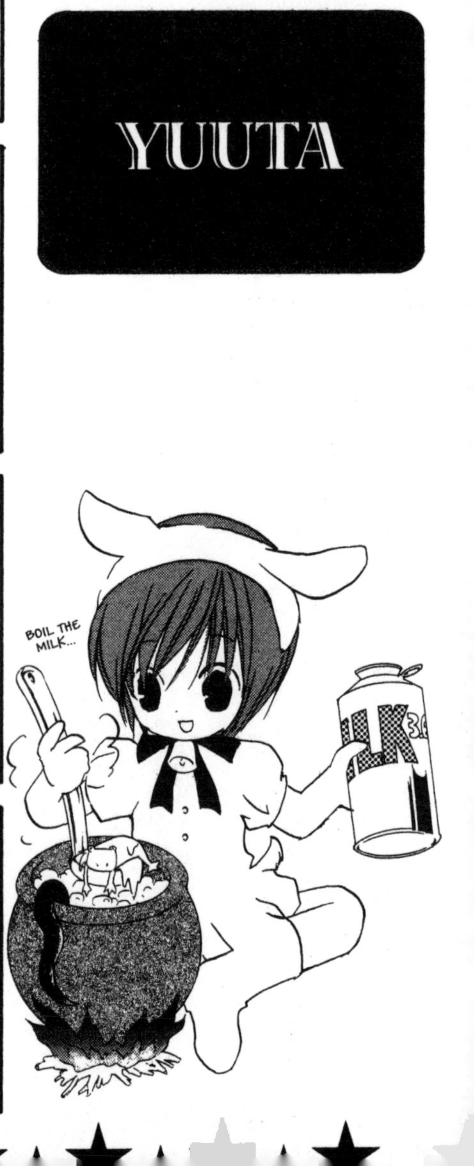
BOIL THE MILK...

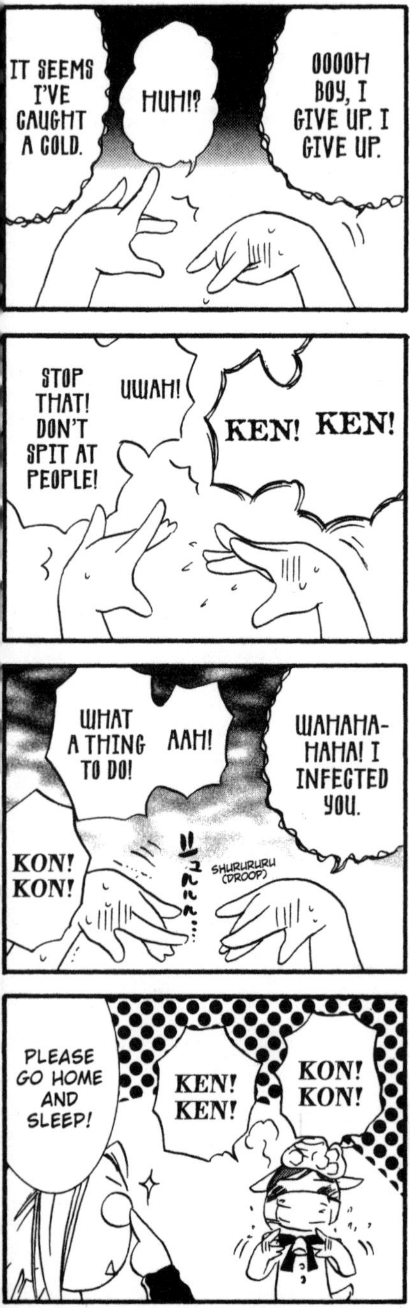
OOOOH BOY, I GIVE UP. I GIVE UP.
HUH!?
IT SEEMS I'VE CAUGHT A COLD.
KEN! KEN!
UWAH!
STOP THAT! DON'T SPIT AT PEOPLE!
WAHAHA-HAHA! I INFECTED YOU.
AAH!
WHAT A THING TO DO!
SHURURURU (DROOP)
KON! KON!
KON! KON!
KEN! KEN!
PLEASE GO HOME AND SLEEP!

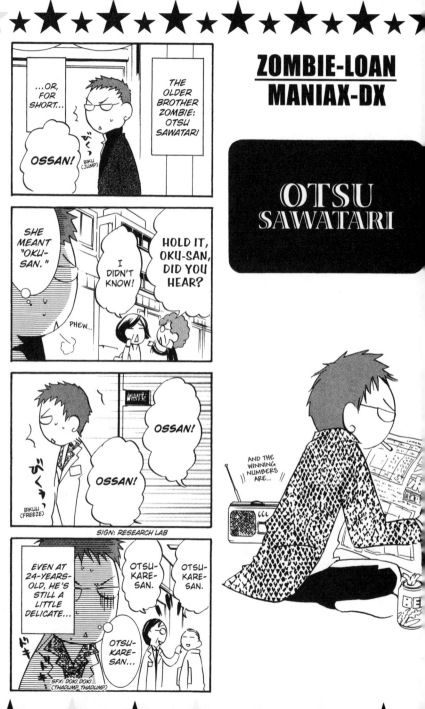

ZOMBIE-LOAN MANIAX-DX

OTSU SAWATARI

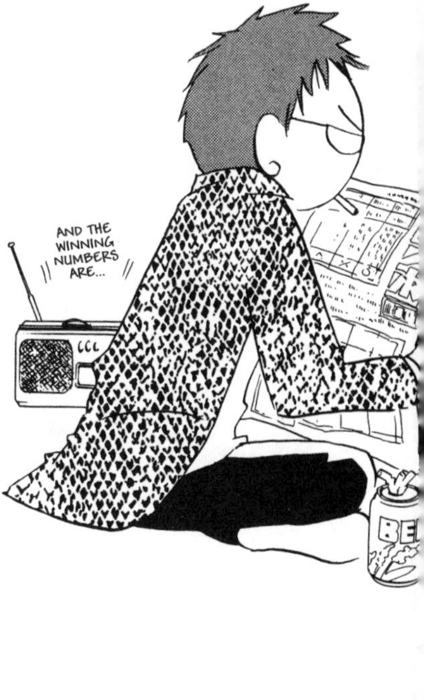
AND THE WINNING NUMBERS ARE...

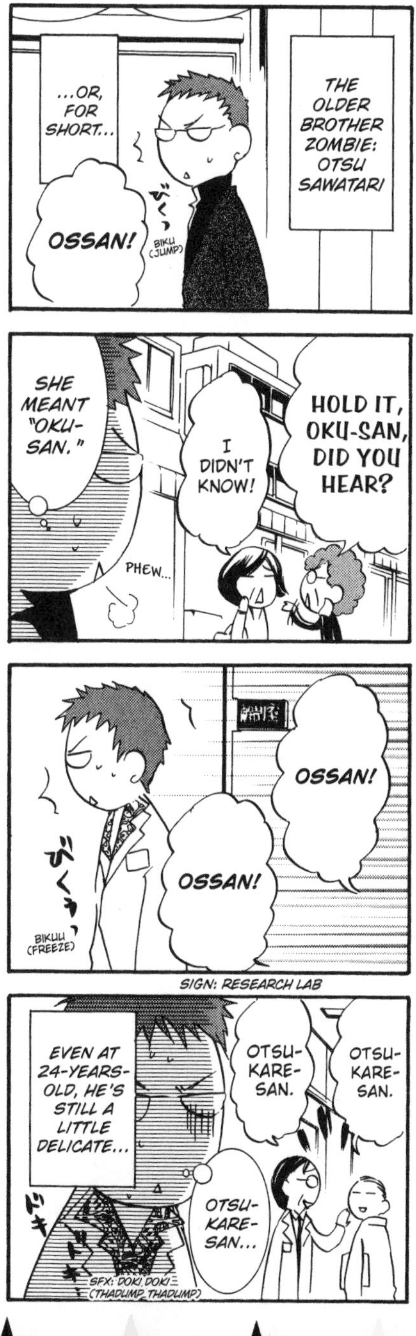
THE OLDER BROTHER ZOMBIE: OTSU SAWATARI
...OR, FOR SHORT...
OSSAN!
BIKU (JUMP)
HOLD IT, OKU-SAN, DID YOU HEAR?
I DIDN'T KNOW!
SHE MEANT "OKU-SAN."
PHEW...
OSSAN!
OSSAN!
BIKUU (FREEZE)
SIGN: RESEARCH LAB
OTSU-KARE-SAN.
OTSU-KARE-SAN.
EVEN AT 24-YEARS-OLD, HE'S STILL A LITTLE DELICATE...
OTSU-KARE-SAN...
SFX: DOKI DOKI (THADUMP THADUMP)

COLLABORATION COMIC PART 1

DearS

ZOMBIE-LOAN **Rozen Maiden**

HYURURURU (ZOOOOM)
RELAXED...
KYA!
GASHAAN (CRASH)
OH? THIS ISN'T JUN'S ROOM.
WH-WH-WHAT ARE YOU!?
I'M SHINKU, THE FIFTH DOLL OF THE ROZEN MAIDENS.
THIS MUST BE THE BATH-ROOM. HOW UNCOMFORT-ABLY SMALL... SHOW ME TO THE GUEST BEDROOM AT ONCE!
B-B-B-BATH-ROOM!?
YOU, SERVANT, POUR ME SOME TEA.
REN'S THE SERVANT.
RAAWR! WE'RE ON A ZOMBIE HUNT!
THERE'S MORE OF THEM!?
MON-EY!!
WHERE IS THE MON-EY!?
GASHA DOSHA (CRASH BAM)
IS THIS A NEWBIE THIEF...?
S-STOP IT...
......
......
JI (STARE)
GASHI (CLASP)
TEA.
SHUT UP!!
SOME-THING JUST WENT ON BETWEEN THEM.
GO HOOOME!!
GASHAA (CRASH)
PARIIN (CRACK)
KYAAH! KYAAAH!

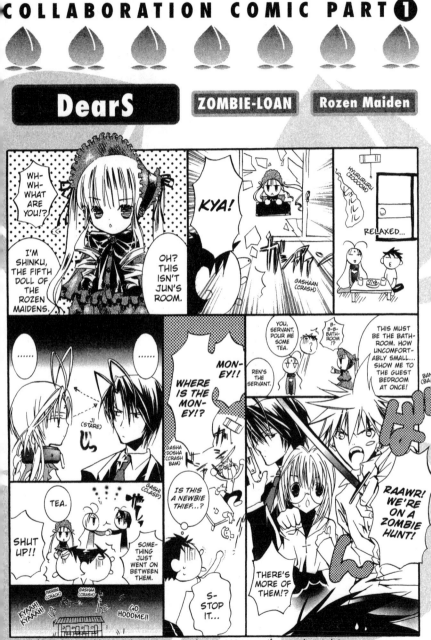

First published in Monthly Dengeki Comic Gao! February 2004 issue (from Media Works)

COLLABORATION COMIC PART 2

DearS

ZOMBIE-LOAN

Rozen Maiden

TODAY IS YET ANOTHER ZOMBIE HUNT!
GOFER, FIND US A BLACK-RINGED ZOMBIE!
YEAH, YEAH...
WHAT'S WITH ALL THE TENSION...?
FOUND ONE! THERE!!
IT'S A HELLUVA COLLAR! ZOMBIE FOUND!
ZOMBIE...?
THAT'S JUST AN ALIEN. ARE YOU GUYS OKAY?
THAT'S RIGHT. REN'S AN ALIEN AND TAKEYA'S A SLAVE.
GO (BASH)
WHERE?
ARE YOU GUYS OKAY?
WHAT WAS THAT!?
S-SORRY, HE'S JUST A BIT OF A HIKIKOMORI...
HE'S A LITTLE GLOOMY AND WILL BUY STRANGE DOLLS BY MAIL ORDER, BUT DEEP DOWN, HE'S A GOOD LITTLE BROTHER.
AH!
FOUND IT! HERE IT IS! THIS TIME, I'VE GOT IT!
A BLACK COLLAR!
THAT'S A RIBBON.
THIS HURTS, YOU KNOW.
DON'T TOUCH ME, YOU VILE GIRL!
BISHI! (SLAP)
THE DOLL SPOKE!
SORRY, THAT DOLL'S CURSED...
HM... A CURSED DOLL, EH? HOW UNSCIENTIFIC.
DON'T, SHINKU-CHAN!
YEAH, WELL, YOU'RE A ZOMBIE.
THE END. THAT WAS THE CO-STARRING OF ZOMBIES, ALIENS, AND CURSED DOLLS! ♥
THIS IS NOT A SANE-SOUNDING SITUATION AT ALL...
FOR THOSE OF YOU WITH AN INTEREST IN THE BIZARRE, GO TO YOUR LOCAL BOOKSTORE NOW! ★
REN LIKES MELON BREAD.

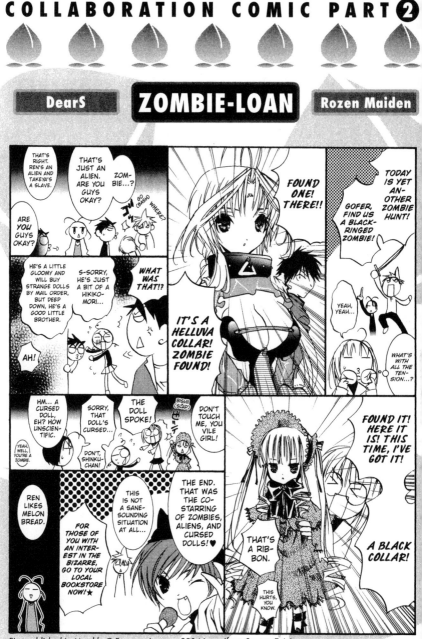

First published in Monthly G Fantasy, January 2004 issue (from Square Enix)

COLLABORATION COMIC PART 3

DearS **ZOMBIE-LOAN** **Rozen Maiden**

TOP: ZOMBIE-LOAN
LEFT: YOUR COLLATERAL'S YOUR LIFE.
PHONE #: 0111-EVERYONE-DIES

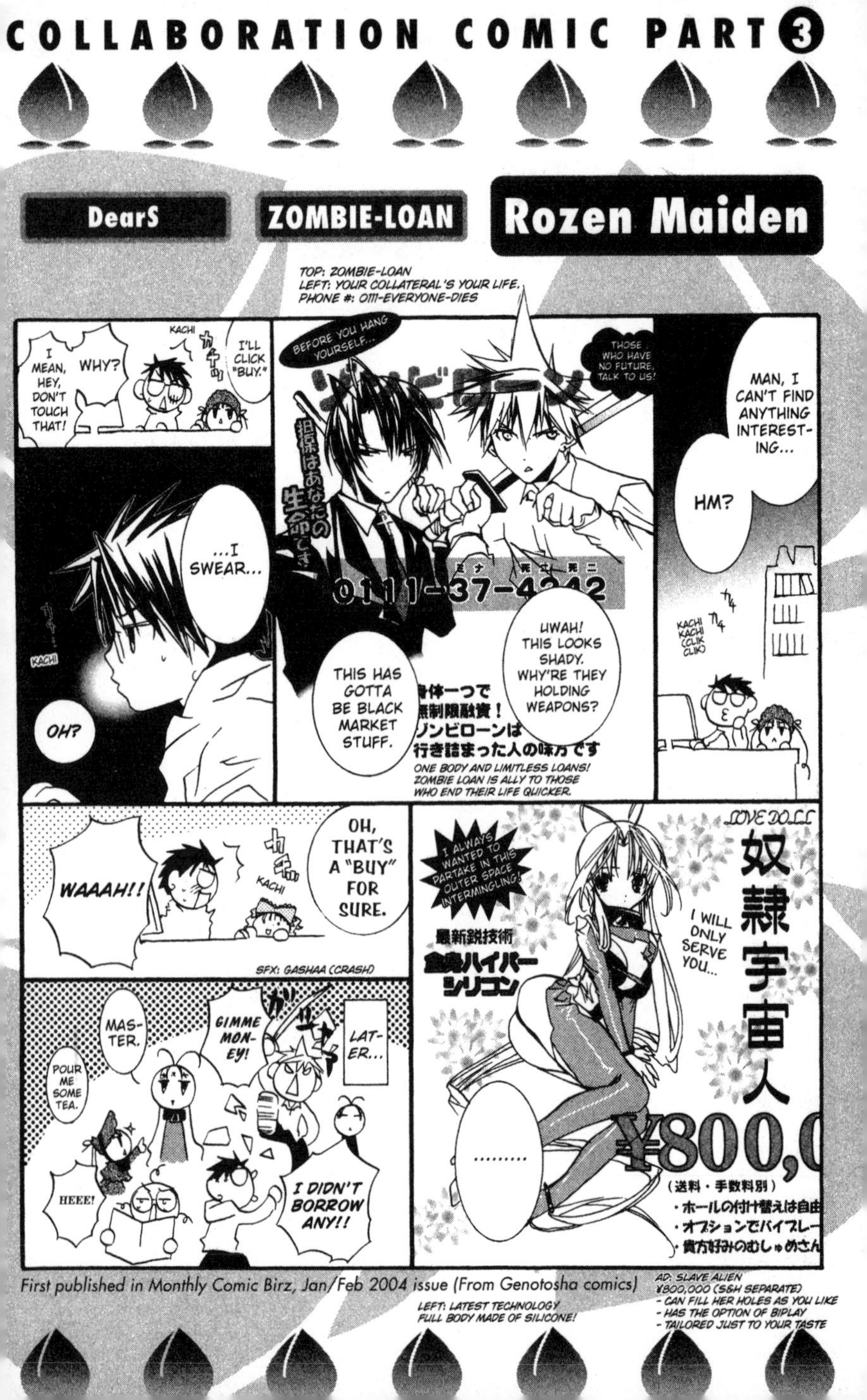

MAN, I CAN'T FIND ANYTHING INTEREST-ING...
HM?
カチ カチ
KACHI KACHI (CLIK CLIK)
BEFORE YOU HANG YOURSELF...
THOSE WHO HAVE NO FUTURE, TALK TO US!
担保はあなたの生命です
0111-37-4242
UWAH! THIS LOOKS SHADY. WHY'RE THEY HOLDING WEAPONS?
THIS HAS GOTTA BE BLACK MARKET STUFF.
身体一つで無制限融資！ゾンビローンは行き詰まった人の味方です
ONE BODY AND LIMITLESS LOANS! ZOMBIE LOAN IS ALLY TO THOSE WHO END THEIR LIFE QUICKER.
I'LL CLICK "BUY."
カチ
KACHI
WHY?
I MEAN, HEY, DON'T TOUCH THAT!
...I SWEAR...
KACHI
OH?
LOVE DOLL
奴隷宇宙人
I ALWAYS WANTED TO PARTAKE IN THIS OUTER SPACE INTERMINGLING!
I WILL ONLY SERVE YOU...
最新鋭技術
全身ハイパーシリコン
¥800,0
(送料・手数料別)
・ホールの付け替えは自由
・オプションでバイブレー
・貴方好みのむしゅめさん
....
OH, THAT'S A "BUY" FOR SURE.
カチ
KACHI
WAAAH!!
SFX: GASHAA (CRASH)
LAT-ER...
GIMME MON-EY!
MAS-TER.
POUR ME SOME TEA.
I DIDN'T BORROW ANY!!
HEEE!

First published in Monthly Comic Birz, Jan/Feb 2004 issue (From Genotosha comics)

AD: SLAVE ALIEN
¥800,000 (S&H SEPARATE)
- CAN FILL HER HOLES AS YOU LIKE
- HAS THE OPTION OF BIPLAY
- TAILORED JUST TO YOUR TASTE

LEFT: LATEST TECHNOLOGY
FULL BODY MADE OF SILICONE!

Preview of the next volume:

Shito's secret becomes clearer... And then what...!?

Shito suddenly disappears. Then a mysterious man appears before Chika and company. What's this secret Shito's hiding!? A new enemy confronts everyone while they're running about trying to get Shito back, and...!?

KNEEL THERE.

Meanwhile, Chika's...!?

FA-THER...!?

F-

SHITO-SAMA.

And new characters keep showing up!!

What's Michiru to do...!?

GAAN (SHOCK)

JUNIOR ...!?

SO WHY IS THERE A JUNIOR HIGH GIRL LIVING HERE?

ONIICHAN, THIS DORM'S FOR A HIGH SCHOOL, RIGHT?

ZOMBIE-LOAN
VOLUME 4 GOES ON SALE SOON!

TRANSLATION NOTES

p91
UMA is an "Unidentified Mysterious Animal." One such
UMA in Japan is an "obokobo." Michiru mistook the Japanese word for virgin ("oboko") for "obokobo" instead.

p93
The God of Entertainment ("Enta no Kami-sama") is a
comedy show on TV.

p119
Revolution is a reversal move in the card game Dai Hin
Min (Poor Man). The Americanized drinking game version
is known as Asshole.

p127
Hot spring eggs ("Onsen Tamago") are simply poached
eggs. They are usually served for breakfast at a hot
springs inn because traditionally eggs were coddled in the
hot springs, as the just-below-boiling temperature was
perfect for cooking them.

p142
Yukata are casual kimono worn in summer.

Kimono are always worn with the left side folded over
the right side, but when dressing the dead for burial, the
kimono is folded with the right side on top.

p165
Gochisousama or *gouchisousama deshita* is a ritualistic
expression said when one is done eating, similar to giving
thanks for food at the end of a meal.

p175
Possession in Japanese is spelled with the words for
"god" and "descent."

Based on what Yomi is discussing, Koyomi's family probably lives in and maintains a traditional Japanese Shinto
shrine. The shrine maidens she speaks of are attendants
for shrines, and they assist the priests in ceremonies,
perform ceremonial dances, do fortune telling, as well as
a wide variety of other tasks.

p183
Enka is a type of Japanese music that became popular in
the early 20th century. The subject matter in the songs
tends to be melodramatic or highly sentimental. It can be
compared to country or folk music.

p187
Oku-san is used to address married women, similar to
"Ma'am."
Otsukare-san is said at the end of a long work day, like
"Good work."

General note:
There are many mentions of various sums of money (in
¥) throughout this volume. Since exchange rates fluctuate
daily, equivalent sums printed here would most likely
be inaccurate. At the time this volume went to print, $1
USD was approximately equivalent to ¥115 JPY. In general, a rough estimate to use is $1 USD to ¥100 JPY.

ZOMBIE-LOAN
3

by PEACH-PIT

Translation: Christine Schilling
Lettering: Alexis Eckerman

ZOMBIE-LOAN Vol. 3 © 2004 PEACH-PIT / SQUARE ENIX. All rights reserved. First published in Japan in 2004 by SQUARE ENIX CO., LTD. English translation rights arranged with SQUARE ENIX CO., LTD. and Hachette Book Group USA through Tuttle-Mori Agency, Inc. Translation © 2008 by SQUARE ENIX CO., LTD.

Yen Press
Hachette Book Group USA
237 Park Avenue, New York, NY 10017

Visit our Web sites at www.HachetteBookGroupUSA.com and www.YenPress.com.

Yen Press is an imprint of Hachette Book Group USA, Inc. The Yen Press name and logo are trademarks of Hachette Book Group USA, Inc.

First Yen Press Edition: June 2008

ISBN-10: 0-7595-2837-3
ISBN-13: 978-0-7595-2837-6

10 9 8 7 6 5 4 3 2 1

BVG

Printed in the United States of America